BRITISH CONSTITUTION Made Simple

The Made Simple series
has been created
primarily for self-education
but can equally well
be used as
an aid to group study.
However complex the subject,
the reader is taken
step by step,
clearly and methodically,
through the course. Each volume
has been prepared by experts,
using throughout the
Made Simple technique of teaching.
Consequently the gaining
of knowledge now becomes
an experience to be enjoyed.

Accounting
Acting and Stagecraft
Additional Mathematics
Advertising
Anthropology
Applied Economics
Applied Mathematics
Applied Mechanics
Art Appreciation
Art of Speaking
Art of Writing
Biology
Book-keeping
British Constitution
Calculus
Chemistry
Childcare
Commerce
Commercial Law
Company Administration
Computer Programming
Cookery
Cost and Management
  Accounting
Data Processing
Dressmaking
Economic History
Economic and Social
  Geography
Economics
Electricity
Electronic Computers

Electronics
English
French
Geology
German
Human Anatomy
Italian
Journalism
Latin
Law
Management
Marketing
Mathematics
Modern European History
New Mathematics
Office Practice
Organic Chemistry
Philosophy
Photography
Physical Geography
Physics
Pottery
Psychology
Rapid Reading
Russian
Salesmanship
Soft Furnishing
Spanish
Statistics
Transport and
  Distribution
Typing

BRITISH CONSTITUTION Made Simple

Colin F. Padfield, LL.B., D.P.A.
of Gray's Inn, Barrister

Made Simple Books
W. H. ALLEN   London
A Howard & Wyndham Company

Made and printed in Great Britain
by Richard Clay (The Chaucer Press) Ltd, Bungay, Suffolk
for the publishers W. H. Allen & Company Ltd.
44 Hill Street, London W1X 8LB

First Edition, September 1972
Second Edition, January 1975
Third Edition, June 1976

ISBN 0 491 01862 2 Paperbound

Preface

This book covers the elements of the British constitution. While the text is primarily designed for students preparing for the General Certificate of Education at 'O' and 'A' levels of the various examination boards, the ground covered also makes it suitable reading for professional examinations in local and central government and in public administration generally.

Additionally, the book will be particularly helpful for student accountants and for all those training for professional positions such as company secretaries, hospital administrators, estate agents, surveyors, and many others.

For the general reader the book provides a thorough background to the political constitution under which we live and a comprehensive, up-to-date insight into its workings.

In short, it is a book about citizenship which gives the layman a clear and concise understanding of his rights, benefits, duties, and responsibilities. As such, it should provide interesting and valuable reading for all of us privileged to be members of a great democracy.

Preface to Third Edition

The Third Edition of this book has enabled me to comment, even if only briefly, on some of the changes that are taking place affecting the subject of British Constitution. Devolution is still under discussion now that a White Paper has been prepared; the Referendum has been used once; the publication of the late Mr. Richard Crossman's diaries breached the convention of cabinet secrecy and prompted a reply from Baroness Sharp, the former Permanent Secretary of the Ministry of Housing and Local Government.

There is a Police Complaints' Bill before Parliament at the time of writing which lays down a new procedure in regard to complaints against police officers; and the question of electoral reform still inspires the Liberal Party and leaves the two major parties somewhat cool. So far as it is possible within the limits of the available pages I have tried to mention the relevant facts to enable the ordinary reader to gain a clearer understanding of the present political scene, and the average student to glean sufficient knowledge to overcome the test of an examination. There is no respite for the student whose task is to learn, understand and know the main principles of the constitution, the institutions involved and how they work.

I am indebted to the Rt. Hon. The Lord Hailsham of St. Marylebone, P.C., C.H., for permission to quote from articles published in *The Times*; to the Clerk of the House of Commons; Mr. Anthony D. Steen, M.P. (Wavertree, Liverpool), for assistance with papers and advice not otherwise obtain-

vi							*Preface*

able; and my colleagues, friends and students who have been so kind in
assisting me with opinions and advice. To all the above I am most grateful.

Robert Postema of W. H. Allen has had the task of trying to fit into limited
space the new and important material. To him and to his secretary, Jane
Williams, I am indebted and thankful.

February, 1976						COLIN PADFIELD

Acknowledgements

I must thank first my colleagues, Tony Byrne and Barrie Foster, both specialists in this field, who read the typescript, criticized it and provided me with valuable source material. In addition, Barrie Foster prepared Appendix Two on study and examination technique, while Russell Pearce, another colleague, also gave me much valuable material.

Ann Fulton and Felix Bourne, students of mine, read and checked the proofs and made useful comments. My wife provided constant encouragement and was of great assistance in arranging the material into chapters and in checking the typescript as it progressed.

I must mention especially David Platt and Margaret Anderson of W. H. Allen & Co. Ltd., who guided the book from its inception to its completion, contributing generous help and comments. I owe them a heavy debt.

I also acknowledge help received from the Clerk of the House of Commons, Sir Barnett Cocks, K.C.B., O.B.E., for providing various forms; from the Rt. Hon. Edward du Cann, P.C., M.P., who also gave me source material; and from various civil servants in numerous Ministries who gave me much help and advice.

Finally, I am indebted to the Controller of H.M. Stationery Office for permission to reproduce various documents in the book; to the Field Enterprises Education Corporation, Chicago, Illinois, U.S.A. for permission to reproduce the illustration on page 93, and, finally, to the Associated Examining Board and the Schools Examination Board, University of London, for permission to reproduce specimen examination questions at Appendix Three.

Any errors and omissions in the book are entirely my own.

COLIN PADFIELD

Table of Contents

Table of Regnal Years of English Sovereigns

Sovereign	From	To	Years	Important Acts and Events
William I	1066	1087	21	Domesday Book (1086)
William II	1087	1100	13	
Henry I	1100	1135	36	
Stephen	1135	1154	19	
Henry II	1154	1189	35	
Richard I	1189	1199	10	
John	1199	1216	18	Magna Carta (1215)
Henry III	1216	1272	57	
Edward I	1272	1307	35	Statute of Westminster I (1275)
Edward II	1307	1327	20	Justices of Peace appointed (1327)
Edward III	1327	1377	51	Justices of Peace Act (1361)
Richard II	1377	1399	23	
Henry IV	1399	1413	14	
Henry V	1413	1422	10	
Henry VI	1422	1461	39	
Edward IV	1461	1483	23	
Edward V	1483	1483	1	
Richard III	1483	1485	3	
Henry VII	1485	1509	24	
Henry VIII	1509	1547	38	Statute of Proclamations (1539)
Edward VI	1547	1553	7	
Mary	1553	1558	6	
Elizabeth I	1558	1603	45	
James I	1603	1625	23	
Charles I	1625	1649	24	Shipmoney Act (1640) Star Chamber Abolition Act (1640)
Charles II	1649	1685	37	Habeas Corpus Act (1679)
James II	1685	1688	4	Bill of Rights (1688)
William and Mary	1689	1702	14	Act of Settlement (1700)
Anne	1702	1714	13	Act of Union (1706)
George I	1714	1727	13	Riot Act (1714)
George II	1727	1760	34	
George III	1760	1820	60	Parliamentary Privilege Act (1770)
George IV	1820	1830	11	
William IV	1830	1837	7	Reform Act (1832)
Victoria	1837	1901	64	Judicature Acts (1873–75)
Edward VII	1901	1910	10	
George V	1910	1936	26	Parliament Act (1911) Statute of Westminster (1931)
Edward VIII	1936	1936	1	
George VI	1936	1952	17	Parliament Act (1949)
Elizabeth II	1952			Life Peerages Act (1958)

CHAPTER ONE

THE NATURE OF THE CONSTITUTION

Introduction

The form or structure of the Government of a society becomes its constitution. The constitution determines the distribution and exercise of the sovereign power within that political society or state. (Professor A. V. Dicey, a learned constitutional lawyer.)

Man is by nature a social being. In early times he formed clans or tribes for the protection and survival of himself and the group of which he was a member. Once a group, clan, or tribe is formed, **rules** are necessary to regulate the relationships of man with man and to ensure **order** and **peace** within the group. A **constitution** may thus be defined as 'the system or body of fundamental principles according to which a nation, state, or body politic is constituted and governed' (*The Shorter Oxford English Dictionary*).

A society cannot exist without such rules. The earliest records show that a King, chief, or leader is chosen or appointed, a council of elders or wise men is formed to assist the King or leader and a **Government** comes into being. In every known form of human society there exists some form of government.

The same basic procedure occurs today, when a group of people wishes to form a football club, an arts group, or a scientific society or similar body. First of all, the members usually arrange a meeting, appoint a committee, choose a chairman, name the officers of the committee—a secretary and treasurer—and then proceed to draw up the rules of the club. These rules usually define the purpose of the club, the powers and duties of the chairman, the committee, the officers, and the individual members. In all essentials a **constitution** is made for that particular group or society.

Obviously a nation or a state is a much more complex body than a small club or society, and each nation or state varies in its constitution. Types of constitutions are discussed further in this book, particularly the British constitution which is, in a sense, unique with its own particular form and procedure. It has, for example, taken over a thousand years to grow and evolve.

It will assist a student to grasp the idea of a political constitution if he remembers his own physical constitution with its skeleton, trunk, limbs, and vital organs such as the brain and the heart. He has a physical structure and framework, and he is able to function as a conscious living person, capable of reasoning and making decisions on which to act.

If we look at Professor Dicey's definition at the start of this chapter we note his reference to 'form or structure' of a Government on the one hand, and the 'distribution and exercise' of **sovereign power** on the other. The phrase 'sovereign power' means for our purposes the highest power in the state, i.e. the power vested in the modern Cabinet as head of the Government charged with the heavy and important duty of governing our lives. In medieval times the 'sovereign power' was vested in the Monarch. In the dictionary definition

1

of 'constitution' we note that emphasis is on the 'system or body of fundamental principles' by which a state is governed. In truth, most definitions of a
'constitution' can be criticized, but for our purposes the above definition
serves to pin-point the essentials.

What is a State?

A state is an independent political society situated within defined limits
whose subjects are bound together with ties of mutual protection and assistance. Belgium, Denmark, France, Italy, Great Britain, Spain, the United
States of America, Venezuela, and so on, are all states and are sometimes
called 'nation-states'.

The main functions of a state are:

(*a*) to repel external aggression; and
(*b*) to maintain law and order within its territories.

These are the two basic functions of a state. We are all aware that there are
many more duties carried out by a modern civilized state, such as the provision of welfare services, poor relief, health services, unemployment relief,
and educational services. The extent of these services is determined by the
wealth of the nation, the wish of the people, and by other factors.

Within a state there is a sovereign power or Government. This sovereign
power may be one person, e.g. a King, a dictator, or leader, or a body of
persons, like a **Council**, a **Parliament**, or a **Congress** having supreme authority.
Subjects of a state owe a duty of allegiance to the sovereign power in the
state of which they are members.

A nation may be united by race or language but this is not necessarily so.
For example, Switzerland and the U.S.A. are each composed of different
races and there is a diversity of speech within each of these states. The unity
which most often binds a nation together is **territorial unity**; that is the occupation by a group of people of a defined geographical area. We may say,
therefore, that people who dwell in the same area and are subject to the same
laws, are citizens of the same nation or state.

Types of State

There are two main types of states: (i) **Federal**, and (ii) **Unitary**. The reason
why the citizens of a state adopt one or the other of these forms is as a result
of the historic development of each state or the wishes of its citizens.

(i) *Federal States*

A Federal State is a group of constituent units which aims to reconcile
national unity and power with the maintenance of individual State rights.
Here power is divided between (i) a National Government which, in matters
of common concern, e.g. defence, is supreme over the whole country; and
(ii) State Governments which are supreme in those matters left to them, e.g.
State schools. For the citizens living under Federal authorities there are in
fact two sets of laws: (i) Federal Law, and (ii) State Law. The main examples
of Federal States are: the United States of America, Australia, Canada, and
Switzerland.

The U.S.A. became federated because, following the War of Independence,
the thirteen States then in existence were too weak individually to carry on the

work of government. They joined together as equals for the common convenience. Though they gave certain powers to the Federal Government, each State preserved its own independence by reserving to itself certain well-defined powers.

These powers which are usually yielded to a Federal Government are those dealing with (i) national defence; (ii) foreign policy; (iii) the control of international trade, through customs duties and tariffs, and similar matters. Powers of a purely local character are reserved to the State Governments.

In Switzerland the cantons (subdivisions of the country) desired unity in matters of common concern such as defence and tariffs. Nevertheless, German, French, and Italian-speaking sections each wished to preserve some measure of individuality.

> Federalism means the distribution of the force of the State among a number of co-ordinate bodies each originating in and controlled by the constitution (A. V. Dicey, *Law of the Constitution*).

(ii) *Unitary States*

In this type of state, power is **concentrated** in one body and the departments of government are **centralized** in one institution. The United Kingdom is a Unitary State. The Norman kings in the eleventh and twelfth centuries set up a strong central government (the *Curia Regis* and the Great Council). They gradually established control over the whole kingdom and created out of the customary laws the common law of England. Thus was built up a solid structure of government, a national Parliament and a legal system.

> Unitarianism, in short, means the concentration of the strength of the State in the hands of one visible sovereign power be that Parliament or Czar (A. V. Dicey, *Law of the Constitution*).

The United Kingdom

The British constitution is the constitution of the United Kingdom of Great Britain and Northern Ireland, and consists of (i) England and Wales, (ii) Scotland, and (iii) Northern Ireland.

Scotland was at one time a separate State, but by the *Act of Union* in 1707, England and Scotland were united and became the **United Kingdom of Great Britain**. Since 1603, both Scotland and England have shared the same Monarch. Moreover, although Scotland and England both had, at one time separate Parliaments, the Parliament at Westminster in London, now legislates for the whole of the United Kingdom.

Northern Ireland, however, has a separate Parliament at Stormont* in Belfast, and an Executive Government. The Northern Ireland Parliament consists of (i) the Monarch, (ii) a House of Commons of fifty-two elected members, and (iii) a Senate composed of two *ex officio* Senators and twenty-four Senators elected by members of the House of Commons. The Stormont Parliament may legislate on certain internal matters only, for example, the peace, order, and good government of Northern Ireland, and has its own Ministries. Parliament at Westminster, to which twelve M.P.s are returned

---

* Temporarily suspended for a year in 1972. Mr. William Whitelaw was appointed Minister for Irish Affairs.

The United Kingdom of Great Britain and Northern Ireland

from Northern Ireland, legislates on the following matters: defence, external affairs, overseas trade, coinage, patents, wireless telegraphy, postal services, and some taxation.

Local Government

The system of local government in the United Kingdom does not make the British Constitution a Federation. Local authorities derive their powers from Parliament (the central legislature) and these are not rightly comparable with those of the individual States of a true Federation. The feature of a State which exists within a Federation is that of **sovereignty** which is what a local authority does not possess or claim. Moreover a local authority in the United Kingdom has no separate Legislature, Executive or Judiciary. In reality, the United Kingdom local authorities are agents of the central Government in carrying out the policies of the Government and administering statutes, such as the *Education Act of 1944*.

British Commonwealth

The Commonwealth is not a Federation for there is no central Government, no common defence force or judiciary and no rigid obligations or commitments between the members. Nevertheless all the members of the Commonwealth have a broad community of interests, and they are bound together by a common sense of ideals and a common interest in the maintenance of peace, freedom, and security. The Queen's legislative power in the Parliaments of the Commonwealth is a formality. As it has been said—'She reigns though she does not rule'. The Queen, as personal Head of the Commonwealth, does provide the element of continuity in administration and her personal influence over the whole group is, of course, very great.

Types of Constitution

Constitutions may be divided into two main classes: (i) **rigid**, and (ii) **flexible**, although both types of political constitutions are of course equally concerned with the distribution of the powers of government between the various organs of both central and local Government.

(i) *Rigid Constitutions*

A rigid constitution may be defined as one which cannot readily be amended. This does not mean, of course, that it cannot ever be amended, but that any amendments that are found to be necessary may only be made by means of a special process provided by the constitution for that purpose.

When a community 'starts from scratch', as it were, an attempt is made by the founders to define as clearly as possible and to make secure the relationship of the various organs of government: the Executive, the Legislature, and the Judiciary. The constitution so framed assumes the character of **fundamental law**. Any other law, whether passed by the central Government or a State or local government, derives from the constitution and is subject to the constitution, i.e. is subordinate to the fundamental law.

Some states attempt to embody these principles in a single document, or a small group of documents. In it will be found the necessary rules and principles for the creation of a **Legislature**, an **Executive** and a **Judiciary**, the election of a **President** or a **Prime Minister** and **principles for the conduct of citizens defining rights and duties.**

The best example of a **written** constitution in this sense is that of the U.S.A. formed in 1787, the *Declaration of Independence* and the *Constitution of the United States*. It is contained in a document of some 12 pages and is freely available for anyone to read and study. The *Constitution of the United States* is the **source of government** authority. It is the **fundamental law** of the land, defines the limits of the sphere of action of the National Government and assigns to its three branches—Executive, Legislature, and Judiciary—specific duties and responsibilities.

In composing such a document the founders of a rigid type of constitution are faced with a very difficult task. They realize that by the very nature of things, by the nature of life itself, change must occur. Nevertheless, the founders who formulate the fundamental laws of the constitution do not want their constitution lightly upset or altered. Any change which is found desirable and necessary must follow a special process. This process is in the nature of a safeguard and usually has four objects:

(i) That the constitution should be changed only after due deliberation.
(ii) That the people themselves should have an opportunity to express their views on a proposed change (e.g. by a referendum if need be).
(iii) In a federal system, the respective powers of central and local (or national and State) Governments should not be changed by one party only, e.g. the central Government alone.
(iv) The protection of minorities in language, religion, race, etc.

Most countries today have written constitutions. These include Australia, Belgium, France, East Germany, West Germany, the U.S.A., and the U.S.S.R. Many former British colonies such as Nigeria, Kenya, and Aden also have written constitutions.

(ii) *Flexible Constitutions*

A flexible constitution is one which can be readily amended without any special procedure.

Britain has no formal constitution in the sense here described. There is no written booklet comparable to that described before. There are, of course, constitutional rules and principles, and some are contained in statutes such as the *Magna Carta* (1215); the *Bill of Rights* (1689); the *Parliament Acts* (1911 and 1949); and the *Peerage Act* (1963). No attempt has been made by Parliament to codify or set down separately (as in the case with the U.S.A.) the constitutional laws and customs by which Great Britain is, in fact, governed. In theory this does appear to be a weakness, as there would seem to be inadequate safeguards to prevent the arbitrary seizure of political power. But this is not necessarily so and may be advantageous. The constitutional history of Great Britain does not show a long line of dictatorships. Rather, it shows growth of individual rights and liberties based not so much on law but on the **ideas** of traditional freedoms and traditional practices (conventions), which have developed organically.

The British Constitution is nevertheless a reality. It has lasted longer than most, has been the model for many new countries, and has been an inspiration to many peoples scattered all over the world. If asked of what does the British Constitution comprise, we may reply that it embraces laws, customs, and conventions all hammered out, as it were, on the *hard anvil of experience*.

Thus no **special** legal procedure need be followed to amend the British Constitution. This is a notable feature of those constitutions which are unwritten and have not been formally codified. This remark is a generalization only. New Zealand has a 'written' constitution, but it is also flexible since it can be amended by a simple majority vote of its Parliament.

Although Parliament may alter our constitution by the passing of a statute in the ordinary way, we should at the same time note that important constitutional changes are brought about only after considerable discussion and patient examination of the proposals. The *Parliament Acts* (1911 and 1949), for example, were not passed into law until a full discussion had taken place both in Parliament and outside, i.e. in the Press and by the general public.

It is increasingly felt by responsible politicians that proposals for constitutional change should be preceded by a general election giving a mandate to a Government to effect the change.

Constitutional Structure

In any scheme of government we find there are three essential types of activity which must be carried out:

(i) Making laws. = The Legislature.
(ii) Executing laws = The Executive.
(iii) Adjudicating when disputes occur = The Judiciary.

We may recall that the Anglo-Saxon and the early Norman Kings personally ruled their Kingdoms and performed all three functions. Naturally they required staff to advise them on their duties and, of course, staff to execute their commands. The Anglo-Saxon Kings had the **Witan** (group of elders or wise men); and the Norman Kings had the *Curia Regis* and the Great Council to assist them in their rule. The Chancellor was the Secretary of State for all departments. He was chief executive officer. But it is interesting to note that The King sometimes sat with his judges at The Bench (as it was called), and dispensed Royal justice to his subjects. This Royal court of the early English common law subsequently became known as the Court of King's Bench simply because the King himself used to adjudicate with the judges at the Bench. The Monarch was and still is 'the fountain of justice' and the Queen today is technically present in all her Courts of Law.

The distribution of the functions of government in the British Constitution is as follows:

(i) *The Legislature*

This means the law-making body (*lex*, *legis* = law, L.) In other words it is 'The Queen (or King) in Parliament'. Laws are made by the **House of Commons** and the **House of Lords** with the assent of **the Queen.**

Some laws of a minor or subsidiary character are also made by subordinate bodies, e.g. Ministers, local authorities, public corporations, and similar bodies to whom power to do so has been delegated by Parliament (see p. 248).

(ii) *The Executive*

Laws are executed or put into effect by H.M. Government or other agencies specially appointed to do so. The nominal head of the Government is H.M. The Queen, but in practice actual responsibility rests with the Prime Minister who heads the Cabinet which makes the policy by which the State is to be governed. There are some Ministers in charge of Departments of Government who are not members of the Cabinet. These, with the whole of the Civil Service, the local authorities and public corporations carry out, or administer, the laws made by the Legislature (see p. 107).

(iii) *The Judiciary*

This Branch of government includes the whole range of H.M. judges and magistrates engaged in the task of punishing offenders and settling disputes. The courts range from the House of Lords, the final Court of Appeal in the country, to magistrates' courts. The courts as a whole deal with civil and criminal cases. A fuller description of the English legal system can be found on page 176.

Sources of the British Constitution

Although we do not have a written constitution we may note that many of ~~OND~~ the sources of the British Constitution are found in documents. There are, for example: (i) **statutes**, which are printed and published; (ii) **legal cases** recorded in Law Reports; (iii) political **conventions** which are described in books and journals; and (iv) opinions of constitutional lawyers, political thinkers and historians which are contained in **treatises** describing constitutional rights and duties and practices.

(i) *Statutes*

There are numerous statutes containing provisions about the Constitution. Nevertheless it is true that only a small part of the total scheme of government is prescribed by statute law. For example, the existence of the House of Lords is not founded on statute, and neither was the House of Commons created by statute. The Cabinet similarly was not created by law and owes its existence to convention. These are the most important institutions of government.

The following statutes should be specially noted:

Magna Carta, 1215. The King promised to refrain from imposing any feudal tax save by the consent of the Common Council of the Realm. The Charter also contained the provision: 'To no man will we deny or delay right or justice.'

The *Petition of Right Act, 1628.* This laid down the important principle that there should be no taxation without the consent of Parliament, and that no one may be imprisoned without lawful cause.

The *Bill of Rights, 1689.* This affirmed very important principles of constitutional liberties.

The *Act of Settlement, 1701.* This established the independence of the judges and regulated the succession to the Crown of England.

The *Parliament Act, 1911.* This curbed the power of the House of Lords to amend and delay Bills sent up to that House from the Commons.

The *Parliament Act, 1949.* An additional Act curbing the power of the House of Lords.

The *Peerage Act, 1963.* This allowed the renunciation of hereditary titles of peers.

The *Race Relations Act, 1968.* This aimed to prohibit prejudice on account of race, colour or ethnic origin.

The *Representation of the People Act, 1969.* This gave the vote to persons of 18 years of age.

In addition to the above there are many more statutes which originate, alter, or abridge the rights and duties of institutions, groups of persons, or individuals, but lack of space forbids their inclusion here.

(ii) *Case Law*

Case law is judge-made law. Its importance lies in the fact that the judgements of the highest courts in the land bind all lower courts in similar cases. Most of the disputes dealt with by judges in the past have been private civil cases between man and man, but some cases have determined constitutional rights and liberties. These cases enshrine the law, and since they will be followed and applied by succeeding judges and magistrates we may say that the cases are an important source of constitutional law.

Examples are numerous, but we may note here the following important decisions:

The *Case of Proclamations, 1611,* which held that the King by his Proclamation cannot create any offence which was not an offence before.

Stockdale v. *Hansard, 1839.* The mere resolution of the House of Commons does not alter the law of the land.

Bowles v. *Bank of England, 1913,* which denied the right to levy a tax merely on the resolution of the House of Commons.

A.-G. v. *Wilts. United Dairies, 1922.* The Executive may not impose a charge on a citizen unless Parliament expressly so authorizes.

Thomas v. *Sawkins, 1936*, which held that police are entitled to enter a public meeting (even if that meeting is held on private premises) if the police have reasonable suspicion that a breach of the peace is likely to occur.

Christie v. *Leachinsky, 1947*. A person who is arrested by the police must be informed of the charge or crime of which he is suspected.

(iii) *Conventions*

Conventions are rules of political practice which the courts of law do not recognize. They are not laws and cannot, therefore, be enforced as such. Nevertheless they are an important source of constitutional law.

In our everyday life in a family, club, a class of students, or society generally there are certain unwritten rules which gradually form in the course of time and are observed. A breach of an unwritten rule (or convention) will disturb the working of a group or society and ultimately, if the breach continues, may cause a breakdown. In political life, and in the actual business of government, conventions gradually evolve and are consistently observed. These conventions also ensure the smooth working of the constitution.

We shall consider these conventions more closely later in our study when we deal with the constituent parts of government, e.g. H.M. The Queen, the House of Commons, the House of Lords, the Cabinet and other important bodies. But here we must observe that in practice conventions are very important. For example, our system of Cabinet government rests entirely on convention. So too does the choice of a Prime Minister, the selection of Cabinet members and the collective responsibility of the Cabinet. These are but a few of the matters in which convention plays a great part.

If, as we have observed, a convention is not law how can it be enforced? The sanction (or force) behind a convention is indirect rather than direct. Breach of a political convention does not result directly in a fine or other punishment in the courts of law. Let us take the following well-known convention: 'Parliament must meet at least once a year.' If Parliament does not meet, several laws will be broken. The *Army and Air Force Act, 1961*, would expire, for this Act must be renewed annually by means of an Order in Council which is subject to affirmative resolution in each House. In other words each House must specifically resolve that the Order be approved. If Parliament does not meet in accordance with the convention the standing Army could not legally be maintained for the defence of the realm. All military discipline would as a consequence cease to exist in the absence of **legal** power to enforce it. A further result would be that the *Finance Act* (an annual Act) could not be passed to enable the collection of revenue, and the appropriation to the various items of public expenditure. Such are the consequences if Parliament does not meet once a year as is required by convention. In effect there would be a breakdown of government, and eventually the law itself would be broken, as described above.

Political conventions include a great deal that is based on custom and expediency. The sanction behind these conventions is ultimately public opinion.

Once established a political convention may form the basis of a law. Thus conventions are a source of law. The following statutes merely embody in written form principles which were previously conventions: the *Statute of Westminster, 1931* (H.M. The Queen is Head of the Commonwealth; the Commonwealth is a free association of equal and independent states) and the *Ministers of the Crown Act, 1937* (the existence of the Prime Minister and his salary). Some examples of conventions are:

(*a*) *The Monarch.* The Queen will exercise the Royal Prerogative (with a few exceptions) only on the advice of a Minister of the Crown.

The Queen must assent to all Bills properly passed through Parliament.

The Queen must invite the leader of the political party having a majority in the House of Commons to form a Ministry. The person so invited is known as the Prime Minister. Other Ministers of the Crown are appointed on the advice of the Prime Minister.

The Queen must act on Cabinet advice.

The Queen dissolves Parliament at the request of a Government which ceases to command a majority in the House of Commons or is defeated in that House on a major issue.

(*b*) *Parliament generally.* In cases of conflict between the two Houses the Lords shall yield to the Commons. (This convention was given statutory recognition in the *Parliament Acts, 1911 and 1949*).

The Government must not flout the generally expressed wishes of Parliament.

The business of the House of Commons is arranged between the Prime Minister and the Leader of the Opposition.

Parliamentary committees are miniatures of the House of Commons as regards party representation in them.

(*c*) *United Kingdom and the Dominions.* The United Kingdom Parliament will not legislate for a Dominion except at its request and with its consent.

Governors-General are appointed by the Crown and act on the advice of the Dominion Prime Minister.

(iv) *Treatises*

Text writers of authority sometimes express their opinions on important constitutional problems. Those opinions do not have the force of law, but sometimes they may assist a judge in a legal case to reach the right decision, particularly where the point is obscure or two constitutional principles are difficult to reconcile. In so far as the opinions are adopted by a court they are a source of constitutional law.

Political philosophers and thinkers affect public and parliamentary opinion. By their writings they may initiate new ideas on legislation, the form or institutions by which government is carried on. We may instance: John Locke (1632–1704), Montesquieu (1689–1755); Blackstone (1723–80); Jeremy Bentham (1748–1832); Edmund Burke (1729–97); A. V. Dicey (1835–1922); J. S. Mill (1806–73); Erskine May (1815–86) the author of *Parliamentary Practice*. All have contributed insights and source material by their writings and have affected our own Constitution and those overseas.

The Separation of Powers

The doctrine of the separation of powers is particularly associated with Montesquieu, the French liberal philosopher, who visited this country and studied the English Constitution which he much admired. His book *L'Esprit des Lois* published in 1748 had wide currency throughout Europe. Put simply, the doctrine is that the three functions of government (legislative, executive, and judicial) should be discharged by separate bodies and that to prevent misgovernment no two of the functions should be entrusted to the same hands. If, for example, the power of making laws were exercised by the same persons as those who execute or interpret them, the result would be tyranny.

The separation of the three institutions (Legislature, Executive, and Judiciary) should enable each to act as a check on the others. Each body should be staffed by its own personnel, and no one person should be a member of any of the other two powers or institutions.

Montesquieu wrote:

> When the legislative and executive powers are united in the same person, or in the same body . . . there can be no liberty; because apprehensions may arise, lest the same Monarch or Senate should enact tyrannical laws, to execute them in a tyrannical manner.
>
> Again, there is no liberty if the judicial power be not separated from the legislative and executive. Were it joined with the legislative, the life and liberty of the subject would be exposed to arbitrary control; for the judge would then be the legislator. Were it joined to the executive power, the judge might behave with violence and oppression.
>
> There would be an end of everything were the same man, or the same body, whether of the nobles or of the people, to exercise those three powers that of enacting laws, executing public resolutions, and trying the causes of individuals.

The germ of the idea was not new. Aristotle had referred to it; John Locke (1632–1704), the English liberal philosopher, also postulated the doctrine in his *Second Treatise on Civil Government*; and Blackstone in his *Commentaries on the Laws of England* (1765) referred to the importance of mutual checks on governmental power and of an independent judiciary in the English Constitution.

The Separation of Powers in Britain Today

The doctrine of the separation of powers does not apply **completely** to the British Constitution, as the functions of the following to some extent overlap:

The Sovereign. The Queen is head of the Administration (Executive), head of the Judiciary and an integral part of the Legislature. The Monarch's constitutional position is unique (see p. 107).

The Lord Chancellor. He is a member of the Cabinet, President (Speaker) of the House of Lords, and head of the Judiciary under the Crown. The three powers are joined in his office and are exercised by the same individual (see p. 214).

The Cabinet. This is the centre of the executive power in the State. It is composed of Ministers who must, by convention, be members of one or other of the Houses of Parliament. A strict application of the doctrine would exclude all Ministers of the Crown (the Executive) from membership of the Legislature. Under the British Constitution the Cabinet and the Legislature are closely and continuously associated, and the relationship may be described as a **partnership** in government, rather than a separation. This, however, is subject to the control vested in Parliament in outvoting the party in power and thus ensuring the discontinuance of the Executive in office and the dissolution of Parliament.

Ministers. Ministers, who in fact constitute the Executive, are frequently empowered by the Legislature to perform (under the authority of statute) legislative duties in the framing of delegated legislation (see p. 248). Moreover certain statutes empower Ministers to perform judicial or quasi-judicial functions which show an encroachment on the essential tasks of the judiciary (see p. 251).

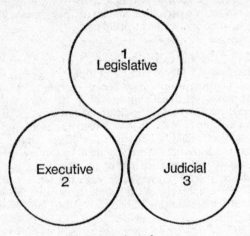

The separation of powers

The House of Lords. The Upper House is at one and the same time a constituent part of the Legislature, the final Court of Appeal for all civil and criminal cases and may adjudicate upon, and punish, breach of its privileges or contempt of the House.

The House of Commons. Primarily a legislative and deliberative body, it is the dominant part of the Legislature, but it may also act in a judicial capacity for breach of any of its privileges and for contempt of the House.

The Judiciary. The independence of the Judiciary is an important characteristic of the British Constitution (*Act of Settlement, 1701*). Nevertheless this independence and separation cannot be complete in practice, for in the last resort judges are removable from office on an address from both Houses of Parliament. Further the Rules of the Supreme Court (detailing how an action shall proceed) are made by the judges of the High Court and Court of Appeal under authority of statute. Moreover, we shall see later (p. 180) that the common law of England was largely judge-made out of the customs of the people. Judges continue to develop the common law by their decisions, and they fulfil the statute law by their interpretation and administration of the law. To that extent, therefore, the judges exercise an indirect power of 'legislating' in the sense of making new rules. Moreover, some of the functions of the judges are administrative in substance, e.g. an order made for the guardianship of an infant, supervision of bankruptcy proceedings, and liquidation of companies.

Conclusion. In the strict sense of the doctrine of the separation of powers, we may say that the theory has no true application. Nevertheless, the doctrine has assisted in forming essential and fundamental ideas concerning the development of the British Constitution. In particular, the independence of the Judiciary is of the greatest import. Parliament does not, for instance, discuss matters which are *sub judice* (i.e. under consideration by a judge at that moment), nor do Ministers of the Crown interfere with the discretion of a judge in any civil or criminal case whatsoever.

The British experience, therefore, may be said to be that it has distributed the power of the State among various bodies of which the Legislature, Execu-

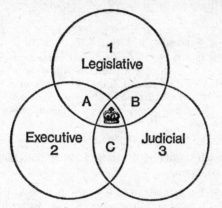

No complete separation of powers

tive, and Judiciary are the main, and that the various bodies act as *checks and balances* to prevent despotism and to ensure that liberty (within the law) and effective government can be simultaneously achieved.

The Separation of Powers in the United States of America

The doctrine of the separation of powers had a deep effect on the thinking of the 'founding fathers' of the U.S.A. in the drawing up of the Constitution of 1787. This well-known document provides the most clear example of a practical separation of the three fundamental powers.

The first three Articles of the American Constitution are important in this respect. Article I vests the federal legislative power in the Congress of the U.S.A. (Congress comprises (i) a Senate, and (ii) a House of Representatives); Article II states that the executive power is vested in the President who shall hold office during a term of four years. Article III vests the judicial power in the Supreme Court of the United States of America.

These three powers seem to have been intended to be mutually exclusive. For example, no member of one branch of government may be a member of either of the others as well. The President of the U.S.A. is not, and cannot be, a member of Congress (the Legislature). Any member of Congress who wishes to become President of the U.S.A. must resign from that body before accepting the Presidency (John F. Kennedy resigned from Congress in 1960 on becoming President). The President may, or may not be, a member of the political party with a majority in Congress.

The *checks and balances* which are necessary to maintain equilibrium are written into the Constitution of the U.S.A. Thus the President may veto legislation of Congress, and such veto may only be over-ridden by a two-thirds majority in the Senate before the legislation may come into effect.

With the exception of the Vice-President (who *ex officio* presides over the Senate) no member of the Government (the Executive) may also be a member of Congress. The President (who heads the Executive) appoints judges to office in the Supreme Court (the Judiciary). This last body is of great importance in that it has overriding power under the Constitution to declare Acts of Congress (or of any State legislature) or the actions of a President to be illegal (or unconstitutional) if they should transgress the provisions of the Constitution itself.

The Rule of Law (or Supremacy of Law).

The Rule of Law is one of the fundamental characteristics of the British Constitution. But, like the word 'constitution' it is difficult to define.

The origin of the Rule of Law is found in Greek and Roman thought. Broadly it was considered that over and above all man-made law (sometimes called 'positive' law) there is a universal law which applies to all men everywhere and at all times.

Bracton, a judge in the reign of Henry III, wrote:

> The King himself should not be subject to any man but to God and the law makes the King.

This universal law (or **natural law** as it was sometimes called) was attributable to God. In the seventeenth century, L.C.J. Coke identified natural law with the **common law of England** which he described as 'the perfection of reason'. Since human reason was given by God, the principles of natural law were deducible by man by the use of his reason.

During the conflict between the King and Parliament in the seventeenth century Coke claimed that the common law was above the King and the Executive (i.e. the King's Ministers). In the struggle for power between the King and Parliament, Coke with other common law judges formed an alliance with Parliament. The Parliamentary forces won the struggle, and finally the supremacy of Parliament over the King and all other bodies was assured by the *Bill of Rights, 1689*.

The doctrine of the Rule of Law (as understood by Coke) had now to be reconciled if possible with the other important doctrine of the **supremacy of Parliament** (or sovereignty of Parliament). Either the law was supreme or Parliament was supreme. The outcome of this contention was the adoption of the theory or principle that the common law was subject to such changes as the King *in Parliament* might make from time to time. Henceforward the law now regarded as supreme was the common law *and* statute law, i.e. the whole of English law.

The important effect of the doctrine was to prevent or preclude any arbitrary action of the Crown in person (i.e. the Monarch) or, indeed, of members of the Government acting as servants of the Crown.

Broadly, therefore, today the Rule of Law is the principle that the process of government is bound up with the law and that the law is supreme. A Government in power must act **according to law**, i.e. within the law. For example, a Home Secretary cannot forcibly enter my house unless he has lawful power so to do; neither may he arrest me unless he has lawful power so to act. The law gives me remedies if my rights are infringed. The Rule of Law may, therefore, be said to prevail when the exercise of all forms of public authority (central government authorities, local authorities, police, and other bodies) is subject to review by the ordinary courts of law to which all citizens have equal access.

The Rule of Law may perhaps best be grasped by contrasting it with its opposite, i.e. the arbitrary use of authority against any person or property, unchecked by any other power or body. This state of affairs leads straight to despotism or anarchy. Most reasonable men prefer order and peace to the confusion and misery of anarchy.

Professor A. V. Dicey, in his work *The Law of the Constitution* (1885), gave three meanings of the Rule of Law thus:

(i) *Absence of Arbitrary Power or Supremacy of the Law*

It means in the first place, the absolute supremacy or predominance of regular law as opposed to the influence of arbitrary power, and excludes the existence of arbitrariness of prerogative, or even wide discretionary authority on the part of the Government . . . a man may be punished for a breach of law, but he can be punished for nothing else.

(ii) *Equality before the Law*

The Rule of Law means again, equality before the law or the equal subjection of all classes to the ordinary law of the land administered by the ordinary law courts.

(iii) *The Constitution is the Result of the Ordinary Law of the Land*

The Rule of Law means with us the law of the constitution, the rules which in foreign countries naturally form part of a constitutional code, are not the source but the consequence of the rights of the individuals, as defined and enforced by the courts; that, in short, the principles of private law have with us been by the action of the courts and Parliament so extended as to determine the position of the Crown and of its servants; thus the constitution is the result of the ordinary law of the land (see p. 16).

Is the Rule of Law Valid Today?

However valid the Rule of Law may have been in Dicey's lifetime (some critics deny its truth even for that period) the doctrine has been subject to criticism in the light of modern developments, particularly in the last thirty years.

We shall take each of the main rules in order:

(i) *Absence of Arbitrary Power*. Today Ministers (and other executive bodies) are sometimes given wide discretionary powers by statute. Thus, a Minister may be empowered by law 'to act as he thinks fit' or 'if he is satisfied'. Such words as 'if necessary', 'requisite', or 'expedient' abound in statutes implementing new services. There is, therefore, discretionary power bestowed by Parliament which is openly and avowedly used even under the 'regular law'. Such discretionary power is sometimes abused, and it is immaterial whether the power is derived from the 'regular law' or not.

During emergencies such as war, much wider powers are given by law to the Executive. For example, the Home Secretary was empowered under *Regulation 18B of the Defence (General) Regulations, 1939*, to imprison any person, 'if he had reasonable cause to believe such person to be of hostile origin or associations'. One person, Liversedge, was detained without trial under *Regulation 18B* and sued the Home Secretary for false imprisonment. It was held by the House of Lords that the court could not inquire into the grounds for the detention; it was a matter for the executive discretion of the Home Secretary in the circumstances of war. Accordingly the imprisonment was lawful.

Difficulty arises as to the meaning of 'regular law'. It is understood that Dicey meant the **common law** and the **statute law,** as it then existed. Today, however, much of the legislation is **delegated legislation,** i.e. rules, orders, or statutory instruments made by Ministers and other bodies and not directly by Parliament. Although such legislation is made under powers conferred by statute, Parliament has little control over the making of such legislation (see p. 248). Many citizens frequently find themselves subject to rules not made by Parliament but by the Executive. These rules hardly existed in Dicey's time.

Certain members of society are subject to special rules in their professions. Thus, solicitors, barristers, doctors, midwives, nurses, members of the armed forces, and the police are all subject to special rules, breach of which renders a member of any of the professions named liable to special punishment, such as fines deprivation of livelihood, or expulsion. Such rules apply to particular classes of people in the community who are treated differently from ordinary citizens. In any case the special rules cannot be treated as part of the 'regular law'.

(ii) *Equality before the Law.* However attractive this formula may be, there are obvious exceptions to it. H.M. The Queen cannot be sued personally in her own courts ('The Queen can do no wrong'). The *Crown Proceedings Act, 1947* (see p. 151) has not affected the personal immunity of the Sovereign.

Certain members of society are obviously exempt from the general law. A child in arms is inevitably treated differently from adult members of society. Children under 10 years cannot in this country be convicted of crime, and those between 10 and 14 only in special circumstances.

More important is the number of officials who have greater legal powers than those possessed by the ordinary citizen. The police, public health inspectors, factory inspectors, medical officers of health, inspectors of weights and measures, customs' officers, and so on, all possess special powers. Some may forcibly enter private premises to inspect or take possession of property; some may be empowered to arrest, and some may prosecute for certain special offences. Although these rights are conferred by law they do, in fact, place the officials mentioned in a special position. To that extent there is no 'equality before the law'.

Foreign sovereigns, ambassadors, High Commissioners, and diplomats enjoy a special immunity from civil and criminal law of the country to which they are officially posted. These constitute a further exception to the principle of 'equality before the law'.

Judges of the High Court enjoy immunity from liability for acts done within their official jurisdiction. This judicial freedom and independence is essential for the proper administration of justice. Nevertheless, judges (and indeed magistrates) provide a further exception to the rule.

(iii) *The Constitution—the result of the Ordinary Law of the land.* We have noted that many countries have written constitutions. In particular we have mentioned the U.S.A. Most modern states adopt written constitutions. We have mentioned already that the constitutions usually provide clauses defining the rights and duties of citizens (see The *Bill of Rights* which constituted the first ten Amendments to the American Constitution). When, therefore, any person unlawfully invades the rights of person or property of a citizen he may consult the constitutional provisions, decide that the invasion is unlawful and sue the offender before the law courts.

Dicey states: 'with us the constitution is the consequence of the rights of the individual as defined in the Courts of Law'. The British Constitution is unwritten: it is the product of the operation of the ordinary law of the land. The legal rights and duties of a British subject are generally found in the common law (there are, of course, certain rules contained in particular statutes). The broad rule of the common law in that no one may interfere with or invade my person or property unless he has lawful power so to do. Otherwise he commits a wrong (contrary to the common law) for which I may sue. There is no guaranteed constitutional rule in writing to this effect; it is merely the rule of the common law which has been hammered out over the centuries by the judges. Any citizen may, therefore, ascertain his rights from the legal cases decided in the past and from statutes.

There are, therefore, no fundamental and guaranteed rights enshrined in some sacred constitutional code or statute.

How secure are the rules of common law in this respect? Under the doctrine of Parliamentary supremacy we have seen that Parliament can make and unmake law to any extent it pleases. It can, therefore, revoke all or any rights of person or property which we may have, and it may do this at any time it pleases. That is theory. In practice it would be unthinkable. The true safeguard against abuse of executive power lies in the vigilance of an informed electorate, a free Press, the responsibility of the Government to Parliament and of Parliament to the electorate, and an independent judiciary.

As has been said: 'The test of a free country is to examine the status of the body that corresponds to Her Majesty's Opposition' (per Sir Ivor Jennings). All we need to note here is that the traditional freedoms which we know in this country are the result (or consequence) of the operation of the common law and are not enshrined in a written form in a constitution. It is impossible to say whether one or the other is the more secure; the only true safeguard lies in the will and spirit of the people to preserve the freedoms they now enjoy.

The Rise of Parliament

To understand the British Constitution one must look at the history of Parliament and its rise to power. We recall that the British Constitution has evolved over the course of 900 years into its present form which is that of a democracy with a constitutional Monarch at its head. By this we mean that although the supreme power in the State lies in the hands of the people, and the representatives they elect, the formal head of the State is the Queen whose actual powers are restricted by constitutional laws, customs and conventions.

The word 'Parliament' meant a talk, and was originally applied in the thirteenth century to the after-dinner gossip of monks in their cloisters which, incidentally, was condemned as unedifying. The word was also used to describe solemn conferences such as that in 1245 between Louis IX of France and Pope Innocent IV. It then came into use for the national assemblies in England after the middle of the thirteenth century.

The Kings of England were once powerful figures who claimed to rule their lands by divine right. A Monarch cannot, however, rule a kingdom by himself.

The Anglo-Saxon kings were assisted by the **Witenagemot**, an assembly of the wisest of men in the kingdom, to give counsel (**rede**) to the Monarch. Even in those times it was an English custom that in important matters such as the interpretation of laws, the King ought not to act alone but should first obtain the advice and consent of the wisest of his people. Custom also required that he hold 'deep speech' with the **Witan**, or council of wise men, two or three times a year. After listening to the speeches of the leaders, the assembly gave a vote for or against a proposition by clashing their arms against their shields.

The Anglo-Saxon Witan appears to have been a small aristocratic body of variable composition with great powers. F. W. Maitland stated:

> It can elect Kings and depose them; the King and Witan legislate; it is with the counsel and consent of the Witan that the King publishes laws; the King and Witan nominate the ealdormen and bishops, make grants of the public lands, impose taxes, decide on peace and war and form a tribunal of last resort for causes criminal and civil. It is a supreme legislative, governmental and judicial assembly.

Here, we may note, was a free assembly of men who, though not elected, were representative of all parts of the country. They came from the **shires** (later called 'counties') and smaller units into which the country was divided. The **ealdormen** were important local figures; the **sheriff** was the King's outpost officer who represented the King's interests and presided in the shire court to do justice and administer the laws. The sheriff was an important powerful figure and his office survived the Conquest.

After the arrival of the **Normans** in 1066 we find a great change took place. The Norman Kings possessed orderly minds and were efficient administrators. They unified the kingdom, administered the local English customs and laws and introduced *feudalism*. Under this system the King made grants of land to his nobles and followers in return for a promise of allegiance, active help in time of war and the payment of feudal dues. The nobles who held their land directly from the King also made subgrants of land to their tenants, again in return for allegiance and the payment of feudal dues. The lord on his part promised protection and justice. William I went further and ordained that all landholders owed a duty of allegiance to him as King. This qualified the immediate allegiance which a landholder owed to his immediate overlord. Thus loyalty to the King was the supreme and universal duty of all English freemen (or **freeholders,** as they were called). This form of feudalism introduced from the continent made for greater unity and cohesion within the kingdom.

The Witan disappeared with the Anglo-Saxon Kings. William I and his successors held **Great Councils** instead. These were assemblies of the King's tenants in chief (i.e. the nobles and others who held their lands directly from the King). 'Thrice a year,' we are told, 'King William wore his crown every year he was in England; at Easter he wore it at Winchester, at Pentecost at Westminster, and at Christmas at Gloucester, and at these times all the men of England were with him—archbishops, bishops and abbots, earls, thegns, and knights.'

During the thirteenth century the 'Councils' began to be called 'Parliaments'. The barons were thus, on occasion, summoned by the King to attend a 'Parliament'. They were the aristocracy and did not represent all the classes of England. The knights and the burgesses (i.e. citizens) in the medieval boroughs were not represented, and these were growing wealthier and more important.

In 1265 **Simon De Montfort** summoned representatives of the 'commons', i.e. the commoners, which included the knights from the counties and two elected burgesses from the independent towns or boroughs with Royal Charters. In 1295 the so-called **Model Parliament** of Edward I was summoned which included barons (the nobility), knights, burgesses, senior clergy, and lower clergy. All were summoned on the principle that 'what touches all should be approved by all'.

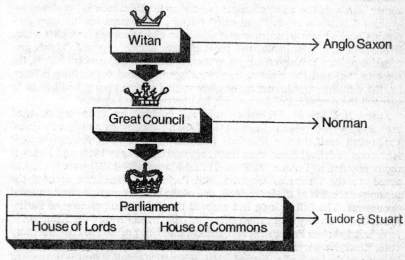

Witan: Great Council: Parliament

These groups of people, comprising the three estates of the Realm (**the Lords Spiritual, the Lords Temporal** and **the Commons**) were summoned by the King to Westminster to some of the Parliaments, particularly when the King required extra money to carry on government or to engage in wars or crusades.

The foregathering of all classes in the country was a big step forward. In the first half of the fourteenth century the practice developed whereby the Lords and the Commons met separately from each other in private assemblies or gatherings to discuss their answers to the King who called them to his presence. These answers were given to the King *in Parliament*.

Most of the discussions or debates took place in these private meetings of the Lords and the Commons. From some time in the middle of the fourteenth century the Commons elected a speaker who presided over the meetings. He acted also as a channel of communication with the King. When the King demanded money from the Commons, the latter began submitting to the King petitions or 'bills' requesting a change in the law of the land. During this time the vital principle of **grievances before supply** was established. When the King asked for financial aid from his people, the Commons chose the moment to strike a bargain with him regarding the redress of grievances which were brought to his notice in Parliament in the form of petitions.

From the time of Henry V (1413–22) a Bill so presented was enacted in the form the Commons desired. Nevertheless for some time afterwards both the

Sovereign and the Lords considered they could tamper with or alter the text extensively without obtaining the approval of the Commons. It was not until the reign of Henry VII (1485–1509) that the practice was established of sending up petitions (apart from Private Bills) to the King in the form of statutes to which the King could either assent or dissent.

The Tudor and Stuart Period

The sixteenth and seventeenth centuries witnessed a great constitutional struggle between the Monarchs on the one hand and Parliament on the other. Henry VIII was the most absolute of Monarchs; Elizabeth I, his daughter, avoided a head-on conflict and ruled through Parliament for her own purposes. Charles I was aristocratic and wished to claim **prerogative rights** which Parliament and, eventually, the common law judges opposed. These prerogative powers included the right to issue ordinances and proclamations, the right to tax, and the right to exercise dispensing and suspending powers, i.e. the right to grant immunity or dispensation to any person he liked or to suspend the operation of laws which had properly been enacted.

James II (1685–8) claimed to rule the country by **divine right**, used arbitrary methods which alienated the Crown's supporters and openly defied Parliament itself. In the *Bloodless Revolution* (or *Glorious Revolution* as it is sometimes called) Parliament finally resisted the King in 1688, and James II thereupon fled to France. William III and Mary (1689–1702) were invited to accede to the throne of England, and Parliament thereupon secured the passing of the *Bill of Rights* in 1689, one of the most important constitutional documents. The Bill at long last ensured the ultimate supremacy of Parliament. One of its most important effects was that henceforward the King would be definitely below Parliament and, indeed, owed his position to Parliamentary vote. Executive government depended upon Parliament for the laws it administered and the funds of money which the Executive required for the purpose of government. We must remember that the Monarch continued to play a leading part for some time as head of the Executive, until the emergence of a Prime Minister and a Cabinet.

The Eighteenth Century

George I (1714–27) and George II (1727–60) could neither speak nor understand English with ease and were less interested in the affairs of England than those of Hanover. Both left the affairs of actual government in the hands of their Ministers. As a result we see the emergence of the office of **Prime Minister** (the first was **Sir Robert Walpole**) and of the Cabinet system of government which continues to this day. George III (1760–1820) tried unsuccessfully to re-establish royal power by using the **pocket boroughs** to create a party of King's friends in the House of Commons.

During the eighteenth century the Sovereign began to summon Parliament regularly. The *Mutiny Act* was passed which legalized a standing army for a year at a time, so that Parliament had to be called or summoned at least once a year. By the *Septennial Act, 1716,* Parliament's life was extended from three to seven years which made for greater continuity.

The main task of Parliament, however, was to consolidate the victory of 1689. There was party strife in Parliament, and there was a war with France to contend with. Further, although Parliament had secured supremacy, there was still considerable legal power left with the King and this had to be reconciled with the power of Parliament itself. The solution was found in new institutions within Parliament, in particular the growth of political parties, the office of Prime Minister and the Cabinet.

Reform Act, 1832

This Act is important because it gave political sovereignty to the electorate. Parliament reformed the corrupt system of pocket boroughs whereby constituencies with small electorates returned as their member of Parliament a nominee of a local magnate. The next hundred years saw the introduction of the **secret ballot**, and the eventual extension of the franchise to all adult persons.

Democracy is the most difficult of all forms of government. How far we have gone along the path to its achievement will be seen in the succeeding chapters which deal with its essential features. But first let us look at the concept of democracy in relation to Britain and other countries.

Democracy and Britain

The word democracy comes from *demos* (Greek) meaning people, and *kratos* (Greek) meaning power. Democracy can be of two kinds: (i) **direct** and (ii) **indirect**.

(i) Direct Democracy

Direct democracy was best observed in classical Greece when it was possible to assemble practically all the citizens in one place, as in the city-states of that time, e.g. Athens. The wise men in those city-states proposed legislation and the measures were put to the citizens who expressed their wishes in the form of a **plebiscite**. A plebiscite is a direct vote of the whole nation, or of the people of a district, on a special point; or an ascertainment of general opinion on a matter.

(ii) Indirect Democracy

This is more suited to modern nation-states which we find in the world today. Indirect democracy is practised through representative institutions such as Parliament. In the seventeenth century England achieved that situation through the events leading up to the *Glorious Revolution* when James II fled the country and Parliament assumed sovereignty, thus replacing the despotic rule of the Monarchs of the preceding centuries. Most civilized nations achieved or adopted democratic institutions by 1850.

Democracy in the sense in which we use the term today in Western Europe, the British Commonwealth, and the U.S.A., is based on certain doctrines. The first is the theory of the **separation of powers** (see p. 10) which involves the following: (i) legislation is made by a freely elected Parliament; (ii) executive power is vested in a Government responsible to the Legislature (Parliament); and (iii) an independent Judiciary. This doctrine implies that there is a free choice at regular intervals between two or more political parties. In the United Kingdom this takes place at least every five years. Elections are held to enable the electorate (the people) to choose or reject one or more parties. If there is only a single list of members of one party we are not using the word 'democracy' in the Western sense here understood.

We may say, therefore, that the separation of powers and free elections are essential characteristics. The other important feature of Western democracy (as in the United Kingdom) is the **Rule of Law** (see p. 14). You will recall that this means in essence that one is free from arrest unless one offends the law. One is free within the law. There is no discretionary power vested in a Minister or the police, for example, to arrest for vague 'political' crimes which are unknown to the law. The Rule of Law presupposes that there is equality before the law. There are certain immunities (e.g. the Crown, certain ambassadors, etc.), but as a broad proposition it represents a bulwark of democracy. We also have courts of law where justice is administered openly and fairly. There are no secret courts. We have freedom of opinion and speech, again within the law. We can, of course, alter the law from time to time, and we do so. But Parliament examines all legislation to ensure that it is good and suitable for the nation as a whole.

The word 'democracy' embraces all the above. It is difficult to describe: it is complex and it is the most difficult of systems to operate. But it is fitted with many *checks and balances* against the abuse of power, and it happens to be the best form of Government which the enlightened thought of man can devise. Abraham Lincoln expressed it thus: 'Government of the people, by the people and for the people.'

The expression 'rule of the people' is understood very differently in the U.S.S.R., China, Bulgaria, and Outer Mongolia. There is no doctrine of the separation of powers; no free elections; no rule of law; and freedom of opinion, speech, and association are not generally accepted. Yet the supporters of these regimes regard them as 'democratic'. Private ownership of the means of production is regarded as 'undemocratic'. State ownership and central planning for the increase of national wealth are the accepted beliefs of the Communist idea. The Communist Governments believe that the subordination of every interest and activity to the State ensures that the common good prevails over private interests.

Sovereignty

Sovereignty is the supreme power within a State. That supreme power in the United Kingdom is Parliament. Sir Edward Coke said:

> The power and jurisdiction of Parliament is so transcendent and absolute, that it cannot be confined, either for causes or persons, within any bounds.

In theory the sovereignty of Parliament is absolute. It is not, for example, subordinate to any other body or group inside the United Kingdom or outside. No Parliament, it is said, can bind its successors in power, for Parliament can make and unmake laws to any extent.

In practice, the 'sovereignty' is a number of rights any one of which can be abstracted. The Crown makes treaties with other countries. The agreements give rights and impose duties (the duties or obligations detract from the concept of sovereignty). Moreover the United Kingdom is a member of international organisations and bodies, e.g. NATO, the Western European Union (WEU), the International Monetary Fund (IMF).

Although it is true that the supremacy of Parliament means that no Parliament can bind its successors in power, in practice the treaties solemnly entered into by previous Governments are honoured by the successors in power and membership of the international organizations is continued.

Sovereignty and the EEC

The ultimate aim of the *Treaty of Rome* (*1958*) is to achieve **economic and political unity.** The Treaty of Rome is intended to be of unlimited duration. Opponents of Britain's accession fear the loss of Parliament's authority. They point to the legislation imposed by the community, which is binding on all member States and means a loss of sovereignty. The supporters of the EEC reply that there is no loss or surrender of sovereignty, but a 'pooling' of sovereignty by all concerned. In renouncing some of our sovereignty we receive in return a share of the sovereignty renounced by other members.

The question resolves into whether we believe in international co-operation or not. If we do, then organization is essential and rules are needed to achieve the economic and political benefits foreseen. In framing the rules for the European Community the British Parliament will contribute its part, but it will also be obliged to follow the rules imposed by the supranational authority. On 1 January 1973 the United Kingdom joined the EEC (*European Communities Act, 1972*).

Exercises

1. Define a 'constitution'.
2. Define a State and indicate its main functions.
3. Distinguish between a Unitary State and a Federal State.
4. Of which countries is the United Kingdom composed?
5. Some States are said to have rigid constitutions while others are described as flexible constitutions. What is meant by these descriptions?
6. What do we mean by (i) The Legislature; (ii) The Executive; and (iii) The Judiciary?
7. What do we mean by 'the sources' of the British Constitution?
8. What is meant by the doctrine of 'the separation of powers'? Has it any validity today?
9. The Rule of Law (or supremacy of law). Has this doctrine any validity today?
10. Give a short account of the rise of Parliament from Norman times to the early nineteenth century.

CHAPTER TWO

ELECTIONS AND THE PARTY SYSTEM

The Electoral System

The United Kingdom is divided into constituencies, each of which contains 60,000 to 70,000 persons who have the right to vote, and each of which returns one member to Parliament as its political representative in Westminster.

All persons, over the age of 18 years, have the right to vote. The actual qualifications and disqualifications are dealt with later.

This voting franchise, 'one man one vote', as it is frequently expressed, is fundamental to our democracy and the British Constitution. We enjoy the privilege of voting for the candidate we prefer; we have secret ballots; an electoral procedure which is fair and just; and an absence of corruption in its administration. All these electoral rights and benefits have been won, step by step, over the past 140 years.

Development of the Franchise

The House of Lords originally contained the aristocratic nobles and barons, and was the predominant chamber until the time of Elizabeth I (1558–1603). The Lords were summoned to the House by writ of summons and duly took their seats. They have at no time in history been elected by the people, and therefore this chamber cannot be described as truly democratic. That position remains substantially the same today.

The House of Commons contained originally in the thirteenth century the knights from the shires and the burgesses from the boroughs. Together these two groups of representatives made up the Commons. At the beginning of the reign of Elizabeth I, two members were elected from each county and two burgesses were elected for each Borough to attend Parliament. These men were squires or landowners from the counties, and landowners of influence and power or members of the middle class from the boroughs.

In the counties of England and Wales the right to vote for a member was laid down in the fifteenth century and was limited to males only having a clear income of 40 shillings per year. The franchise was based on wealth. In the boroughs this rule did not apply; the voting franchise varied from borough to borough, but here also the vote was generally limited to those persons with landed interests which resulted in a small electorate. In 1800 only three persons out of every 100 possessed the vote. That could not be described as just or democratic.

In the eighteenth and nineteenth centuries the rich landowners exercised considerable influence over the electorate. Many county members of Parliament were simply the nominees of the wealthy aristocrats. Some villages or hamlets with only a handful of residents returned a member to Parliament. They became known as **rotten** or **pocket boroughs**. Bribery, corruption, and intimidation of voters were common features of the electoral system of the day. Monarchs used the opportunity to persuade powerful landowners to return to Parliament those members upon whom the King could rely to manipulate the Commons to further his own ends. The members who lent themselves became known as 'King's Friends'.

In the early nineteenth century, however, the industrial revolution effected a great change in the country: coal- and iron-mining increased greatly, railways were constructed, and factories were erected on, or near, the great coalfields in the Midlands and the North of England. Large towns, e.g. Manchester, Leeds, Sheffield, and Birmingham, sprang up. None had proper representation in Parliament. Yet at the same time small hamlets such as Old Sarum (Wiltshire) with six voters, returned two members to Parliament; and Okehampton, Devon, a small town, sent to Parliament as many members as the whole of Yorkshire.

From the industrial revolution emerged a much larger and wealthier middle class who condemned the inefficient political system that excluded them from political power. After considerable agitation and struggle, during which riots broke out in most of the large towns, the *Reform Act, 1832*, was passed. This laid down the foundation for a remodelled franchise. All reforms of the electoral system after this important act followed as natural steps in the process towards universal franchise which exists today.

The stages are noted as follows in more detail:

The Reform Act, 1832:
  (i) This Act disqualified fifty-six small boroughs from returning members to Parliament, and thirty other boroughs were deprived of all but one member;
  (ii) The seats taken from boroughs in (i) above, were transferred to the growing industrial centres—Birmingham, Manchester, and the County of Yorkshire.

In addition to the above, the Act laid down for the boroughs a uniform **occupation franchise** for any male who occupied as (*a*) owner or (*b*) tenant, any house, shop or other building of an annual unfurnished value of £10.

The county franchise was extended to long leaseholders and copyholders (i.e. those who held their lands by right of a copy of the rolls in the Court manor) of property of the annual value of £10, to all male leaseholders who held land for terms of not less than twenty years and to occupiers of property of £50 annual representation.

The Act produced 215,000 new voters, mainly of the middle class, making a total voting population of 500,000.

Representation of the People Act, 1867
This made for another redistribution of seats. Some forty-five boroughs, each with a population of less than 10,000, lost one member to the new large towns. The Act reduced the property qualification of the leaseholder and copyholder to £5, and introduced as an additional qualification the occupation of a tenement (premises) of a minimum rateable value of £12. In the boroughs the working man was enfranchised, i.e. if he was a male householder occupying for one year a separate dwelling house and paying the poor rate, or a lodger who occupied for a period of one year lodgings of unfurnished value of £10. The total number of voters reached 2,000,000.

Ballot Act, 1872
This Act introduced the vital principle of the **secret ballot** and made intimidation of voters an offence.

Representation of the People Act, 1884

This Act made three changes:

(i) It extended the householder and 'lodger' franchise to the counties (bringing the counties into line with the boroughs under the 1867 Act above).

(ii) In the counties and the boroughs any person occupying any land or tenement of a clear annual value of £10 obtained the vote.

(iii) It gave the vote to any servant (e.g. a gardener) living separately from his employer, i.e. not living in the house of his employer as would a butler or a valet.

The main effect of this Act was to give the vote to the working man in the county. The total number of voters now reached 5,000,000.

(1) Presiding Officer checking name of voter
(2) Clerk issuing Voting Slip
(3) Voter receiving ballot paper
(4) Voter in polling booth
(5) Voter in polling booth
(6) Voter putting slip in Ballot Box (locked)
(7) Police Officer preserving law and order

A polling station

Redistribution of Seats Act, 1885

This Act also redistributed seats to provide more equal electoral areas on the basis of one M.P. for every 50,000 of population. The cause of this was the influx of new inhabitants from the rural areas to the Northern and Midland towns. Some 134 seats were taken from boroughs with small populations, and these seats were allocated to the large towns insufficiently represented in Parliament. The number of M.P.s increased to 670.

Representation of the People Act, 1918

This was an important Act whose provisions may be summarized as follows:

(i) The voting qualification was laid down as six months' residence or occupation of business premises.

(ii) The vote was given to any woman over 30 years, provided she or her husband was qualified to vote at local government elections.

(iii) Disqualification for the receipt of poor relief was abolished.

(iv) All Parliamentary elections must be held on the same day; and no elector may vote in more than two constituencies.

(v) Any Parliamentary candidate must deposit £150 with a Returning Officer. This sum was forfeit if the candidate did not poll one-eighth of the total votes cast.

(vi) Seats were redistributed on the basis of one M.P. to every 70,000 of population.

Representation of the People Act, 1928

This introduced a uniform franchise for men and women of 21 years and over provided they were qualified by:

(i) Residence for qualifying period of three months.

(ii) Occupation of land or premises for business purposes of annual value of £10 or more for three months.

(iii) Being the spouse of an occupier of land as at (ii) above.

(iv) Being a graduate of a British university.

Representation of the People Act, 1948

The main provisions included:

(i) Abolition of the business premises' qualification to vote (see (ii) above).

(ii) Abolition of the graduate vote (see (iv) above).

Representation of the People Act, 1969

The main provisions of the above Act are as follows:

(i) Voting age for Parliamentary and local government elections now 18.

(ii) The non-resident qualifications for voting at local government elections and the property qualifications for candidates at local government elections are abolished.

(iii) Candidates' election expenses in Parliamentary elections are now: £750 plus 5p for every 6 entries in the register in a county constituency and 5p for every 8 entries in a Borough constituency. Maximum expenses: £1,250 in counties and £1,125 in boroughs.

(iv) Polling hours on election days are extended to 10 p.m.

(v) Political descriptions (maximum six words) may now appear on ballot papers. A central register of political descriptions is kept.

The lowering of the voting age added approximately 2,500,000 voters to the register. With respect to point (v) above over eighty different party labels have been used since 1945.

The Voters

Table 1 on the next page illustrates the proportion of the electorate to the population of the United Kingdom.

By the *Representation of the People Act, 1969* the voting age for Parliamentary and local elections is now 18 years. The 1974 total electorate was 39,798,899.

Table 1
Electorate and populations

Year	Total Electorate	Population Aged 20 and over	Electorate as percentage of population aged 20 and over
1831	438,000	10,207,000	4·4%
1832	720,784	10,207,000	7·1
1864	1,130,372	13,051,816	9·0
1868	2,231,030	13,625,658	16·4
1883	2,955,190	16,426,233	18·0
1886	4,965,618	17,394,014	28·5
1914	7,483,165	24,969,241	30·0
1921	19,984,037	26,846,785	74·0
1931	29,175,608	30,096,135	96·9
1946	34,320,351	34,516,000	99·3
1949	33,545,221	34,981,000	95·9
1959	34,523,000	37,211,000	92·8
1964	35,003,000	36,372,000	96·2

OND

Criticism of the Electoral System

The candidate at a Parliamentary election who receives most votes wins the election and becomes the Member of Parliament for the Constituency. Whether he wins by 1 vote or 10,000 it does not matter: the man with the most votes gets in.

This system has merit; it has been well tried and satisfies the electorate as a whole. In effect, the election has the appearance of a race past the winning post. But there are criticisms. We may note the following.

M.P.s with Minority of Votes

Let us suppose that in the Camford constituency there are three candidates: Raymond Redd (Lab.), Basil Blew (Con.), and Leslie Liberty (Lib.). The election vote may reveal the following result:

Raymond Redd (Lab.)	26,000
Basil Blew (Con.)	24,000
Leslie Liberty (Lib.)	10,000
	60,000

Mr. Redd (Lab.), the successful candidate, has the support of 26,000 voters. But most of the voters, i.e. 34,000 (24,000 (Con.) and 10,000 (Lib.))

voted against Mr. Redd. In effect, therefore, a member is returned to Parliament on a minority of the total number of voters in that constituency. This may be looked upon as a weakness if we accept the principle that an M.P. ought to have the support of the majority of the voters in his constituency. This criticism does not apply in contests between two parties only, i.e. where there is a 'straight fight' between two contestants. For example:

Raymond Redd (Lab.)	36,000
Basil Blew (Con.)	24,000
	60,000

The Reflection of Public Opinion

The present electoral system is said to be 'unfair' to minority parties. The House of Commons is composed of those members who attract most votes in their constituencies. The leader of the party returning most members to Parliament forms H.M. Government. If we look at the election results of the country as a whole we may say that the House of Commons constituted in the usual way does not represent the true balance of feeling in the country.

This is best seen by Table 2 below. The figures are based on percentages.

Table 2
Percentage of M.P.s per Party and percentage of votes cast

Party	1966		1970		Feb. 1974		Oct. 1974	
	No. of M.P.s (%)	Total votes cast (%)	No. of M.P.s (%)	Total votes cast (%)	No. of M.P.s (%)	Total votes cast (%)	No. of M.P.s (%)	Total votes cast (%)
Con.	40	42	52	46	47	38	44	36
Lab.	58	48	46	43	47	37	50	39
Lib.	2	9	1	8	2	19	2	18

These figures show the difference in the **feeling of the voters** throughout the country, and the **actual party representation** in the House of Commons. The Labour Government took office in 1966, but, as will be seen from the above table, it polled only forty-eight per cent of the total votes cast. Strictly speaking, therefore, the majority of persons did not vote for the party which assumed power.

In the election of October 1974 the Liberal Party obtained 5,346,800 votes (18 per cent), but gained a mere 13 seats (2 per cent of the seats); the Conservatives obtained 10,464,675 votes (36 per cent) and 276 seats. The Labour Party obtained 11,456,597 votes (39 per cent) and obtained 319 seats. The Labour majority was 5.

Reform of the Electoral System

The electoral system of this country has been the subject of official inquiries of one kind or another for the past seventy years. A Royal Commission was set up in 1910: conferences were held in 1916, 1930, and a Committee on

OND

Electoral Law Reform was constituted in 1948. The most recent inquiry was a Speaker's Conference which was held in 1967. This last conference recommended against the introduction of a new system. No fundamental change may be anticipated, though we may remember that the constituency boundaries are continuously under review by a Commission.

No system, however, is perfect, and it is fitting here to consider the alternative suggested forms of electoral representation.

The Second Ballot

This system is based on the principle that a successful candidate must obtain an **absolute majority** of the votes cast so that there will be no minority M.P.s. Let us suppose there are three candidates, *A*, *B* and *C*. The result of the contest is:

A polls	25,000 votes
B „	20,000 „
C „	10,000 „

A second ballot is held. Candidate *C* is eliminated since he obtained the lowest vote. At the second ballot *A* and *B* only are the contestants. The contest now resolves itself into a straight fight. Either *A* or *B* will be the winner. In the second vote the 10,000 votes could of course be distributed between the two. It is more than likely that *A* will win, but not necessarily so, since the 10,000 votes cast for *C* may be given to *B* who would then have 30,000 (20,000 + 10,000).

The criticism of the second ballot is that it would eliminate minority M.P.s and there would be no representation of minorities. The holding of a second ballot is also tedious, and can be inconvenient to the public.

The Alternative Vote

This procedure is similar to the second ballot, but the election is carried out at one election. Voters under this system mark on the voting slips the numbers 1, 2, or 3 against the candidates' names in order of preference. The first count is taken on first choices. Let us suppose Candidate *A* has 25,000 with a '1' against his name; Candidate *B* has 20,000 with a '1', and Candidate *C* has 10,000 similarly marked. If no candidate has an absolute majority on first preferences (i.e. polls more than half of the total number of votes in the constituency), the candidate with the lowest number of votes (i.e. *C*) is eliminated from the contest. The votes cast for *C* are distributed to the remaining candidates (*A* and *B*) on the basis of second preference. One of these contestants will win the election on the basis of the majority of votes. In the event of a tie at an election a recount can be asked for and, if another tie results, the issue can be decided by the spin of a coin.

Proportional Representation

The principle of proportional representation is based on the idea that each party should obtain representation in proportion to the number of votes cast for it. To operate the system the country would be divided into large constituencies, or the whole country could be regarded as one large constituency in which each party would be represented in proportion to the votes it secured. Generally it is assumed that the country would be divided into large constituencies.

Each constituency would return a number of M.P.s to the House of

Commons. Each party then puts up several candidates. The elector would vote for the candidates in order of preference, marking his voting slip in numerical order. Any candidate who obtains a certain quota of first preferences would be immediately elected. His surplus votes would be distributed to other candidates according to the second preferences expressed on the voting slips. Again, any candidate then obtaining the quota would be returned, and a similar distribution of his surplus votes would take place.

Example. Let us assume that three seats are available to a large constituency and that there are five candidates contesting the election. (There could, of course, be more.) Let us also assume that a quota of 40,000 votes are needed for the election of any candidate.

The result on first preferences could then be:

Attlee	50,000
Burke	40,000
Churchill	30,000
Disraeli	20,000
Gladstone	10,000

Attlee and Burke are both elected for each has acquired the necessary quota. But the election so far has not given to Churchill, Disraeli, or Gladstone the requisite number, viz. 40,000.

The next step in the process is to take the excess of Attlee's votes, i.e. 10,000, and to divide these according to the second preference marked on them. The result might then be:

Attlee	40,000
Burke	45,000
Churchill	35,000
Disraeli	20,000
Gladstone	10,000

We note that Churchill, Disraeli, and Gladstone have not acquired the necessary quota. The next step is to take the surplus votes of Burke (i.e. 5,000). These are distributed among Churchill, Disraeli, and Gladstone. If this distribution does not produce the desired result the candidate with the fewest votes is eliminated from the contest and his votes (let us say Gladstone's) are redistributed according to the next choice. The process is repeated until a candidate gets the quota of 40,000, when he is declared elected to join Attlee and Burke. This form is known as the single transferable vote.

The advantages of proportional representation are first, that it gives a greater opportunity to minority parties to obtain seats in the House. (The Liberal Party supports proportional representation because of the discrepancy between the total number of votes cast throughout the country and the actual number of Liberal M.P.s elected.) Secondly, if there is a range of candidates of varying abilities the electors are given a choice for particular individuals. Moreover, if there are within a party (let us say the Labour Party) certain members belonging to opposing factions, e.g. Left Wing and Right Wing, an elector would be able to express his preferences for the faction within the party which he (the elector) supports.

The disadvantages of proportional representation are as follows:

(i) It is complicated and confusing to the electors.
(ii) It is unlikely to produce better government.

(iii) Many small parties could arise, so that it would be rare for one political party to obtain a majority of seats overall. This would lead to a coalition (grouping of parties to form a government) which produces weak and unstable governments.

(iv) The link between an M.P. and his constituents would be broken since the small area, with a single M.P., would disappear in the large constituencies with more than one member.

Most European countries have adopted some form of proportional representation. However, it does not appear to rouse deep enthusiasm in this country and since in modern times political power is 'monopolized' between two main political parties and since there are no fundamental differences between their policies in this respect (the Speaker's Conference of 1967 recommended against any new system of representation) it is most unlikely that proportional representation will be adopted here.

Development of the Party System

Edmund Burke (1729–97), a great Irishman, statesman, writer, and orator, defined a political party as:

a body of men united for promoting, by their joint endeavours, the national interest upon some particular principle in which they are all agreed.

This definition is clear and memorable. It shows us also that the modern idea of party political organization had taken root before the end of the eighteenth century. In the following pages we sketch in broad outline the history of the influential parties which have shaped the destiny of the Constitution.

History

Towards the end of Charles II's reign (1660–85) the Exclusion Bill debates in Parliament (1679–80) were notable in that they gave rise to the birth of two parties in the political life of the nation. These two parties became known as **Whigs** and **Tories**. These names were given by each party to the other, more as terms of reproach, but they were subsequently accepted by each as its label. Later in the 1830s the two parties changed their names again: Whigs became **Liberals**, and Tories became **Conservatives**.

The earliest Parliaments had no party system in anything like the form we have today. Members were called by the Monarch to attend upon him at Westminster mainly to obtain grants of money or to gain practical support in the government of the country. His primary functions as Monarch in the early days were to maintain peace and good order at home and to preserve the kingdom from foreign aggression.

In the reign of **Charles I** there was a division in Parliament between the supporters of the Monarch, called the **Royalists**, and his opponents, the **Roundheads**. In the Civil War, Charles I was executed in 1649, and **Cromwell** (1599–1658) became a virtual dictator until the **Restoration** in 1660 and the accession of **Charles II**.

Right until the end of the seventeenth century the principal Officers of State were chosen by and responsible to the Monarch—not to Parliament or the nation at large. This was a matter within the Royal Prerogative. The officers appointed sometimes acted in concert with one another, but more often they acted independently. The fall from power or resignation of one officer did not necessarily or automatically involve the resignation of the others. Each Officer of State was liable to be dismissed by the Sovereign at any time.

Originally, the Whigs in the late seventeenth century represented the rising merchant class and the new middle class. The Tories represented the landed aristocracy and the squirearchy (country gentry). There was no clear definition of political aim or philosophy. Whigs and Tories were groups, each of which was influenced by royal power and patronage and by the religious questions of the period.

In 1693 a change took place. Both **William III** and **Mary** (1689–1702), found that mixed ministries of Whigs and Tories would not work. The mixture was incompatible with the growth of the political parties now forming definite ideas and policies of their own. The Whigs wished to limit the power of the Royal Prerogative, to extend religious freedom to Protestants, and to favour the monied interests (in London and the provinces) as opposed to the landed gentry, who were the main supporters of the Tories.

In 1693 **William III** was advised by the Earl of Sunderland to select a Ministry from the political party which enjoyed a majority in the House of Commons. The first united Ministry (of the same political party) was appointed in 1696 from the Whigs. The Ministry so formed included Russell (the Admiral), Somers (Advocate), Lord Wharton, and Charles Montague, who afterwards became **Chancellor of the Exchequer**. This group of Ministers became known as the **Junto**. It was made up of a small section which met in secret apart from the main body of Ministers. It attracted some suspicion: people frowned upon the separation into groups or cliques, for they had been dangerous in the past. Nevertheless, the Ministry so formed continued, though it was looked upon as a novelty in the political life of the nation.

The Junto was the forerunner of the modern **Cabinet**. In due time it accepted the principle of a common aim and the joint responsibility of Ministers. If there were internal disagreement in the group this would involve a change of personnel (e.g. where one or two members resigned) or the resignation of the whole body of Ministers. This, of course, happens today.

George I (1714–27), the first of the Hanoverian Kings, could not speak English well. His unfamiliarity with the language was a handicap and he was disinclined to attend and preside at meetings of his Ministers whose business he did not fully understand. The King's absence led to the appearance of a **Prime Minister** who presided over the group in the King's place. **Robert Walpole** (1676–1745), a Whig, acquired the position first in 1721 and retained office without interruption for almost twenty-one years.

In the eighteenth century both parties, Whigs and Tories, were united by family and local ties rather than by a unity of political aims or philosophy. There was no effective party discipline, and there was no Opposition Party in the sense in which it operates in Parliament today, for the simple reason that it was not organized.

The Growth of the Liberals

In about 1830 the old party of the Whigs became known as Liberals. This name also was given to the Party by its opponents, and implied laxity of political principles. Gradually, however, the name was accepted by the Party itself to manifest its claims to be pioneers and champions of political and social reform and progressive legislation.

In 1836 the **Reform Club** was founded as a centre and meeting place for

Liberal M.P.s and sympathizers outside Parliament. In 1861 a **National Liberal Registration Association** was founded, and Liberal Associations sprang up throughout the country. These associations organized lists of local voters after the *Reform Act, 1832*. In 1877 a **National Liberal Federation** was established with Headquarters in London.

During the second part of the nineteenth century the Liberal Party under **W. E. Gladstone** (1809–98) (the founder of modern Liberalism) was in power for long periods. However, during the **Irish Home Rule** crisis of 1886, a group known as **Liberal Unionists** seceded from the Party because of disagreement (the group later on joined the Conservatives). This division within the Party was maintained during the first quarter of the twentieth century. Then a further split occurred into **National Liberals** and **Independent Liberals**. This further weakened the Party with the result that only fifty-nine Liberal M.P.s were returned to Parliament at the general election of 1929. After the 1945 election the number was reduced to twelve, and after the 1950 election it was further reduced to nine. After the 1951, 1955 and 1959 elections the number of Liberal M.P.s fell to six. The 1970 election which yielded six Liberal M.P.s again reflected the great change which has come over the Party since its heyday in the nineteenth century. In 1974 the Party gained 14 seats.

The Conservative Party

At the same time as the Whigs changed their name to Liberal we find the Tory Party assuming the name 'Conservative'. This name was reputedly invented by one J. W. Croker in 1830 and became generally adopted at the time of the passing of the *Reform Act, 1832*, to demonstrate the leading principle of the party, namely the preservation of the national institutions.

In 1832 the Tories founded the **Carlton Club** which was the centre and meeting place of the Tory M.P.s and their followers and adherents outside Parliament.

After the *Irish Home Rule Bill of 1886* (as noted above) certain dissentient Liberals (Liberal Unionists) entered into a compact with the Conservatives and, eventually, in 1912, this group united with the Conservatives under the title **National Unionist Association of Conservative** and **Liberal Unionist Organizations**. The members became known as 'Unionists'. The name Conservative is the more popular one by which the Party and its members are today referred to.

The Conservative Party has held power for considerable periods during the present century; e.g. 1951–5; 1955–9; 1959–64; and 1970–74.

Edmund Burke (1729–97) and **Benjamin Disraeli** (1804–81) (first Earl of Beaconsfield) exercised most influence on Conservative political theories. Disraeli, Prime Minister from 1874–80, is commonly regarded as the founder of modern Conservatism. One of his aims was to harmonize the 'two nations' (the rich and the poor), an aim which he combined with progressive social reform.

After 1945 the Conservative Party has modified its policy to accord with modern times and generally a more equitable spread of wealth. The party's industrial policy seeks to reconcile the need for central direction with its traditional encouragement of individual and private enterprise which has sometimes been named 'welfare capitalism'.

The Conservative Party was defeated in 1964, but regained power in 1970 under Mr. Edward Heath.

The Labour Party

The Labour Party has grown to power over the last hundred years. It is distinguished from the other parties in that it sprang up outside Parliament and was limited, until it could operate politically through the enlargement of the franchise. The Liberals and the Tories were groups of M.P.s who formed parties within Parliament. Moreover, it may be said that the Labour Party originally represented the working classes. Its present membership has broadened to include others.

The main beliefs of the Party are socialist and are said to derive from about 1834 when **Robert Owen**, a social reformer, established his 'village of cooperation' at New Lanark. He was followed by **Charles Kingsley (1819–75)**, priest and writer, and others who established **Christian Socialism**. These were followed by **William Morris**, **John Burns**, and other reformers who were passionately concerned with social justice.

Towards the close of the nineteenth century three socialist organizations were formed:

    (i) The Social Democratic Federation (1881).
    (ii) The Fabian Society (1883).
    (iii) The Independent Labour Party (1893).

At about the same time **Trade Unions** were recognized by law (*Trade Union Act, 1871*). These were combinations of workmen and were vitally concerned with the improvement of the wages, welfare, and conditions of employment of the working classes. The Trade Unions allied themselves to the Labour Party, in sympathy with their aims.

Fabianism was the system of beliefs of certain notable intellectuals (Sidney and Beatrice Webb, Graham Wallas, H. G. Wells, G. B. Shaw, to name only some) who held that social change could be brought about by **gradual parliamentary means**. The Fabian Society collaborated with the Labour Party, the trade unions, and the Co-Operative Movement, and was concerned with political education of men and their representative organizations.

The British Labour Party believes in peaceful and constitutional change to socialism by democratic methods based on popular support and consent. The party believes also in a planned economy and public (i.e. State) ownership of certain vital industries. This State-ownership of important industries was largely brought about by the Labour Government of 1945–51 which also introduced a comprehensive system of social security, creating, in effect, a **'Welfare State'**.

The Parliamentary Labour Party

The first appearance of Labour candidates at a general election was in 1892 when there were twenty-seven candidates standing as Labour or Liberal–Labour. At the general election of 1895 there were twelve successful candidates, and at the election of 1900 there were eleven.

In 1900 the **Labour Representative Committee** was set up to establish a unified Labour Group in Parliament with its own **Whips**, its own policy and a willingness to co-operate with any party which might be engaged in promoting legislation in the direct interest of labour (i.e. the working classes of the country at the time). In 1906 the L.R.C. became known as the **Labour Party**.

In 1918 some 74 members were returned to Parliament. This number was almost doubled in 1922, and in 1929 some 287 members were returned. In

1931 there were 65, but from then on it has gradually increased its members until, in 1945, after World War II, there were some 396 Members in Parliament representing the Labour Party with its greatest ever majority. In 1966 Labour returned 363 members, again with a sufficient majority to form a Government. It was defeated in 1970 by the Conservatives.

This briefly is the history of the three contestants for power in the Parliamentary arena. The Liberals are struggling to be a serious contender for Parliamentary power. The two main contestants are Labour and Conservative.

The Scottish Nationalist Party

This was formed in 1928. Its first success was in 1945 when one M.P. was returned for Motherwell. In November 1967 Mrs. W. Ewing was successful in a by-election at Hamilton. In February 1974 seven Members were elected. In October 1974 ten members were elected.

Welsh Nationalist Party (Plaid Cymru)

Founded in 1925 this party has fought elections continuously since then, and in a by-election at Carmarthen in 1966 Mr. G. Evans became the first Party candidate to be returned to Parliament. In February 1974 two Members were elected. In October 1974 three were elected.

The Government and Opposition Parties

The Party system of Government in this country is the practice of placing the exercise of the executive authority of the State in the hands of Ministers who are Members of Parliament and belong to one political party whose members have gained a majority of the Parliamentary seats at a general election.

Immediately the result of a general election is known, the leader of the dominant party selects his Cabinet. He chooses members from his own party in either House (Lords or Commons). A wise leader will select the most able men with whom he is in political agreement. Together they will form a united team. The 'Administration', as it is sometimes called, thereupon conducts the business of governing the country and its affairs as efficiently as it can.

The essential feature, however, is the **duality** of the parties: (i) The Government, formed from the majority party, and (ii) the Opposition, comprising the defeated party leader and his party members. The Leader of the Opposition also forms a 'Shadow Cabinet' ready to take over the reins of government at any time if need be.

There may, of course, be more than two parties in the House of Commons. Today at a general election both major parties (Conservative and Labour) contest most constituencies. The Liberal Party fights in as many constituencies as it can. In 1964 the Liberals put 365 candidates 'in the field' and won 9 seats. In 1966 it returned 12 M.P.s, and over the whole country the party polled 2,327,533 votes. In 1970 the corresponding figures were 6 M.P.s and 2,117,638 votes. In modern times we may expect, therefore, some Liberal M.P.s, a Welsh Nationalist M.P., a Scottish Nationalist, and perhaps one or two Independent Members. Altogether these will be few. But there must be two main parties: (i) the Government, and (ii) the Opposition.

The Opposition is only slightly less important in the Constitution than the Government, because it may 'if the balance of party power shifts become or be willing to follow Her Majesty's Ministers' (Sir Courtenay Ilbert). On the same theme Walter Bagehot (1826–77) wrote:

The House of Commons lives in a state of perpetual choice; at any moment it can choose a ruler or dismiss a ruler. And therefore party is inherent in it, is bone of its bone, and breath of its breath.

Coalitions

Where no party obtains an overall majority (i.e. has more M.P.s than all other parties put together) a difficult position arises. In the 1920s we had three parties: a major party (the Conservative), and two minor parties—Liberal and Labour. In these circumstances an Administration can only be formed if a major party (with many, but not an absolute majority of M.P.s) agrees to combine with one or other of the minor parties to form a Government. A compromise must be made over policies. Inevitably disagreements arise and dissentient members may resign from the coalition government. This weakens the administration and eventually the Government resigns and an appeal is made to the electorate. Another general election is then held. In peacetime coalition governments tend to be weak in policy and may fall apart, ending in resignation or dissolution. Vacillating policies and numerous changes of Government produce cynicism and disillusionment in the people.

In times of emergency, however, coalition governments may be successful. During World War II (1939–45) a National Coalition Government made up of members of all parties (Conservative, Liberal, and Labour) held the keys of power. Parties and party members sank their political differences in the national interest and presented a united front against the common enemy. It had one aim—the prosecution of war in defence of the realm. The existence of the State and its people was at stake and the national interest overrode all others. This is common sense and was the best thing to do.

It is a necessary part of the working of the party system in this country for the parties to know when to suspend party controversy. (Viscount Samuel (1870–1963). *Our Parliament* by Strathearn Gordon.)

Coalitions are commonplace in some countries. Thus in 1974 France, West Germany, Italy, Holland, Finland, and Canada had coalition governments. Denmark, Norway, and Sweden each had a **minority** government, that is a government which has the most seats of any party, but fewer than the combined seats of two or more other parties.

In March 1974 the Labour Government was able to form a minority government. In that situation the Government party has to act circumspectly, dropping those proposals which would be opposed by the other two parties acting in unison.

A Council of State

If a National Coalition Government comprising the most able men in the State can wage a mighty war and protect the lives and rights of its people why may not this form of government be equally successful in time of peace? The proposition is simple and attractive. It is difficult to justify its opposite. Why not a Government of the best men in the State elected by all the people to govern our lives, free of party squabbles and ties, and free to devote themselves to producing the 'good' life for all in justice, equity, and peace?

In a small State such as Athens (population roughly 35,000) it was possible in classical times to assemble all the citizens to ensure the election of the best candidates fitted to govern in the interest of the State and its members—a 'Government of the people, by the people, for the people'. This is an oversimplification of Athenian government, but the germ of the democratic ideal was there found.

The 'Council of State' style or form of Government pre-supposes facts which do not accord with the harsh realities of life. There is no agreement as to who are, or what is meant by, 'the best men'. All have faults and weaknesses. Moreover history shows that even when such elite groups are formed there is no certainty that the best people will agree among themselves. Without parties we would have 635 M.P.s with varied backgrounds and interests and widely different policies. Dissensions and disagreements arise among the best of men. Frequently the disagreements are deep and the differences of policy are irreconcilable.

It is impossible to assemble 55 million together to vote. The electors have diverse interests, opinions, and views both as to their representatives and the policies they should follow. Let us now suppose a group of the 'best men' do succeed to power. Would the group give it up once in the saddle? Political power has always had a fatal attraction for ambitious men. '**All power corrupts, and absolute power corrupts absolutely,**' said Lord Acton.

History provides astonishing examples, and England has had its share of despotic monarchs and its taste of a dictator in Cromwell (1599–1658). The country remembers its experience.

Criticisms of the Two-Party System

No system of government is perfect. The experience of Parliamentary government in this country has been one of continuous adaptation to the challenges, changes, and crises which are the lot of man and of nations. We may applaud the virtues of a two-party system while acknowledging certain weaknesses.

(i) The expression of minority views which are not a part of any one of the major parties is limited. Party discipline in the House, party loyalty, and the self-discipline of party members prevent individual M.P.s who are members of one of the major parties from supporting minority views.

(ii) Independent M.P.s (who disclaim allegiance to any party) are handicapped. An independent may not afford now to become an M.P. if he depends on his Parliamentary salary alone. This was raised, however, in 1972. An independent would not be promoted to ministerial rank. He loses the assistance of a party 'Whip' and the consequential party assistance, e.g. in being kept informed by literature, research, data, and notices. An independent has to frame his own Private Member's Bill—if he has one. For all their value in Parliament itself (we remind ourselves of the late Sir Alan Herbert, W. J. Brown, and others) 'the writing is on the wall'. The independent M.P. will be squeezed out by the monolithic major parties. That is a loss. A lone voice may be a wise one.

(iii) If a voter casts his vote for a party and not for the individual candidate on his merit and personal qualities there can be danger in ignoring the personal element in politics. Essentially a Member represents constituents; there is a personal and human relationship, an identification with the people of an area.

(iv) The *raison d'être* of the small minority party (e.g. Liberals) is similar to that of the independent M.P. Each has a value. A minority party should be kept in being: its policy may be right and good and may yet appeal to the best in men to give it the necessary support to grow. A minority party is an insurance against having no Government at all (e.g. if both parties fall apart, disagree, and disintegrate). Men, like bees, may regroup.

Advantages of the Two-Party System.

For some two hundred years there has been virtually a two-party system:

(i) Whigs and Tories, (ii) Liberals and Conservatives; and (iii) Labour and Conservatives.

We may justify the system on the following grounds:

(i) *Natural Division.* The two-party system follows the basic division existing between men: (*a*) **radicals**, i.e. those who wish to reform thoroughly and immediately; and (*b*) **conservatives**, i.e. those who prefer gradual change within existing institutions which may be adapted to change.

(ii) *It Works.* The two-party system is now one of the main features of the constitution. It has been tried and found **successful**, it has developed empiric-ally—by experience.

(iii) *The Will of the People.* The electorate chooses a Government and also, in effect, lays down the broad lines of policy which the electorate expects a Government to follow, e.g. as expressed in a party's manifesto. The system is democratic, and the elector himself can compare the actions of a Government with its party programme announced before election.

(iv) *Provides Strong Government.* The two-party system ensures stable and strong government during its term of office—usually five years. During this period the Government has virtually unlimited powers to legislate as it will.

(v) *Ensures Strong Parties.* Each major party has an efficient party political organization (see p. 40) and each has a declared policy. The Opposition Party has its Shadow Cabinet ready to accept office immediately on failure of the Government. This system therefore allows for continuous and strong Government. Weak parties with few M.P.s, or a party which is divided by dis-agreement and dissension cannot form an Administration though it may join in a coalition which may be unstable in peace-time.

(vi) *For and Against.* Voters have a simple choice between two rivals—'For' or 'Against'. If there were many parties and policies confusion may arise in the electorate.

(vii) *Floating Voters.* These voters who can be instrumental in changing a Government do not generally like voting for a party unable to form a Govern-ment.

(viii) *Right and Left Wings.* Each major party has a right and a left wing. Each party can, therefore, absorb factions and persons holding widely differ-ent views and coming from different areas of society. There are Trade Union-ists in the Conservative Party; professional men and industrialists in the Labour Party. Each party has its cross-section of social and religious groups. A third political party finds difficulty in framing a distinct policy of its own different from the other two parties.

(ix) *The Debating Chamber and the Houses of Parliament.* People are affected by the buildings or institutions in which they live and work. 'We shape our buildings, and afterwards our buildings shape us,' said Winston Churchill in 1943 (October) in the Debate on the rebuilding of the House of Commons. The seating arrangements of the House of Commons (see p. 56) and the lobby arrangements (separating 'Ayes' and 'Noes') support or pre-serve a two-party system of Government and Opposition. The **structural form encourages good debate**. A Government can be criticized openly, and its weaknesses or strengths can be exposed or appraised in full view of all members, the Press, and the public. It has been proved by actual experience; it is satisfactory and it works well. Moreover, the atmosphere of the House can tame the wildest spirits and induce respect for constitutional method.

These are some of the points which justify a two-party system of Government. There are others.

> The two-party system is the natural concomitant of a political tradition in which Government as such is the first consideration and in which the views and preferences of voters and of members of Parliament are continuously limited to the simple alternative of 'for' and 'against'. (L. S. Amery: *Thoughts on the Constitution.*)

Party Organization Today

All three major parties are organized to maintain their existence, fight elections, win voters to their cause, and return members to Parliament. We shall deal with (i) the Conservative Party, (ii) Labour Party, and (iii) the party organization in Parliament.

The Conservative Party Organization

(i) *The Constituency Association.* The constituency is the unit of the party organization. Each is divided into wards or polling districts.

The objects of a Constituency Association are:

(*a*) to recruit members;
(*b*) to fight elections;
(*c*) to select prospective candidates (usually with the approval of an Advisory Committee of the National Union);
(*d*) to raise election funds (by subscriptions, donations, bazaars, etc.).

The constituency appoints its own executive committee and Chairman, and has various sub-committees (Trades Union Committee, Young Conservatives' Committee, Women's Advisory Committee, Education Committee).

The Constituency Association appoints a certificated agent (see p. 41) to carry on the full-time work of the constituency. He is assisted by a woman organizer and office staff.

(ii) *The Area Councils.* There are twelve Area Councils in England and Wales. Each Area comprises several constituencies, and these are linked together on a provincial basis by the Area Council which co-ordinates the resources of the Area to advise the Central Office in London.

(iii) *The Central Council of the National Union.* The Central Council is composed of (*a*) the Leader, (*b*) the Officers of the Party, (*c*) the Parliamentary Party, (*d*) all adopted candidates, and (*e*) four representatives from each constituency association. This group amounts to nearly 6,000. Only about 3,500 attend the Central Council. Theoretically, the Central Council is the governing body at national level, but in practice it is too large to carry out executive functions, and it merely acts as a two-way link between M.P.s and the rank and file in the country. It also serves as a centre for Conservative interests. It does not control the Central Office of the Parliamentary Party. One standing committee of the Central Council vets prospective Parliamentary candidates.

(iv) *The Executive Committee of the National Union.* This comprises 150 members mainly from the provincial Areas. The body includes the Leader and other principal officers of the Party. It deals with the affairs of the Central Council. There are important sub-committees, e.g. Local Government, Trade Union Advisory Committee, Young Conservatives' Committee, Central Women's Advisory Committee, and the Conservative Political Centre Committee.

(v) *The Leader.* The Leader of the Party is elected by the Parliamentary Party, adopted prospective Parliamentary candidates and the Executive Committee of the National Union. He selects the Chairman of the Conservative Party who heads the Central Office. The Leader determines the Party programme and policy on the issues of the day. He must always consult with the other leading members of his party and must also have regard to the views of backbenchers in the '1922 Committee'.

(vi) *The Central Office.* Founded in 1870 by Disraeli, this office is under the control of the Leader. As its name implies the office is the permanent Headquarters of the Party. It co-ordinates preparations, workers and the resources for an election campaign. It supplies information, arranges speakers for the Party for local Constituency Associations. It carries out studies of public issues. It has charge of the Party's finances, and makes grants to constituencies, if needed. It also vets prospective candidates. It is responsible for recruiting and training the paid agents and organizers in the constituencies.

(vii) *Conservative Research Department.* This body undertakes long term research to assist in party policy. It also provides official secretaries for Parliamentary Committees and prepares briefs on issues coming before Parliament. It provides party members with information and guidance, and assists all departments of the Central Office. The Research Department comes within the framework of the Party Headquarters.

(viii) *The Election Agent.* These are the full-time officials employed by each constituency. They are trained by Central Office, which conducts examinations for them and issues them with certificates of proficiency.

The main duties of an agent are:

(*a*) To act as link between the M.P. and his constituency.
(*b*) To account for money spent at an election.
(*c*) To inform the M.P. of local matters of importance requiring his attention.
(*d*) To arrange the M.P.s speaking engagements.
(*e*) To arrange for the M.P. to meet electors who wish to see him.
(*f*) To inspire local voluntary workers and co-ordinate the ward and the constituency activities.
(*g*) To provide an efficient administrative office.
(*h*) To get his Parliamentary candidate returned at the next general election (i.e. *to win*).

(ix) *The Annual Party Conference.* About 4,000 persons attend the Annual Party Conference. The conference comprises all the members of the Central Conference of the National Union, election agents, and an additional three representatives from each constituency association. Delegates representing various groups put forward motions which are debated by the conference and replied to by the leaders of the Conservative Party. Although resolutions may influence the Leader in forming his policy they are not instructions and are not binding on him. The Conference is virtually a 'sounding board' of opinion and a Party rally. The Conference gives the party members a sense of unity and renews their enthusiasm.

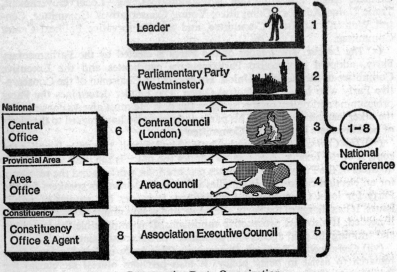

Conservative Party Organization

The Labour Party Organization

(1) *The Constituency Organization.* Each local Labour Party is in fact a federation of a number of organizations, including the Young Socialists, local trade unions, representative socialist societies, and local branches of the co-operative societies. Representatives of all affiliated groups serve on a General Management Committee which elects the officers, viz. Chairman, Secretary. The objects of the constituency organization are similar to those of the Conservative Association listed above.

The constituency appoints its Secretary, and where the constituency employs an agent he usually occupies both posts.

(ii) *Regional Councils.* There are eleven Regional Councils with full-time staff controlled by Transport House.

(iii) *National Executive Committee.* The Annual Party Conference elects the National Executive Committee, which comprises 12 members elected by various groups of Trade Unions, 7 by constituency parties and regional federations, 1 by socialist and co-operative societies, and 5 women are appointed to represent the women's sections of the party. The Leader and Deputy Leader of the Party are *ex officio* members. The Treasurer of the Party is elected by the whole Party Conference.

The National Executive Committee meets regularly and its functions are:

(*a*) To interpret and implement Annual Party Conference decisions.
(*b*) To manage the party finances.
(*c*) To maintain liaison with the Parliamentary Party.
(*d*) To supervise local associations.
(*e*) To enforce discipline.

(iv) *The Leader*. He is elected by the Parliamentary Labour Party for a year at a time. The leader is customarily re-elected and is rarely opposed. He exercises considerable influence, but is not so dominant as the Conservative leader. He does not control the officials of Transport House (the Party Head Office).

(v) *The Head Office (Transport House)*. This is the counterpart of the Central Office of the Conservative Party. It is headed by the General Secretary, who is appointed by the N.E.C. The Head Office is the national Headquarters of the Party and deals with the same matters as those carried out by its Conservative counterpart. The Head Office provides the full-time staff for the Regional Councils.

(vi) *Annual Party Conference*. Over 1,100 delegates from the affiliated organizations attend the Annual Party Conference. Delegates vote according to the number of 'due-paying' members in the group they represent. The Trade Unions dominate the 'card-vote'. Members of Parliament, prospective candidates, members of the National Executive, and local agents are *ex officio* members of the conference.

A programme is drawn up by the National Executive Committee; motions are debated, and the conference determines the Party's general policy. The conferences are widely reported in the Press and on radio and television so that the public may see the main issues of the day debated and the Labour Party's leaders called to account.

Party Organization in Parliament.

Each political party in the House of Commons has what is called a Parliamentary Party, made up of M.P.s of the same political persuasion. These groups are:

(i) The Parliamentary Labour Party.
(ii) The 1922 Committee (Conservative).
(iii) The Liberal Parliamentary Party.

The groups of M.P.s meet once or twice weekly during a session to discuss the business of the House and in particular important matters of the moment, some of which may be controversial.

First, we recall that the two major political parties will form the Government and the Opposition. The Government will have its Cabinet (twenty or more members), the Opposition will have its 'Shadow Cabinet'. All M.P.s who are not members of the Cabinet or Shadow Cabinet are known as 'backbenchers' (Government backbenchers or Opposition backbenchers).

We shall discuss a Government Party and its Parliamentary Party, (the same general principles apply to the Opposition Party in its relation with its Parliamentary Party.) A Government Minister may be invited to attend a Parliamentary Party meeting and will meet and hear the views of backbenchers. The Government policy on an issue may have been or be about to be decided in the Cabinet, and the Minister will explain this to the party group and expect and encourage support. Party members may not, of course, always agree with Cabinet policy. In this situation the Minister must handle the issue skilfully and carefully. The Cabinet must have behind it the strong support of its party members (i.e. the backbenchers) if it is going to push its policies through Parliament. It cannot afford a defeat on a division of the House. Backbenchers, for their part, seek to know what is the policy of the

Cabinet and to be kept 'in the picture'. Communication between a Minister (and his colleagues in the Cabinet) and the backbenchers is vital. This is a two-way matter. Both sides must try to co-operate, and there must be give and take or compromise on occasions.

A Parliamentary Party group may not instruct or control a Cabinet. The basic constitutional doctrine is that the Cabinet is responsible to the House of Commons as a whole. A Government's (i.e. a Cabinet's) essential duty is to govern, but it can only do this if it has the solid support of its party members. Hence the need to obtain harmony with its backbenchers and to present a united team in the event of a Division of the House. If an individual M.P. feels strongly about an issue he can abstain from voting or vote against the policy of his own party. This is attended by certain risks as we shall see later (p. 66).

In addition to the full meetings of Parliamentary Parties there are numerous committees or meetings to discuss particular matters, e.g. trade, economic affairs, industrial relations, agriculture, education, and so on. These committees are sometimes attended by a Minister (or Shadow Minister in the case of Opposition Parliamentary Parties) or a representative of a Minister. In addition, the Whips (see p. 65) will also attend to get to know the feelings, views and interests of party members on the various committees such as those mentioned above.

We mention here that although the term Opposition Party suggests continual obstruction, contest, and contention, this is not in fact the case. Many matters are dealt with in agreement with the Opposition, and the House does not divide. Moreover, on occasions a free vote may be taken when M.P.s of all parties may vote according to their own consciences free from the party line, as in the vote on the Referendum Bill.

Exercises

1. Give a short historical account of the development of the franchise up to the present century.

2. What are the main provisions of the *Representation of the People Act, 1969*?

3. What criticisms may be made of the electoral system?

4. What do you understand by: (i) The second ballot; (ii) The alternative vote; (iii) proportional representation?

5. How did Burke define a political party?

6. What, in your opinion, has contributed to the decrease in the number of Liberal M.P.s to the House of Commons?

7. Account for the growth of the Labour Party since its inception.

8. Coalitions seem to work in war but not in peace. Why is this?

9. What are the advantages of the two-party system in the British Constitution?

10. Describe the party organization of (i) the Conservative Party; and (ii) the Labour Party.

CHAPTER THREE

THE LEGISLATURE

The British Parliament comprises (i) H.M. The Queen, (ii) The House of Lords, and (iii) The House of Commons. It is sometimes technically described as The Queen in Parliament. The Legislature is **bi-cameral**, i.e. it consists of two chambers: the House of Lords and the House of Commons.

The House of Lords

This is the older of two Houses. Originally the Anglo-Saxon Kings were advised and assisted by the Witan; and the Norman Kings by the Great Council (the *Magnum Concilium*). This latter body was an assembly of feudal barons, nobles, and vassals, together with the bishops whose appointments were in the gift of the Monarch. All were powerful magnates summoned by the King and consulted by him on matters of importance.

Another Norman institution—the *Curia Regis* (the Court of the King)— comprised a smaller group of advisers who carried on day-to-day government and thus ensured continuity. The *Curia Regis* had two main functions which tended to separate: one was **judicial** which, in the time of Henry II (1154–89), gave rise to the Courts of Law (see p. 183); the other was **administrative and advisory** to give continuous governmental advice to the King. The House of Lords is the successor of the old *Curia Regis*, a feudal body.

The Norman Kings summoned not only the barons on matters of great importance, but after 1265 another group—the 'Commons'—which included the knights from the shires and the burgesses from the cities and boroughs. These two groups met separately from each other in private assemblies— the Lords in one group and the Commons in another. Each body was constituted on entirely different principles.

The period between the seventeenth and nineteenth centuries witnessed the rising power of the wealthy commercial class who became the middle class. Members of this group of people pressed for reform of the Commons to ensure fairer representation in Parliament. Eventually, after a period of great political agitation, the *Reform Bill* of 1830–2 was passed. The Bill was strongly opposed by the House of Lords mainly because of the threat to their own political power and influence. The Lords rejected the Bill twice. When, however, Lord Grey's Government induced the King to agree to create enough peers in favour of reform to swamp the Lords, the Upper House at last gave way and the Reform Bill was finally passed. This was a strong indication that the power of the Lords, great as it may have been in the past, would have to give way in face of the rising power of the Commons.

The Period 1832–1911

The *Reform Act, 1832*, introduced a wider voting franchise, and the House of Commons became more representative of the people. The *Reform Acts of 1867 and 1884* introduced an even wider franchise which resulted in an increased representative and democratic House of Commons. Some politicians in the nineteenth century pressed for the reform or abolition of the House of Lords which was described as an undemocratic anomaly.

Changes were, however, slow. Prime Ministers were still largely peers. Their presence and that of other leading Ministers of the Government in the House of Lords lent authority to the proceedings in that chamber. But, towards the end of the nineteenth century the number of peers (as distinct from commoners) in the Government became fewer. The last peer to be Prime Minister was the Marquess of Salisbury who resigned in 1902.

The Commons continued to grow in status and power, and the debates and struggles in the Lower House determined the course of political life and growth. The Lords' power was still in theory equal with that of the Lower House except that, by convention, the Lords did not interfere with financial questions. Meanwhile many old Whig peers joined the Tories in the House of Lords and this increased the Conservative strength of that chamber. In the Commons the party division between Liberals and Conservatives became more bitter. Social change was needed and many industrial problems arose. This state of affairs precipitated another crisis which resulted in the *Parliament Act, 1911*, by which the power of the House of Lords was much curtailed.

The Parliament Acts of 1911 and 1949

Theoretically, the Lords' power of veto over measures proposed by the Commons used to be unlimited. In 1909 **Mr. David Lloyd George,** Chancellor of the Exchequer under **Mr. H. H. Asquith**, Prime Minister, tried to push forward a programme of democratic legislation. The Finance Bill which contained the financial proposals was passed by the Commons, but was rejected by the Lords. This rejection infringed the convention that the Lords ought not to oppose a **Money Bill** sent up by the Commons. The Bill was introduced again, dissension followed, and eventually the Prime Minister threatened that unless the Bill were passed by the House of Lords he would arrange for the King to create a sufficient number of Liberal peers to ensure its passage. In the circumstances the Bill was finally passed by the Lords and became law.

The Government felt that it ought not to be baulked in this way and thereupon introduced a Bill to curtail the powers of the House of Lords itself. This Bill was passed by the House of Lords under the same threat as before of 'flooding' the Upper House with sufficient Government peers to ensure its passage. The *Parliament Act, 1911*, is the result of the struggle and provides that:

> If a Money Bill, having been passed by the House of Commons and sent up to the House of Lords at least one month before the end of the session, is not passed by the House of Lords without amendment within one month after it is so sent up to that House, the Bill shall, unless the House of Commons direct to the contrary, be presented to His Majesty and become an Act of Parliament notwithstanding that the House of Lords have not consented to the Bill.

This in practical terms meant that the House of Lords no longer had any power to interfere with the policy of the Government so far as finance was concerned. If, therefore, the House of Lords does not pass a Money Bill as it stands within one month, the Bill may receive the Royal Assent without the concurrence of the House of Lords.

A 'Money Bill' is defined as:

A Public Bill which, in the opinion of the Speaker of the House of Commons, contains only provisions dealing with the imposition, repeal, remission, alteration or regulation of taxation . . . or subordinate matters incidental to those subjects or any of them.

Every Money Bill must be endorsed by the Speaker to the effect that it is a Money Bill. The Speaker's decision is made after consultation with two members of the Chairman's Panel.

To fall within the provisions of the Act, Money Bills certified by the Speaker must be sent to the Lords at least one month before the end of the session.

Other Bills. The *Parliament Act, 1911,* made certain provisions regarding Bills other than Money Bills. The Act laid down:

If any Public Bill (not a Money Bill) is passed by the House of Commons in three successive sessions and is sent up to the House of Lords in each of those sessions, that Bill on rejection by the House of Lords a third time be presented to His Majesty and become an Act of Parliament provided that two years have elapsed between the date of the Second Reading in the first of these sessions of the Bill in the House of Commons and the date on which it passes the House of Commons in the third of these sessions.

The effect of this was that the Commons could get their own way and that the House of Lords could only delay, not prevent, legislation.

After 1911

The House of Lords accepted their minor role in the legislature, and there was less disagreement between the political views of the Government and the majority of the Lords. The decline in the importance of the Upper House was reflected in fewer peers holding Government office. Moreover the **convention** now emerged that the Prime Minister must be a member of the House of Commons. **Lord Curzon** was passed over for Prime Minister in 1922 and **Mr. Stanley Baldwin** was chosen in compliance with the convention.

Another struggle, however, lay ahead. In 1947 a Labour Government was obstructed by a mainly Conservative Upper House over the proposals to nationalize steel. Accordingly another Parliament Bill was introduced which provided that a Bill rejected or amended by the Lords can go for the **Royal Assent** provided it has been passed by the Commons in two successive sessions (not three as provided in the Act of 1911). As two successive sessions may be held in one year, the *Parliament Act, 1949,* reduced the delaying period of the Lords from two years to one.

Composition

The House of Lords consists of two classes: **the Lords Spiritual** and the **Lords Temporal.** For our purposes there are, however, four main groups:

(i) *The Lords Spiritual.* There are twenty-six Spiritual Lords who hold office by virtue of being bishops of the established Church of England. They comprise:

(a) The Archbishops of Canterbury and York and the Bishops of London, Durham and Winchester who are each entitled to a seat.

(b) Twenty-one diocesan bishops being the senior bishops of the Church. When one of this number dies or resigns his seat he is succeeded by the next most senior diocesan bishop of the Church.

(ii) *Hereditary Peers.* These number about 950 and are peers of the United Kingdom or of Scotland. Under the *Act of Union, 1707*, the Scottish peers elected sixteen of their number to represent them in the Lords. Now, however, by s. 4 of the *Peerage Act, 1963*, all Scottish peers are entitled to a seat.

Peerages are occasionally granted immediately to ladies of distinction or the widows of distinguished men. Peeresses in their own right (as they are called) frequently acquire their title by lineal inheritance which means that females succeed to the title in default of males. The rank of peeress in her own right is inherited by her eldest son (or perhaps daughter). In 1971 there were twenty-one peeresses in this rank.

(iii) *Lords of Appeal in Ordinary.* These are sometimes referred to as the Law Lords. They number eleven, hold the rank of baron and are appointed for life (*Appellate Jurisdiction Act, 1876*, as amended). They perform the judicial work of the House of Lords when sitting as the final Court of Appeal.

(iv) *Life Peers.* These are men and women appointed to the rank of baron or baroness under the *Life Peerage Act, 1958*. There are about 250 at the present time.

Creation and Renunciation of Hereditary Peerages

The creation of peerages is one of the Monarch's prerogatives. Originally the method adopted was to issue a writ of summons to an individual to the House of Lords followed by his taking a seat. This conferred a hereditary peerage, i.e. the right to attend descended to the Lord's heir at law. Since the fifteenth century the creation of hereditary peerages has been by **Letters Patent** which enabled descent to be directed into a certain line of heir different from those ascertained by reference to feudal customary law. Today all hereditary and life peerages are conferred by the Sovereign on the advice of the Prime Minister.

The Scottish peers are those who held titles which existed before the *Act of Union, 1707*. Since that time there has been no power to create Scottish peers as such though they may be created peers of the United Kingdom.

There is a common belief that most of the peerages date from feudal times. In fact only about sixty can be traced to a date before the eighteenth century; the rest have been created within the last two hundred years.

The *Peerage Act, 1963*. Before 1963 a hereditary peerage could not be surrendered or disclaimed. The Act now permits this, so that a person who succeeds to a peerage, or a person who had succeeded to a peerage before the law was changed, may disclaim that peerage for his or her lifetime and thereby becomes a commoner. Any person who disclaims his peerage loses his right to sit in the House of Lords, but he is able to vote at Parliamentary elections and is now eligible for election to the House of Commons.

The Act was passed as a result of the case of Mr. Anthony Wedgwood Benn who, in 1960, was M.P. for the constituency of Bristol South-East. His father, Viscount Stansgate, died in 1960. Mr. Wedgwood Benn, an able politician, became a peer immediately and was automatically disqualified from membership of the House of Commons. His seat was accordingly declared vacant, and a by-election was held. The new Viscount Stansgate stood as a candidate, was re-elected by a large majority and presented himself

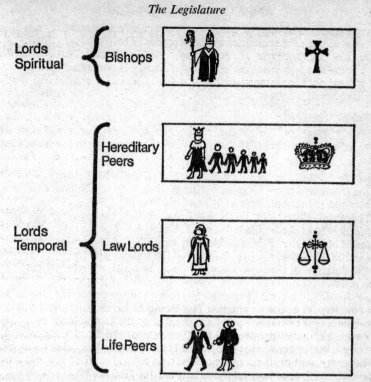

Lords Spiritual { Bishops

Lords Temporal { Hereditary Peers

Law Lords

Life Peers

Peers of the Realm

as a member of the House of Commons. He was refused entry to the House and his opponent (who had in fact lost the election) was declared the member for the constituency. As a consequence of the publicity attending the case the Government introduced the *Peerage Act, 1963,* which provided (as we have noted above) for disclaimer and renunciation of a peerage. The Act enabled Viscount Stansgate to resume his former status and to become again Mr. Anthony Wedgwood Benn. The existing member gallantly resigned his seat and a further by-election was held. Mr. Wedgwood Benn won the seat and took his place once more as the duly elected member for Bristol South-East.

Sir Alec Douglas-Home (formerly Lord Home) and Mr. Quintin Hogg (formerly Lord Hailsham), both prominent politicians also took advantage of the Act and became members of the House of Commons. Mr. Quintin Hogg (a distinguished lawyer and politician) was in 1970 made Lord Chancellor and once again resumed his former title of Lord Hailsham—as a life peer under the 1958 Act.

The *Peerage Act, 1963,* does not extinguish a peerage when a disclaimer is made. The next heir upon the death of his father can either elect to assume the peerage or to disclaim.

Disqualification. There are certain categories of persons who are disqualified from membership of the House of Lords. These are:

(i) Persons who are aliens, bankrupts, or infants.

(ii) Persons convicted of treason or felony (serious crime) may not sit or vote until the sentence has been completed or pardoned.

(iii) Civil servants who are peers may sit in the House of Lords, but they may not speak or vote on issues. This rule is contained in a Treasury Minute. On resignation from the Civil Service he may resume the full rights of his peerage.

Officers of the Lords

Both Houses of Parliament have some members concerned with the management of business. The most important of these in the House of Lords are:

(i) *The Lord Chancellor.* Presides over the House in his capacity as **Speaker of the House** and takes his place on the **Woolsack**, the traditional name given to a broad red-covered seat in front of the Throne.

The Lord Chancellor is recommended for appointment by the Prime Minister who is not required to consult the House. The Lord Chancellor is a member of the Government and usually a member of the Cabinet. As a member of the Executive, the Legislature, and the Judiciary he forms an exception to the doctrine of the separation of powers to which we referred previously (see p. 10).

As Speaker, the Lord Chancellor has fewer and less important powers than his counterpart in the Commons. The House of Lords is master of its own procedure, and matters of order are decided by the House itself.

As an important member of the Government the Lord Chancellor frequently takes an active part in debates. He may speak and vote as a member of his party, and on these occasions he rises from the Woolsack and moves a few feet so that he may be technically 'in' the House.

The Lord Chancellor is responsible for the control of services and accommodation in that part of the Palace of Westminster and precincts occupied by or on behalf of the House of Lords. In the absence of the Lord Chancellor a Deputy Speaker presides. The Crown appoints several peers, in order of precedence, to the office of **Deputy Speaker**.

(ii) *The Chairman of Committees.* The first of the Deputy Speakers is the **Lord Chairman of Committees** who is appointed by the House at the beginning of each session. His duties include the following:

(*a*) He takes the chair in all Committees of the House.

(*b*) He is *ex officio* chairman of all other Committees of the House.

(*c*) He acts as Speaker in the absence of the Lord Chancellor. He does not usually take part in the debates on ordinary topics.

(iii) *The Clerk of Parliaments.* He is appointed by the Crown and is removable only on an address of the House. His duties include keeping the records of proceedings and judgements and administering the judicial business of the House. He also pronounces the words by which the Royal Assent to Bills is signified (see p. 94).

The Clerk Assistant and the Reading Clerk record the daily attendances and read the Commission for Royal Assent.

(iv) *The Gentleman Usher of the Black Rod.* He is a member of the Royal Household. He enforces the orders of the House.

(v) *The Serjeant-at-Arms.* He attends the Lord Chancellor and carries the Mace.

Organization of the House of Lords

Attendance. Although the actual membership is over 1,000, the average daily attendance is 270, but in the course of a year some 700 take part. More attend when some matter of special interest is under discussion. Recently in proceedings the average length of a sitting is just over five hours.

During the session the House of Lords meets on most Mondays, and on Tuesdays and Wednesdays at 2.30 p.m., and on Thursdays at 3 p.m.

To ensure that only those peers who are interested in the general work of Parliament attend, holders of hereditary peerages are asked at the beginning of each session whether they will attend the sittings of the House as often as they reasonably can, or whether they wish to be relieved of the obligation to attend. If they so desire they are requested to apply for leave of absence either for the duration of a particular Parliament or for a single session. During that time they are expected not to attend the sittings of the House. A peer who wishes to terminate his leave of absence may do so on giving a month's notice.

Peers in constant attendance at the House of Lords are generally elder statesmen and other who have spent their lives in public service.

Peers receive no salary for their parliamentary work. They are, however, entitled to (i) travelling expenses from their homes to the Palace of Westminster (provided they attend at least one-third of the number of sittings); and (ii) expenses incurred for the purpose of attendance within a maximum of £13·50 a day.

The minimum number of members required to form a duly constituted House is three, but a vote cannot be taken unless there are thirty peers present.

Political Parties in the Lords. Like the Commons, the House of Lords has a Government bench and an Opposition bench. There are, however, a number of peers who have no party affiliations who sit on the 'cross-benches'. There are, too, the Law Lords and the Lords Spiritual whose special position excludes party politics.

On the Government side there must be by law at least three Ministers of the Crown as members of the House of Lords in addition to the Lord Chancellor. One of the three will be the Leader of the Government party in the House, and one will be the **Chief Whip** who is in charge of the party organization in the Lords. The Government Ministers in the Lords deal with all questions or debates on behalf of the Government, and inevitably they will have to cover a wide parliamentary field, not necessarily those subjects falling within the sphere of their own department.

The Opposition Party in the Lords follows the usual party organization found in the Commons, with a Leader, Chief Whip, and party spokesman.

Superficially there are certain resemblances to the Commons, but we must remember that the power of the Upper House has been much eroded (*Parliament Acts, 1911 and 1949*). Moreover, peers do not have the risk of elections and loss of their seat or status.

As to the conduct of business we have already noted that this falls to the Lord Chancellor who is **Chairman** of the House. He differs from the Speaker in the Commons in that he (the Lord Chancellor) is not impartial for he is a member of the Government, and may take part in debates. He may vote, but has no casting vote.

The procedure for the passing of legislation is dealt with on page 92.

The Present Functions of the Lords

OND

The main duties of the House of Lords, bearing in mind the limitations imposed by the *Parliament Acts, 1911 and 1949*, are summarized as follows:

(i) *Initiation of Legislation.* As we have noted the House of Commons is the chamber which initiates almost all the important Bills. The only Bills introduced first in the House of Lords are (*a*) those of a legal character, (e.g. the *Courts Act, 1971*), (*b*) Bills of a non-financial or non-controversial character, and (*c*) those of a minor character. The House of Lords contains many distinguished lawyers, including the Law Lords, in addition to experienced politicians well acquainted with the legislative process of Parliament, and they are therefore well qualified to deal with all of the above types of Bills. Moreover this duty saves the time of the Commons.

As to the procedure, we should note that the same legislative process applies in the Lords as in the Commons: Bills are read three times, and there is a **Committee stage** and a **Report stage**. Where Bills are received from the Commons, the Lords now content themselves with making minor changes only, such as verbal alterations.

(ii) *Revision of Legislation.* Formerly, where the House of Lords held fundamentally different views about a particular Bill the ensuing disagreement could precipitate a constitutional crisis, as we have already noted (see p. 46). Today this does not present a serious problem. The main Bills are introduced first in the Commons and constitute part of the political programme or mandate of the Government. The Upper House must therefore content itself with making only those amendments designed to improve the proposals.

Where disagreement does occur over a particular Bill, it is submitted for the Royal Assent without the concurrence of the House of Lords. If, however, the Lords decide to amend the Bill it must be returned to the Lower House where it originated for consideration of those amendments. If the Commons reject the amendments made by the Lords, a committee is set up to show the reasons for the disagreement, and a message is sent to the Lords. The amendment may then be dropped, or alternative ones adopted. Negotiation proceeds until agreement is reached. Only if it is impossible to reconcile the different points of view would the Commons invoke the powers of the *Parliament Acts, 1911 and 1949*, to present the Bill for Royal Assent after one year (with the exception of Money Bills).

Notwithstanding these technical procedures to achieve agreement, we must not forget that the House of Lords *is* the second stage in the legislative process and that this allows time for reflection, eliciting new points of view and for detecting errors not discovered in the Commons.

(iii) *Discussion on Current Affairs.* Most persons would say that the Commons has too much to do and too little time in which to do it. Because of this it follows that the Commons cannot give many hours to discussing current affairs. The Upper House is not pressed in this way. Many peers have wide experience and knowledge, and some are specialists. The debates in the Upper House are usually informed with good sense, of high quality and (because peers do not fight elections) they are disinterested. The contribution of Life Peers has added to the standard, and a reading of *The Times*, *The Daily Telegraph*, or *The Guardian* will reveal the general level attained and the detachment which the Upper House achieves.

All institutions have their critics, and the House of Lords is not exempt. These allege long-windedness, a lack of urgency and sense of reality. Critics point also to the high average age of the members and conclude that this reflects a lack of modernity in thought, approach, and attitude.

Reform of the House of Lords

The reform of the Upper House has agitated the minds of thoughtful persons for many years. In 1649 the House was abolished on the grounds that it was 'useless and dangerous to the people'. It was restored in 1660.

Since then it has been commonly attacked on the ground that the hereditary principle (of feudal origin) is incompatible with representative democracy. A Conference on the Reform of the Second Chamber was held in 1918, presided over by Lord Bryce. He stated:

> The need of two chambers has been an axiom of political science based on the belief of the innate tendency of an assembly to become lazy, tyrannical and corrupt, a tendency which can only be checked by the co-existence of another house of equal authority.

Even if all these points were true it is extremely doubtful whether the House of Lords would be the corrective to re-establish industry and efficiency, benevolence and propriety, particularly having regard to the present diminished powers of the Upper House. We have already noted (p. 46) that the *Parliament Acts, 1911 and 1949*, have considerably reduced the effectiveness of the House of Lords as part of the supreme legislative assembly.

The main criticisms may be listed thus:

(i) *The House of Lords is unrepresentative.* Most members claim noble birth or are there by reason of past political service, church office or as Law Lords. The majority are drawn from a special section of the people.

(ii) *Conservative bias.* Members tend to belong to a property-owning class and are conservative. Labour peers are generally but a small proportion of total membership. They are, therefore, ineffective in voting power.

(iii) *Unsuitable Membership.* Some peers have not the interest or capacity for politics. Most are hereditary peers, and this is not a satisfactory qualification for deliberative or legislative duties. Some hereditary peers must earn a living, and may be prevented from attending the House for that reason.

(iv) *Attendance.* Many of the peers do not attend regularly and their attendance is sparse.

The result of these and similar criticisms is that there has been a decline in the public esteem of the Upper House as a second chamber.

Is the Lords as a Second Chamber Necessary? There is no general agreement on this point for the following reasons. It is generally held that a second chamber should not:

(a) Be a duplication of the other chamber and should differ in qualifications for membership.

(b) Represent a single or a few classes or interests.

(c) Predominantly favour any of the parties which alternately govern the country.

It is frequently held that a second chamber should:

(*a*) Have a fixed term of life.
(*b*) Be independent, without fear of punishment for the expression of opinion.
(*c*) Represent all bodies of opinion, even those who do not accept the whole programme of any party.
(*d*) Provide opportunity for 'second thoughts', reconsideration and deliberation.

The question of reform was debated in the House of Lords itself in 1946. Some twelve years later the *Life Peerages Act, 1958*, was passed, which overcomes, to some extent, the criticism of the hereditary character of the House. The Crown may now confer peerages on men and women who have proved themselves worthy of the honour in public service and in many walks of life including industry, commerce, the professions, and the Commonwealth. A life peerage, as its name implies, terminates on the death of the recipient of the honour.

The *Government White Paper* (*Cmnd 3799*) *of 1968*. This document, issued in November 1968, represented the agreed conclusions of a joint party conference established in November 1967.

The Government stated four propositions on which reform should be based:

(*a*) The second chamber has an essential role to play, **complementary** to, but not rivalling, that of the Commons.
(*b*) The present composition and powers of the House of Lords prevent it from performing that role as effectively as it should.
(*c*) The reform should therefore be directed towards promoting the more efficient working of Parliament as a whole.
(*d*) Once the reform has been completed the work of the two Houses should become more closely co-ordinated and integrated, and the functions of the House of Lords should be reviewed.

The White Paper further stated that reform should achieve the following objectives:

(*a*) The hereditary basis of membership should be eliminated.
(*b*) No one party should possess a permanent majority.
(*c*) In normal circumstances the Government of the day should be able to secure a reasonable working majority.
(*d*) The powers of the House of Lords to delay public legislation should be restricted. to 6 months
(*e*) The Lords' absolute power to withhold consent to subordinate legislation against the will of the Commons should be abolished.

2-TIER SYSTEM

The Labour Government introduced the *Parliament* (*No. 2*) *Bill, 1969*, to give effect to the proposals in the White Paper, but it was withdrawn. Neither the Government nor the Opposition regarded the Bill as of much importance, and it was realized that legislation might create additional problems.

Conclusion. There is no special sanctity in a second Chamber. New Zealand manages her affairs successfully without one. Sweden abolished its second Chamber in 1971. The U.S.A., however, has a Senate (Upper House) made up of 100 members on the basis of two members for each State. The Federal Constitution makes special provision for this, and it is unlikely under the rigid constitution of the United States that there will be a change to a single Chamber.

Lord Shinwell said:

> Let us face the problem frankly. Either we create an elected senate sharing authority with the Commons or leave the subject alone. As a debating chamber the House of Lords can do no harm and may even do some good. (*The Times*, 7 November 1970.)

He went on to suggest a revival of the old cut and thrust of debate customary in the Commons fifty years ago; fewer speeches which were sometimes read word for word from a script. The Lords would then qualify as a useful national forum for the discussion of national and international affairs.

The English have a habit of not doing away with institutions unless they become objectionable or harmful. The House of Lords will continue so long as it 'behaves itself' (as one spokesman has put it) in its relationship with the Commons.

The House of Commons

We have already traced the history of the House of Commons from the time of Simon de Montfort in 1295 and the so-called Model Parliament, and have noted the great constitutional struggles of the seventeenth century which culminated in the *Bill of Rights, 1689*, and the *Act of Settlement, 1701*. These two documents finally assured the supremacy of Parliament over the Monarch and all other institutions, and settled the succession to the English throne.

Democracy, as we understand the word, was not attained overnight. Our institutions and procedures have grown step by step for some 250 years following the Bill of Rights.

In this chapter we shall examine the existing House of Commons to which Members of Parliament are elected and where the will of the people finds its highest democratic expression.

Composition

The House of Commons is a representative assembly of men and women who are Members of Parliament. There are at present 635 seats in the House of Commons and these are distributed as follows:

England	516
Wales	36
Scotland	71
Northern Ireland	12
	635

Constituencies. The United Kingdom is divided into constituencies each of which returns one member to the House of Commons.

Parliament itself determines where those constituencies are located. Under the *House of Commons* (*Redistribution of Seats*) *Acts, 1949 and 1958*, there were set up four permanent **Boundary Commissions** for England, Scotland, Wales, and Northern Ireland. The Chairman of each Commission is the Speaker of the House of Commons. The Vice-Chairman is a judge.

The duty of the Commissions is to keep constituencies constantly under review, to submit periodic reports at intervals of not less than ten years nor more than fifteen years and to recommend changes in the boundaries of any constituency. Broadly, each constituency should be for an area containing 60,000 to 70,000 people. Some of the constituencies are rural and some urban. Roughly half of the 635 members represent boroughs, and half the counties. A city (or borough) with a population of half a million inhabitants may return to Parliament seven or eight members.

The reason for the constant review of constituency boundaries is the shift or changes of population arising from new or expanding industries, the building of new towns, new housing estates, and similar factors. The reports of the

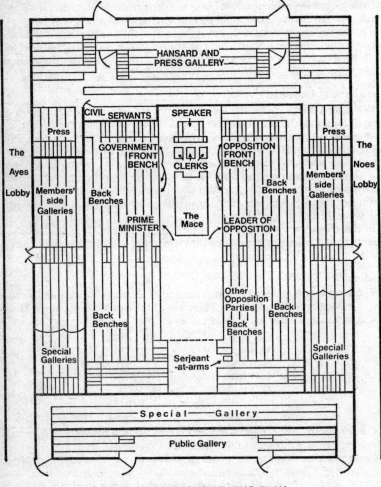

HOUSE OF COMMONS SEATING PLAN

House of Commons

Boundary Commissions are made to the Home Secretary and require Parliamentary confirmation.

The constituencies of Northern Ireland are larger than the average English counterpart. We have already mentioned that Northern Ireland has its own self-government at Stormont (temporarily suspended in 1972) which deals with local internal matters, and as a result the electors of that country have correspondingly less interest in the activities of the Parliament at Westminster.

Qualifications for Membership of the House of Commons.

Any adult British subject or citizen of the Irish Republic over 21 may be a member of the House of Commons.

The following persons are, however, disqualified:

   (i) Aliens.
  (ii) Infants, i.e. persons under 21.
 (iii) Mental patients.
 (iv) Members of the House of Lords.
  (v) Clergymen of the Churches of England, Scotland, and Ireland, and the Roman Catholic Church.
 (vi) Bankrupts (usually for a period lasting until five years from their discharge).
 (vii) Persons convicted of treason provided they have not been pardoned.
(viii) Persons convicted of corrupt or illegal practices at Parliamentary elections.
 (ix) Persons disqualified by the *House of Commons Disqualification Act, 1975.* The principal persons in this category are—
    (*a*) Judges and stipendiary magistrates.
    (*b*) Civil servants.
    (*c*) Members of the regular Army, Navy and Air Force.
    (*d*) Police Officers (except Special Constables).

Any dispute as to qualification for membership is decided by the House of Commons, not a court of law. Thus, the **Committee of Privileges** (which exercises the jurisdiction) held that when Lord Stansgate (formerly Mr. Anthony Wedgwood Benn) wished to claim his seat in the Commons in 1961 it was decided that he was disqualified by reason of his peerage (see p. 48).

Generally, practically anyone (with the above exceptions) is entitled to stand for election as a Member of Parliament. In practice, there are many factors which affect candidature. Primarily, a candidate must possess certain important personal attributes, an interest in people, politics, and a capacity for hard work. But, apart from these factors, there is the need for financial backing and the support of a political party. These matters are referred to later in more detail (see p. 84).

Attendance

The House of Commons meets in Westminster from Mondays to Fridays throughout the year. There are 160 sitting days per year, and these are divided roughly into four periods:

(*a*) From November to Christmas	30–40
(*b*) From January to Easter	40–50
(*c*) From Easter to Whitsun	30
(*d*) From Whitsun to end of July	40

When Parliament is not sitting it is said to be **in recess**.

Hours. On Mondays, Tuesdays, Wednesdays and Thursdays the official hours of sitting are from 2.30 p.m. to 10.30 p.m. There are certain classes of Parliamentary business which are always exempt from normal closing time. Moreover, if the House so desires and chooses any other business may necessitate going on longer than 10.30 p.m. If the business of the House is urgent or important (as is frequently the case) the sittings continue much later. All-night sittings sometimes occur.

Fridays are exceptional in that the House assembles at 11 a.m. and usually rises at 4.30 p.m. This enables Members to return to their constituencies, some of which are far distant from Westminster. Most members engage in political activities, e.g. attending to complaints, etc., of constituents, on Saturday mornings, and attend other local functions.

Only in exceptional circumstances does the House of Commons sit during the mornings of Mondays, Tuesdays, Wednesdays, and Thursdays.

Members of Parliament are not expected to be in constant attendance in the debating chamber. Some are members of the numerous committees of the House, and all have many and varied duties to perform. When, however, specially important business is to be dealt with such as a vote on important legislation, special steps (through the Whip system, see p. 65) are taken to ensure that members are present. Apart from these times the House of Commons chamber may be relatively full or empty, dependent on the speakers and the subject-matter of the debate. The majority of members remain within the precincts of the House so that they may be available to reach the lobbies within a few minutes of being called. Some members may leave the House of Commons altogether for a few hours.

Formerly, if members desired to be away from the House for some days at a time during the session they had to apply formally for leave of absence. This is not now considered necessary. But, if an official delegation of members of the House of Commons is visiting a foreign country, for example, formal permission to be absent is granted.

Ministers in the Commons

All Ministers of the Crown must sit in one or other of the Houses of Parliament. The *Ministers of the Crown Act, 1965*, and the *House of Commons Disqualification Act, 1957*, governs the number of Ministers who may sit in the Commons. At the present time ninety-one holders of Ministerial office are entitled to sit and vote in the House of Commons at any one time.

Resignation of Members

A member elected to the House of Commons may, for some reason, e.g. ill health, incapacity, wish to resign during a Parliament. One might suppose that a letter sent direct to Mr. Speaker and the Chairman of his constituency party might dispose of this matter, but this is not so.

Technically speaking, a Member of Parliament cannot resign his seat. The reason is historical. At one time the Crown wanted to ensure that members of the House would not escape their important responsibilities to vote money (i.e. to impose taxation on the public) for carrying on the government of the country simply by resigning from the House. Taxes had to be imposed, and the **Royal power** was applied in earlier times to ensure that the reluctant member did not evade his duty.

Today a member resigns by an indirect method of applying for 'an office of profit under the Crown'. The holding of such an office (except Ministerial office) has been a disqualification for membership of the House of Commons since the *Act of Settlement, 1701*. The application is automatically granted and the member vacates his seat.

The two appointments to 'an office of profit' are: (i) Steward of the Chiltern Hundreds, or (ii) Bailiff of the Manor of Northstead. Both are ancient offices, though neither exists in fact today. Both are nominally in the gift of the Chancellor of the Exchequer who may grant them in quick succession where more than one member wishes to vacate his seat at the same time. No remuneration attaches to the two posts, and, in practice, a request is never refused. The former M.P. thereupon resumes his status as an ordinary citizen.

Officers of the Commons

The Speaker

The office of Speaker dates back to Simon de Montfort and the Model Parliament of 1295, and we know from the Parliamentary Rolls that the office has been held continuously from 1377.

From the earliest times the Speaker was the spokesman of the Commons to the King. But his exact relationship *vis-à-vis* the Crown was anomalous and precarious, for the Speaker was at one and the same time the spokesman (hence the name Speaker) *to* the House of Commons on behalf of the Crown. We know that in the sixteenth century he was appointed by and paid by the Crown and was, therefore, looked upon as the agent of the King. The Tudor and Stuart sovereigns ensured that all Speakers should be of their choosing. They were, therefore, compliant to the Royal wish, managing Royal business in the Commons and reporting on the attitude of members. This was not satisfactory to the Commons.

In 1629 Mr. Speaker Finch was held down in his chair by the Commons while resolutions were passed condemning the Crown's taxation of 'tunnage and poundage', whereupon (we are told) the Speaker stated: 'I am none the less the King's servant for being yours'.

In 1642, however, the attitude of the Commons stiffened. When Charles I came into the House to arrest five members of the Commons he demanded of the Speaker where the members were. The Speaker replied bravely: 'I have neither eyes to see nor tongue to speak in this place, but as the House doth direct me whose servant I am.'

The constitutional struggles of the seventeenth century finally resulted in the *Bill of Rights, 1689*, and the supremacy of Parliament over the King. Thenceforward the Speaker was undoubtedly the servant of the Commons. From that time forward his modern duties as spokesman of the Commons to the Crown and as chairman have evolved.

Such in broad outline is the history, and it is small wonder that the office and 'Mr. Speaker' himself are accorded traditionally great respect by the public and by all members of the House. Thus, when during proceedings the Speaker rises to his feet all other members in the Chamber must sit down; when he speaks in the proceedings all other members remain silent. If a member disobeys the Speaker he will first be given a warning. If the member persists he may be ordered to leave the House. This is effected traditionally by stating the name of the offender instead of referring to him by the customary manner of 'The Honourable Member for . . .' (the constituency for which the member stands). At this point the Government Minister in charge of the business being debated will move a resolution that the offending member be expelled. The resolution is carried usually unanimously and the offender must leave the House for a certain period (usually five days for a first offender.)

In 1968 Dame Irene Ward, Conservative Member for Tynemouth, who first entered the House in 1931, made a protest during a debate on the Finance Bill. During the division she took a stand before the mace at the foot of the clerks' table, obstructed the tellers when they returned to announce the voting figures and failed to obey the Speaker's request, several times repeated, to resume her seat. The Speaker eventually 'named' Dame Irene, and the Leader of the House moved her suspension. This motion was carried, and as Dame Irene persisted in trying to voice her protest from where she stood the Speaker directed the Serjeant-at-Arms to escort her from the Chamber. She went quietly, and was debarred from entering the Chamber for a week.

Present Functions of the Speaker. The Speaker is the chief officer of the House of Commons, and his main duties are as follows:

(i) He is the mouthpiece of the House of Commons in its relation with (*a*) the Crown, (*b*) the House of Lords, and (*c*) other representative bodies and organisations.

(ii) He presides over the House in its debates, and enforces the rules for preserving order in its proceedings.

In addition, the Speaker has a number of administrative and statutory duties in relation to the function of the Commons. Among these are the following:

(*a*) He certifies whether a Bill is a **Money Bill** for the purposes of the *Parliament Acts, 1911 and 1949.*
(*b*) He executes the Orders of the House.
(*c*) He signs warrants for the issue of writs for by-elections.
(*d*) He issues warrants for committal for contempt of the House, and warrants for witnesses to attend the House to give evidence.
(*e*) He issues reprimands to members or 'strangers' (i.e. members of the public) for contempt of the House or breach of privilege.
(*f*) He supervises and controls all the departments of the House of Commons.

Election of the Speaker. The Speaker is elected by the House from among M.P.s. Usually the Prime Minister and the Leader of the Opposition consult together and agree to propose a member who has taken no recent part in party controversy and who is acceptable to all sections of the House. Qualities of good temper, common sense and scrupulous fairness are looked for.

When elected, the Speaker must, in his chairmanship of the most important and powerful body in the country, be impartial. He does not, therefore, take part in debates (i.e. he does not speak on party political matters). This practice has been observed by all previous Speakers over the last hundred years. He has a casting vote, but, in the event of a tie, he uses that vote to keep the issue open.

When the House of Commons sits, for certain purposes, 'in committee' the chair is occupied by the Chairman of Ways and Means, the Deputy Chairman of Ways and Means, or a temporary chairman. The debates and business done by the House 'in committee' are more informal.

Residence. The Speaker may be called upon to chair a meeting of the House at any time of the day or night, and should as servant of the House be available to perform his important duties. He is given an official residence within the precincts of the Palace of Westminster.

Salary. The Speaker receives a salary of £20,000 per annum, payable out of the Consolidated Fund (see p. 59). On retirement the Speaker is offered a peerage and is awarded a pension.

The Chairman of Ways and Means

This officer is elected by the House from among its members at the beginning of each Parliament. He presides over the House when it is in Committee and maintains order in its business. He must be impartial in the chair. He acts as Deputy Speaker of the House as do the three Deputy Chairmen of Ways and Means.

The Chairman of Ways and Means and the Deputy Chairmen are party appointments and the holders receive salaries for their work in the House.

The Clerk of the House

This office dates from 1388. The Clerk is appointed by the Crown and is removable on an Address from the House. The Clerk keeps the records, prepares the journals, endorses Bills sent or returned to the Lords.

He is assisted by two Clerk Assistants who are similarly attired in wig and gown and sit at the Table of the House and formally record the proceedings.

The Clerk of the House controls a staff of about thirty officers whom he appoints. The Clerk's experience, knowledge of procedure and advice are available to the House, its committees and members.

The Serjeant-at-Arms

He is the officer who ceremonially attends the Speaker with the Mace (the symbol of the Speaker's authority). He executes the Speaker's warrants for commitment to prison (if need be), maintains order in the galleries, controls the messengers and porters, and arranges the policing of the House.

The Serjeant-at-Arms is appointed by the Crown and he is provided with an official residence in the House.

The Speaker's Counsel

This is a lawyer whose duty is to assist the Chairman of Ways and Means in the examination of Private Bills (see p. 90).

The Librarians

Their duties include the provision of literature, journals, books of reference and similar material for the use of members.

Parliamentary Privilege

The House of Commons and the House of Lords enjoy certain rights and privileges. These privileges are part of the common law and are enforceable as such.

Broadly the privileges of Parliament govern the relation of each House with (i) each other, (ii) the Crown, (iii) the Courts, and (iv) the public.

The rights (or privileges) have been won largely as the result of the former struggles of Parliament with the Crown over the question of the 'supremacy' of Parliament and with the Courts over the question of jurisdiction. The main object of Parliamentary Privilege is to protect the rights of the House of Commons and its members inside Parliament to enable them to do their duty. Parliamentary Privilege ensures the efficiency of Parliament. In a sense it forms a special law which is interpreted and administered in each House and not in the ordinary courts of law. It is nevertheless part of the law of the land and is recognized constitutionally by the Courts of Law.

Privileges of the House of Commons

At the opening of Parliament the Speaker lays claim to the privileges in the name of the Commons thus:

their ancient and undoubted rights and privileges; particularly that their persons may be free from arrests and all molestations; that they may enjoy liberty of speech in all their debates; may have access to Her Majesty's Royal person whenever occasion shall require; and that all their proceedings may receive from Her Majesty the most favourable construction.

To this request the Lord Chancellor, acting for Her Majesty, replies:

Her Majesty most readily confirms all the rights and privileges which have ever been granted to or conferred upon the Commons, by Her Majesty or any of her royal predecessors.

The main privileges may, therefore, be listed thus:

   (i) Freedom from arrest.
   (ii) Freedom of speech and debate.
  (iii) Right of access to the Queen.
  (iv) Right to regulate its own proceedings.
   (v) Right to regulate its own composition.
  (vi) Right to have the most favourable construction placed on the deliberations of the Commons.
 (vii) The power to punish for breach of privilege or for contempt.

(i) *Freedom from Arrest.* This has lost much of its former importance. M.P.s are not exempt from the criminal law and, if they commit arrestable criminal offences they may be arrested if need be at any time. The privilege relates to civil arrest, i.e. arrest for civil cause. A member may not be arrested on a civil matter during a session and forty days before and forty days after a session. The privilege is practically obsolete. It was formerly invoked when a member was arrested for civil debt (*Ferrer's Case, 1543*), but since the *Debtor's Act, 1869*, which precludes arrest for civil debt, the privilege is not now of importance, and a Select Committee on Parliamentary Privilege in 1967 recommended its abolition.

Where a member is convicted of crime the judge notifies the Speaker, and the House may if, the crime be of a serious nature, pass a motion expelling the member concerned.

(ii) *Freedom of Speech*. This is one of the main freedoms which is jealously guarded. The *Bill of Rights, 1689* (*Article 9*) declares:

That the freedom of speech and debates on proceedings in Parliament ought not to be impeached or questioned in any court or place out of Parliament.

No legal proceedings have since then been taken by the Crown or a private person against any member for words spoken in the House. So a member may not be prosecuted for sedition nor may he be sued for libel or slander in respect of anything said by such member during proceedings in the House or published on its order paper. Members are also exempt from the provisions of the *Official Secrets Acts, 1911–1939*, in respect of anything said by them which would in other circumstances be a criminal offence.

The privilege of freedom of speech is not a personal right of an individual M.P. but a necessary protection and guarantee that a member should be able to defend to the full the interests of the electors, and is, therefore, an indirect constitutional privilege of every citizen.

Allied to the right of freedom of speech is the right of the Commons to debate (*a*) in private, and (*b*) in secret session. The Commons may at any time exercise the right to exclude strangers (i.e. the public) from the public galleries. The right may be exercised by the Speaker on his own initiative or on a motion by a member that strangers be ordered to withdraw. A vote is then taken and the Speaker may thereupon order members of the public to withdraw from the Chamber.

A secret session is one in which vital matters of national importance are discussed, e.g. shipping losses in time of war, the revelation of which would be helpful to an enemy. The House may resolve that its proceedings or debates be held in secret and that the public (including the Press) be excluded.

(iii) The *Right of Access to H.M. The Queen*. In the thirteenth and fourteenth centuries the Commons were sometimes admitted to the Royal presence to give answers to the demands or requests put before them. The privilege is formally requested today by the Speaker. It is a collective right and is exercised through the elected representative of the House, namely the Speaker.

(iv) The *Right to Regulate its own Proceedings*. The House of Commons has the right to determine its own constitution, e.g.:

(*a*) To settle disputed elections where irregular practices are alleged.

(*b*) To suspend or expel a member.

(*c*) To decide what it will discuss and the order of so doing.

(*d*) To settle its own procedure in the chamber and in the House as a whole.

Bradlaugh, an atheist M.P. for Northampton, refused to take the oath on his admission to the House of Commons and claimed the right to make an affirmation instead under the *Evidence Acts, 1869 and 1870*. The House refused to permit this and Bradlaugh challenged the ruling in the Courts of Law. He also sought an order to restrain the Sergeant-at-Arms (Gossett) from preventing him from entering the House and a declaration that the resolution of the House was void. The Court held that: 'For the purpose of determining on a right to be exercised within the House itself, and in particular the right of sitting and voting, the House and the House alone could interpret the Statute'. Bradlaugh was subsequently allowed to affirm in 1886 and took his seat. *Bradlaugh* v. *Gossett* (1884).

(v) *The Right to Regulate its own Composition.* This privilege is closely allied to the previous one. The right is best exemplified by the right:

(a) To fill a casual vacancy by the Speaker issuing a warrant instructing a writ to be issued authorizing an election to be held in a constituency when a casual vacancy occurs.

(b) To decide disputed elections. This is done by an order of the House to H.M. judges who are directed to hear the petition. The House invariably accepts the determination of the judges.

(c) To determine whether a person claiming to be lawfully elected is or is not legally disqualified. See the case of Mr. Anthony Wedgwood Benn (p. 48).

(d) To expel a member or suspend a member.

(vi) *The Right to have the Most Favourable Construction placed on its Deliberations.* This is a reminder of former times when the business of the House was reported to the Monarch by the Speaker in his own words. This was sometimes a very tricky duty demanding the utmost tact and discretion. The privilege is now of no great practical importance.

(vii) *The Power to Punish for Breach of Privilege or Contempt.* The privileges are those listed above. Contempt means 'any act which offends the dignity of the House or which obstructs or impedes any member or officer of the House in the discharge of his duty or which tends to produce such a result', e.g. disorderly conduct in the House, abuse of the Speaker, throwing a tomato at him.

Enforcement. The House may punish offenders by imprisonment, fine, reprimand, admonition, or, in the case of a member, expulsion or suspension. Imprisonment may be for a specified time or until the end of the session when the committal automatically lapses. The prison itself is located in the Clock Tower. Warrants for the arrest of a member or non-member are drawn up by the Speaker and executed by the Serjeant-at-Arms with the aid of the civil police.

Complaints of breach of privilege or contempt are investigated by the **Committee of Privileges** which has power to summon witnesses and hear evidence. The House itself decides what amounts to breach of privilege. Nevertheless the Courts of Law have laid it down that it is for the Courts, as a matter of law, to determine the existence and the limits of a privilege claimed by a litigant. The Courts will not consider mere resolutions of either House as sufficient justification for a privilege, for a resolution as such is not law. The following case is relevant to the privilege of freedom of speech and debate (No. (ii) above):

The House of Commons ordered the publication by its printer (Hansard) of certain matters which were defamatory of Stockdale (plaintiff). Copies of Hansard were sold outside Parliament and Stockdale sued Hansard in defamation. Hansard's defence was that an order of the Commons granted privilege from action in the Courts of Law and that a resolution of the Commons and a declaration of its privilege excluded the Courts of Law from jurisdiction. *Held:* That the mere resolution or order of the House will not justify an act otherwise illegal, and that the House had no privilege to authorise publication of libel outside the House. *Stockdale* v. *Hansard* (1839).

The *Parliamentary Papers Act, 1840*. As a result of the decision in *Stockdale* v. *Hansard* (1839) the *Parliamentary Papers Act, 1840*, was passed which extended absolute privilege to any publication made by authority of either House of Parliament. Accordingly an action for defamation in any such publication will be stayed on production of a certificate from an officer of the relevant House.

Privileges of the House of Lords

The House of Lords is the descendant of the medieval Council. The Lords were in those early days the tenants in chief of the Crown. One of the incidents of feudal tenure was that a tenant had a right or duty to attend his lord's (i.e. the King's) court, known as suit of court. The Lords attended court and gave advice to the Crown personally, if need be.

The privileges of the Lords are practically the same as those enjoyed by the Commons, namely:

(i) Freedom from arrest.
(ii) Freedom of speech and debate.
(iii) Right of access to the Crown. This is a personal right since each peer is a Counsellor of the Sovereign.
(iv) The right to regulate its own proceedings and composition.
(v) The right to enter a protest in the journals against a resolution of the House.

The Whips

The name 'Whip' derives from the hunting field. Many M.P.s of former days were country gentry and rode to hounds. The 'whipper in' kept the hounds in a pack or in line. The 'Whip' is a well-known parliamentary term and has two meanings. It refers to:

(i) An important party official (Government and Opposition):
(ii) A written notice or direction to an M.P. to attend the House to vote.

Party Official

After a General Election each major party appoints a Chief Whip and assistant Whips. The Government Chief Whip usually holds the office of Parliamentary Secretary to the Treasury, a salaried post. The holder has few departmental duties. Assistant Whips (8–10) are also appointed to lesser Government posts as Junior Lords of the Treasury. These also are salaried, and some are sinecures (i.e. with few departmental or ministerial duties). The freedom from departmental duties enables the Whips to manage their party politically within Parliament.

The main duties of the Government Whips are *managerial*. They include the following, namely to:

(*a*) Arrange the business of the House and its time-table.
(*b*) Advise M.P.s how to vote and of the relative importance of a motion or debate to the Government.
(*c*) Inform the leaders of the feelings and views of backbenchers on party policy.
(*d*) Discipline M.P.s if need be.
(*e*) Arrange 'pairing' of M.P.s.
(*f*) Act as 'Patronage Secretary' (Government Chief Whip).

The Whips are the agents through whom the party machinery is used for the conduct of the business of the House. They are the eyes and ears of the party chief. It is their business to try and discern the direction in which sections of opinion are moving, to hear any mutterings of discontent, and to suggest methods for mitigating them. (Sir Courtenay Ilbert.)

The Opposition leader also appoints an **Opposition Chief Whip** and assistant Whips. Their duties correspond with those of their counterparts on the Government side. They are salaried appointments.

(*a*) *Arranging business.* The Government Chief Whip consults with (i) the Prime Minister and the Leader of the House (a senior politician) as to the time-table of the business, and (ii) the Opposition Chief Whip who also confers with the Leader of the Opposition. When done and agreed the Government Chief Whip confers with the Speaker for his approval of the time-table of business.

This is not always easy. Sometimes a Government party wishes to get an important Bill through Parliament quickly, e.g. an Industrial Relations Bill. The Opposition may require to debate the Bill to which it is fundamentally opposed. A compromise has to be reached to enable the Opposition to debate and object while also enabling the Government to pass the Bill with its majority.

(*b*) *Advising M.P.s.* The Whips usually attend the Parliamentary Party meetings each week, and there outline the business of the following week indicating the relative importance of pending matters. The Chief Whip sends formal notices (also called 'Whips') to all members of the Parliamentary Party detailing the matters to be dealt with in the House.

The notices are underlined in three ways: one-line; two-line; and three-line, in ascending order of urgency or importance, thus:

One-line whip = least vital.

Two-line whip = a division is expected. M.P.s must attend (unless firmly 'paired'—see p. 68).

Three-line whip = attendance vital. Only seriously ill M.P.s will be excused.

(*c*) *Informing the Leader.* M.P.s of a particular party will be expected to follow the main policies of the party, in or out of office. The Cabinet or the Shadow Cabinet each gives a lead, but neither of these groups may expect automatic obedience from its M.P.s in the Parliamentary Party. The leaders require to know how the rank and file feel about a particular matter, and the Chief Whips must inform them of the views of M.P.s. The aim is to achieve agreement and unity.

Nevertheless it is true that a Government and an Opposition may each act unwisely. Neither claims final wisdom. Where a substantial group within a party disagrees with its leaders a dangerous situation arises. A house divided against itself will fall; and so will a Government or Opposition Party.

Where an individual M.P. disagrees with his party he may say so. The Whip will try to alter his view by discussion, persuasion, or advice with a view to compromise or agreement. In the final resort an M.P. may on conscientious grounds refrain from voting or vote against his own party.

(*d*) *Discipline.* The basic principle of the party system is that each party

PRIVATE AND CONFIDENTIAL   PARLIAMENTARY LABOUR PARTY

ON MONDAY, 25th October, 1971, the House will meet at 2.30 p.m.

DEBATE ON THE UNITED KINGDOM
AND THE EUROPEAN COMMUNITIES (3rd day)

Speakers: (Mr. G. Rippon to open for the Government)
(Mr. M. Foot to open for the Opposition)
(Mr. Douglas Jay to wind-up for the Opposition)
(Mr. Robert Carr to wind-up for the Government)

A GOOD ATTENDANCE THROUGHOUT IS REQUESTED

ON TUESDAY, 26th October, the House will meet at 2.30 p.m.

DEBATE ON THE UNITED KINGDOM
AND THE EUROPEAN COMMUNITIES (4th day)

Speakers: (Mr. W. Ross to open for the Opposition)
(Mr. G. Campbell to open for the Government)
(Mr. G. Thomas to wind-up for the Opposition)
(Mr. P. Thomas to wind-up for the Government)

A GOOD ATTENDANCE THROUGHOUT IS REQUESTED

ON WEDNESDAY, 27th October, the House will meet at 2.30 p.m.

DEBATE ON THE UNITED KINGDOM
AND THE EUROPEAN COMMUNITIES (5th day)

Speakers: (Mr. A. Barber to open for the Government)
(Mr. Wedgwood Benn to open for the Opposition)
(Mrs. B. Castle to wind-up for the Opposition)
(Mr. John Davies to wind-up for the Government)

A GOOD ATTENDANCE THROUGHOUT IS REQUESTED

ON THURSDAY, 28th October, the House will meet at 2.30 p.m.

DEBATE ON THE UNITED KINGDOM
AND THE EUROPEAN COMMUNITIES (final day)

Speakers: (Mr. Harold Wilson will open for the Opposition)
(Mr. R. Maudling will open for the Government)
(Mr. J. Callaghan will wind-up for the Opposition)
(Mr. E. Heath will wind-up for the Government)

A VITAL DIVISION WILL TAKE PLACE AND YOUR ATTENDANCE

AT 9.30 P.M. IS ABSOLUTELY ESSENTIAL

NOTE: Suspension of the Rule—Members may like to know that on Monday, Tuesday and Wednesday, suspension will depend on the number of Members who have indicated to Mr. Speaker their intention to take part.

ON FRIDAY, 29th October, the House will meet at 11 a.m.

PROROGATION WILL TAKE PLACE

BOB MELLISH

ON TUESDAY, 2nd November, Her Majesty The Queen will open the New Session of Parliament.

Example of a 'Whip'

accepts certain defined policies, and that M.P.s of the party act in concert to present a united front, voting 'Aye' or 'Nay' in accordance with the agreed policy. Nevertheless, each M.P. has, in the final resort, after pondering the issues at stake, a freedom to act as his conscience dictates even if this amounts to a vote against his own political party.

If no compromise can be reached with a dissentient M.P. the question arises as to how far and how long a party may carry a rebel within its ranks. If an M.P. consistently votes contrary to the direction of the Whip he will first be tactfully warned against continual opposition. If the M.P. persists the ultimate sanction is expulsion from the party and the withdrawal of the Whip and the benefits from adherence to a politically powerful party group. The M.P. then virtually becomes independent. How long that lasts depends on many factors. Sometimes an expelled member is re-admitted later. Certain M.P.s have even after expulsion achieved great prominence and Cabinet rank.

(*e*) *Pairing*. If an M.P. is out of the country or attending an important function a system of 'pairing' is applied, i.e. the Whips of both Government and Opposition agree that e.g. Mr. *A*, M.P. (Con.) who is away, shall be paired with Mr. *B*, M.P. (Lab.) also away; or that Mr. *C*, M.P. (Con.) is paired with Mr. *D*, M.P. (Lab.) who are both members of a Parliamentary delegation or ill, etc. If each party loses an equal number of members the majority in a division of the House will not be affected.

(*f*) *Patronage Secretary*. The Government Chief Whip is known as the Patronage Secretary. As we have seen, the appointment is an important one (his official office is at 12 Downing Street, London) and the holder exercises considerable influence in the award of honours. Moreover, since the Government Chief Whip is the 'eyes and ears' of the Prime Minister he may recommend to the leader any M.P. with the necessary ability and character for advancement to Ministerial office.

Moreover, where a M.P. is competent in a particular subject and wishes to speak in debate as a backbencher the Government Whip will make arrangements for him to be given the opportunity—sometimes called 'catching the Speaker's eye' if circumstances of the business of the House permit.

Committees

Both Houses of Parliament have an organized system of committees. This is inevitable. Parliament does what any other institution does when faced with a formidable amount of work: it distributes its work to smaller bodies which report back to the main body—the House of Commons or the House of Lords.

Parliamentary committees serve two distinct purposes:

(i) To represent the whole House in the detailed scrutiny of legislation:
(ii) To inquire into matters which may only be satisfactorily investigated by a small number of persons.

Another important feature which we may mention here is that committees are constituted to enable Parliament to consider matters in a less formal atmosphere than that which obtains during an ordinary sitting of the House.

The Committee system of the House of Commons is made up of:

(i) Committees of the Whole House.

    (ii) Standing Committees.
    (iii) Select Committees.
    (iv) Joint Committees (i.e. committees of (*a*) the Commons and (*b*) the Lords).
    (v) Committees on Private Bills.

In addition to the above we should note the existence of Parliamentary Party Committees (referred to on p. 72) the Scottish Standing and Grand Committees, and the Welsh Grand Committee (see p. 70).

(i) *Committees of the Whole House*

A Committee of the Whole House is the technical name given to the whole House presided over by the Chairman of Ways and Means (or a Deputy) instead of the Speaker. It constitutes itself in this form by resolution to enable the House as a whole to consider important Bills in detail, clause by clause, after their second reading.

The procedure generally in a Committee of the Whole House is the same as that when the House sits formally, except that the Committee operates under more flexible rules. Thus a member may speak more than once on the same motion. The mace is placed by the Serjeant-at-Arms under the Speaker's table, signifying the proceedings are of less formal character.

Committees of the Whole House are appointed for a specific purpose (e.g. the consideration of a particular Bill) and with limited powers. When the matter to be dealt with is completed and the deliberations ended a report is made to the House formally (the Speaker then resuming his chair and the mace being replaced). The report to the House is made by the Chairman of the Committee.

(ii) *Standing Committees*

Public Bills which, after a second reading, are *not* committed to Committees of the Whole House, to Select Committees, to Joint Committees or to the Scottish and Welsh Grand Committees (see below, p. 70) are sent to Standing Committees.

A Standing Committee considers and amends Public Bills. Standing Order 38 requires that all public Bills, except:

    (*a*) Bills for imposing taxation and Consolidated Fund and Appropriation Bills, and
    (*b*) Bills confirming Provisional Orders,

shall be committed to a Standing Committee unless the House otherwise directs. Bills of first class constitutional importance would be dealt with by a Committee of the Whole House, as would those which are required to be passed quickly into law.

Today the House of Commons appoints eight Standing Committees designated Standing Committee *A, B, C* to *H*. Any number of Standing Committees may be appointed by the House, but it is rare for more than five such committees to sit simultaneously.

Constitution. An ordinary Standing Committee consists of a Chairman and not fewer than twenty nor more than fifty members nominated in respect of each Bill the committee is to consider. Members are appointed by the Com-

mittee of Selection, regard being had to the interest and experience of members
and to the composition of the House, i.e. party strengths.

Scottish Standing Committee. This consists of thirty members nominated
from Scottish constituencies with up to twenty other nominated members.
In its plenary (i.e. full) form the committee is known as the Scottish Grand
Committee and comprises *all* the members for the Scottish constituencies and
not less than ten nor more than fifteen others. These committees consider
Scottish estimates and other matters relating exclusively to Scotland as well
as Scottish Bills.

Welsh Grand Committee. Consists of thirty-six members for constituencies
in Wales and Monmouthshire, with up to five other nominated members.
This committee considers Welsh estimates, and matters relating exclusively
to Wales in addition to Welsh Bills.

Procedure in Standing Committees. This is similar to that followed by a
Committee of the Whole House.

(iii) *Select Committees*

These are committees which are *not* (i) Committees of the Whole House,
or (ii) Standing Committees.

Select Committees are set up to take evidence on some particular matter
and to report their opinion to the House. As the name implies the committees are called 'Select' merely because the House selects the names of those
who become members. A further note on the constitution appears below.

Select Committees may be grouped under three heads:

(i) Committees supervising Government Administration.
(ii) *Ad hoc* committees.
(iii) Domestic committees.

(i) *Committees Supervising Government Administration*. Examples of these
include the following:

(a) Public Accounts Committee (see p. 102).
(b) The Select Committee on Expenditure (see p. 100).
(c) The Statutory Instruments' Joint Committee (see p. 250).
(d) The Committee on the Nationalized Industries (see p. 164).
(e) The Select Committee on Race Relations.
(f) The Select Committee on Immigration.
(g) The Committee for the Parliamentary Commissioner (see p. 269).
(h) The Select Committee on Science and Technology.
(i) The Select Committee on Overseas Development.

(ii) *Ad hoc Committees*. These are set up on a short-term basis to investigate a particular matter (i.e. *ad hoc*). A recent example in 1971 was the Committee on the Civil List (see p. 108). This Committee was appointed to investigate the expenses of the Royal Family. The Chairman was Lord Boyle and the
Committee reported in December 1971, as a result of which the House approved the revised allowances shown on page 108.

Another example was the Select Committee set up in February 1969, to
investigate certain claims made by Sir Gerald Nabarro, M.P., that he had
'irrefutable evidence' of the Chancellor's intention to increase the price of
Road Fund Licences for motor-cars in the impending Budget of 1969. The

matter was investigated and the claims made by Sir Gerald were rejected as unfounded.

After an *ad hoc* committee has investigated and reported upon the particular subject matter within its terms of reference it ceases to exist.

(iii) *Domestic Committees*. These are constituted to enable the House to manage and run its own affairs more efficiently. One finds in a college usually a Library Committee or Restaurant Committee and so on; such committees being 'domestic' to the particular institution. It is in this sense that we use the word domestic committee in relation to the House of Commons. Examples of these committees include:

(*a*) The Committee of Selection. (This names the members of the Standing Committees and other committees mentioned above.)

(*b*) The Committee of Privileges (see p. 64).

(*c*) The Select Committee on Procedure. (This makes recommendations in the rules and orders giving the procedure of the House to ensure more efficient administration.)

(*d*) The Select Committee on Debates and Reports. (Arranges publication of official matters for the members, the House and the public.)

(*e*) The Kitchen and Refreshment Rooms Committee. (Makes provision for and supervises running of kitchens, etc.)

(*f*) The Standing Orders Committee.

(*g*) The Select Committee on Members' Interests (Declaration) (p. 89).

Powers of Select Committees. The Select Committees of the House of Commons have certain important powers. Thus a committee may:

(i) Summon witnesses to give evidence to the committee (e.g. civil servants of any department, expert witnesses such as scientists or technologists).

(ii) Order production of documents, such as reports made to Government Ministers of an official nature.

In the Lords these powers are not given automatically. Witnesses may be requested to attend there or to produce documents to its Select Committees. If need be an Order of the House of Lords may be made to ensure compliance.

Attendance of Public. Members of the public may be allowed to be present while evidence is being given before a committee. During the deliberating stages, e.g. when members discuss the truth, value, or worth of the evidence given, or the contents of their report and their recommendations the public may be excluded. M.P.s (not members of the committee) may be present during the deliberative stages, though they usually withdraw as a mark of courtesy. When a committee reports to the House the document is made public and is usually reported in the Press as part of the Parliamentary proceedings.

(iv) *Joint Committees*

These are committees composed of (i) members of the House of Commons and (ii) members of the House of Lords, usually in equal numbers. Such committees may be appointed to deal with (*a*) a particular subject, (*b*) a particular Bill, or (*c*) Bills of a particular kind.

A joint committee to consider a particular subject may be appointed at the instance of either House. A proposal that a particular Bill should be committed to a joint committee must come from the House in which the Bill originated.

Constitution. Members of a joint committee are chosen by each House in equal numbers. The Chairman is elected by the joint committee from among members nominated by either House. Decisions are taken by vote in the normal way.

A joint committee has only that authority which is given to it by both Houses. The time and place of meetings are fixed by agreement between the two Houses. An example is the Statutory Instruments Committee.

The report of a joint committee is presented to both Houses by the Chairman to the House of which he is a member, and by a member selected by the committee for the purpose to the other House.

(v) *Committees on Private Bills*

Private Bills are those which are usually of a local character and are most commonly presented by a local authority, a Port authority, or similar body requiring an extension of its powers (see p. 90).

Private Bills may be opposed or unopposed. An opposed Bill is one which is opposed, e.g. by a group of persons, another local authority, or a private company whose rights may be adversely affected were the Bill to become law. Opponents thereupon present a petition to the House against the Bill. But, even where no petition has been presented against a Private Bill the Chairman of Ways and Means for the Commons and the Lord Chairman of Committees for the Lords may report that any particular Bill should be treated as opposed.

The committee on an opposed Bill before the Lower House consists of four members of the Commons (who are appointed by the Committee of Selection). The members must have no local or personal interest in the Bill since their function in relation to the Bill is quasi-judicial.

In the case of an unopposed Bill the committee comprises the Chairman of Ways and Means, the Deputy Chairman and three other members chosen by the Chairman from a panel appointed by the Committee of Selection at the beginning of each session.

In the House of Lords the committees on opposed Bills consists of five members, while unopposed Bills are referred to the Lord Chairman of Committees.

Parliamentary Party Committees

In addition to the above committees, we must also note that both the Government and the Opposition have their own **Parliamentary Party Committees.** Thus, in 1971 the Conservative backbench Parliamentary Committees appointed committees for each of the following subjects: Defence; Transport Industries; Housing and Construction; Employment; Home Affairs; Foreign and Commonwealth Affairs; Trade; Agriculture; Fisheries and Food; Legal; and Finance. Each committee has its Chairman, Vice-Chairmen, and secretaries chosen from backbench M.P.s. The Parliamentary Labour Party has its committees constituted in broadly the same way and covering the same subjects. The Shadow Cabinet stands at the apex of the Opposition committee structure.

Comment on Committees

It follows from the description and number of the committees already mentioned that all M.P.s will serve as members of some of them. Certain committees are directly concerned with legislation (e.g. Standing Committees) but some will be concerned with the administration of the Government itself, i.e. the use of its executive power, and some will be concerned with finance.

One of the problems facing the House today is its weakness to control the Government. In effect the Government has its way, whether in legislation, finance, or administration. The growth of powerful party loyalties has meant that the Commons has virtually lost its capacity to defeat a Government. The influence of the House has, therefore, diminished. Some critics suggest that as a result of this poorer candidates stand for Parliament and (perhaps more important) public confidence in the old institutions has declined.

Some thinking persons have suggested ways to restore the influence and power of the Commons, particularly to enable the Commons to discuss policy before decisions are taken and the stamp of party approval has been applied. On the one hand we say the Government must govern; on the other we say the House should control the Government or at least the Government should be responsible to the House of Commons.

One remedy which has been suggested is to appoint small 'specialist' committees, e.g. on Education, Immigration, Race Relations, Science and Technology, Overseas Development. Such committees have been appointed since 1966 (some are still in being) and they are of two kinds:

(i) 'Subject' committees (to consider a range of related subjects).
(ii) 'Departmental' committees (to consider the work and activities of a particular Government Department, such as the Home Office).

The Committees have been given powers to call for papers and to call witnesses, e.g. civil servants and experts outside the service. Membership of these committees will broaden an M.P.'s experience and awareness of the difficulties of administration and of the problems to be solved. M.P.s will, therefore, be able to ask more pertinent questions on the floor of the House or to suggest possible remedies which a Government ought to apply. Nevertheless, the final decision rests with the Cabinet and the individual Ministers (see Collective and Ministerial Responsibility on p. 118). These are the executive Ministers in their Departments, fed with up-to-date information, continuously trying to solve their departmental problems, and inevitably the Government's policy will prevail by reason of its majority upon which it can rely. The question remains whether the 'specialist' or 'departmental' committees are effective and useful. The observations of John Mackintosh, M.P., are as follows:

If diversions are required each M.P. has his constituency work, and the need to make his own mark in his party, none of which is furthered by spending time trying to nibble at the edges of executive power.

We may note here the **Committee on Expenditure** set up at the beginning of 1971 which examines the estimates and the expenditure for five years' ahead. This Committee ranges over a wide field. Finance and policy are closely interwoven. It follows, therefore, that this important Committee will inevitably cover much of the territory to be investigated by the Specialist Committees enumerated above.

A Green Paper (1971) states:

> The Government sees this dual system (i.e. Specialist Committees and the Expenditure Committee) providing an effective machinery of scrutiny without impairing the responsibility of Ministers to Parliament or detracting from the importance of proceedings on the floor of the House of Commons.

One can only hope that this will be so. The fact remains that the problem facing all M.P.s is the enormity and variety of the problems facing Government as a whole. The most that a backbench M.P. can do is to specialize in a few fields and make himself reasonably competent in those. Otherwise he might, in ignorance or confusion, be a mere automaton, responsive to the 'Whip' alone.

The Commons at Work

The Cabinet and the Government Ministers hold the keys of power at the head of the State. They wield the executive power, making decisions which may affect the lives of millions.

The House of Lords and the House of Commons together have an essential role to play in the constitution in (1) considering Bills (legislation), (2) voting of supplies, (3) the application of moneys voted, (4) questioning Ministers, and (5) debating issues of public importance which arise constantly in national and international affairs. All these matters will be dealt with in more detail later.

In this chapter we consider the House of Commons at work. First we sketch in broad outline the normal year's work, and then we consider the daily routine followed on each 'sitting day' of the House.

The Year's Work

A Parliamentary session lasts for one year approximately, i.e. from October to October. Each session is usually broken up by adjournments to allow for vacations. When Parliament is not sitting it is said to be in recess.

During each session there are approximately 160 'sitting days'. This amounts to thirty-three weeks of the year during which M.P.s carry on their work at Westminster. At the beginning of the present century Parliament was in full session for some twenty-six weeks only. In 1939 the number of weeks increased to twenty-nine. Parliamentary work increases year by year, it becomes more complex and exacting and consequently more time is needed.

Parliament is summoned by the Queen in October and it is prorogued or dissolved by the Queen. The modern practice is that the same Royal proclamation dissolves a Parliament and summons a new one.

Each Parliamentary session is officially opened by the Queen. In the speech from the Throne the achievements of the Government during the past year (if it has been in office during the year) are briefly reviewed. Then follows the future intentions of the Government and its legislative programme. The speech is usually delivered by Her Majesty in person; otherwise it is read by the Lord Chancellor or by a Royal Commission. The place where the speech is delivered is in the House of Lords where the Commons are summoned to hear it.

Then follows what is described as the 'grand inquest of the nation', i.e. a general debate and discussion on the political situation, domestic and foreign, takes place. But, before an address is moved in answer to the Speech, a formal first reading of an obsolete Bill is performed in both Houses. In the Commons this is known as a 'Bill to prevent Clandestine Outlawries'. This quaint formula or document acknowledges the rule of 'redress of grievances before supply'. In other words, before the Commons is prepared to vote the money necessary to carry on government the Crown must attend to the grievances of subjects. Once that formality is over a full scale 'inquest' or inquiry into the state of affairs of the nation takes place when backbenchers on the Government side move the address in reply to the Speech.

The work of the House is roughly divided into three parts: legislative, control of finance, and the checking of the work of the Government by questioning of Ministers (administration). The time devoted to each of these subjects is as follows:

(i)	Legislation	50 per cent
(ii)	Finance	30 per cent
(iii)	Administration	20 per cent

This is a broad analysis of the time. We shall deal with each of the headings in more detail later, in particular considering the steps in the enactment of legislation, the raising of finance by taxation, and the apportionment or distribution of the monies so raised to Departments of Government. The checking by the House of the administration of Government is the last of three duties, and this involves questions raised in the House or a full-scale debate and, if need be, a vote of censure on the Government. The object of this is to ensure that the Government Ministers and their departments or agencies are working efficiently, are subject to the control of Parliament, and ultimately to the people of the country.

Question Time

At about 2.45 p.m. Question Time begins. For 45 minutes members may ask questions of Ministers who reply 'on the floor of the House'.

Question Time is a useful Parliamentary device to enable any member to:

(a) Obtain information.

(b) Publicise a grievance.

(c) Stimulate, challenge or embarrass a Minister.

(d) Show that the member asking the question is active in the House.

All M.P.s receive complaints and information from constituents. Some disclose injustices or maladministration and may be genuinely critical of Government. A member may, after verifying the facts, direct a question to the appropriate Minister and ask for an explanation in Parliament. A member may have certain information gained from his own resources which warrant a question in the House. He need not wait to be moved by a constituent.

Parliamentary questions are of four types:

1. 'Oral', requiring an oral answer in the House.
2. 'Non-oral' or 'written' requiring a written reply.
3. 'Private Notice',—in effect oral questions of an urgent nature which by special permission from the Speaker receive a reply at the end of Question hour, even on the day when first raised.

4. 'Supplementary', which follow replies to 'oral' questions. The supplementary questions are presumed to arise impromptu in the mind of the questioner, though in fact they are often prepared for previously by the member.

Most proceedings in Parliament are governed by rules. Question Time has evolved its rules. Thus a question must be written on paper and handed to the Clerks of the House who may rephrase it in parliamentary language. A question must relate to the department of the Minister questioned, and forty-eight hours' notice to a Minister is required. A questioner must verify his facts and figures, if any, which he quotes. Hearsay and rumour should be avoided. A question must be interrogative in form, not a statement or a speech. It must not be argumentative or merely rhetorical and must not refer to a debate in the current session or be critical of a decision of the House; nor must it contravene constitutional usage or etiquette.

As noted above, the supplementary question is the chief counter to an unsatisfactory, vague, or evasive reply. Although a Minister will be briefed by his Department, the supplementary question may be an accurately aimed blow which the Minister must parry as deftly as he can or reply to as best he can with the information available. Sometimes a supplementary question may result in a minor debate particularly if other members join in the fray. However, we must note that a Minister is not bound to reply to a question, and (rarely) he may refuse to do so on occasion, e.g. on security grounds.

Question Time is limited to three-quarters of an hour. Consequently time is short, and if long answers are required this necessarily means that fewer questions can be answered. Where questions on the list are not answered on a particular day they receive a written reply.

If a member is not satisfied with an answer given by a Minister he may 'raise the matter on the adjournment'; that is, in the half-hour debates which take place at 10 p.m. each evening. This can only be done if the questioner secures a place by ballot to raise the matter.

During Question Time a member may move the immediate adjournment of the House under Standing Order No. 9 (a procedural rule of the House) to 'discuss a specific and important matter that should have urgent consideration'. This depends on whether the Speaker allows the motion. If he does the motion is moved and a speech is made involving the point of the question to which a reply is made by a Government Minister on behalf of the Government. If the matter is of sufficient importance the Prime Minister or Leader of the House may reply.

By the nature of things Opposition front- and backbenchers ask more questions than members on the Government side. No Government backbench member would wish to embarrass his side if he can by discreetly securing a written reply obtain the required action or information.

There is never a division during Question Time. Consequently there is no motion which is likely to bring down a Government. Nevertheless questions do ensure that a Government is kept on its toes; that faults are brought to light; inefficiencies exposed and malpractices prevented. The right of any subject to petition the Crown or a Government is beyond doubt; the right of a member to question the Government is another freedom which should be jealously guarded.

Answers. On receiving a question the Minister passes it to civil servants of the Department to obtain details and facts for a reply. The Minister is then 'briefed' with information to enable him to answer clearly and accurately the point raised. Civil servants also provide background information in case supplementary questions are asked. The Minister is politically responsible for his Department and the civil servants for their part try to ensure that their chief makes a good showing when on his feet facing a critical House.

Ministers appear in the House and answer questions on a rota system. Normally two Ministers appear each day and take all the questions relating to both Departments. The Prime Minister and the Leader of the House answer questions on two days a week, at 3.15 p.m. on Tuesdays and Thursdays.

Generally the questioners are Opposition front- and backbenchers and, to a lesser extent, Government backbenchers. It sometimes happens, however, that the Government may itself arrange for a question to be asked to enable a Prime Minister or other Minister to disclose certain information of importance which the House and the public ought to know.

All Oral Answers are reported in Hansard (the official Report of the House of Commons) and sometimes in *The Times* and other newspapers. A study of Hansard is necessary to reveal the kind of question to which Government Ministers are exposed.

The Debate on the Adjournment

In addition to Question Time (2.45–3.30 p.m.) a member may raise a matter on the motion 'that the House do adjourn' which is moved at the end of the day's business at 10 p.m. The last half-hour before the House rises at 10.30 p.m. will then be devoted to debating any important topic a member seeks to introduce.

The normal rule since 1945 is that the main business of the House is finished at 10 p.m. Any debate which is then allowed takes place between that hour and 10.30 p.m.

Where an 'all-night' sitting occurs the ten o'clock rule is thereupon suspended, in which case no one may take advantage of a debate on a motion which he seeks to move.

Many members have matters which they seek to raise. Consequently a ballot is held or the Speaker makes a decision as to the member who will be allowed to move a motion.

The Ten-Minute Rule

This is another method of raising a subject in Parliament. A member may introduce a Bill under what is called the 'Ten-Minute Rule' which is the time allotted at certain specified times during a session to enable a member to introduce a Bill with a ten-minute speech. A ten-minute speech may be allowed in reply, and the House may vote or accept the Bill unopposed. Even if the Bill is not accepted the member has the satisfaction of bringing public attention to his cause as contained in the Bill.

Procedure

All institutions in which groups of men reach decisions and take action on those decisions have rules of procedure for the conduct of business. The rules of the House of Commons are contained in:

(i) Acts of Parliament (e.g. *Parliament Acts*, 1911 and 1949).

HOUSE OF COMMONS

Wednesday, 8th December, 1971

*The House met at half-past
Two o'clock*

PRAYERS

[Mr. SPEAKER *in the Chair*]

ORAL ANSWERS TO QUESTIONS

POSTS AND TELECOMMUNICATIONS

B.B.C. Wales

1. Mr. Gwynoro Jones asked the Minister of Posts and Telecommunications what percentage of the population of Wales receive the British Broadcasting Corporation Wales Channel ; and what is the figure for Carmarthenshire.

The Minister of Posts and Telecommunications (Mr. Christopher Chataway) : The B.B.C. tells me that, providing efficient sets and aerials are used, 74 per cent. of the population of Wales and 48 per cent. of the population of Carmarthenshire should be able to receive the very high frequency transmissions of B.B.C. Wales.

Mr. Jones : I thank the Minister for that reply, but is he aware that there is a great deal of concern in Carmarthenshire, basically a Welsh-speaking county, with 70 per cent. to 75 per cent. speaking Welsh, at the inability of half of the population there not only to receive Welsh language programmes but even to receive English language programmes relating to Wales? Will the Minister indicate when the Carmel U.H.F. station, now transmitting B.B.C.2, will be able to transmit B.B.C. Wales programmes, and what will be the increase in the coverage? Further, is the Minister aware that in areas of North Carmarthenshire and Mid-Wales there is a great deal of concern, regarding not only B.B.C. Wales but all channels, at the poor reception or lack of coverage?

Mr. Chataway : I am not able to give a date for the Carmel transmissions of B.B.C. Wales, but when they are available they will be receivable, I am told, by 62 per cent. of the population of Carmarthenshire. On the more general point, 97 per cent. of the population of Wales can now receive either B.B.C.1 or B.B.C. Wales. Many people in the rest of Great Britain would be surprised to know that a substantial number of people in Wales have the choice between three B.B.C. stations and two I.T.V. stations.

Post Offices (Private Companies)

2. Mr. William Hamilton asked the Minister of Posts and Telecommunications whether he will initiate legislation to provide for a network of local post offices operating as private companies.

Mr. Chataway : No, Sir, but there are nearly 23,000 sub-postmasters engaged in private enterprise.

Mr. Hamilton : But not in relation to postal services. Does not the right hon. Gentleman recall that he expressed a distaste for monopoly conditions in radio and broadcasting generally? Does he not apply the same criteria to postal services, or does he think that monopoly services are desirable and efficient?

Mr. Chataway : I have never disguised my view that for postal services, in this country as in all others, a monopoly is desirable. One continually has to look at the scope of such monopolies. But when it comes to broadcasting, I am glad to say that there is no such necessity for a monopoly.

Mr. Geoffrey Finsberg : Will not my right hon. Friend welcome the belated conversion to the theories of private enterprise shown by the hon. Member for Fife, West (Mr. William Hamilton)?

Mr. Chataway : It is most encouraging.

Television Channels

3. Mr. Whitehead asked the Minister of Posts and Telecommunications what proposals he has received from the Director-General of the Independent Television Authority relating to a fourth television channel.

12. Mr. Golding asked the Minister of Posts and Telecommunications whether

(ii) Standing Orders of the House.

(iii) Precedents in the Journals of the House and in text books.

(i) *Statutes.* We have already referred to the rules relating to Money Bills and the particular rules which apply to these as laid down in the *Parliament Acts, 1911 and 1949* (see p. 46). Another statute containing procedural rules is the *Parliamentary Papers Act, 1849*.

(ii) *Standing Orders.* These number over a hundred and have been hammered out over the years to ensure efficient dispatch of the business of the House. Only three orders date back to before 1832. The orders lay down the time-table for each day (see p. 82), the manner in which motions may be moved, the form of debate, the rules for adjournment, the rules for the closure of a debate (see p. 81).

The Speaker or the Chairman of the House for the time being or of a Committee of the House enforces the rules. Thus a Speaker may 'name' a member who refuses to desist from interrupting the proceedings or for disobedience of the rules. 'Naming', i.e. calling the member by his name rather than the Honorable Member for . . .' entails automatic suspension from the House. This particular rule was first formed in 1641 by Mr. Speaker Lenthall and has been followed since as the accepted procedure for suspension of a member.

The standard work on Parliamentary Procedure was written by Thomas Erskine May (a former clerk of the House of Commons) in 1844 and was entitled *A Treatise upon the Law, Privileges, Proceedings and Usages of Parliament*. This work which is shortly referred to as 'May' is still the standard authority and is periodically revised.

The justification of these procedural rules is that they:

(*a*) Ensure fairness in the conduct of the proceedings.

(*b*) Protect the rights of the Opposition and minorities.

(*c*) Promote efficient and orderly dispatch of business.

Just as the common law has evolved over the years to form the basis of an efficient legal system so too have the Parliamentary Rules of Procedure emerged. They are flexible and allow for growth and modification to enable the House to meet the demands of modern Parliamentary life. Yet at the same time they produce certainty, and represent 'the distilled common sense of centuries'.

Sir Reginald Palgrave ('The House of Commons') said:

The House conducts both its business and its manners according to chance remarks, or casual rules, recorded in journals of about three centuries ago; which rules were, in their turn, founded upon custom and usage of immemorial antiquity.

Under this heading we may include 'Sessional Orders' which, as their name implies, are special orders applicable during the session for which they are laid down and are therefore temporary.

Ceremony still continues to play its part in national and Parliamentary life. The ceremonial procedure of the House, e.g. (1) the summons of Black Rod to attend the House of Lords to hear the Queen formally opening Parliament; (2) the Speaker's Procession to the Lords; (3) The Royal Assent to Bills which is given in Norman-French, all conduce to dignity and tradition.

Those procedures (quaint though they may appear to other eyes) are a constant reminder of the history and the continuity in English Parliamentary democracy, and an acknowledgement of the debt owed to the figures of the past by those to whom the heritage has now fallen.

(iii) *Precedents* in the Journals of the House are kept by the Clerks of the House of Commons and are the 'case law' of the operative rules of the present.

Motions

The business of the House of Commons is conducted by means of motions. A motion is merely a proposal which a member wishes to submit to the House. If the motion is agreed it may result in (1) an Order by which the House gives an instruction to some person or official; or (2) a Resolution by which the House expresses its corporate opinion.

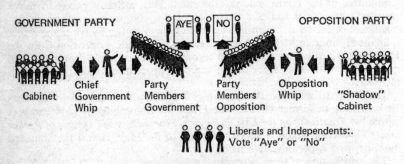

Division of the House

Motions may be moved by the Government or the Opposition or a member. Most frequently in important debates the two major parties are involved. In some debates only one motion is moved, e.g. a motion of censure, and the battle ensues on the single proposal and is resolved by a division almost always in the Government's favour. Amendments are merely alterations to a motion. Amendments may be moved by an opponent.

The procedure of a debate follows well-defined rules as applied in debating societies. The Government side puts its case through speakers selected for their particular position as Cabinet Minister, Departmental Minister, or by reason of special experience and interest. The motion will be opposed by the Opposition whose speakers will be selected practically on the same principles as the Government speakers.

Backbenchers in the House who wish to speak in the debate try to catch the Speaker's eye so that they too can contribute their knowledge, insight, and relevant comments for or against the motion. If the Government moves a motion and the Opposition has replied with its speakers the Government spokesman proposing the motion is entitled to wind up the debate by replying to the points made against the motion and recapitulating the reasons for the motion.

After a debate the House may divide; those members for the motion go into the Government lobby (the 'Ayes'); those against go into the Opposition lobby (the 'Noes'). The number of members voting is counted and the result is recorded in the journals of the House together with the names of voting members. To ensure accuracy 'tellers', i.e. pairs of members (one Government and one Opposition) are posted at each of the lobby doors and count members as they pass through.

The result of a debate on most issues and in all major matters is a foregone conclusion, if the Government has a majority and uses it to ensure that its will prevails. Parliamentary debates on important issues are reported in the Press, on the radio and television, and the electorate is kept well informed of the issues and the outcome. All the speeches are recorded in Hansard, the official report of the proceedings, and this is on sale to the general public.

Terminating Debates

In the eighteenth and nineteenth centuries any member who wished to speak on an issue could do so. Nowadays it is well known that a Government is committed to the passage of a number of Bills as outlined in the Queen's speech, and that Parliamentary time is limited.

In the nineteenth century the Irish Nationalists adopted filibustering tactics, i.e. speaking for long periods with the object of preventing the enactment of legislation. In 1881 in a Parliamentary session of 154 days fourteen Irish members delivered 3,828 speeches, and asked numerous questions. Although within the rules of the House at that time, these tactics threatened to wreck the entire business of the House.

Accordingly, means have been evolved to prevent such obstruction by the Opposition. There are three devices to overcome delaying tactics. By these means Bills can be given speedy passage through the House. They are:

1. The Ordinary Closure.
2. The Kangaroo.
3. The Guillotine (or Closure by Compartment).

The Ordinary Closure. The origin of this is traceable to 1881 and a resolution emanating from W. E. Gladstone (Prime Minister) and approved by the House. It has now been incorporated in Standing Orders (No. 29). At any stage in the debate any M.P. may move 'that the question be now put'. If the Speaker (or Chairman of the House if it is in Committee) permits, the motion is put to the House. If the motion that the debate shall end is carried, the debate is brought to an end. The mover of the motion in the full House must have the support of 100 members. The rule of the Ordinary Closure applies to Standing Committees though in those assemblies only twenty members are needed to support the motion.

The Kangaroo. This form of closure applies to the Committee Stage and Report Stage of the consideration of Bills. The Speaker (on the Report Stage) and the Chairman (in the Committee of the Whole House or a Standing Committee) may select a certain number of clauses of a Bill which he considers important. Only those clauses are discussed, the remainder are not debated. This procedural rule evolved from 1919 and is now incorporated in Standing Order No. 31.

The Guillotine. This form of closure is adopted if the House by resolution so ordains. It is usually invoked when a comprehensive or a long Bill is debated. Such a Bill may be divided into compartments, and any debate on the Bill or a part of the Bill may be 'cut off' ('guillotined') at a predetermined time. The 'guillotine' has been used increasingly by all Governments in modern times. A recent example occurred in the passage of the *Industrial Relations Bill, 1971.*

The objections to the closure devices named above are that they restrict consideration of a Bill and, therefore, prevent Parliament fulfilling its essential role. The Opposition naturally find the devices unpopular. Moreover, legislation hurried through Parliament may be defective in clarity and meaning and difficult to enforce. On the other hand a Government must in an emergency ensure that legislation is passed without delay (e.g. the *Emergency Powers Act, 1939*). Moreover a Government is pledged by its mandate to pass legislation and may claim that it is acting efficiently if it goes ahead and enacts speedily those Bills which it promised to introduce. The use of its political majority in the House is a constitutional means to that end.

The Daily Time-Table of the House of Commons.

The time-table of the House of Commons is regulated by Standing Orders. The following is the usual order of events:

Time:	Business.
2.30 p.m.	House meets.
	Prayers.
	Mr. Speaker in the Chair.
2.35 p.m.	**Preliminary Business.**
	Motions for new writs, e.g. to fill vacant seats in constituencies.
	Unopposed Private Business (Bills).
	Presentation of public petitions to House.
2.45 p.m.	**Questions to Ministers. Oral answers given by Ministers.**
	'Private Notice Questions' (i.e. Questions allowed to be asked on grounds of urgency).
	Requests to move the Adjournment of House under Standing Order 9. (i.e. to debate a specific and important matter which should have **urgent** consideration).
	Ceremonial speeches, statements by Ministers in personal explanation, or ex-Ministers giving reasons for resignation.
3.30 p.m.	**Public Business.**
	Presentation of Public Bills.
	Government Business Motions (e.g. on Public Expenditure).
	Public Business: 'Orders of the Day'.
	Motions for Leave to introduce Bills.
10.10 p.m.	**Public Business ends.**
	Minor business,
	Motion for the Adjournment of the House.
10.30 p.m.	**House Adjourns.**

Note: The above applies generally from Mondays to Thursdays. On Fridays the House meets at 11 a.m. and adjourns at 4.30 p.m.

Criticism of Procedure

Since the beginning of the present century Government activities have increased greatly. More parts of the public sector are brought within the jurisdiction of the Government, and at the same time most of them have become more technical. All Government Departments have advisory committees feeding Ministers with information and data. The total number of these committees alone is 900.

Since 1964 several prominent politicians (Mr. R. S. Crossman was one) have advocated a closer examination of the Commons' procedure in managing its work. The fact remains that the Commons has too much to do and too little time in which to do it. The following, however, are some of the recent suggestions and changes which have been made to ensure a better use of Parliamentary time:

(i) *Improved Voting Methods.* This was examined by the Select Committee on Procedure during 1966/7, but was rejected. Press-button voting (as occurs in the U.N.) was not accepted. Moreover the saving in time was held to be small.

(ii) *An Increase in the Number of Days Parliament Sits.* This was also rejected by the same committee. Ministers would be overworked, and M.P.s must have time for constituency duties. They need rest as do all other individuals.

(iii) *Morning Sittings.* Morning sittings were introduced in 1967 when the House met on Mondays and Wednesdays to deal with unopposed Bills, Ministerial Statements and adjournment debates. It was, however, not successful and the experiment has ended.

(iv) *Question Time.* The aim is to increase the number of questions asked. Only a certain number can possibly be asked. The M.P. who asks long questions may get long answers. The moral is for a brisker approach by both M.P.s and Ministers. A further recommendation, now implemented, is that questions should be answered more quickly. The maximum limit is now twenty-one days from notification of the Question.

(v) *Improving Public Bill Procedure.* It has been recommended that the Second Reading stage of a Public Bill of a non-controversial character be dealt with by a Second Reading Committee (i.e. upstairs). This is now the practice, subject to the proviso that if twenty M.P.s object the Bill will be dealt with in the normal way.

The Select Committee on Procedure recommended that there should be a carry-over of bills from one session to the next. (At present Bills not passed in one session must be reintroduced in the following and pass through all stages again.)

A third recommendation was that more preliminary discussion take place before a Bill is introduced, through White Papers, Specialist Committees, *Ad hoc* Committees. This would ensure that Bills would be better drafted to take account of the feeling and views of the House.

The Report Stage of *minor* Bills should be taken in Committee. This was implemented in 1968.

The Third Reading stage should be without amendment or debate. This recommendation was not implemented.

(vi) *Improving Financial Procedure.* It was recommended that the Committee Stage of the Finance Bill should go to a Standing Committee. In 1967 the Government persuaded the House to agree to the whole Bill going to Committee. In 1968 the Finance Bill was dealt with wholly by a Standing Committee. In 1969 the Bill was split between a Standing Committee and a Committee of the Whole House.

The Committees of Supply and Ways and Means have been abolished; the object being to make financial procedure more intelligible to the public and increasing flexibility. The new Expenditure Committee now exists (see p. 100).

(vii) *Increasing Opportunities for Private Members*. Standing Order No. 9 (see p. 76) should be interpreted more liberally. This has been put into effect.

The suggestion was made that sittings on Fridays be lengthened. This has not been accepted. Members return to their constituencies usually at weekends and must have time to do so.

The Member of Parliament

There are 635 M.P.s in the Commons. This group is made up of men and women from all walks of life: lawyers, doctors, ex-service men, teachers, lecturers, financiers, businessmen, farmers, trade union leaders, and so on. A variety of people decide to devote themselves to politics. Today it is interesting to note that a majority of M.P.s are middle class and have had a university education. Roughly 1 in 6 M.P.s will be a journalist, teacher, or university lecturer. Men outnumber women by 25 to 1, but this imbalance is likely to be corrected as more women take up active professional careers.

There are two main parties: Conservative and Labour. In 1974 the Liberals returned 14 members only. Included in the 635 M.P.s are Ulster Unionists, Scottish Nationalists (7 members), Welsh Nationalists (2), Independents (5) and the Speaker.

Part-time or Full-time M.P.s

Should M.P.s be full-time or should they be part-time representatives, i.e. able to carry on other work outside Parliament? One view is that part-time occupation while an M.P. increases the M.P.'s usefulness in the House. He is more 'in touch' with life, more keenly aware of the pressures and problems of industry, for example, if he is a Trade Unionist or a company director; more conscious of the problems of education if he is a teacher or lecturer, and so on. In effect he broadens his outlook by practical experience in life generally over which he exercises political control or leadership. The other view is that the work of an M.P. is itself so exacting and the responsibilities so heavy and complex that he cannot, by the very nature of political life today, discharge those essential duties unless he gives himself wholly to his work as M.P. We shall consider these duties more closely later.

The salary of an M.P. is £5,750 a year, plus £3,200 for secretarial expenses. The salary is small by comparison with that received by professional men whether company directors, administrators, trade unionists, and so on. Some M.P.s may feel compelled and justified in earning extra money to maintain a standard of living compatible with a member's duties and position. Some write for the Press, take part in radio and television discussions. M.P.s may, as a concession, claim income tax relief for expenses actually incurred. The general view, however, is that British M.P.s are not well paid in comparison with those in other countries.

To avoid public disquiet when M.P.s vote increases in their salaries it is suggested that their pay be linked with an appropriate Civil Service grade, e.g. Assistant Secretary of State, enabling automatic increases.

The M.P.'s Duties

The duties of an M.P. are so varied that it is convenient to classify them:

(a) The M.P. and the Nation.

The first duty of a Member of Parliament is to do what, in his faithful and disinterested judgement, he believes is right and necessary for the honour and safety of our beloved country. His second duty is towards his constituents, of whom he is the representative and not the delegate. It is only in the third place that a man's duty lies to the party organisation or programme. (Sir Winston Churchill in an address to his constituents in 1955.)

Every one knows that, by our Constitution, after a gentleman is chosen, he is the representative, or, if you please, the attorney of the people of England, and as such is at full freedom to act as he thinks best for the people of England in general. He may receive, he may ask, he may even follow the advice of his particular constituents; but he is not obliged, nor ought he, to follow their advice if he thinks it inconsistent with the general interest of his country. (A speech by Sir William Yonge, M.P., in 1745.)

It follows, therefore, that the over-riding duty of an M.P. is to play his part in safeguarding the security and prosperity of the United Kingdom and its peoples. That security includes making the Constitution work, observing the rules of Parliament, attending its committees, debates, etc., and using his judgement in the best interests of the nation. If an M.P. is in charge of a Government Department he will have much to do in an executive capacity; if he is a backbencher he should learn as much as possible of national and international affairs, the pros and cons of the cases and problems on which he must decide and vote. 'The prerequisites of the successful politician are: common instincts combined with uncommon ability.' (W. Bagehot)

(b) The M.P. and his Constituency.

Once elected to Parliament an M.P. becomes the representative of some 50,000 to 70,000 electors within his constituency. All persons, whether they voted for him or not, may look to him. It is his duty to serve them. Accordingly most M.P.s hold their 'clinics' or 'surgeries' (usually on Saturdays) where constituents may bring their complaints, problems, difficulties, or alleged injustices. Some may seem trivial, some are important. *A* may have received no Old Age Pension to which she is entitled; *B* may have been refused redundancy payment; *C* may be unable to find accommodation for her family, or is destitute; *D* may seek the member's support in a national wage claim about which the Minister has done nothing or has delayed setting up the necessary machinery for settlement; *E* may wish to become a naturalized British subject and does not know how to proceed.

The consultations may be dealt with by personal advice; sometimes by referring the constituent to a local authority official, sometimes by writing a letter to a Minister or his Department, sometimes by personal representation to the Minister. If no other method is suitable and the matter is important enough an M.P. may raise a question in the House of Commons or the point may be made on the ten o'clock adjournment of the House. Ordinary people like to be able to meet their M.P. face to face, to get to know him, to feel that he is interested in them. An M.P. increases his standing if he gets things done for his constituency.

He must concern himself with local industry. If an important local industry collapses or fails (e.g. Rolls-Royce, Ltd., Derby in 1971) numbers of persons may be unemployed. The local M.P. must press for Government help, if necessary, draw attention to the circumstances, call for help for the unemployed, in finding new jobs, retraining, rehabilitation, etc.

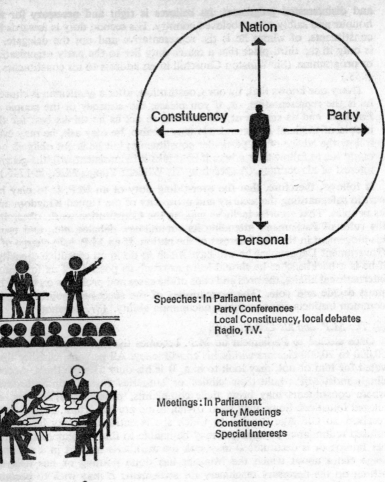

Nation

Constituency   Party

Personal

Speeches : In Parliament
           Party Conferences
           Local Constituency, local debates
           Radio, T.V.

Meetings : In Parliament
           Party Meetings
           Constituency
           Special Interests

Consultation : In Parliament
              Constituency "clinics"
              Groups (Chambers of Commerce,
              pressure groups etc.)

Correspondence : With Constituents
                Pressure Groups
                Government Departments
                Ombudsman

Responsibilities of an M.P.

An M.P. must attend local civic and social functions. A Royal visit may be planned, a new Mayor may be installed, a new school opened, a new factory is built, receptions, dinners, bazaars are held, and to most of these the Member of Parliament will be invited.

The constitutional position of an M.P. in relation to his constituency and the electorate was well expressed by Edmund Burke, the distinguished Irishman, in his address to the electors at Bristol in 1774:

> Certainly, gentlemen, it ought to be the happiness and glory of a representative to live in the strictest union, the closest correspondence, and the most unreserved communication with his constituents. Their wishes ought to have great weight with him; their opinion high respect; their business unremitted attention. It is his duty to sacrifice his repose, his pleasures, his satisfactions, to theirs; and above all, ever, and in all cases, to prefer their interest to his own. But, his unbiased opinion, his mature judgment, his enlightened conscience, he ought not to sacrifice to you, to any man, or to any set of men living. . . . *Your representative owes you, not his industry only, but his judgment; and he betrays, instead of serving you, if he sacrifices it to your opinion.*
>
> To deliver an opinion is the right of all men; that of his constituents is a weighty and respectable opinion, which a representative ought always to rejoice to hear, and which he ought always seriously to consider. *But authoritative instructions, mandates issued, which the member is bound blindly and implicitly to obey, to vote and to argue for, though contrary to the clearest conviction of his judgment and conscience—these are things utterly unknown to the laws of this land, and which arise from a fundamental mistake of the whole order and tenor of our constitution. . . . You choose a member indeed; but when you have chosen him, he is not a member for Bristol, but he is a Member of Parliament.*

So, a Parliamentary constituency elects an M.P. to Parliament as a representative, not a delegate (i.e. one subject to instructions from his constituency). Actually, an M.P. must consider the views of his constituents as a matter of common prudence. All agree that he is not absolutely bound by their instructions. It is a matter of degree, adopting the mean between extremes.

The tension between an M.P. and his constituents is always present. Thus when Mr. Nigel Nicholson, M.P. for Bournemouth East, did not support the Government in the Suez crisis of 1956 his decision incensed the local constituency party representatives. In the 1959 election he was not readopted by the local constituency party. In 1972 Dick Taverne, Q.C., M.P., socialist member for Lincoln, disagreed with his party and the local constituency leaders over Britain's entry to the EEC. In March 1974 he campaigned as a social democrat and was re-elected. These are examples of the power wielded by a local party and the sanction which the constituency party can apply.

Where there is a 'free' vote in Parliament a member can vote as he chooses free from the party line and in accordance with his conscience and good judgement. The general rule is that where there is a division in the House the Whips are on.

No one should minimize the difficulties surrounding the judgements which an M.P. has to make in his voting and decisions. There are occasions in all our lives when on a point of principle and rightness a stand must be made. This takes courage; men are not gifted with foresight. The judgement as to what best to do in the complexities of modern life is the common problem of all politicans.

(c) *The M.P. and his Party*

An M.P. is in Parliament because he is a member of a party. Today the Independent M.P. who owes allegiance to no party is rare indeed. Usually a prospective candidate chooses the party which reflects most closely his own political philosophy, Conservative, Labour, or Liberal. If adopted as a candidate at a political election the prospective M.P. will get the support of the party machine (see p. 40). He is thereupon expected to support the party view, its political manifesto, and, if successful at the election, he will take his place as a member of the House of Commons pledged to support the party in the Government or Opposition as the case may be. Accordingly he votes in the Divisions of the house in compliance with the instructions of the party.

Where a 'free' vote in the House is decided upon an M.P. may vote as his conscience dictates. Where an M.P. disagrees with his own party he may vote against it, but this course is attended with the risk of an admonition or warning from the Whips. No party can afford recalcitrant members in important issues when a division occurs, particularly where a Government has a small majority only. Party unity is vital, and it takes courage to ignore the Whips. An M.P. must also bear in mind the reaction his adverse vote may have on his local Constituency Party group (cf. Mr. Nigel Nicholson's experience, see p. 87). Usually, therefore, an M.P. must compromise, and seek other means to bring his views to notice, e.g. in the Parliamentary Party meetings, at Party Conferences and among other unofficial groups of M.P.s with similar views in Parliament.

M.P.s are not 'rubber stamps', automatons, members of a regiment, acting in accordance with instructions on all conceivable occasions. Democracy recognizes the existence of minorities, and political parties do likewise. Each has groups, e.g. Left and Right wing of a party, and a centre group. All parties have meetings, conferences or groups where policy can be thrashed out, and it is here that an M.P. may find opportunity to get his particular viewpoint accepted by the leaders. Additionally, an M.P. may be a member of the specialized party committees, e.g. on trade unions, foreign affairs, economic policy, where he may seek to air his views in an attempt to change the accepted party policy.

(d) *The M.P. and his Interests.*

In addition to (i) the national interest (which has overriding claim on his vote), (ii) party interests, and (iii) constituency interests, an M.P. may have special personal interests. Thus he may be interested in reform of abortion laws, liquor licensing reform, the abolition of blood sports, crime prevention, protection against pollution, consumer protection, and so on. He may represent a particular section of workers, e.g. consultant or adviser to the Police Federation, a particular professional body or trade union, from which he receives a fee in return for any assistance he may give in the conduct of their affairs or in achieving particular objects. Thus he may make speeches in debates in the House, make representations to a Government Minister for the particular group whose special interests he protects or furthers. He may produce a Private Member's Bill and endeavour to get that through the House. He may, or may not be, successful but he will certainly draw public attention to the subject matter in which he is personally interested. Examples of Private Members' Bills which have become law are cited on page 90.

Where a Government is committed to a heavy legislative programme there is scant opportunity for the debate of sectional or minority interests or the enactment of Private Members' Bills which may be important to an individual M.P. but relatively unimportant nationally. Government is the art of the possible, and what is possible is conditional on the capacity of Parliament, time and finance, and other factors.

Declaration of M.P.'s Interests. Where an M.P. speaks in the Commons he is expected, by convention, to declare any financial interest or pecuniary relationship he has in the matter under debate. The convention has been shown to be too narrow in scope particularly having regard to the growth in public relations and consultancy work undertaken by some M.P.s.

A compulsory Register of Members' Interests published by HMSO began in November 1975 and is available for public inspection. The convention is transformed to a Rule of the House. The registrable interests are:

1. Directorships.
2. Employment of office.
3. Trades or Professions.
4. Clients.
5. Financial sponsorships.
6. Overseas visits.
7. Payments, etc., from abroad.
8. Land and property.
9. Declarable shareholdings.

The Register follows the lines of the Select Committee's Report which was agreed to by the House on 12 June 1975. The Registrar is an officer of the House of Commons.

On one hand the public have a right to know the 'interests' of an M.P. and on the other he has a right to privacy. It was a question difficult of satisfactory solution. Some felt it should be left to an M.P.'s own judgement.

Legislation

We have already noted that the Legislature comprises the Queen, the House of Lords, and the House of Commons, and that one of the chief duties of Parliament is the enactment of legislation.

Legislation first finds expression in the form of a Bill, which is in effect draft legislation. A Bill is divided into clauses and sometimes sub-clauses. During the process of passing through Parliament a Bill undergoes scrutiny and debate, and changes, called amendments, are often made to a Bill. When a Bill passes into law it becomes a statute and the clauses become sections (sub-clauses become sub-sections). A specimen first page of a Bill appears on page 322. A copy of the first page of a statute appears on page 323. You will observe from the statute that underneath the official reference and the short description of the object of the statute there follows the *enacting clause* which normally reads thus:

Be it enacted by the Queen's Most Excellent Majesty, by and with the advice and consent of the Lords Spiritual and Temporal, and Commons in this present Parliament assembled, and by the authority of the same, as follows:

Kinds of Bills

There are four types of Parliamentary Bills, viz.:
  (i) Public Bills.
  (ii) Private Members' Bills.
  (iii) Private Bills.
  (iv) Hybrid Bills.

In addition to the above classification we have also noted that there are (a) Money Bills (see p. 47), and (b) Non-Money Bills, not requiring the expenditure of money.

(i) *Public Bills.* These alter the general law of the land and are normally introduced by the Government. We recall that when a Government is returned with a mandate to pass certain legislation the electorate will expect the promise to be kept. Examples of Public Bills include the *National Health Service Act, 1946*, the *Race Relations Act, 1965*, the *Sex Discrimination Act, 1975*.

(ii) *Private Member's Bill.* This type of Bill differs from a Public Bill (above (i)) only in being introduced by a member of either House who is not a member of the Government. A ballot is held for the opportunity to introduce such Bills. The first twenty members are successful, and certain Fridays in each session are allocated to enable members successful in the ballot to introduce their Bills. It must be remembered, however, that Government Bills (i.e. Public Bills) are most important and since Parliamentary time is limited there is little time left for Private Members' Bills.

Apart from the ballot method a private member may seek leave to introduce a Bill under the 'ten-minute' rule which permits the proposer enough time to make a brief speech outlining the case for his Bill. An objector member is permitted a few minutes to oppose the Bill saying why the Bill should not go forward. Following this the question is put to the House that leave be given to bring in the Bill.

The increasing pressure on Parliamentary time precludes many Private Members' Bills from being debated, and even some that are debated do not reach the stage of Second Reading. A few Bills do become law, and we may mention far-reaching measures such as the *Matrimonial Causes Act, 1937* (introduced by the late Sir A. P. Herbert, and the *Murder (Abolition of Death Penalty) Act, 1965*, introduced by Mr. S. Silverman.

It may be considered that too little time is allowed for Private Members' Bills, some of which are of greater importance than the time spent on them might suggest, and they do provide the ordinary M.P. with the opportunity to introduce legislation which is not necessarily of importance to the Government of the day.

(iii) *Private Bills.* Private Bills are (a) **Local**, and (b) **Personal**.

(a) **Local Bills** deal with (i) the construction or alteration of works, e.g. bridges, canals, docks, ports, roads, railways, tramways and waterworks, and (ii) others—e.g. extending the powers of local authorities, and of gas, electricity and other public utility undertakings; altering the powers of charters of public corporations, and dealing with Crown and Church property.

(*b*) **Personal Bills** are now rare and must be started in the House of Lords. They relate to estates, names, naturalization, divorce, peerage, and other matters not classified as 'local'.

As to (*a*) Local Bills we should note that during the eighteenth and nineteenth centuries this was the only means by which local authorities were able to acquire legal powers to initiate new schemes. Parliament was forced to develop some procedure to protect private interests against the excessive powers which local authorities and other *ad hoc* bodies acquired.

Today a local authority (or other public body) may wish to acquire additional powers not available under the general law. To do this it may promote a private Bill. The procedure is complicated, lengthy, and expensive. The Standing Orders of both Houses must be complied with as well as certain Acts. Procedure requires that notice of the intention to present a Bill should be given to the public, and in some cases to individuals affected by the Bill. If opponents of the Bill wish to challenge it in Parliament they may do so before the Private Bill Committee. The proceedings here are judicial in character; the contest is between the promoters (represented by lawyers) and the opponents who may also be legally represented. Witnesses for and against the Bill may be examined or cross-examined as in a court of law. The committee then decides for or against the Bill on the evidence adduced. The main interest of the Committee is to resolve or reconcile the clash between the private and the public interest. The Committee has powers of alteration or amendment of a Bill, and finally the Bill is reported to the House.

(iv) *Hybrid Bills*. These partake of the characteristics of (*a*) Public and (*b*) Private Bills, i.e. they alter the general law, but have particular effect upon certain bodies or individuals, e.g. the *Parliament Square Improvement Act, 1949*, the *British Museum Act, 1964*, the *Severn Bridge Tolls Act, 1965*. Hybrid Bills are referred to a Select Committee for examination, but at a later stage in the legislative process they proceed as Public Bills. An important point to note in these Bills is that persons affected by a Bill may lodge a petition against it, as in the case of a Private Bill. The Committee Stage is taken as for a Private Bill, i.e. a quasi-judicial procedure is followed with an opportunity to make petitions of objection.

The Origin of Bills

Legislation springs from many and varied sources: a declared policy of a political party which seeks power; a declared Government policy (i.e. once it is in power); a departmental policy; a Royal Commission; a committee appointed *ad hoc* by the Government (to consider one particular matter and to make recommendations); a research group.

Whatever the source of a Bill, there will certainly be discussions, negotiations, consultations (sometimes taking months), and meetings before the Bill is drafted. Groups and interests affected will be approached and their views ascertained. Thus legislation on health matters would involve medical organizations representing the medical profession, nursing societies, local authorities; law reform would be preceded by discussion with the Law Society, the General Council of the Bar; road traffic law would involve motoring organisations, A.A., R.A.C., local authorities, police, highway surveyors, motor manufacturers, and so on. This time given to discussion with affected groups and interests is the period of gestation of the Bill.

Once a Minister adopts an idea, or policy, or scheme for a Bill he must obtain Cabinet approval that it is a suitable measure. The proposed Bill is drafted and perused by a committee of the Cabinet at which the draftsman and the Government Chief Whip are normally present.

Out of the 160 days in a parliamentary session only sixty are available for public legislation. It follows, therefore, that only a certain number of Bills can find room in the legislative programme. The most that Parliament can manage during one year is between sixty and seventy Public Bills. Some of these are large comprehensive measures (e.g. the *National Health Service Act, 1946*, the *Sex Discrimination Act, 1975*); others merely amend, or consolidate previous Acts, or merely deal with small (though important) matters.

Drafting. This is a skilful and sometimes a long process if the proposed Bill is complicated. The task is undertaken by lawyers (known as Parliamentary Counsel) attached to the Parliamentary Counsel's Office at the Treasury. Amendments and redrafts are made and, when completed, the draft Bill is considered by the Cabinet who scrutinize it to ensure it accords with intention and purpose. A memorandum is attached to the draft Bill to explain its objects.

Stages in Legislation for Public Bills

A Bill passes through the following stages to enable Parliament to consider and reconsider its provisions as thoroughly as possible.

    (i) First Reading.
   (ii) Second Reading.
  (iii) Committee Stage.
  (iv) Report Stage.
   (v) Third Reading.
  (vi) Amendments in the Upper House.

(i) *First Reading.* This is a formality. The Clerk of the House reads out the short title of the Bill and the Minister names a day for Second Reading. This is formal acknowledgement that the Government intends to bring in a Bill. The Bill is then printed and published. The Opposition may then study it with a view to criticism and amendment if need be.

(ii) *Second Reading.* This is the effective stage at which there is the first opportunity for debate on the Bill and its principles. The Minister or member in charge of the Bill explains its purpose and the main issues of policy involved, and he moves that the Bill be read a second time. The debate is limited to the purpose of the Bill and the means proposed for giving effect to it. Detailed discussion, which includes criticisms which could be met by amendment, is reserved for the Committee Stage or Report Stage.

If the Opposition decide to vote against the Bill an amendment is moved by one of their number to prevent the Bill being read a second time. If the amendment is defeated the Speaker declares the Bill to be read a second time.

In the Commons a **non-controversial Bill** may be referred to a '**Second Reading Committee**' to recommend whether or not it should be taken as read a second time. This procedure saves the time of the House as a whole.

(iii) *Committee Stage.* The next stage in the legislative process is the reference of the Bill to a Committee. This is composed of between twenty-five and forty-five members.

Most Bills are sent to a Standing Committee for detailed consideration and amendment, if need be.

We consider the part played by committees generally in the House on page 68. All we need to remark here is that the House of Commons has six Standing Committees, *A* to *F*. The committees are made up of between twenty-five and forty-five members and the members are appointed by another committee called the Committee of Selection (an all-party committee run by the

First reading of a Bill in the Commons

Whips). The Standing Committees are not permanent committees (or 'standing' for a considerable time) but are constituted afresh for each Bill as it arises. The membership of the Standing Committee is in **proportion to the respective political parties** and where a member has special interest or experience in the subject of a Bill he will usually be appointed to a committee. Thus let us suppose that a House of Commons is made up of:

Conservative	400
Labour	200
Liberal	35
Total members	635

A Standing Committee might be made up thus:

Conservative	18
Labour	9
Liberal	2
	29

The Government (Conservative) would have a majority in the Committee and would thereby ensure its will prevails.

The purpose of the Committee Stage is to consider the **details** of a Bill, clause by clause and word by word. The Chairmen of the Standing Committees are appointed from a panel of twelve members. Debates in Committee are freer, a member may speak on a point more than once, but business is conducted expeditiously and, if need be, the debate may be closed by resolution. The Standing Committees meet in the morning usually twice a week.

(iv) *Report Stage*. Having passed the Committee Stage the Bill is formally reported to the House by the Chairman of the Committee. The House then considers the Bill as amended, and it may then make any additional amendments needed. The Report Stage is similar, in practice, to the Committee Stage, except that, in the House of Commons, the amendments are discussed rather than the clauses of the Bill.

(v) *Third Reading*. At this stage, the Bill is reviewed in its final form after the amendments have been made at earlier stages. The debate is confined to the contents (as opposed to the principles) of the Bill, and verbal amendments only may be made in the Commons. This is a purely formal stage.

(vi) *Amendments in the Upper House*. A Bill may originate in either House. Normally legislation starts in the Commons and is then sent to the Lords. A Bill which deals with taxation or expenditure (i.e. a Money Bill) must be introduced in the Commons.

Legislation of an intricate, but not of controversial character, may be introduced in the House of Lords where it may be fully discussed before being sent to the Commons, e.g. the *Crown Proceedings Act, 1947* (see p. 152) and the *Courts Act, 1971* were dealt with in this way. The Lower House may then deal with the Bill more quickly.

After a Bill has passed the third reading in the House of Commons it is ready for sending to the House of Lords. An order is made by the Commons that the Clerk of the House carry the Bill to the Lords and desire their concurrence. If the Bill originated in the House of Lords it goes to the Commons after the third reading there. If there is no disagreement between the two Houses the Bill is submitted for the Royal Assent (see below). If, however, the second House amends the Bill it must be returned to the House where it originated for consideration of the amendments. If the first House rejects the amendments made by the second House, a committee is set up to show the reasons for the disagreement. A message embodying the reasons is sent to the second House. The amendments disputed may then be dropped, or alternative ones adopted. This process continues until agreement is reached. If agreement proves impossible, the Commons may make use of their powers under the *Parliament Acts, 1911* and *1949* (see p. 46) to present the Bill for Royal Assent after one year without the concurrence of the Lords.

The Royal Assent

The Royal Assent is given (*a*) by the Sovereign in Letters Patent and is declared to both Houses by their Speakers, or (*b*) periodically by Royal Commission. The Royal Commission is composed of three Lords Commissioners who sit before the throne in the House of Lords. The Speaker and Commons are summoned by Black Rod to the bar of the House of Lords, the title of the Act is read out and the Royal Assent is signified by the Clerk of Parliaments in Norman–French thus:

1. Public Bills (except Money Bills) La reyne le veult.
2. Money Bills La reyne remercie ses bons sujets, accepte leur bénévolence, et ainsi le veult.

Formerly a Monarch could veto a Bill, but this power has not been exercised since Queen Anne and has fallen into disuse. By convention the Royal Assent is never withheld.

If a Bill is urgent it will be presented for Royal Assent forthwith after passage through the Commons and the Lords. Otherwise Bills are presented in batches before a long adjournment or at the end of a session.

The stages through which a Bill is passed occupy a long process. Nevertheless, in an emergency such as an outbreak of war, emergency legislation may be passed through all stages in a few hours, as occurred with the *Defence of the Realm Act, 1914* and the *Emergency Powers Act, 1939.*

Finance

All Governments need money to carry on their essential functions. The very existence of Parliament is due primarily to the need of the early Norman and later Monarchs to obtain money from their subjects. Kings taxed the people to pay for wars or to provide for the King's courts and their amenities.

Today money is needed to carry on the essential functions of Governments, e.g. maintenance of order, and defence against external enemies. These are in themselves costly but, in addition, all modern Governments expand their control over the economy to maintain a high level of employment, to raise the standard of living of all inhabitants, year by year. A Government must, among other things, organize a prices and incomes policy; it must assist local authorities to provide essential services such as housing and education, for which they are responsible in partnership with the central Government, and, above all, these economic activities must be fitted within the international scene by trying to ensure the country's balance of payments stands at a proper level.

In 1900 taxation took ten per cent of the nation's income. Today taxation takes over forty per cent of the nation's income, which indicates the growing cost of all the activities of Government in controlling the affairs of the nation as a whole.

The Main Principles of Parliament's Control

We have already mentioned the long struggle between the Crown and Parliament from the Middle ages to the seventeenth century when Parliament gradually established the principle that taxation could not be imposed by the Crown (by prerogative) at its will. Parliament grudgingly voted or granted the money, but always insisted that its grievances be met or answered before any grant was made. To justify its demands to Parliament for money the Crown had to specify in detail the reasons for the expenditure it proposed to make. We see therefore that today we have the principle that the estimates of expenditure of the Crown (i.e. the Government departments) must be published to Parliament before Parliament will vote the income (in the form of taxation) to meet the proposed expenditure.

By the seventeenth century after the *Bill of Rights, 1689,* Parliament firmly established the principle that taxation could not in future be imposed by the Crown or Monarch but must be approved by Parliament. Moreover, a Minister is no longer responsible to the Monarch, as was formerly the case, but he is responsible to Parliament as the supreme authority in the State. We have already mentioned that the House of Commons achieved supremacy in Parliament, so that the next principle to note is that only a Minister (as a member of the House of Commons) could propose the spending of money by the Government.

The House of Commons is today the effective chamber which controls national finance both as to (*a*) raising money, and (*b*) spending it. The House of Lords has practically no powers now in this regard (see p. 46), in that the House of Lords is powerless to reduce or veto a Money Bill.

During the course of time Parliament has evolved three important financial or accounting principles to control the expenditure of moneys by the Crown:

   (i) Any sum granted is a **maximum** and may not be exceeded.
  (ii) Money authorized to be spent for one purpose may not be spent on another purpose.
 (iii) Money granted for any purpose may be used only during the financial year for which it is voted. Surpluses may not be carried forward but must be paid over to the Exchequer (i.e. the Treasury).

Control by the Treasury

The nation's financial year begins on 1 April and ends on 31 March of the following year. A Parliamentary session runs from October to October. Thus one session straddles two financial years.

The tax year runs from 6 April each year to 5 April of the following year. These two dates determine the schedule of time to which Government Departments and Parliament work.

Each Government Department prepares its estimates during October and November. The estimates show what the particular Department requires during the following financial year.

The estimates are sent to the Treasury where they are checked during December. By January all the Departmental Estimates from the various Government Departments will be ready for discussion by the Cabinet. The estimates are then published in February. During February and March the House of Commons considers the published estimates. In these estimates the Chancellor of the Exchequer will have information on which he will be able to base his Budget which he will present to the Commons early in April. This is one of the important events in the Parliamentary session, and equally important to the public.

We recall that the Commons must know the details of expenditure proposed (the estimates) before it will grant supply of money to cover the needs. The place of the Treasury in the scheme of financial control is crucial. It co-ordinates on the one hand the estimates after scrutinizing them to prevent waste or excess by consulting the Permanent Under-Secretary of a Government Department (or his Accounting Officer). With modern technology advancing apace, costing presents very great difficulty.

Having collated the estimates, the next duty of the Treasury and the Chancellor is to consider means by which the sums required will be met, i.e. by taxation, the main source, or borrowing money.

How the Chancellor will meet the requirements will depend on a number of factors. In particular he will pay regard to whether the nation is in an inflationary situation or its opposite, deflationary. There is inflation when prices and incomes are rising. In that case the Chancellor must budget for more income to cover this situation. He may increase taxation to meet the proportionate increase in the expenditure of the Government Departments.

If he increases taxation he will thus take from the public their spending power, for the public will have less money to spend.

The Chancellor possesses the facts and figures from the Central Statistical Office, from the Department of Trade and Industry, The Board of Trade and from his own Ministry. The Chancellor analyses the nation's position and forms his policy. He discusses with the Prime Minister his recommendations for raising the extra money required. The Chancellor may recommend: (i) raising the income tax; (ii) surtax; (iii) road fund (car) tax; (iv) purchase tax, and so on. Most of us will be familiar with the problem and dilemma. If he taxes necessities the Government will be unpopular; if he taxes cigarettes, tobacco, wines, spirits, and luxuries he will also be unpopular. No tax is popular with the payer. Someone will be disappointed, inevitably. The Prime Minister may suggest amendments to the Chancellor's proposals.

Supply Debates

Once the estimates for the ensuing financial year have been finally agreed between the Chancellor and the Cabinet they are published at the beginning of February. This leaves six weeks before the Chancellor presents his Budget proposals to the House of Commons.

The estimates are presented in tabulated form to the Commons under three main heads: (i) the Defence Departments; (ii) the Revenue Departments; and (iii) the Civil Estimates. The whole of the estimates covers 450 pages. Hence it is highly technical.

The House of Commons comprises 635 members. This is much too large a body to examine in detail the provisions of the estimates. Moreover, only twenty-nine working days are allowed between the publication of the estimates and some time in August by which the Appropriation Bill must be passed. The House also lacks the necessary expert and technical knowledge to criticize properly the estimates. Accordingly the House sets up a committee to do its work. This task was formerly allotted to the Estimates Committee consisting of members drawn from all parties. However, in 1969 the **Select Committee on Procedure** recommended that the **Estimates Committee** should become a **Select Committee on Expenditure**.

Broadly, this Committee is charged with the duty of examining closely all areas of Government expenditure to consider whether the sums asked for are indeed necessary. Do we, for example, need nuclear submarines? If so, are they built to the best specification, and are they built economically without waste? What equipment is needed today by the Army and Air Force and Navy for their tasks? Is that equipment the best available and is it costing too much? How many people must be employed? Crime is increasing, more prisons are required as well as better security. What type of prison is the best, how many do we need, and are they built economically? How many prison officers are required? The financial implications of all such questions is considered and immediately policy is involved. The task, therefore, of considering estimates is highly important. The composition and functions of the new **Expenditure Committee** is discussed in detail on pages 100 and 101.

The twenty-nine 'Supply Days' of the House of Commons are devoted to general discussions on matters of policy. At the end of the allotted time, usually by early August of each year, all the remaining items are voted through the House without discussion and are approved by the annual Appropriation Act.

The Interim Period

If the Appropriation Act is not passed until early August how are the Government Departments financed between 1 April (the beginning of the financial year) and August? We must remember that no expenditure may be made without the approval of the Commons. The answer is that the House passes a Vote on Account with a *Consolidated Fund Bill* immediately after the Budget. This will enable the Government Departments and the Defence Forces to draw enough money on account until the Appropriation Act is passed in August.

We have mentioned that the estimates are very detailed. The need for this is justified by the fact that money authorized for one purpose may only be spent on that specific purpose. Moreover, strict control is maintained by the Comptroller and Auditor-General. And he may only do this if he knows specifically for what purpose money is being used. Virement is a technical term and in practice means merely that it is permissible to transfer a sum of money voted for one branch of the Armed Forces to another. Virement has been extended to a limited extent in Departments other than the Defence Services. In all cases, however, Treasury approval must first be obtained.

The Budget

In all matters of finance the lead must be taken by the Government. The Government proposes how it intends to spend money and the Government proposes how it will raise money. A Government may, of course, borrow money, e.g for capital expenditure such as loans to local authorities or to the nationalized industries. But the main source of supply is taxation.

The Chancellor of the Exchequer prepares his Budget, the details of which are disclosed only to the Cabinet a few days before presentation to the House of Commons. Strict secrecy is maintained as to the details right up to the moment the Chancellor makes his speech in early April to the House of Commons. Any leakage may cause the resignation of the Chancellor himself, as was the case with Dr Hugh Dalton who made a chance remark on his way into the Commons itself to a lobby correspondent.

The manner of presentation is usually a report on the financial year just ended. He then compares the result with the forecast. There follows a review of the general economic situation anticipated during the year just beginning. The Chancellor then sets out his proposals for alterations in taxation.

Until 1967 all work in the Commons relating to new or altered taxation was dealt with by a committee of the whole House (called the Committee of Ways and Means). A new procedure was implemented in the Budget in 1968 following a recommendation of the Select Committee on Procedure. The Budget speech and Budget debate now take place in the House of Commons itself. The House considers the Budget statement over a number of days and must vote upon proposals for new or altered taxation, including income tax, which has to be approved each year. Customs and excise taxes, estate duty and stamp duties, continue automatically from year to year unless altered by Parliament.

The House of Commons, after debate finally approves the Chancellor's proposals and, subject to any minor amendments, the results are enacted in the Finance Act which then becomes law.

Some time elapses between the announcement of the Budget proposals and

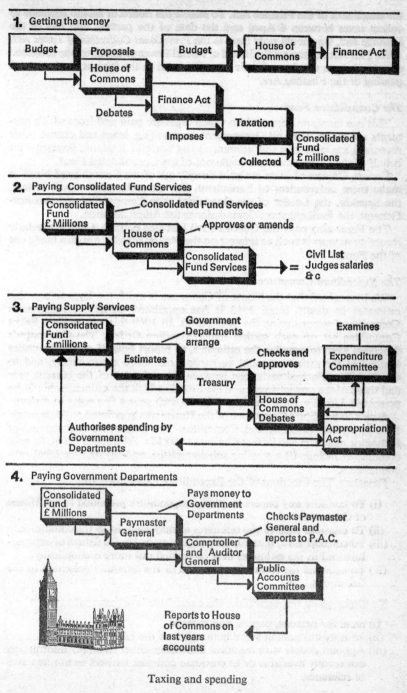

1. Getting the money

Budget — Proposals — House of Commons — Debates — Finance Act — Imposes — Taxation — Collected — Consolidated Fund £ millions

Budget → House of Commons → Finance Act

2. Paying Consolidated Fund Services

Consolidated Fund £ Millions — Consolidated Fund Services — House of Commons — Approves or amends — Consolidated Fund Services = Civil List Judges salaries & c

3. Paying Supply Services

Consolidated Fund £ millions — Estimates — Government Departments arrange — Treasury — Checks and approves — Expenditure Committee — Examines — House of Commons Debates — Appropriation Act

Authorises spending by Government Departments

4. Paying Government Departments

Consolidated Fund £ Millions — Paymaster General — Pays money to Government Departments — Comptroller and Auditor General — Checks Paymaster General and reports to P.A.C. — Public Accounts Committee

Reports to House of Commons on last years accounts

Taxing and spending

the enactment of the Finance Act. To enable the Board of Inland Revenue to collect taxes between 6 April and the date of the passing into law of the Finance Act, we should note there is the *Provisional Collection of Taxes Act, 1913*. This Act authorizes the Board of Inland Revenue to collect the proposed new taxes from the date of their announcement in the Budget to the date of passing of the Finance Act.

The Consolidated Fund

This is a common account into which taxes are paid and from which payments are made. Thus all Government receipts (e.g. taxes and certain other revenues) are paid into this account at the Bank of England. Payments on behalf of the Government are made out of the Consolidated Fund.

Certain Officers of State are paid directly out of the Consolidated Fund to make them independent of Parliament. For example, High Court Judges, the Speaker, the Leader of the Opposition, the Comptroller and Auditor-General, the Parliamentary Commissioner for Administration.

The Fund also pays the Queen's Civil List (see p. 108). Certain regularly recurring payments such as interest on the National Debt, are also made out of the Fund.

The Expenditure Committee

We have noted that the House of Commons is much too large to examine estimates in detail. Since 1912 it has appointed annually an Estimates Committee (except during the War years). In 1960 this was made a Select Committee set up each session under Standing Orders. The Committee's functions were to examine the estimates, to report how, if at all, the policy implied in the estimates could be carried out more economically, and to consider the principal variations between the estimates of the current year and those of the previous year and the form in which the estimates should be presented. Usually, the committee selected each year a few votes to review.

A new Expenditure Committee of the House was appointed on 21 January, 1971 to replace the Estimates Committee. The Committee is composed of forty-nine members and its first Chairman was Mr. Edward du Cann. Its sub-committees include (i) a steering sub-committee, and (ii) six functional sub-committees.

Functions. The functions of the Expenditure Committee are:

(i) To consider any papers on public expenditure presented to the House of Commons.
(ii) To consider such of the estimates as may seem fit to the committee.
(iii) To consider how, if at all, the policies implied in the figures of expenditure and in the estimates may be carried out more economically.
(iv) To examine the form of papers and of the estimates presented to the Commons.

To discharge its responsibilities the committee is empowered to:

(i) Send for persons, papers, and records.
(ii) Sit notwithstanding any adjournment of the House.
(iii) Appoint people with technical knowledge either to supply information not readily available or to elucidate complex matters within its terms of reference.

(iv) Appoint sub-committees to which the main committee may refer matters relating to expenditure.

(v) Admit the public, unless the Committee orders otherwise.

Sub-Committees. The sub-committees (in addition to the steering sub-committee) appointed by the Expenditure Committee are:

(i) Public Expenditure (General).

(ii) Trade and Industry.

(iii) Employment and Social Services.

(iv) Defence and External Affairs.

(v) Education and Arts.

(vi) Environment and Home Office.

Each of these sub-committees has eight members, including the Chairman. The titles of the sub-committees are not intended to be restrictive, but merely indicate the general area of administration assigned to each. The work of each sub-committee and the main committee is of high importance. Those M.P.s concerned with a particular sector of public administration (e.g. Home Office, or Trade and Industry) will need first of all to inform themselves of the general civil service practices of financial control and budgeting which are carried out in the various Government Departments and of the relevant **policy** decisions.

The Public Expenditure (General) sub-committee will concern itself mainly with studying the central area of government financial control (*a*) at Treasury level, (*b*) Cabinet levels, and (*c*) within the Civil Service Department. If this committee is to be successful (as one hopes it will) it must adapt the most modern financial techniques employed in successful enterprises (private or public) here or abroad.

The main point of the committee is to give much more detailed consideration to the estimates than can the entire House of Commons. The estimates for the current year under discussion by the committee are not in practice affected, but the committee does its best to ensure that the money voted by the House for the estimates is properly used and that the expenditure allowed for each item is not exceeded. Additional Parliamentary time has been allocated for discussion of the reports of the committee.

The Comptroller and Auditor-General

This post was created first by Gladstone in 1866. The Comptroller and Auditor-General is not a civil servant, he is an Officer of Parliament. His salary is charged on the Consolidated Fund which gives him a certain independence of Parliament.

The Comptroller and Auditor-General has two functions:

1. As Comptroller he controls receipts and issues of public money to and from the Consolidated Fund and the National Loans Fund.

2. As Auditor-General he audits departmental accounts and submits his report on the Appropriation Accounts and other accounts, as required by statute, to Parliament.

His statutory function is to ensure that all expenditure is properly incurred (e.g. that no payments are made which go beyond any relevant statutory authority) and that Treasury sanction has been obtained whenever necessary.

In addition, however, he has been encouraged by successive Public Accounts Committees (see below) to examine Departmental expenditure with a view to drawing attention to any case of apparent waste or extravagance.

The Public Accounts Committee

This is a Select Committee of the House of Commons. It was first set up under Mr. Gladstone in 1861 to ensure that expenditure was properly incurred in accordance with the purpose for which the expenditure was voted and with any relevant statutes.

We note that the accounts of each Government Department are examined by the Comptroller and Auditor-General who reports on them. The Public Accounts Committee (PAC) have the duty to examine the accounts also. This duty is widely interpreted by the PAC to ensure that full value has been obtained for the sums spent by the Government Departments. The PAC have examined cases where the administration has been faulty or negligent. The PAC is, therefore, another 'watchdog' to expose waste and inefficiency.

The PAC sits weekly throughout the Parliamentary session, and prepares reports which are then presented to the House of Commons. The Committee has power to call for persons (e.g. civil servants) or papers (the actual accounts if need be). Questions may be put to the individual concerned and any papers examined. The PAC is advised by the Comptroller and Auditor-General and his professional staff to assist in the analysis and investigation of the public accounts.

The PAC operates 'after the fact' as it were. Its main effect is that it is critical of expenditure already made. Its work, therefore, lacks the interest of current events. Any recommendations made by the PAC are considered by the Treasury which may accept them and put them into effect to avoid the pitfall the following year.

The Report of the Comptroller and Auditor-General in January 1962 drew attention to the excessive profit made on a Government contract for making Bloodhound missiles by Ferranti, Ltd. The matter was investigated and the company finally agreed to repay £4,500,000.

Supplementary Estimates

These are necessary when during a financial year a Department finds it has underestimated the cost of a particular service, or it has not made provision for something which arises unexpectedly or which could not reasonably be foreseen. Thus a crisis in the Middle East (compare Suez crises of 1956) could well involve a Supplementary Estimate for the Defence Services. Where a demand is thus made by a Department it is passed to the Treasury, and the Chancellor may (if he approves) then place before the House of Commons a Supplementary Estimate. This would pass through the same Parliamentary process as that for the annual estimates. Supplementary Estimates arise usually in the latter part of the financial year.

Excess Votes

These are necessary when a Department has underestimated an item of expenditure and the mistake is discovered after contract has been made. Money must, therefore, be voted to avoid breach of contract by the Government. An Excess Vote must be obtained from the House of Commons. In practice, of course, the money is invariably found. The occasion for the vote does, however, provide a chance for the Opposition to criticize the Government for its failure in budgeting or for its maladministration. Excess Votes are usually for comparatively small sums. They differ from Supplementary Estimates in that Excess Votes arise from over-spending which has already occurred, the fact being revealed when accounts are presented at the end of the financial year. Supplementary Estimates provide for foreseen additional expenditure.

The Paymaster-General

The Paymaster-General is a political post, not of Cabinet rank. The holder is responsible for signing documents permitting a Government Department to receive money from the Consolidated Fund after the Treasury has given authority for payment.

The office has few responsibilities attached to it (other than the above). This enables a Prime Minister to appoint some person to this junior post who is allocated some additional responsibility in the Government.

Normally the appointee is a male. In October 1968 Mrs Judith Hart was appointed to the post in the Wilson Government. Under that administration Mrs. Hart was given a seat in the Cabinet.

Forward Planning

In the past a Government was concerned with the estimates for the ensuing financial year. The estimates were, and still are, difficult to analyse and control. Parliament debates the Annual Estimates for the next financial year beginning 1 April, and the reports submitted to Parliament by the Expenditure Committee (which has replaced the Estimates Committee). The Opposition may propose a motion criticising the Government on its inadequacy and mishandling. Naturally the Government, Opposition, and individual M.P.s are interested in what is happening now.

But Government should be concerned with the future. If A is managing an industry efficiently he will (1) study the available data, information, statistics and trends; (2) look at his resources; and (3) plan for the future, setting himself targets or objectives. If something unforeseen happens the plans can, if flexible, be altered to cope with the event.

Forward planning is now essential for Government. A Government on assuming office may look forward to holding the keys of power for five years. It will have its broad plan of what it hopes to accomplish during each Parliamentary session. But it can only put through its policies if there are sufficient resources to pay for them. Hence the need for long-term financial plans.

In 1969 the Government published a Green Paper (i.e. a publication giving tentative ideas for discussion) entitled *Public Expenditure: a New Presentation*. Broadly this suggested the production of figures (estimates); (*a*) for the preceding financial year; (*b*) the next financial year; and (*c*) for each of the three years following that. On the figures or estimates supplied by all Government Departments the Treasury would be able to assess the probable demands which will be made on it for finance over a period of some five years.

The next problem facing the Treasury is to devise the probable tax changes or borrowing of money which will enable the Government to pay for the estimates over the five-year period.

The Expenditure Committee (referred to on p. 100) is concerned with this matter and has until 1971 (December) produced White Papers which are

Table 3

Public expenditure by programme, with adjustments to 1971-72 outturn prices and relative price effect attributed to individual programmes 1970-71 to 1975-76

£ million

	1970–71 provi-sional outturn	1971–72 estimate	1972–73 estimate	1973–74 estimate	1974–75 estimate	1975–76 estimate	Average annual percentage increase 1971–72 to 1975–76
At 1971–72 outturn prices							
DEFENCE AND EXTERNAL RELATIONS:							
1. Defence Budget	2,750	2,725	2,751	2,816	2,837	2,887	1·4
2. Other military defence	51	73	56	58	62	79	2·0
3. Overseas aid	206	216	234	245	266	290	7·6
4. EEC and other overseas services	147	148	180	284	319	322	2·3(1)
COMMERCE AND INDUSTRY:							
5. Agriculture, fisheries and forestry	424	485	475	413	366	368	—6·7
6. Research Councils, etc.	123	129	137	142	146	152	4·2
7. Trade, industry and employment:							
Investment grants	595	503	267	129	69	34	—49·0
Other	706	768	736	696	592	412	—14·4
NATIONALISED INDUSTRIES:							
8. Nationalised industries capital expenditure	1,817	1,837	1,829	1,834	1,837	1,923	1·2
ENVIRONMENTAL SERVICES:							
9. Roads	880	867	959	1,038	1,096	1,166	7·7
10. Surface transport	216	233	245	242	241	233	0·0
11. Housing	1,219	1,272	1,411	1,339	1,301	1,281	0·2
12. Miscellaneous local services	976	1,012	1,086	1,131	1,193	1,257	5·6
13. Law and order	665	708	768	824	878	931	7·1
14. Arts	24	30	30	34	37	41	8·1
SOCIAL SERVICES:							
15. Education	2,953	3,092	3,269	3,391	3,526	3,690	4·5
16. Health and personal social services	2,482	2,553	2,709	2,848	2,980	3,110	5·1
17. Social security	3,793	4,426	4,615	4,654	4,676	4,700	1·5
OTHER SERVICES:							
18. Financial administration	273	286	304	315	318	322	3·0
19. Common services	237	268	299	323	350	369	8·3
20. Miscellaneous services	84	103	98	97	94	104	0·2
21. Northern Ireland	526	598	629	640	655	671	2·9
TOTAL OF SPECIFIC PROGRAMMES	21,147	22,332	23,087	23,493	23,839	24,342	2·7(2)
22. Debt interest(3)	2,335	2,225	2,200	2,175	2,150	2,125	—1·1
23. Contingency reserve	—	—	125	250	375	500	
24. Shortfall	—	—100	—100	—100	—100	—100	
25. Price adjustments(4)	341	13	—140	—136	—119	—127	
TOTAL	23,823	24,470	25,172	25,682	26,145	26,740	2·7(2)

(1) This figure excludes contributions to the European Communities
(2) This figure excludes investment grants
(3) The estimates of debt interest rest on certain conventional assumptions
(4) For a description of the content of this item see Notes on Methodology, paragraph 10, page 102.

presented to Parliament by the Chancellor of the Exchequer. These reports are debated in the House.

All Government Departments are called upon to forecast proposals and expenditure for five years ahead. The Department of Education and Science will indent for new schools, replacing old ones and catering for the raising of the school-leaving age. A new Government faced with rising crime may promise to 'strengthen the forces of law and order'. The Home Office will have to state its requirements for more police, more motor-cars, training establishments, radios, and personal equipment. The prison service will be considered. More prisons will be required, and better arrangements for after-care of prisoners and so on. The Lord Chancellor may require new courts (*Courts Act, 1971*) and staff to man them. The Defence Minister must look ahead and plan for new defence equipment, to match the needs of modern defence. The Minister for the Environment will have to forecast the new motorways and roads which will be required in five years' time. Entry into the European Economic Community must be paid for. A forecast must be made as to that.

The new Expenditure Committee examines, with the help of Treasury officials and other experts, the demands on the national resources. This Committee splits up into sub-committees to examine the expenditure projected for the various subjects referred to (see p. 101). White Papers are prepared by the Committee for presentation to the Chancellor. The Papers are then debated in Parliament. In the past critics have complained that the Commons is unable to exercise any influence upon the economic decisions of the Government.

Long-term planning is an obvious need for efficient government. The White Papers so far produced have been helpful and well prepared. *Public Expenditure to 1975–76 (Cmnd. 4829)* is an insight into the future. But accuracy in costing is difficult in the economic climate of today. Many things may go awry. The Government in power today may, of course, not be in office in five years' time.

Broadcasting Parliament

The broadcasting of Parliamentary proceedings has been debated since 1960.

On 24 February, 1975, the Commons decided to permit a four-week experimental *radio* broadcast of their proceedings. The House rejected (275 to 263) a three-week experimental televising of their proceedings. Both were free votes.

The main reason for broadcasting proceedings was that the British people were missing history every day because the workings of Parliament were shrouded and kept from the public view. Today democratic parliaments need broadcasting just as much as broadcasting needs Parliament. This would lead to more open government.

The reasons advanced against the experiment were that the presence of television cameras might change the nature of parliamentary proceedings; that in editing recordings for transmission the broadcasters might attach too much importance to the frivolous and eccentric; and editors would select portions of speeches which were dramatic, entertaining and sensational. A fair and balanced summary posed difficult problems.

The experimental four-week period for radio broadcasting began on 9 June, 1975. The House has yet to decide on its continuance.

Exercises

1. Describe the composition of the House of Lords.
2. Why was the *Life Peerage Act, 1963*, passed into law?
3. Who are disqualified from being members of the House of Lords?
4. Write notes on: The Lord Chancellor; the Lord Chairman of Committees; the Clerk of Parliaments; the Gentleman Usher of the Black Rod; the Serjeant-at-Arms.
5. The House of Lords should be reformed or abolished. What views have you on this matter? Give reasons for your suggestions.
6. The *Parliament Act, 1911* and the *Parliament Act, 1949*, were important Constitutional statutes. Write what you know of each.
7. What are the disqualifications for membership of the House of Commons?
8. Describe the process of resignation from the House of Commons.
9. Describe (i) the election, and (ii) the functions of the Speaker of the House of Commons.
10. Write what you know of: The Chairman of Ways and Means; the Clerk of the House; the Serjeant-at-Arms; the Speaker's Counsel; the Librarians.
11. What are the privileges of the House of Commons?
12. The House may punish for breach of privilege. How does The House do this?
13. The 'Whips' are important Party Officials. Explain to an alien what these persons do in the House of Commons.
14. Distinguish between (i) a Sessional Committee; (ii) an *ad hoc* Committee, and (iii) a Standing Committee.
15. What is a Joint Committee?
16. Explain the different types of questions, e.g. (i) Oral; (ii) Written; (iii) Private Notice; and (iv) Supplementary questions.
17. What is meant by 'The Debate on the Adjournment'?
18. What do you understand by 'The Ten-Minute Rule'?
19. All large institutions must have rules of procedure. Describe to a foreign subject where these rules are found.
20. Who was Erskine May? Why is he important to a student of the British Constitution?
21. Imagine yourself an M.P. Draft a motion on an important political topic on which you feel the Government should act.
22. Describe and distinguish between (i) the Ordinary Closure; (ii) the Kangaroo; and (iii) the Guillotine.
23. What do you understand by 'the P.L.P.' and 'the 1922 Committee'?
24. Discuss critically: 'M.P.s should be full-time professionals not "gifted amateurs".'
25. State Edmund Burke's views on the constitutional position of an M.P. in relation to his constituency.
26. Can an M.P. safely defy his own Political Party in the House of Commons?
27. There are said to be four types of Parliamentary Bills. What are they?
28. Distinguish between a Private Bill and a Private Member's Bill? Give examples.
29. How many days are allotted in a Parliamentary session to the subject of public legislation? Roughly how many Public Bills are passed each year?
30. Describe the various stages through which a Bill must pass before it finally receives the Royal Assent.
31. How are amendments made by the Upper Chamber resolved?
32. May a Bill first be introduced into the House of Lords before being sent to the Commons?

CHAPTER FOUR

THE EXECUTIVE

The Monarchy

The United Kingdom is a monarchical State, sometimes described as a limited hereditary Monarchy. The origin and history we have already noted on page 17.

The Crown

When we use the phrase 'the Crown' we must distinguish two meanings:

(i) The Crown may mean the Monarch or Sovereign, who personally holds office, or

(ii) The Executive, i.e. the Prime Minister, Cabinet and Ministers with the Civil Service who exercise governmental powers in the name or on behalf of the State.

The Crown is the visible symbol of supreme executive power which is vested in the Queen but exercised by her Ministers who, as we have noted, are responsible to Parliament and ultimately the electorate for their actions. It is, therefore, a 'constitutional' Monarchy: 'The Queen reigns, but does not rule.' The Queen may be said to be the personification of the State.

Tenure

The Queen occupies the throne by virtue of statute, viz. the *Act of Settlement*, *1701*, whereby in default of issue of Princess Anne of Denmark and of William III, as provided by the *Bill of Rights*, *1689*, the Princess Sophia Electress, daughter of James I, and the heirs of her body being Protestant.

Title

The Royal Title is now: 'Elizabeth II, by the Grace of God of Great Britain, Ireland and the British Dominions Beyond the Seas, Queen, Defender of the Faith' (*Royal Titles Act*, *1953*). The Coronation took place on 2 June 1953, at Westminster Abbey, London.

Regency

By the *Regency Acts*, *1937–1953*, provision is made for certain contingencies. (e.g. illness, incapacity of mind or body). Thus, if on accession to the Crown the Sovereign is under the age of 18 years, or is incapacitated through illness of performing the Royal functions, a Regent may be appointed to exercise the powers of the Sovereign. The first potential Regent should be the Prince Philip, Duke of Edinburgh.

The *Regency Act*, *1943*, amended the 1937 Act by providing that Counsellors of State may be appointed to whom the Royal functions may be delegated if the Sovereign is ill or absent from the United Kingdom (e.g. on a prolonged visit to a Commonwealth country). The Counsellors shall be the wife or husband of the Sovereign, and the four persons next in line of succession to the Crown, or, if those persons are less than four, then all such persons.

The heir apparent or presumptive to the throne if not under 18 shall not be disqualified from being a Counsellor of State. The *Regency Act, 1953*, provided for the Duke of Edinburgh to act as Regent in the event of the Heir Apparent acceding to the throne before he reached the age of 18 years.

Demise of the Queen

The death (demise) of the Sovereign does not now affect the duration of Parliament (the *Representation of the People Act, 1867*), nor the termination of Parliamentary Offices (*Demise of the Crown Act, 1901*).

The Civil List

In medieval times a Monarch paid all expenses of government (i.e. court expenses, army, navy, and government officers) out of feudal dues payable by the tenants of land to the Lord Paramount (the King). Taxes were then (and still are) burdensome, and the Royal claim to impose taxes by right of his prerogative was one of the main causes which precipitated the struggle between the Crown and Parliament in the seventeenth century. Finally, this struggle resulted in the House of Commons claiming the exclusive right to tax, and then the right to complete control of how the revenue raised should be spent.

If royalty was to be maintained, the King had to have some money to keep him in existence. Charles II was granted the proceeds of the duties on spirits, cider, and beer, and these dues became part of the Royal income. In the reign of William III this grant of money by the Commons became known as the 'Civil List'. The grant is still in being and now includes the money allocated by Parliament and charged on the Consolidated Fund (see p. 100).

Today the Civil List covers the personal income of the Sovereign, together with expenses of the Royal Household and any allowance which Parliament may make for other members of the Royal Family. The Civil List is embodied in a statute (*Civil List Act, 1952*) which granted the Queen £475,000 per annum, and the Duke of Edinburgh £40,000.

In December 1971 the **Commons Select Committee on the Civil List** made recommendations increasing the figures above as follows:

H.M. The Queen	£980,000
Queen Elizabeth the Queen Mother	£70,000
The Duke of Edinburgh	£65,000
Princess Anne	£15,000
Princess Margaret	£35,000
The Duke of Gloucester	£45,000

The recommendations came into effect on 1 January 1972. To meet contingencies of rising costs, the Committee suggested a system in which the Treasury could bring forward Orders in Parliament to make any necessary adjustments. The Committee found that the Queen's household was run very economically, and the increases above were justified.

Crown lands are those lands owned by the State (or the Crown in its executive capacity). The Queen may hold private property, e.g. the Sandringham Estate in Norfolk, and such land is liable for rates and taxes.

Duties of the Sovereign

Our State may be described as a representative Parliamentary democracy in a monarchical framework. The real rulers are 'Her Majesty's Ministers' i.e. the

Cabinet and Ministers in whom are vested the executive powers of government which were once claimed by the Kings of Britain. Today the Queen by convention always acts on the advice of Her Ministers, and never vetoes a statute enacted by Parliament. As we have observed 'the Queen reigns but does not rule'.

Bagehot said that the King had three rights: 'the right to be consulted, the right to encourage, and the right to warn'. 'And,' Bagehot adds, 'a King of great sense and sagacity would want no others.'

In brief, the main functions of the Queen today may be listed thus:

  (i) To open and close Parliament.
 (ii) To dissolve and summon Parliament.
(iii) To appoint a Prime Minister.
 (iv) To be the Fountain of Justice.
  (v) To be the Fountain of Honour.
 (vi) To be the Head of the Commonwealth.
(vii) To exercise the right of advice to Her Ministers.
(viii) To take part in the formal and ceremonial events observed by the Constitution.

(i) *Opening and Closing of Parliament*. The dates on which Parliament is opened (summoned) and closed (prorogued), i.e. the beginning and end of a Parliamentary session, are fixed by Parliament itself. The Queen attends the formal opening of Parliament which is characterised by traditional pomp and pageantry. The Queen drives in State from Buckingham Palace to Westminster accompanied by the Household Cavalry. The event is an important event constitutionally and is notable for its traditional ceremony and dignity.

Her Majesty sits on the Throne in the House of Lords which is crowded for the event. The Commons are summoned to the bar of the upper chamber to hear the Queen's Speech. The Speech is, in fact, prepared by the Prime Minister and Cabinet and, as we have noted (see p. 74), is usually a review of the past with proposals for new legislation in the ensuing Parliamentary session.

(ii) *Dissolution and Summoning of Parliament*. Parliament is dissolved at the end of a five-year period (*Parliament Acts, 1911 and 1949*). If, however, a Government is defeated on a major issue in the House of Commons during the five-year period the Prime Minister must, by convention, resign. Parliament is thereupon dissolved and a general election is held.

A Prime Minister may at any such time during the five-year life of a Parliament request a dissolution. The Sovereign may not constitutionally refuse the request. Normally, however, where a Government has a workable majority in the House of Commons a Prime Minister will not wish to dissolve Parliament. But, where this is not so and a Government has only a small majority a Prime Minister may feel that an appeal should be made to the electorate to enable strong and effective government to be carried on. Accordingly a request is made to which the Monarch accedes.

Sir Alan Lascelles (Private Secretary to King George VI) considered that a Sovereign could not refuse dissolution unless three conditions were fulfilled:

(*a*) The existing Parliament was still vital, viable and capable of doing its job.
(*b*) A general election would be detrimental to the national economy.

(c) The Sovereign could rely on finding another Prime Minister who could carry on his Government, for a reasonable period, with a working majority in the House of Commons.

It is very seldom that the above three conditions will co-exist.

The problem of a request for dissolution sometimes arises where a Government has a small majority. A Prime Minister in this situation may request dissolution if the Government is not strong enough to carry on or carry out its policies. If a request by a Prime Minister for dissolution is refused by the Sovereign the Prime Minister may, of course, resign. His successor, nominated by the Sovereign, would in the circumstances face the same problem as before, and, if he also requests a dissolution this would place the Sovereign in a difficult situation and, in the event, the Sovereign would have to accede to the dissolution.

(iii) *Appointment of the Prime Minister*. The Prime Minister is chosen and appointed by the Queen by right of her prerogative. The choice is frequently automatic, and her appointment is bound by convention. Thus:

(a) Where a party has a majority in the House of Commons and a recognized leader in the House that person will be appointed to the office of Prime Minister.

(b) If the Government is defeated in the Commons and the Prime Minister resigns, the Monarch must send for the leader of the Opposition who will be asked to form a Government. If, by reason of a lack of a majority in the Commons, he is unable to form a Government a general election will be held, in which case the recognised leader of the majority party in the Commons will be appointed.

If a Prime Minister dies in office and there is no recognized leader of the party to succeed him, the Monarch must make a personal choice. Normally this is the person recommended to the Monarch by the Prime Minister before his death. Winston Churchill, for example, recommended two successors (1) Mr. Anthony Eden; and (2) Sir John Anderson. If both Churchill and Eden died, Sir John Anderson was to succeed.

If a Prime Minister wishes to resign (e.g. if he is too ill to perform his office) the Monarch may ask his advice as to his successor. This situation arose on the resignation of Sir Anthony Eden in 1957. There were two contenders for the position: Mr. R. A. Butler and Mr. Harold Macmillan. As a result of her own inquiries, and after consultations with Sir Winston Churchill and Lord Salisbury, Mr. Macmillan was appointed.

Where the political situation is confused the Sovereign may intervene. Thus in 1931 no one party had a clear majority. At the time the Liberal Party had a stronger membership in the Commons. The Labour Party Prime Minister, Mr. Ramsay MacDonald, could not secure agreement within the Labour Party on the means to combat the economic crisis of the time and he tendered his resignation, but recommended to King George V that the King should consult with the leaders of the other two parties, namely Mr. Stanley Baldwin (Conservative) and Sir Herbert Samuel (Liberal). As a result of the King's intervention a conference of the three party leaders was held and a National Government under Mr. Ramsay MacDonald was formed. The coalition so formed was, however, weak due to basic differences in political philosophies.

Where the Sovereign has, in the particular circumstances of the times, to make a personal decision he may consult whom he pleases. Normally, as we have noted, the practice is to consult the Prime Minister who resigns or seeks to resign. But there is no rule to this effect, and sometimes the Sovereign may consult Privy Counsellors or the Monarch's Private Secretary. Thus, we are told, it was as a result of meetings between the Private Secretary to George V, Mr. L. S. Amery and Mr. Bridgman that Mr. Stanley Baldwin was chosen in 1923 to accept the premiership in place of Lord Curzon.

Appointment of Ministers. Originally the Ministers of the Crown were appointed by and dismissed by the Sovereign to whom they were personally responsible for carrying out the Royal commands. Since 1832 the appointment of Ministers has been the responsibility of the Prime Minister who selects his team of Ministers some of whom will be of Cabinet rank and some not.

The list of Ministers is by convention submitted to the Sovereign for approval. Queen Victoria made her opinions known, but today the appointments are little more than a formality. We know, however, that a Sovereign may still make his or her opinion known. George VI, we are told, preferred Mr. Ernest Bevin as Foreign Secretary to Dr. Hugh Dalton, and that recommendation took effect. Ultimately, however, the responsibility is the Prime Minister's, not the Sovereign's.

Dismissal of a Government. Formerly it was within the prerogative of a Sovereign to dismiss a Government. The last time this was done was in 1783 when George III dismissed C. J. Fox and Lord North who were replaced by Pitt.

Since the *Reform Act, 1832*, the effective political power reposes with the Prime Minister and the Cabinet responsible to Parliament. By convention the Monarch is now above party politics.

In theory, a Sovereign could still invoke the prerogative to dismiss a Government, which was acting unconstitutionally. But this presupposes a great deal, since all Governments today are democratically elected and therefore responsive to the will of the people. If a Government acts constitutionally there would be no need for intervention by the Sovereign. In this respect Sir Ivor Jennings comments:

> It (the Constitution) functions in a normal manner so long as the electors are asked to decide between two competing parties at intervals of reasonable length. She (the Queen) would be justified in refusing assent to a policy which subverted the democratic basis of the Constitution, by unnecessary or indefinite prolongations of the life of Parliament, by gerrymandering of the constituencies in the interests of one party, or by fundamental modification of the electoral system to the same end. (*Cabinet Government.*)

This leaves open many questions, and a dismissal of a Government would in fact be a last resort, as, for example if a Government after a vote of censure in the House of Commons on a vital matter refused to resign, or resolved to continue in power indefinitely.

Generally (as Bagehot states), the Monarch is entitled to be informed and consulted, and in practice the Prime Minister has audience with Her Majesty frequently. The Queen on her part develops considerable experience of Constitutional matters. Elizabeth II has had seven different Prime Ministers, has visited all the Commonwealth countries and has therefore a store of useful wisdom and advice which she may impart to her Ministers which may be heeded in the national interest.

(iv) *Fountain of Justice.* The Queen is the 'fountain of justice'. The Courts of Law are the Royal Courts, and Justice is administered by Her Majesty's Judges, appointed by the Crown. Senior counsel who are senior members of the Bar are known as 'Queen's Counsel'.

The Queen can, by prerogative, remit all or part of any sentence or penalty inflicted on a person convicted of crime. Formerly persons sentenced to death for murder could be reprieved. In all such cases where a sentence is remitted or a pardon granted Her Majesty acts on the advice of one of her Ministers—the Home Secretary—who makes his own inquiries, reads the files and advises Her Majesty accordingly.

(v) *Fountain of Honour*. In exercise of her prerogative, Her Majesty confers peerages, baronetcies, knighthoods, and other honours. Most honours are, however, conferred by the Sovereign on the advice of the Prime Minister. Under this heading we include all important state offices to which the Sovereign makes appointments, for example, judges, officers in the Armed Forces, Governors of Commonwealth countries or colonies, diplomats, and the leading positions of the established Church of England. We have noted already the Queen's consent and approval of the appointment of Cabinet and other Ministers.

Notwithstanding the above list, there are a few honours which are the personal gift of the Sovereign. These are the Order of Merit, the Royal Victorian Order, the Most Noble Order of the Garter, and the Most Noble and Most Ancient Order of the Thistle.

(vi) *Head of the Commonwealth*. The Queen is Head of the Commonwealth (see the Royal Title on page 107). The Commonwealth has been described as a free association composed of some thirty independent nations which owe allegiance to the Queen as the symbol of their free association.

The seat of the Monarchy is the United Kingdom. In the nations of the Commonwealth the Queen is represented by a Governor-General, Lieutenant-General or Governor. In Northern Ireland the Queen is represented by a Governor; in the Channel Islands and the Isle of Man, by a Lieutenant-Governor. In the other member nations of the Commonwealth the Queen is represented by a Governor-General who is appointed by the Crown on the advice of the Ministers of the country concerned and is wholly independent of the U.K. Government.

In dependencies the Queen is represented by Governors appointed by the Crown. These have varying legislative and executive functions, but are responsible to the U.K. Government for the good government of the countries concerned.

(vii) *To Exercise the Right of Advice to Her Ministers*. As Bagehot has stated, the Sovereign has three rights: 'the right to be consulted, the right to encourage, the right to warn. And a King of great sense and sagacity would want no others.' The broad rule is that by convention the Monarch always acts on the advice of her Ministers, but this ignores certain important aspects and practices.

First, the Prime Minister has audience with the Queen once a week, while Parliament is in session, usually at 6 p.m. on a Tuesday evening before a Cabinet meeting. He explains when and why he desires the exercise of the prerogative powers of the Queen, e.g. in the summoning, prerogation, or dissolution of Parliament, the conferment of peerages, titles, and honours. This is essentially an important constitutional event. The Queen may make her own observations on proposals.

The Queen today has much work to do. She must read a great deal. Thus, Sir Michael Adeane, Private Secretary, stated:

> This is reading of all sorts—not only familiarizing herself with the Government papers which are produced in this country, which she does with great regularity, but keeping fairly well in touch, though perhaps not in so much detail, with what is going on in a great many other countries. This is mainly done by reports from governors, governors-general, ambassadors and so forth . . .
>
> The Queen is fortunately a quick and accurate reader and the many people who have audiences with her during the year find that she is remarkably well informed on all these important matters. If she is not, I can guarantee that it is because I have not given her the right papers. . . . But she can be relied upon to read the papers and to remember them.
>
> This goes on 365 days in the year and it is something which cannot be skipped, and is not skipped, and something she does very well. But it is something which has increased and goes on increasing.
>
> (Report from the Select Committee on the Civil List 1971) (*The Times*, 3 December 1971.)

Governments and Prime Ministers come and go. The Monarch is the continuing element. Queen Elizabeth has had seven Prime Ministers, and it is clear that her knowledge and experience in the affairs of state are invaluable. Moreover she has visited all parts of the Commonwealth, knows personally the leading figures there and in many foreign countries. Again that experience is unique. The Queen is above party politics, yet at the same time (as Sir Ivor Jennings put it) the Monarch is 'the nearest approach to the ordinary man provided by the British constitutional machine' (*Cabinet Government*). Any advice the Queen may give in a particular situation is disinterested and not partisan. How far a Prime Minister accepts or bows to that advice is a matter for him in the final event. Mr. Asquith's memorandum to George V runs as follows:

> In the last resort the occupant of the Throne accepts and acts on the advice of his Ministers. . . . He is entitled and bound to give his Ministers all relevant information which comes to him; to point out objections which seem to him valid against the course which they advise; to suggest (if he thinks fit) an alternative policy. Such intimations are received by Ministers with the utmost respect and more deference than if they proceeded from any other quarter. But, in the end, the Sovereign always acts upon the advice which Ministers, after (if need be) reconsideration, feel it their duty to offer. They give that advice well knowing that they can, and probably will, be called upon to account for it by Parliament.

(viii) *Pageantry, Pomp, and Circumstance.* Any brief sketch of the Sovereign's function is incomplete without reference to the role which the Monarchs in the last two hundred years have played in the British Constitution. All have set an example of service to the nation and, at the same time, taken a leading part in the pageantry and the traditional ceremonies which are part of the British scene.

British subjects support the Monarchy with respect and affection. They delight in the ancient forms with which Parliamentary government, national, and state affairs are preserved and carried on. The Monarch symbolizes the unity of the State and imparts dignity to its proceedings. The pageantry is merely the visible splendour of the important occasions in national life. Behind the outward splendour lies the difficult, strenuous, and exacting work of ensuring that the rights and duties inherent in democracy are upheld and preserved.

Notwithstanding the fact that the Crown has lost its original great powers it can be said, certainly of the present century, that as those powers passed and the Monarchy became strictly constitutional, the Monarch has become increasingly popular in the hearts and minds of the British people. (Lord Morrison: *Government and Parliament*.)

The visits made by the Sovereign to Commonwealth countries are always notable for the friendly way in which Her Majesty is received. These overseas activities help in uniting the independent members of the Commonwealth and their peoples and serve to reinforce friendships and loyalties to the common ideals which underlie the free association of member States.

The Cabinet

The Privy Council was at one time the formal source of executive power in the State. In medieval times there were the *Magnum Concilium* (the Great Council), a smaller body, the *Curia Regis*, and in addition a body known as the Privy (Private) Council of the King made up of those people on whose advice the Monarch depended and on whom he relied to carry out his decisions and commands.

In the seventeenth century the Monarch held conferences or meetings with his leading Ministers apart from the Privy Council. These meetings were confidential and took place in the King's 'cabinet' (derived from the French *'cabinet'* meaning a private room set apart for interviews).

Charles II and William and Mary did not attend some of the meetings, and, although George I, of Hanover, attended cabinet meetings at the beginning of his reign he could not speak English, did not understand English institutions or our way of life and was not interested in political affairs. By the end of his reign he attended only rarely, and ceased to attend after 1717.

The following factors influenced the growth of cabinet power: (i) the withdrawal of the Sovereign from active politics; (ii) the development of organized political parties; and (iii) the extension of the franchise following the *Reform Act, 1832*.

As the Cabinet grew in importance the Privy Council declined. Many of the former powers of the Privy Council were transferred to the Cabinet, and many of the executive duties of the Privy Council were transferred to newly formed Government Departments.

The link between the Privy Council and the Cabinet is today preserved, however, in that all Cabinet Ministers and other Senior Ministers are Privy Councillors.

The centre of the political power of the State at the present time is the Cabinet which is presided over by the Prime Minister and meets usually at No. 10 Downing Street, London.

Composition

The Cabinet is a group of party representatives which depends for its continued existence in power upon the ability to command the support of a majority of Members of Parliament in an elected legislature, the House of Commons. That support is derived from members of the same political party or a group of parties, e.g. in the event of a coalition of parties.

Most members of the Cabinet are appointed to head Government Departments. The numbers of members forming a cabinet varies. In 1886 there were fourteen members; in 1971 seventeen; in 1974 twenty-one. These form the 'inner core' of the ruling political party.

The Cabinet has the following main characteristics. The Cabinet:

(i) Consists of M.P.s of the same political views.
(ii) Is chosen from the party with a majority in the elected House of the Legislature.
(iii) Carries out a concerted or agreed policy.
(iv) Has a common responsibility to resign collectively in the event of parliamentary censure on a vital issue.
(v) Acknowledges a common leader in the Prime Minister.

Walter Bagehot observed:

The Cabinet is a combining committee—a hyphen which joins, a buckle which fastens the legislative part of the State to the executive part of the State. In its origin it belongs to the one, in its function it belongs to the other. (*The English Constitution*.)

Bagehot also described the constitution as:

The efficient secret of the English Constitution may be described as the close union and nearly complete fusion of the executive and legislative powers.

Functions of the Cabinet

Policy Forming. The main task of the Cabinet is to form the policy of H.M. Government with regard to (*a*) home affairs, and (*b*) foreign affairs. This task faces all governments, but it is essential here to bring it into focus.

The broad outlines of a Government's policy will have been laid before the electorate in its political manifesto before a general election. A programme of legislation will, therefore, be drawn up and followed so far as possible. Industrial relations, unemployment, housing, the reform of local government, the question of joining the European Common Market, immigration, and race relations are a few of the matters to be decided.

Relations with foreign states, international co-operation with such bodies as the United Nations Organization, are continuous. All governments are concerned with protecting vital national interests, maintaining the peace and at the same time meeting the challenge of the inevitable changes and events which occur in the world scene.

The Cabinet governs the country as a whole in the interests of the entire nation. The leaders must be wary of too doctrinaire an attitude against which the electorate may react unfavourably, thus leading to defeat at the next general election.

Filling in Details of Policy. Where a broad policy only is decided upon before an election, the Cabinet is faced with the task of filling in the details. For example the reform of Industrial Law relating to trade unions is a policy matter, but the form of the changes in the law is a matter for the Cabinet, with the assistance of its advisers.

Frequently, lack of time and finance dictate necessary limitations on what the Cabinet can approve. Government, as has been said, is 'the art of the possible'.

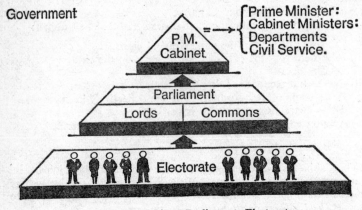

Government: Cabinet: Parliament: Electorate

Co-ordination of Policy. Effective and convenient government requires that all Government Departments concerned with the same problems work together. Thus, for example, the raising of the school-leaving age involved:

(i) The Secretary of State for Education and Science.
(ii) The Secretary of State for Social Services.
(iii) The Secretary of State for the Home Department.
(iv) The Chancellor of the Exchequer.
(v) The Secretary of State for Trade and Industry, and President of the Board of Trade.

The broad dovetailing of policy is achieved at Cabinet level while the lower executive authorities in the provinces, e.g. the local authorities, act in concert with the policy laid down.

Major Unforeseen Problems. Granted that a Government proposes certain reforms which it hopes to carry through during its five-year period of office, some, perhaps all, will be achieved, but it is certain there will also be many emergencies or contingencies which cannot be foreseen. Thus there may be a revolution in the Middle East, a break in East–West relations or the reverse, a capture of an ambassador by terrorists, unrest or violence in Ulster. All such matters fall within the purview of the Cabinet, and evoke response and, if need be, immediate action, as in the oil crisis of 1974.

The world seethes with problems: over-population; pollution of earth, seas, and the atmosphere; the threat of war with its vital and complicated defence plans and, last but not least, the effect which Britain's entering the European Common Market will have on the Commonwealth and its constituent members.

The Cabinet lays down its short- and long-term policies. But it must do even more by giving to the country as a whole a dynamic lead, energizing the

Executive (Civil Service and Local Government) and demonstrating that it can govern. 'The cabinet pushes a stream of tendency through affairs' (per Professor H. J. Laski). Once the dynamic is lacking, government stagnates.

Principles of Cabinet Government.

There are certain well-established principles on which the Cabinet works.

Cabinet and Parliamentary majority. The exercise of the important functions of the Cabinet, for example, its supreme control of the national executive, is vitally affected by the fact that the Cabinet is a group of party representatives depending for its existence upon the support of a majority of members in the House of Commons. As we have noted, it is an important convention that a cabinet which loses that support must resign. This is, in fact, rare.

The value of this convention is that the Cabinet, through its control of the Commons, can frame policies and pass them into law, or raise any funds necessary for governmental purposes.

Some critics describe this system as 'Cabinet dictatorship'. The charge of 'dictatorship' suggests uncontrolled or absolute powers, leading to tyrannical government. The view ignores the checks which operate in the British Constitution in fact. Thus, we have noted that the Cabinet is dependent upon its majority in the House of Commons which can only be maintained by keeping the support of M.P.s, and, through M.P.s, the general public (the electorate) who have entrusted them with power. Moreover, a cabinet which heads a Government must know that its power will end at the expiration of five years in any event (*Parliament Acts, 1911 and 1949*).

A dictator relies on armed force, a state-controlled police, repressive laws, an absence of a rival political party or group, and an absence of free elections. The dictator may, of course, go to the lengths of destroying 'unhealthy' factions.

The power of the British Cabinet rests ultimately on the will of the people and the support of M.P.s of the same political beliefs. All Cabinet Ministers are subject to the law of the land (see the Rule of Law) in the same way as ordinary citizens. They have no power to imprison arbitrarily or destroy the opposition, and may indeed be prosecuted for crime or sued for their wrongs even in purported execution of their lawful powers. Dictators are above the law by definition.

Party Composition. All Cabinet members must be members of the same political party, or at least agreed upon a common policy. Unless there is membership of a party or fundamental agreement upon a common policy a Government cannot command a majority in Parliament to pursue a consistent policy.

In time of war, coalition Governments have been formed from the leaders of the different parties. This form of Government has worked mainly because all M.P.s have sunk their differences in pursuit of the over-riding united purpose of winning the war.

In peace, however, coalitions have not worked well. For example, in the financial crisis of 1931, at a time of trade recession and mass unemployment there was a national emergency. The coalition Government formed at the time was an uneasy combination and was not successful. One half of the Government thought that expansion of financial credit was essential while the other thought restriction of credit was the cure for the prevailing crisis.

It appears, therefore, that only in war is a coalition Government likely to work. In peace a coalition cabinet is ineffectual if it lacks a common policy and aim and is composed of members of fundamentally divergent philosophies.

Collective Responsibility and Ministerial Responsibility. 'Ministerial responsibility' means:

(a) The **collective** responsibility which Ministers share for the policy and actions of the Government.

(b) The **individual** responsibility of Ministers to Parliament for the work of their departments.

'*Collective Responsibility*' became accepted as a doctrine by the middle of the nineteenth century. It means that the Cabinet is bound to offer unanimous advice to the Sovereign even when its members do not hold identical views on a given subject. It implies, therefore, that the policy of Departmental Ministers must be consistent with the policy of the Government as a whole. In principle it means that once the Government's policy on a particular matter is decided each Minister is expected to support it. If he cannot agree with his colleagues on a matter of general policy or on a single major issue he should resign. In February 1938 Mr. Anthony Eden (now Lord Avon) resigned as Foreign Secretary because he disagreed with the appeasement policy of the Prime Minister Mr. Neville Chamberlain. In October Mr. Duff Cooper (later Lord Norwich) resigned from his office of First Lord of the Admiralty because of his disagreement with Chamberlain's Munich Agreement with Nazi Germany, and the dismemberment of the democracy of Czechoslovakia. Similarly, Mr. Aneurin Bevan resigned in 1951 from his office of Minister of Labour over disagreement with the Labour Government's policies of rearmament and with its proposals to impose charges for medical prescriptions under the hitherto 'free' National Health Service. Sir Edward Boyle resigned from his appointment as Economic Secretary to the Treasury because of his disagreement with the invasion of Egypt during Suez crisis of 1956. Mr. George Brown, similarly resigned in 1968 from the Labour Government.

'*Individual Responsibility*' of a Minister means that as political head of his Department he is answerable for all its acts or omissions. He must also bear the consequences of any defect of administration, any injustice to an individual or any aspect of policy which may be criticized in Parliament, whether or not he is *personally* responsible. There is some doubt as to the validity of this doctrine today.

The majority of Ministers are members of the House of Commons. They are there able to answer questions and to defend themselves against criticism in person. Departmental Ministers who are in the House of Lords must be represented in the Commons by someone qualified to speak on their behalf for the Department, usually by their Parliamentary Secretaries (who are, of course, M.P.s).

The work of the various Government Departments is examined in more detail later (see p. 127). Normally Departmental Ministers decide all matters within their responsibility. For example, the Home Secretary deals with all matters relating to police and prisons and their administration. On important matters, however, e.g. a proposal to 'nationalize' the police or the C.I.D., a Minister will usually wish to consult his colleagues collectively through the Cabinet or a Cabinet committee. Any decision by a Departmental Minister binds the Government as a whole.

The responsibility of Ministers for their departments is one effective way of bringing the Government under public control. The knowledge that any departmental action may be reported to and examined in Parliament discourages the taking of arbitrary, ill-considered, or irresponsible decisions and high-handed action.

Cabinet Secretariat. All committees must have secretarial staff to record the business transacted. It is surprising, therefore, to notice that there was no true secretariat of the British Cabinet until 1916 when Lloyd George, as Prime Minister, created one. He transferred the then Secretary of the Committee of Imperial Defence (Colonel M. Hankey) to become the first secretary to the Cabinet. The secretary's main duties were to take charge of all cabinet papers, prepare agendas for meetings, prepare summaries of evidence, provide information of previous decisions of the Cabinet, to record decisions, and to notify Government Departments concerned. All such work was and still is highly confidential.

During the course of the past sixty years Cabinet responsibilities have grown increasingly complex. The work of the Cabinet has been divided and allocated to specialist committees. All such committees require the best and most accurate information available on which to reach decisions. Accordingly the Cabinet office staff has increased (531 in 1975) and now includes scientific and specialist advisers. The Central Statistical Office is one of the most important of the offices used by the Cabinet and its sub-committees for the supply of statistics and data on which the best decisions can be reached.

The Secretarial staff today includes one Secretary of the Cabinet, five Deputy Secretaries and seven Under-Secretaries plus several Assistant Secretaries. All assist by attending at and servicing the numerous committees of the Cabinet which are set up for particular purposes.

Today the Cabinet Office is an extremely important body. It is at the very centre of Government, recording decisions and precedents and co-ordinating the work of the various Cabinet committees. The secretariat provides an element of permanence and continuity to the Cabinet (which must itself change at least once in every five years), and provides also considerable knowledge and experience which inevitably carry great weight. For these reasons the official Secretary to the Cabinet is now one of the leading and most important appointments in the Civil Service.

Cabinet Office Advisers. As part of the reorganization made by the Prime Minister in October 1970 we note the creation of a 'Central Policy Review Staff' (also known as the 'capability unit' or, more colloquially, a 'think-tank'). The purpose of this group of people is to enable Ministers (particularly Cabinet Ministers) to take better policy decisions.

The team of advisers is headed by Sir Kenneth Berrill (1976). The members are drawn from many specialized fields. Their function is to question and challenge policies put to the Cabinet by Government Departments.

The White Paper produced by the Government stated that this unit would enable Ministers:

to take better policy decisions by assisting them to work out the implications of their basic strategy in terms of policies in specific areas; to establish the relative priorities to be given to them; . . . and to ensure that the underlying implications of alternative courses of action are fully analysed and considered.

The Central Policy Review Staff has produced reports on energy and energy conservation, the British computer industry, counter-inflation, presenting information to Ministers, nuclear reactors, race relations, regional policy, decision-making under stress, worker participation, U.K. population trends, coal, and long-term prospects for the British motor industry when British Leyland and the Chrysler Company were in trouble in 1975. British Leyland became Government-owned in 1975 and Chrysler were given great financial assistance from the public purse. The 'think tank' appears now to be a permanent group of talented officials to aid cabinet decision-making.

Cabinet Committees. The Cabinet is composed of the principal officers of State. All Cabinets include the Lord Chancellor, the Foreign Secretary, the Home Secretary, the Chancellor of the Exchequer, the Minister of Defence. There is no fixed composition. It rests with the Prime Minister to decide who has a seat in the Cabinet. Most members are placed in charge of important Ministries, but sometimes holders of minor offices and Ministers without Portfolio (i.e. having no Departmental responsibilities) are appointed members of the Cabinet. Much depends on the personality and capacity of the individual, the availability of Government offices at the time and, of course, the handling of a particular problem or project of the times. Thus, in 1970 the Rt. Hon. Geoffrey Rippon, Q.C., M.P., was appointed Chancellor of the Duchy of Lancaster (a Cabinet appointment with few duties) to handle negotiations for Britain's entry into the European Economic Community.

Cabinet meetings are held roughly twice a week, and usually last for two hours. Everything depends on the state of affairs at home and abroad. The agenda, prepared by the Secretariat, is discussed, the decisions recorded and notified to the Government Departments concerned or affected by the decisions. Each member of the Cabinet is free to express his views on topics introduced by the Prime Minister or other Ministers. All cabinet business follows that general pattern.

Government problems become increasingly complex. The machinery and institutions of government must change to cope with the problems and opportunities which constantly arise. The Cabinet has resorted to the use of committees. These smaller bodies relieve the burden on the main Cabinet. They also provide opportunity for more detailed discussion not suitable for the full Cabinet. Moreover, Cabinet Committees enable non-cabinet Ministers to be associated with policy decisions on matters affecting their own Departments; an important point in itself since so many Government members would not otherwise be linked with the Cabinet.

Cabinet Committees (like the parent body) are secret. Their existence, scope, and composition are not in practice revealed during the life of a particular Government. However, there are certain well-known ones. Thus the Defence Committee exists. It replaced the former Committee on Imperial Defence, and its importance in the provision of men and equipment for the external defence of the nation needs no stressing here. The Committee is composed of the principal members of the Cabinet, the Service Ministers, and the Chairman of the Chiefs of Staff Committee who is the military head of the Forces. All defence matters are dealt with by this Committee and only major matters are reported to the full Cabinet with recommendations for approval.

The Legislation Committee considers draft Bills and watches their progress through Parliament. The Leader of the House of Commons, and the Departmental Minister specially concerned with the subject-matter of a Bill attend the Committee. The Future Legislation Committee considers policy on **future** proposals and Bills to be considered by Parliament. The Lord President's Committee is a General Purposes Committee, i.e. one dealing with matters not specially assigned to a special committee. Of course, as need arises special committees may be appointed to consider some particular matter, e.g. Housing and the National Health Service. These may take decisions without reference to the full Cabinet, but all important matters must be decided by the full Cabinet to whom the committee reports. As noted above, the special committees consist of the Parliamentary Secretaries of the Ministries concerned together with senior civil servants. The Chairman of a special committee is usually the Minister primarily concerned with the problem, or his Parliamentary Secretary.

The committee system of the Cabinet has tended to alter the conduct of proceedings. Formerly all Cabinet Ministers attended all Cabinet meetings and contributed their store of common sense and judgement to the solution of the current problems. The Committee system has been adopted on the ground of efficiency. The Prime Minister keeps in touch with all committees, a fact which reinforces his position as leader since he may well be the only member who is in touch with all. The justification of the committee system is that the complexity and pace of modern life demand a division of responsibility and specialization. Its disadvantage is that full Cabinet meetings may tend to become mechanical and unduly formal, save in the crucial matters such as the outbreak of war.

Co-ordination. The chief co-ordinator in the Cabinet is, of course, the Prime Minister whose task is to adjust and harmonize the work of the various constituent committees and individual members of the Cabinet. Senior members of the Cabinet also co-ordinate the work of the various committees of which they are appointed Chairmen. The Chancellor of the Exchequer must co-ordinate the work and decisions of all committees involving finance. The Secretary of State for Defence also co-ordinates defence matters and the work of the service Ministers who are not members of the Cabinet.

Another means to achieve co-ordination is to group related Departments or Ministries in one Department. The Secretary of State for the Environment is now responsible for: (i) Local Government and Development; (ii) Housing and Construction; (iii) Transport Industries, each in the charge of a Minister. The Foreign Secretary is responsible for (i) Foreign, and (ii) Commonwealth and Colonial affairs.

In 1951 Sir Winston Churchill appointed three Ministers (known as 'Overlords') to supervisory positions in the Cabinet: (i) Lord Woolton (Lord President of the Council) to supervise Agriculture and Food; (ii) Lord Leathers (Secretary of State for the Co-ordination of Transport, Fuel and and Power) to supervise Transport, Fuel and Power; (iii) Lord Cherwell (Paymaster-General) to supervise Research and Scientific policy. This followed the pattern set during World War II when Churchill appointed Ministers without departmental duties, e.g. Lord Privy Seal, The Chancellor of the Duchy of Lancaster, the Paymaster-General and a Minister without Portfolio, whose main task was to act as Chairmen of two or three closely connected Cabinet committees and the co-ordination of a group of related services. In 1953, however, the practice of appointing peers (hence the name 'Overlords') was criticized by Labour spokesmen mainly because the holders of such powerful positions were not responsible to the Commons. Moreover there was a blurring and confusion of political responsibility. Was the Minister responsible (see p. 118) or the co-ordinator (the 'Overlord')? Accordingly, the arrangement was withdrawn in 1953.

Co-ordination involves (i) a clear objective to be achieved; (ii) a plan and time-table; (iii) efficient administrative machinery (committees, sub-committees, and administrative staff); and (iv) effective leadership in the persons of the Prime Minister and leading Ministers who can issue directives to members, reconcile differences in the achievement of the overall policies and master the art of getting things done.

THE CABINET: 1976

1. Prime Minister and First Lord of the Treasury and Minister for the Civil Service.
2. Secretary of State for the Home Department.
3. Secretary of State for Foreign and Commonwealth Affairs.
4. Lord Chancellor.
5. Chancellor of the Exchequer.
6. Lord President of the Council.
7. Secretary of State for Defence.
8. Secretary of State for Social Services.
9. Chancellor of the Duchy of Lancaster.
10. Secretary of State for Employment.
11. Secretary of State for Education and Science.
12. Secretary of State for Scotland.
13. Lord Privy Seal.
14. Secretary of State for the Environment.
15. Secretary of State for Wales.
16. Minister of Agriculture and Fisheries.
17. Secretary of State for Trade.
18. Secretary of State for Northern Ireland.
19. Secretary of State for Prices and Consumer Protection.
20. Secretary of State for Energy.
21. Secretary of State for Industry.
22. Minister for Overseas Development.
23. Parliamentary Secretary, Treasury.
24. Minister for Planning and Local Government.

Ministers Not in the Cabinet

Paymaster General.
Minister of State for Foreign and Commonwealth Affairs (2).
Chief Secretary, Treasury.
Financial Secretary, Treasury.
Minister of State, Treasury.
Minister for Transport.
Minister for Housing and Construction.
Minister of State, Department of Energy.
Minister of State, Department of Education and Science.
Minister of State, Privy Council Office.
Minister of State, Ministry of Defence.
Minister of State, Civil Service Department.
Minister of State, Home Office (2).
Minister of State for Sport and Recreation.
Minister of State, Department of Employment.
Minister of State, Department of Prices and Consumer Protection.

Minister of State, Department of Health and Social Security (2).
Minister of State, Department of Industry (2).
Minister of State, Scottish Office (2).
Minister of State, Northern Ireland Office (2).
Minister of State, Ministry of Agriculture, Fisheries and Food.

Law Officers

Attorney General.
Lord Advocate
Solicitor General.
Solicitor General for Scotland.

In addition there are 45 Parliamentary Under-Secretaries.

The Prime Minister

History

When political parties began to form in the eighteenth century certain dominant personalities emerged as leaders. Sir Robert Walpole who headed the Government from 1721 to 1742 is generally regarded as the first Prime Minister. There was, however, no clearly defined office as such nor was the Cabinet constituted as it is today. English institutions have grown from experience and need. The former executive powers of the Sovereign in the early Privy Council were transferred to a Prime Minister and a Cabinet. This body (the Cabinet) is now the effective apex of the political power in the State.

This transfer of power was more a gradual evolution. Thus in Walpole's administration the King selected the Ministers, not Walpole. Nevertheless, Walpole unified the group of Whigs, and dissentient members unable to support his policies were dismissed or compelled to resign. This foreshadowed the later principle of 'collective responsibility' (see p. 118). When Walpole resigned in 1742 his Ministers did not, however, resign with him. The only resemblance between Walpole and a Prime Minister today is that the latter still holds the office of First Lord of the Treasury and resides at 10 Downing Street, London, W.1.

William Pitt, the Younger, who was in office between 1783–1801 and 1804–6, was a strong Prime Minister, and further consolidated the work of Walpole. In 1834 Sir Robert Peel became Prime Minister and formed a Cabinet of fourteen members. He was able to oversee all the government business of the day whether home or overseas affairs.

The *Reform Act 1832*, and the extension of the franchise had a great effect on the general political scene, and the modern Cabinet began to take shape.

During the nineteenth century W. E. Gladstone (Liberal) and Benjamin Disraeli (Conservative), were the important Prime Ministers who both further developed the office. Disraeli signed the *Treaty of Berlin* in 1878 as 'Prime Minister of England' the first time the office was officially named. In 1905 the Prime Minister was granted by Royal Warrant precedence next after the Archbishop of York.

The Prime Minister is now normally the acknowledged head of the party commanding a majority in the House of Commons. We have noted (see p. 110) that it is only on occasions when no party commands an absolute majority in the House, or when the majority party has no acknowledged head that the Royal discretion as to choice of a Prime Minister may be exercised.

Offices held

There is no salary assigned to the office of 'Prime Minister'. He draws the salary of whatever **other** office he holds. The Lord Treasurer was regarded at the end of the seventeenth century as the most important Government official, and the leading Minister (i.e. the Prime Minister) has normally held the office of First Commissioner (or First Lord) of the Treasury since that time. By virtue of this post the Prime Minister draws his present salary of £20,000 per annum as laid down in the *Ministers of the Crown Act, 1937*, as amended.

The Earl of Chatham (Prime Minister in 1766) was Lord Privy Seal; the Marquess of Salisbury (Prime Minister in 1895) was successively Foreign Secretary and Lord Privy Seal. Winston Churchill during World War II was First Lord of the Treasury **and** Minister of Defence. Mr. Edward Heath, held the offices of (*a*) First Lord of the Treasury and (*b*) Minister for the Civil Service (with the Lord Privy Seal). Mr. Harold Wilson followed suit in March 1974.

Residence

The official residence of the Prime Minister is 10 Downing Street, London. He also has the use of *Chequers*, a country mansion in Buckinghamshire.

The P.M. as an M.P.

In the eighteenth century Cabinets consisted almost solely of peers, though the Leading Minister (the Prime Minister) was recruited from the Commons. In the nineteenth century, however, M.P.s formed the bulk of the Cabinet and, curiously enough, the Prime Minister was frequently a peer.

With the expansion of the franchise and the reduction of the powers of the Lords (by the *Parliament Act, 1911*) it became difficult for a peer to exercise the premiership from the House of Lords. The last peer to be Prime Minister was Lord Salisbury who resigned in 1902. In 1923 Lord Curzon (a contender for the post) was passed over in favour of Mr. Stanley Baldwin. This showed decisively the need for a Prime Minister to be a member of the Commons and thus answerable to that Chamber. In 1963 Lord Home was appointed Prime Minister. He thereupon immediately disclaimed his peerage, and was subsequently elected to the House of Commons as Sir Alec Douglas-Home, M.P.

The Power of the Prime Minister

In considering the power of a Prime Minister we look first at his main functions. These may be enumerated thus:

    (i) He is leader of the majority party in Parliament.
   (ii) He is Head of the Government (i.e. the Administration).
  (iii) He selects Cabinet Ministers.
  (iv) He appoints other members of the Government (i.e. non-Cabinet Ministers), numbering about 100.
   (v) He may move Ministers from one post to another (a reshuffle).
  (vi) He may dismiss a Cabinet Minister or lesser Minister, or call upon a Minister to resign from the Government.
 (vii) He is Chairman of the Cabinet and the important Cabinet Committees.
(viii) He co-ordinates policy and supervises the work of the various Ministries.

(ix) He is the nation's chief spokesman in international and domestic affairs.

(x) He is ultimately responsible for party discipline. He appoints the Chief Whips who maintain close contact with him.

(xi) He exercises patronage (i.e. has the power to appoint to a variety of offices, including judicial and ecclesiastical), dispenses titles, peerages.

(xii) He is political head of the Civil Service, and collaborates with the Head of the Home Civil Service over senior Civil Service appointments and promotions.

(xiii) He communicates the Government's decisions to H.M. The Queen, and advises when Parliament may be dissolved.

This is a considerable list of powers vested in the Prime Minister under the Constitution. When one adds to these the fact that the Prime Minister is frequently in the public eye, on television and radio and in the Press, his impact on the public can be very great, particularly if he has a 'good public image'. There is a tendency nowadays to personalize organizations and ideas, e.g. the Wilson era, the Heath Government, and the leader's performance as Prime Minister can influence the people's voting decisions.

The Limits of Power of the Prime Minister

Providing a Prime Minister has the support of his Cabinet colleagues and commands a majority in the House of Commons he may expect to serve out his five-year period of office. If, however, a Government is defeated on a major issue in the Commons then, by convention, the Prime Minister must request a dissolution of Parliament, whereupon a general election will be held.

A Prime Minister may be forced to resign from his office by his own party. In 1917 Mr. Asquith was forced to resign as Prime Minister following great dissatisfaction within the Cabinet over his conduct of the war of 1914–18. Similarly Mr. Neville Chamberlain was forced to resign in 1940 by dissentient members in the Cabinet and Parliament, again over his leadership in war. There was discontent over Eden's policy in 1956, and Mr. Macmillan's in 1963.

If a Prime Minister becomes ill he may of course resign. But if he does not do so, pressure may be brought to bear on him to resign.

Although a Prime Minister is legally free to select whomsoever he will to be a member of the Cabinet there are practical and political limits to this power. One is the availability of talent within his own party. For example, if a party has been in opposition for some time there will be few M.P.s with previous Cabinet experience (cf. Attlee's Labour Government of 1945).

Another limitation on Cabinet composition is the standing of certain members in the party. Some may have a large following and cannot be omitted for fear of alienating sympathizers within the party. Some M.P.s are outstanding personalities and have obvious political abilities. If such are omitted they may cause splits or splinter groups to form within the party. A Prime Minister must be careful to avoid giving important ministerial posts to minor figures. Friendship is important in all walks of life. Hence to be friends with a Prime Minister is an asset, but that alone is insufficient and there is little evidence that well qualified politicians (unfriendly to a Prime Minister) have been deliberately excluded from office on that account alone.

Some M.P.s, particularly if they have had successful Cabinet experience already, are able by their importance to nominate their own departments in which they would be prepared to serve.

Dismissals

Clearly, a Prime Minister may dismiss a weak and ineffectual Minister. It has been said that a Prime Minister must be a 'good butcher'. Macmillan, in 1962, for example, dismissed one-third of his Cabinet, i.e. seven Cabinet Ministers, and the loyalty of the Conservative Party endured that strain. But a Prime Minister cannot go too far for fear that the dismissals may recoil on his own head by spreading discontent among backbenchers and insecurity among the remaining Cabinet Ministers. A Prime Minister must, in the last resort, **earn** the support and confidence of his party members. He cannot compel it.

Policy Determination

A Prime Minister cannot alone determine policy. Each Minister, e.g. the Chancellor of the Exchequer, Foreign Secretary or Home Secretary, will have a strong brief for certain action or policy. Moreover, policy formation occurs within the party, research bodies, Cabinet Committees, and many decisions are formed before reaching the Cabinet when it is too late for the Prime Minister to alter them. A Prime Minister will, therefore, be unwise to drive through a policy which is disagreeable. A Minister whose particular view or policy is already made public can, of course, resign, thus weakening the Cabinet. We must not forget that Ministers' political careers and party unity are at stake if a Prime Minister over-rides an accepted or formulated policy.

A Prime Minister cannot, in the complex situations and flux of modern life, keep in touch with all aspects of administration. Peel, in the nineteenth century, was able to know all that was going on in Government. It is different today.

The power of a Prime Minister to take decisions himself or after consulting an individual Minister is limited. Important decisions (i.e. those likely to affect the nation as a whole) must go through the whole Cabinet. Similarly where there is no unanimous agreement in a Cabinet Committee the matter must be decided by the full Cabinet.

Generally we may say that the power of a Prime Minister varies with the times (e.g. in war or peace), with the style and aptitude of the Prime Minister, and the ability, experience and determination of his colleagues in the Cabinet.

Qualities of Leadership

A Prime Minister is the leader of his political party which wins an election. What, we may ask, are the specifications for the ideal Prime Minister? No clear answer can be given to this question. History shows that each occupant of the office has different capacities and skills. Moreover the times and circumstances may call for different personalities: a good war-time leader, e.g. Lloyd George or Winston Churchill, may not be equally effective in peace time.

The demands of office, both physical and mental, are extraordinarily heavy. It follows that a Prime Minister must be physically strong and have a good constitution. He must be able to work twenty hours a day on occasion, and be able to eat and drink at all hours of the day. He must be able to snatch a few moments sleep whenever possible, relaxing completely.

Educationally it is not necessary that he hold a first-class honours degree or have high academic qualifications. Ramsay MacDonald, Lloyd George, and Winston Churchill did not have a university education. Nevertheless any Prime Minister today must have the capacity to assimilate much knowledge and possess an orderly vigorous mind.

He must be industrious and able to work under pressure. He must possess initiative, be able to organize others and get his policies accepted and pushed through Parliament. In short an ability to get things done.

He must possess judgement in public affairs, knowing when and where to intervene in a political situation. He must on occasions be patient. When political storms and crises arise (e.g. a threat of war) he must show courage. He must also possess the strength of mind not to worry, and a sense of humour capable of riding out the daily rebuffs and criticism which are the lot of all politicians in a free democratic society. He must have the strength to dismiss Cabinet colleagues (even friends) if the national need so dictates.

Finally we may mention the ability to use television and radio effectively. When a Prime Minister speaks on the television he is watched by millions at home and possibly overseas. A good 'public image', as it is sometimes put, is a useful asset.

Cabinet Ministers, no less than a Prime Minister, must show leadership and possess the qualities mentioned above. A Prime Minister cannot make all decisions; certain important ones are left to a Departmental Minister. For example, the Home Secretary formerly had the awesome responsibility of deciding life or death when a convicted murderer appealed to the Monarch for reprieve.

Government intervenes more and more in public and social affairs, and the actions and decisions of Government Ministers vitally affect the lives of millions. The pace and stress of life are reflected in Government, making more and greater demands on those persons in whom political power has been lawfully vested to act in the best interests of the nation. A study of the newspapers will reveal current topical issues at home and abroad to which Government must react and in respect of which vital decisions must be made.

Government Departments

Government Departments are the main instruments for putting into effect Government policy after Parliament has passed the necessary legislation. The Government Departments (i.e. Ministers and civil servants) are required to ensure that services already in existence are carried on efficiently and smoothly until such time as the Cabinet or Minister thinks fit to change them by legislation. In practice there is a continuum of Government services in those spheres where general satisfaction is given, e.g. the protective services such as police, fire brigades, customs and excise, and similar services.

A change of government does not necessarily affect the number or general functions of Government Departments, though a change in policy may be accompanied by organizational change. The scope of Government activity has, however, in the last fifty years led to the formation of many new Departments. In 1970, for example, Mr. Heath created two new posts, both of Cabinet rank: (i) Secretary of State for Trade and Industry and President of the Board of Trade, and (ii) Secretary of State for the Environment (their functions and responsibilities are described below). A few Departments such as the Home Office, the Foreign Office and the Treasury have existed for over two hundred years.

The work of some Departments, e.g. the Board of Customs and Excise, covers the United Kingdom as a whole. Other Departments such as the Department for Trade and Industry cover Great Britain (England, Wales, and Scotland, but not Northern Ireland) and the Department of Housing and Local Government (which now falls under the general control of the Department of the Environment) covers England only. There are separate Departments for Scotland and Northern Ireland. There is also a separate Department with responsibility for affairs in Wales.

A Department is usually headed by a Minister. There are, however, certain Departments in which questions of policy do not normally arise and which are headed by a permanent official, a Minister with other duties being responsible for them to Parliament. Thus, Treasury Ministers are responsible for a number of Departments, e.g. Her Majesty's Stationery Office, the Central Office of Information, the Treasury Solicitor's Department, the Department of the Government Actuary, the Royal Mint, the National Debt Office, the Public Works Loan Board, and the National Savings Committee. The staff of the Departments are all members of a body of Crown servants known as the Civil Service (see p. 147).

Internal Organization of Government Departments

Departments of Government vary in size and in the volume, type and complexity of their work. Each Department makes its own arrangements for discharging its duties and there are variations in internal organization. However, most Departments have certain features in common.

The Minister is, of course, at the head of his Department and is politically responsible to Parliament. Under the Minister there is usually a Permanent Secretary. In those departments where the Minister is a 'Secretary of State', the chief civil servant in the Ministry is known as Permanent Under-Secretary of State. Below this office there will be one or more Deputy Secretaries; below these a number of Under-Secretaries and Assistant Secretaries.

Major Departments (e.g. the Home Office) have a Principal Finance Officer and Organization Officer. A number of Establishment Divisions within a Ministry have their own Organization and Methods Branch (O. and M. Branch), the members of which act in an advisory capacity to the Permanent Under-Secretary. Many Government Departments also have their own legal advisers or solicitors, and their own Information Divisions.

Some Government Departments maintain a regional organization, and some have direct contact with the public throughout the country by maintaining local offices, e.g. The Department for Employment which maintains employment exchanges for employers seeking labour, for workers who are unemployed or who wish to change their jobs, and also for the payment of unemployment benefit.

Advisory Bodies

One of the devices adopted today to ensure that a Minister is adequately informed on matters falling within his Department is the Advisory Council or Committee. Most Government Departments are assisted by such bodies which now number over 600. This in itself gives an indication of the complexity of public administration. The object of these bodies is to enable the Minister to be the better informed so that any executive action or proposed legislation is taken on the best available information or professional opinion.

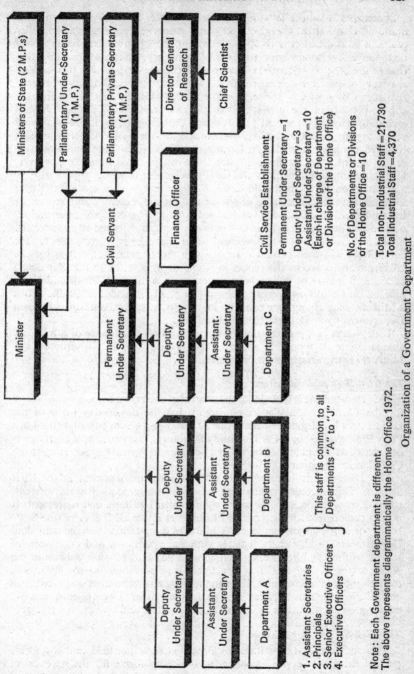

Ministers of State (2 M.P.s)

Parliamentary Under-Secretary (1 M.P.)

Parliamentary Private Secretary (1 M.P.)

Director General of Research

Chief Scientist

Minister

Civil Servant

Permanent Under Secretary

Finance Officer

Deputy Under Secretary

Assistant Under Secretary

Department C

Deputy Under Secretary

Assistant Under Secretary

Department B

This staff is common to all Departments "A" to "J"

Deputy Under Secretary

Assistant Under Secretary

Department A

1. Assistant Secretaries
2. Principals
3. Senior Executive Officers
4. Executive Officers

Civil Service Establishment

Permanent Under Secretary = 1

Deputy Under Secretary = 3

Assistant Under Secretary = 10
(Each in charge of Department or Division of the Home Office)

No. of Departments or Divisions of the Home Office = 10

Total non-Industrial Staff = 21,730
Total Industrial Staff = 4,370

Note: Each Government department is different. The above represents diagrammatically the Home Office 1972.

Organization of a Government Department

Sometimes a statute lays down that a Minister is required to consult a Standing Committee; on other occasions he may seek their advice. In either case the final decision is the Minister's, not the Committee's. Examples of these advisory bodies are: (i) Central Advisory Councils for Education (*Education Act, 1944*); (ii) Police Council (*Police Act, 1914*); (iii) Central Advisory Council for Science and Technology; (iv) National Insurance Advisory Committee (*National Insurance Act, 1946*).

Membership of the advisory committees varies. Some contain experts including scientists, medical practitioners, pathologists, agriculturalists and veterinary surgeons and the like, while others include civil servants (who serve to act as a link with a particular Government Department) and representatives of various interests, e.g. industrialists, trade unionists, educationists, lawyers, local government councillors and local government officers.

In addition to these committees a Minister may set in motion a Royal Commission with a chairman of some standing and a membership representing informed opinion from various walks of life. A commission examines written and oral evidence from Government Departments and other interested organizations—official and unofficial—and individuals. A commission (or committee) will then submit a report with recommendations. It is for the Government to accept the report in whole or in part, or to take (or defer) action as a matter of policy. A recent example is the Redcliffe–Maud Commission on Local Government Reform (see p. 309). In addition to the above a Minister may at any time cause an inquiry to be undertaken within his own Department by a 'Departmental Committee'.

Today there is a proliferation of reports and an abundance of advice, all emanating from reputable sources. The problem of the Government (or Minister) is the arrangement of priorities.

The Civil Service Department

This Department is now under the control of the Prime Minister as Minister for the Civil Service. The responsibility for the day-to-day work of the Department is delegated by the Prime Minister to a senior Minister (the Lord Privy Seal) assisted by a Parliamentary Secretary. The Permanent Secretary is designated as 'Head of the Home Civil Service and Permanent Secretary to the Civil Service Department'.

The Department is responsible for personnel management in the Civil Service. This includes policy and central arrangements for recruitment, training, promotion, general career management, welfare, and retirement. It is also responsible for the control of numbers in the Civil Service (the State being one of the largest employers) and for grading standards in the individual Departments. Additionally it deals with pay, pensions, and conditions of service in the Civil Service, as well as with pay and pension policies in the public sector as a whole. The Department is responsible, too, for promoting the development of administrative and managerial techniques and provides a central management services consultancy to other Departments, e.g. by advising on such matters as O. and M., computers and operational research.

The Civil Service Commission

This body was first constituted by Order in Council in 1855, and now forms part of the Civil Service Department. It is responsible for the selection of permanent civil servants, and in the discharge of this function specific and formal arrangements have been made to ensure its independence and impartiality in the performance of its task of selection of recruits.

The Treasury

The nominal heads of the Treasury are the Lords Commissioners, viz.:

The First Lord of the Treasury (now always the Prime Minister).
The Chancellor of the Exchequer.
Five Junior Lords.

In practice the Lords Commissioners never meet as a board, and their responsibilities are carried out by the Chancellor of the Exchequer who is assisted by:

The Chief Secretary to the Treasury.
The Financial Secretary.
A Minister of State.

All the above are political posts.

There is also a Parliamentary Secretary to the Treasury, who is the Chief Government Whip in the House of Commons whose duties have been outlined on page 65. The Treasury, as its name implies, is the Government Department primarily responsible for the development of Britain's overall economic strategy. The main body of its work is carried by three large groups of divisions, viz.:

   (i) *The Public Sector Group.* This controls the level of public expenditure
       in relation to the general economic strategy and ensures that resources
       are efficiently used within the public sector (e.g. local authorities).
  (ii) *The Finance Group.* This is responsible for ensuring that financial and
       monetary policy in all its aspects is consistent with the overall strategy.
 (iii) *The National Economy Group.* This is responsible for the preparation of
       short-term and medium-term economic forecasts and the co-ordination
       of long-term forecasting work; for the formulation of a co-ordinated
       economic strategy based in part on these forecasts; and for the surveil-
       lance of certain areas of economic policy administered primarily by
       other departments—namely fiscal (i.e. tax) policy, incomes and prices
       policies, and industrial policies.

Parliamentary Counsel to the Treasury. The Office of the Parliamentary Counsel is responsible for the drafting of all Government Bills (legislative), except those Bills or provisions of Bills exclusively affecting Scotland, which are dealt with by the Lord Advocate's Department. The Office drafts all financial and other Parliamentary motions and amendments moved by the Government during the passage of Bills. It also advises Departments on questions of Parliamentary procedure, and its officials (lawyers) attend sittings and committees in both Houses. The Office also drafts subordinate legislation (see p. 248), and advises the Government on legal, parliamentary, and constitutional questions falling within its special experience.

The Ministry of Agriculture and Fisheries

This Department is responsible in England and Wales for administering Government policy for agriculture, horticulture, and fishing. The Ministry administers deficiency payments schemes and various grants and subsidies designed to improve the efficiency of the industries, and gives free technical advice.

The Ministry is also responsible for administering schemes for the control and eradication of animal and plant diseases (e.g. foot and mouth disease). In addition it deals with certain questions relating to legislation about food, including labelling and advertising, slaughterhouses, and the quality and cleanliness of milk and questions concerning the supply and manufacture of food, e.g. its consumption, composition, preservation, and nutritional qualities.

The Ministry maintains relations with other Commonwealth and foreign countries, and co-operates in certain of the activities of a number of international organizations concerned with agriculture, fisheries, and food, e.g. the Food and Agriculture Organization of the United Nations, the Organization for Economic Co-operation and Development, and the General Agreement on Tariffs and Trade (GATT).

Certain of these activities and responsibilities devolve on the Secretary of State for Wales and the Secretary of State for Scotland in respect of those countries.

The Board of Customs and Excise

The primary duty of the Board is to collect and administer the customs and excise duties as laid down in the annual Finance Acts or by other legislation. The Board also advises the Chancellor of the Exchequer on any matters connected with customs and excise, and is also responsible for preventing and detecting the evasion of the revenue laws.

The Board also performs miscellaneous duties for other Departments such as the enforcement of prohibitions and restrictions on the import and export of certain classes of goods, exchange currency control, and the compilation of U.K. overseas trade statistics from customs export and import documents.

The Ministry of Defence

This Government Department is responsible for (i) defence policy, and (ii) the control and administration of the three fighting Services—the Navy, Army, and Air Force.

The Secretary of State for Defence has a seat in the Cabinet and is in charge of the Department. He is assisted by a Minister of State for Defence who is responsible for personnel and logistics (moving men and supplying them with equipment, etc.), research, development and production. There are also three Parliamentary Under-Secretaries with responsibilities for the respective Services.

The Department of Education and Science

This falls under the control of the Secretary of State for Education and Science (a Cabinet post). The Department is organized into various branches (i) schools; (ii) further education (including vocational, recreational, and adult education and the youth service); (iii) teachers, and kindred subjects in England and Wales; (iv) universities; (v) civil science; and (vi) support for the arts throughout Great Britain. The Department is also responsible for National Libraries policy and all general policy matters relating to libraries. There are specialist branches within the Department which advise on health, building, planning (e.g. educational research and statistics), law. The Department also has an information service.

The Department's responsibilities for the development of Primary, Secondary, and Further Education, include dealing with the supply, training, and superannuation of teachers, the building of new schools and other institutions, the school health service, the special educational treatment of handicapped children, and the provision of school meals.

The Department works in co-operation with local education authorities who are required to secure adequate facilities for all forms of education in their areas. The Department's relations with the universities are conducted through the University Grants Committee. Its activities in the field of civil science are discharged through five research councils: the Medical Research Council, the Agricultural Research Council, the Natural Environment Research Council, the Social Science Research Council, and the Science Research Council. The Council for Scientific Policy advises the Secretary of State. Two Parliamentary Under-Secretaries assist the Secretary of State in the discharge of the duties of the Department.

The Department of Employment

This Department is generally in charge of planning and promoting the efficient use of Britain's manpower resources. Its responsibilities include: manpower policy; employment services; vocational training; industrial relations; safety; health and welfare; and the administration of the Government's productivity policy.

The Department also undertakes agency work for other Government Departments in connection with (i) the payment of unemployment benefit and other social security benefits; (ii) the repayment of income tax to unemployed workers; and (iii) the issue of passports.

The DEP is responsible for the relations of the British Government with the International Labour Organization in Geneva and for providing representation on employment and related matters at sessions of all other international bodies. Labour attachés in British embassies and consulates abroad deal with questions about labour and employment in Britain.

It is also responsible for the administration of legislation on monopolies and mergers and restrictive trade practices.

The Secretary of State for this Department has a seat in the Cabinet. He is assisted by one Minister of State and one Parliamentary Under-Secretary.

The Foreign and Commonwealth Office

The Secretary of State for Foreign and Commonwealth Affairs is one of the most important officials and is a member of the Cabinet. The Department acts as a channel of communication between the British Government and the governments of foreign and overseas Commonwealth countries for the discussion and negotiation of all matters (including economic issues) falling within the sphere of international and Commonwealth relations. One of its functions is the drawing up of international treaties and agreements.

The Department provides the means by which the British Government is represented in the United Nations Organization and other bodies and by which it is kept informed about developments in countries overseas; by which British subjects and interests abroad are protected and trade promoted; and by which British policy explained to governments and peoples overseas. It also discharges the British Government's responsibilities in the Associated States (e.g. Antigua, Dominica, Grenada, St. Kitts–Nevis–Anguilla and St. Lucia) and the Dependent Territories of the Commonwealth. In the cases of the Associated States the British Government's responsibilities relate mainly to defence and external affairs. In the Dependent Territories, each of which has its own internal administration, the British Government is finally responsible for good government and for the relations between these territories and other countries.

The Secretary of State (the Foreign Secretary) is assisted by a Minister of State, two Parliamentary Under-Secretaries, and a Minister of Overseas Development.

The Department of Health and Social Security

This Department is under the charge of the Secretary of State for Social Services (a Cabinet post). The Department is responsible (in England) for the administration of the National Health Service, the welfare services provided by local authorities for the elderly and handicapped, welfare foods and certain aspects of public health, including hygiene. Throughout Great Britain the Department is responsible for (i) the payment of benefits (e.g. sickness benefits), (ii) the collection of contributions under the national insurance and industrial injuries' schemes, and (iii) the payment of family allowances. The Department also makes reciprocal social security arrangements with other countries, and represents the United Kingdom on the World Health Organization (WHO) of the United Nations.

Through its Supplementary Benefits Commission the Department is responsible (i) for determining awards of non-contributory benefits (e.g. for the destitute); (ii) for reception centres (e.g. for vagrants or those having no home to go to); and (iii) for assessing the means whereby people can apply for legal aid (see p. 208). In addition, the Department has responsibilities in connection with pensions and welfare services (including in some cases medical and surgical treatment) for war pensioners in the United Kingdom, the Channel Islands, the Isle of Man, and the Republic of Ireland, and for U.K. war pensioners living in Northern Ireland or in countries overseas.

The Secretary of State is assisted by a Minister of State and two Parliamentary Under-Secretaries.

The Home Office

The Ministerial head of the Home Office is the Secretary of State for the Home Department (the Home Secretary) who is always accorded Cabinet rank by virtue of the importance of his responsibilities. First we should observe that all matters of national administration not specially assigned to other Ministers are entrusted to the Home Secretary. For this reason he is sometimes described as the 'residuary legatee'. His duties are now practically restricted to the domestic affairs of England and Wales, the Channel Islands, and the Isle of Man.

The Home Secretary's duties may be classified thus:

(i) He is the recognized channel of communication between the Crown and the subject in all cases where no other special procedure is laid down.
(ii) He is responsible for the maintenance of internal law and order.
(iii) He administers much statute law, particularly in regard to the welfare

of the community, though some of this work has been redistributed to other Departments: the Department of Health and Social Security; the Department of Employment and Productivity.

The chief matters falling within the scope of the Home Office are:

(i) *Police*. The Home Secretary is directly in control of the Metropolitan Police and assumes indirect control of provincial forces.

(ii) *Administration of Justice*. The Home Secretary has control over the organization of magistrates' courts, the appointment of Metropolitan magistrates and stipendiary magistrates; the introduction of legislation on criminal justice; the criminal injuries' compensation scheme.

(iii) *Extradition*. The Home Secretary exercises control over the extradition of criminals.

(iv) *Prerogatives of Pardon and Mercy*. The Home Secretary advises the Monarch on these matters.

(v) *Immigration and Aliens*. The Home Secretary is responsible for immigration and for the admission, supervision and deportation of aliens. He also grants certificates of naturalization to aliens desirous of becoming British subjects.

(vi) *Prisons, Probation, After-care of Prisoners*. The Home Secretary is responsible for these services.

(vii) *Fire Service*. The Home Secretary maintains central control of the Fire Service.

(viii) *Parliamentary and Local Government Elections*. The Home Secretary is responsible for the administration of the law relating to these matters.

(ix) *By-laws of Local Authorities*. The Home Secretary is responsible for sanctioning by-laws made by local authorities in so far as they relate to 'law and order' and 'good governance'.

(x) *Petitions and Addresses to the Sovereign*. The Home Secretary is responsible for receiving and submitting addresses and petitions to the Sovereign and preparing presentations to Parliament.

(xi) *Miscellaneous*. These matters include preparing patents of nobility for peers and formal proceedings for the bestowal of honours; granting licences for scientific experiments on animals; ordering the exhumation and removal of bodies; supervising the control of explosives, firearms and dangerous drugs; deciding general policies on the law of liquor licensing and of shops; the general policy on the law relating to music and dancing; racial integration problems; the regulation of employment of children and young persons.

Finally, the Home Secretary controls the relations with Northern Ireland, the Channel Islands, and Isle of Man, and is the medium of communication between the Established Church and the Crown.

In the discharge of his important duties the Home Secretary is assisted by two Ministers of State (not of Cabinet rank) and one Parliamentary Under-Secretary.

The Central Office of Information

This is a common service Department which produces information and publicity material, and supplies publicity services required by other Government Departments. In the United Kingdom it conducts Government press, television and poster advertising, produces booklets, leaflets, films, television material, exhibitions, photographs and other visual material, and distributes Departmental press notices.

For the Foreign and Commonwealth Office it supplies British information posts overseas with similar publicity material, and manages schemes for promoting the overseas sale of British books, periodicals, and newspapers.

It is responsible for British pavilions at world exhibitions (e.g. Expo' 70) and for exhibition services on behalf of the Board of Trade at overseas trade fairs and British Weeks. It also organizes tours for visitors officially invited to Britain. Nine regional information offices are maintained in England, which provide services for the Home Departments and assist the overseas services by providing material.

The Central Office of Information is administratively responsible to Treasury Ministers, but the Ministers whose Departments it serves are responsible for the policy expressed in its work.

The Board of Inland Revenue

The Board administers the laws relating to (i) income tax and surtax; (ii) corporation tax; (iii) capital gains' tax, (iv) stamp duty; (v) estate duty, and certain other direct taxes. It also advises the Chancellor of the Exchequer on any matters connected with the taxes. The Board of Inland Revenue is also responsible for the valuation of real property (i.e. land and buildings for such purposes as compensation for compulsory purchase) local rates in England and Wales and for estate duty. It also collects tithe redemption annuities.

The Department of the Environment

This is a new Department created in October 1970, and is under the charge of the Secretary of State for the Environment, of Cabinet rank. The new Department unifies into a single Department (i) the former Ministry of Housing and Local Government; (ii) the Ministry of Public Building and Works; and (iii) the Ministry of Transport.

The Secretary of State for the Environment is assisted by the following:

(i) A Minister for Local Government and Development.
(ii) A Minister for Housing and Construction.
(iii) A Minister for Transport Industries.

Each of these Ministers (whose status is that of a Minister in charge of a Department not represented in the Cabinet) has full charge of his functional wing of the Department by delegation from the Secretary of State, and has subordinate Ministers working to him within the field of policy which falls to each.

(i) *The Minister for Local Government and Development* is generally responsible for local government in England, and he exercises powers in regard to the administration of the Planning Acts concerning the use and development of land, sewerage, and other services administered by local authorities. The Minister is responsible also for the sanctioning of loans for most purposes for which local authorities require to borrow money and for acting as the link between local authorities and the central Government.

(ii) *The Minister for Housing and Construction* is responsible for supervising the housing statutes and the national housing programme. His officers keep in close touch with the local housing authorities. Local authority proposals for dealing with slum clearance are also submitted to him.

(iii) *The Minister for Transport* has powers and duties relating to inland transport in Britain. These include certain statutory duties concerning railways, roads, road transport, and inland waterways. He is responsible to Parliament for the nationalized transport undertakings, e.g. the British Railways Board, the British Transport Docks Board, the British Waterways Board, the Transport Holding Company, the National Freight Corporation, and the National Bus Company. The Minister appoints the members of the Boards of these organizations and may determine the broad policies to be pursued, including the formulation of capital investment programmes. He is the highway authority for motorways and trunk roads in England, allocates the funds provided by Parliament for road expenditure (including grants for principal roads vested in local authorities) and has many powers relating to road traffic and road safety.

The Minister is also responsible in Britain for general policy in connection with the development of ports and for their operation in the event of war.

The Department of Industry

This is a new unified Department set up in October 1970. The Department is in charge of the Secretary of State for Industry, who also holds the office of President of the Board of Trade. The Secretary of State (of Cabinet rank) is assisted by three Ministers: (i) the Minister for Trade; (ii) the Minister for Industry; and (iii) the Minister for Aerospace. The status of each of these Ministers is that of a Minister in charge of a separate Department not represented in the Cabinet.

(i) *The Minister for Trade* is responsible (under the President) for overseas trade and export promotion, and for trade and commerce within the United Kingdom. In overseas trade, including the many activities contributing invisible earnings to the balance of payments, the Minister is responsible for external commercial policy (including tariff policy), export policy and services, invisible earnings to the balance of payments. He is also responsible for shipping and tourism, hotels and insurance. Within the United Kingdom, the Minister is concerned with the distributive and service trades, including retail distribution, newspapers, printing, publishing, and films. He has a number of general responsibilities in relation to commerce, including the administration of the Insurance and Companies Acts, patents and copyrights, weights and measures, and hire-purchase legislation.

(ii) *The Minister for Industry* is responsible, under the Secretary of State, mainly for industry in both the public and private sectors. Its functions may be divided into three groups relating to (*a*) industry, (*b*) regional development, and (*c*) research.

(*a*) *Industry*. This group deals with nationalized gas, coal, electricity, and steel industries.

(*b*) *Regional development*. This includes responsibility for regional industrial development, particularly for such aspects as the Local Employment Acts, grants and loans, and industrial development certificates.

(*c*) *Research*. This includes the running of the Department's research establishments, of which seven are concerned with defence supply, and ten are industrial establishments.

The objective of the new Department of Industry is to advise and assist

British industry and commerce to improve their economic and technological strength. It has been charged with establishing a general framework of requirements, incentives, and restraints within which firms and companies will be able to operate as freely as possible to their individual advantage. One of the main functions of the Department is to review the size and methods of the various services now provided to help industry in order to determine whether they are a proper charge on the State and, if so, whether the present system of organization is cost-effective and likely to produce the required result.

(iii) *The Ministry for Aerospace*. This is a newly created Department in the charge of a Minister to take over all the aerospace functions of the aviation group of the former Ministry of Technology, both civil and military. The new Ministry is responsible for research, development and procurement of aircraft, guided weapons and electronic equipment, and for the development and support of civil aircraft. The Minister for Aerospace is responsible to the Secretary of State for Defence for the defence aspects of the work of his Department.

The Paymaster-General's Office

This office acts as a banker for Government Departments (except the Boards of Inland Revenue and Customs and Excise for which separate arrangements exist). Money granted by Parliament is transferred, in such sums as may be required from day to day, from the Exchequer account to the account of the Paymaster-General at the Bank of England. Most payments of Government Departments are made by means of payable orders drawn on the Paymaster-General's Office. The orders are similar to cheques and the recipients (i.e. payees) obtain payments through the commercial banks, whose accounts at the Bank of England are in turn reimbursed by the Paymaster-General's Office.

The Paymaster-General's Office is also responsible for the regular payment of many public service pensions, including those of civil servants, teachers, and members of the National Health Service, as well as the retired pay and pensions of officers of the Armed Forces, their widows and dependants.

The Ministry of Posts and Telecommunications

The Minister is responsible to Parliament for the General Post Office (established as a public corporation in 1969). He is also responsible generally for national broadcasting policy and is the Parliamentary spokesman in regard to the British Broadcasting Corporation under its charter and licence, and to the Independent Broadcasting Authority under the *Television Act, 1964*. Each of these bodies has considerable autonomy.

The Ministry carries out the functions of the former Post Office under the *Wireless Telegraphy Act, 1949*, has regulatory control of radio transmission and reception, and is responsible for the issue of radio licences, including the sale of broadcast receiving licences through the Post Office.

The Stationery Office

Her Majesty's Stationery Office (HMSO) is responsible to the Chancellor of the Exchequer. The office is the central Department for providing Government printing, binding, and publishing, and for providing Government

Departments with office machinery, equipment, and supplies, together with desk stationery.

The Controller of HMSO is the Queen's Printer of Acts of Parliament. The Stationery Office maintains thirteen printing and binding works where about one-third of all official printing is done, the remainder being carried out under contract with private printers. The Stationery Office maintains eight Government bookshops for the sales of official publications.

The Welsh Office

This office is the responsibility of the Secretary of State for Wales, assisted by a Minister of State.

The Secretary of State has full responsibility in Wales for Ministerial functions relating to health, housing, local government, town and country planning, new towns, water and sewerage, roads, forestry, tourism, national parks and historic buildings, and shared responsibility (with the Minister of Agriculture, Fisheries, and Food) for agriculture in Wales. The Secretary of State maintains general oversight of Government policy in Wales, and has certain duties relating to national parks, the National Library and National Museum of Wales. The Department maintains close relationships with other Government Departments in regard to economic and social planning through the Welsh Planning Board and Welsh Council.

The Welsh Office is at Cardiff, but a small Ministerial office is maintained in London.

Scotland

The Secretary of State for Scotland is responsible for a number of functions which, in England and Wales, are distributed among a number of Government Departments. The Secretary of State is assisted by a Minister of State and three Parliament Under-Secretaries of State. The Scottish Law Officers are: (i) The Lord Advocate, and (ii) the Solicitor-General for Scotland.

The Secretary of State's duties are discharged by four main Departments (each of equal status):

(i) The Department of Agriculture and Fisheries for Scotland.
(ii) The Scottish Development Department.
(iii) The Scottish Education Department.
(iv) The Scottish Home and Health Department.

The Secretary of State is responsible for preparing and implementing economic plans for Scotland. He is advised as to this by the Scottish Economic Planning Council and the Scottish Economic Planning Board, together with officials of Government Departments concerned.

Day-to-day administration is carried on in Edinburgh, but each Department has representatives in London (where the Scottish Office is located) for liaison and Parliamentary duties.

The Lord Chancellor

The Lord High Chancellor of Great Britain, more usually known as the Lord Chancellor, ranks eighth in order of precedence in England after the Queen, a status which reflects his importance as a Minister of the Crown chiefly responsible for the administration of justice.

The Lord Chancellor is appointed by the Crown on the advice of the Prime

Minister. His position combines duties which are legislative, executive, and judicial. It is, therefore, an exception to the constitutional doctrine of the 'separation of powers'.

In his legislative capacity the Lord Chancellor presides over the House of Lords. He may take part in its debates and can vote in all of its divisions.

As an executive or administrative officer he is a member of the Cabinet, its chief legal and constitutional adviser and one of its representatives in the House of Lords. He is the Ministerial head of the Land Registry, the Public Record Office and the Public Trustee, and he provides assistance in cases of difficulty in the administration of these departments. He is also responsible for the custody and use of the Great Seal which authenticates important legal documents such as Letters Patent.

In his judicial capacity the Lord Chancellor is head of the judiciary, President of the House of Lords (in its appellate capacity) and President of the Supreme Court. He is the most important member of the Judicial Committee of the Privy Council, and is head of the Chancery Division of the High Court. However, he rarely sits as a judge other than in the House of Lords and the Judicial Committee of the Privy Council. He appoints, in the name of the Crown, the following judicial officers: puisne judges of the High Court, Crown Court, and Circuit Judges, and magistrates. The appointments of legally qualified chairmen of certain administrative tribunals are subject to his approval.

The Lord Chancellor is served by a staff of professional assistants and his office is in the House of Lords. His salary is £20,000.

The Law Officer's Department

The Attorney-General and the Solicitor-General are together known as Law Officers. They are political appointments, and the holders are precluded from private practice.

(*a*) *The Attorney-General* is usually a member of the House of Commons. His duties comprise the following:

(i) He represents the Crown in the courts in civil matters, and may prosecute in important and difficult cases in the criminal courts.

(ii) He advises Government Departments on important legal matters and may take part in many judicial and quasi-judicial proceedings affecting the public interest, e.g. the administration of charities and patent law.

(iii) Certain criminal offences must be reported to the Attorney-General (e.g. by the police) and his consent is necessary before criminal proceedings may be taken in certain cases, e.g. bribery, incest, corrupt practices, and offences against the *Official Secrets Acts, 1911 and 1939*, the *Dangerous Drugs Act, 1951*, the *Public Order Act, 1936*, the *Prevention of Violence (Temporary Provisions) Act, 1939*, and various other Acts.

The Attorney-General superintends the work of the Director of Public Prosecutions. He is head of the English Bar, and points of professional etiquette may be referred to him.

(*b*) *The Solicitor-General* is deputy to the Attorney-General and his duties are similar. He is a barrister-at-law and is usually a member of the House of Commons. By the *Law Officers Act, 1944*, any functions authorised or required to be discharged by the Attorney-General may, unless expressly excluded, be discharged by the Solicitor-General if the office of Attorney-General is vacant, if the Attorney-General is absent or ill, or if the Attorney-General authorizes his deputy to act in any particular case.

The Civil Service
History

Kings, Presidents, dictators, and Governments of all kinds require officials to enforce the orders or laws made by the rulers. In early times the civil servants (clerks and administrators) were employed directly by the King or by his Ministers. Appointment was by patronage, in the gift of the King (or his Ministers) and depended on personal relationship, or friendship or knowing the 'right people'.

Some posts were often given as a reward for political services and were regarded as part of the 'spoils' of office. Many posts were sinecures, the appointee receiving a salary but performing no real work. Sometimes the holders of Government posts were empowered to charge fees for their services to the public.

Such was the broad picture until the end of the eighteenth century, when there was a movement for reform. Royal patronage was reduced, sinecures became fewer and the charging of fees was abolished. The *Reform Act, 1832* left the Civil Service untouched; but attacks were made on its inefficiency and corruption by J. S. Bentham (1748–1832) and J. S. Mill (1806–73). Important reformers, e.g. Benjamin Jowett, Macaulay, Trevelyan and Northcote, became interested in the reform of the Civil Service, particularly following the changes in recruitment by competitive examination to the Indian Civil Service and the reform of the examination system at Oxford and Cambridge.

Parliament appointed a Select Committee to inquire into the cost of the civil administration, and as a result of evidence given to the committee Trevelyan and Northcote were asked to prepare a report on the reorganization of the Permanent Civil Service to ensure its efficiency in administration. This report (the Northcote–Trevelyan Report) of 1854 made 4 main recommendations which laid the foundation of the present Civil Service:

  (i) Recruitment should be by competitive examination.
 (ii) Promotion should be by merit and not seniority.
(iii) The separation of the 'intellectual' from the 'mechanical' side of administration.
(iv) The unification of the Civil Service; the unification of recruitment and inter-departmental promotion.

During the next seventy years these recommendations were all adopted.

In 1855 the Civil Service Commission was set up by Order in Council as an independent body controlling the recruitment of civil servants. It established rules regarding age, ability, knowledge, health, and character of entrants. Originally the Civil Service Commission tested by examination only those nominated by Departmental heads, but after 1870 open competition became the only method of entry to the Civil Service, except for the Foreign Office and Home Office. The Commission is today made up of six Commissioners (with a staff of roughly 1,000) and continues its main function in the appointment of Civil Servants. Formerly the Treasury answered in Parliament for the Commission, but in 1968 the Civil Service Department incorporated the Civil

Service Commission and took over certain former Treasury functions in relation to the Civil Service as a whole, viz. personnel policy, recruitment, training, promotion, pay and conditions of service.

Description Today

Definition. 'A civil servant in Britain is a servant of the Crown (not being the holder of a political or judicial office) who is employed in a civil capacity and whose remuneration is found wholly and directly out of the money voted by Parliament.'

Civil servants are of two kinds: (*a*) non-industrial, and (*b*) industrial. Non-industrial civil servants are members of the staffs of the Government Departments, home and overseas, who are employed as administrators and clerks. The total number in post on 24 November 1975 was 719,000.

Certain industrial workers are also civil servants. These number about 200,000, and include persons working in Royal Ordnance Factories, making weapons, ammunition, etc., and Royal Dockyards such as those at Plymouth, Portsmouth.

Civil servants are 'established', i.e. they are permanent and have a right to a pension on completion of a number of years' service, and 'unestablished', i.e. temporary, having no right to a pension.

For our purposes we shall be mainly concerned with 'non-industrial' civil servants who are concerned with administration, and the first point to note is that since 1945 the work of government has increased greatly in volume and complexity. This is reflected in a considerable increase in the number of people employed and the variety of specialists needed to perform the more complex tasks which fall to modern Governments in civilized states the world over.

Civil Service Classes

It was recognized quite early on that certain administrative work demanded a high level of ability and that other duties were largely routine. In 1920 this division was linked with the educational system and gave rise to three main classes, known as 'Treasury Classes': viz.:

Class	Education	Age
1. Administrative	Degree	22
2. Executive	'A' Levels (G.C.E.)	18+
3. Clerical	'O' Levels (G.C.E.)	15/16

This is the broad division of classes still recognized for entrants. However, we should also note the inclusion into the Civil Service of the important 'professional, scientific, and technical staff' (known as 'Specialist Classes') which are today increasingly important.

In effect, therefore, there are four classes, as follows:

1. Administrative ⎫
2. Executive ⎬ Treasury Classes
3. Clerical ⎭
4. Professional, Scientific and ⎫ Specialist Class
   Technical Staff ⎭

(i) *Administrative Class.* The number of civil servants in this top class is 2,900, plus 1,000 in the Diplomatic Service.

The duties are highly important and include (i) formulation of policy and advising the Minister; (ii) preparing answers to Parliamentary questions; (iii) briefing the Minister with material for public speeches in Parliament and outside; and (iv) administering the particular Government Department.

Most entrants (60 per cent) to the Administrative Class are appointed soon after leaving university. The remainder (40 per cent) are mature entrants

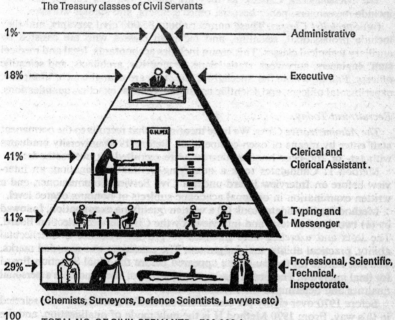

The Treasury classes of Civil Servants

1% — Administrative

18% — Executive

41% — Clerical and Clerical Assistant.

11% — Typing and Messenger

29% — Professional, Scientific, Technical, Inspectorate.

(Chemists, Surveyors, Defence Scientists, Lawyers etc)

100 TOTAL NO. OF CIVIL SERVANTS = 500,000 Approx

Civil Service structure

either as a result of promotion from other classes (mainly from the Executive Class) or by direct entry from outside the service, e.g. from industry, local government, etc.

There are certain ranks within the Administrative Class, viz. Permanent Under-Secretary, Deputy Under-Secretary, Assistant Secretary, Principal, and Assistant Principal.

(ii) *Executive Class.* This class numbers 90,000. Their duties include the day-to-day conduct of government business within the framework of established policy. Executive classes deal with higher work of accounts, revenue collection, management of regional or local offices. Some of the work of the Executive Class overlaps into that of the Administrative Class, there being no absolute dividing line. As we have noted government work itself has expanded in amount, scope and complexity.

(iii) *Clerical Class.* This class numbers 127,000, and the staff undertake the usual clerical work common to all offices, e.g. keeping records, handling particular claims in accordance with established rules, summarizing reports and assisting seniors.

Below the Clerical Class is the Clerical Assistant group. There are some

71,000 Clerical Assistants, and they perform the simpler clerical duties of accounts, operating office machines and registry work such as the filing of documents and the dispatch of files and records.

In addition to the above there is the **Typing Class** (numbering some 26,000) and the **Personal Secretary Class** (about 3,600).

The **Messengerial Classes**, as they are called, number 26,000, and they include messengers, paper keepers, office cleaners, and similar workers.

(iv) *Specialist Classes.* These number about 85,000 civil servants, and they include professional, scientific, and technical classes who are assisted by ancillary technical classes. This group includes accountants, legal and medical staff, engineers, surveyors, statisticians, economists, architects, and scientific officers. Falling within the Specialist Class, too, are draughtsmen, librarians, experimental officers, and scientific assistants with less exacting qualifications.

Recruitment Today.

The Administrative Class. We have mentioned that recruits to the permanent staff enter by means of open competition. Before 1970 university graduates with 1st- or 2nd-class honours degrees were recruited by two methods:

Method I: Candidates took a qualifying written examination, an interview before an Interview Board under a Civil Service Commissioner, and a written examination in optional academic subjects at honours degree level.

Method II: Candidates took (*a*) a written qualifying examination, followed by (*b*) two days' of tests and interviews by the Civil Service Selection Board. The tests and exercises were intended to provide evidence of intellectual ability, practical ability, and judgement. The candidate was awarded marks. The last hurdle (*c*) the candidate appeared before the Final Selection Board for final interview. The Board made its evaluation of the candidate's personal qualities and determined the successful ones.

Before 1970 over eighty per cent of the successful candidates were selected in this way. From 1970 Method II is the only mode of qualification, and the requirement of a 1st- or 2nd-class honours' degree for eligibility is abolished. Method II was used for the selection of mature candidates from outside the service (e.g. from industry, local government, etc.) and will be continued after 1970 for this class of entrant in view of its superiority over the alternative Method I.

Since 1964 members of the Scientific Officer Class who wish to transfer to the Administrative Class have been allowed to apply, and these entrants also take Method II.

The Executive Class. Recruitment is by the following methods:

(i) Open competition for persons between $17\frac{1}{2}$ and 28 years who have two 'A' levels or a degree (those with a degree make up ten per cent of the total recruited in this way).

(ii) A qualifying written examination followed by interview for candidates serving in H.M. Forces and former members of Overseas Civil Service.

(iii) An annual limited competition by written examination and interview open to permanent officers in the Clerical Class between 19 and 24 years.

(iv) Promotion by a Departmental board of clerical officers aged 25 and over.

The Clerical Class. These are recruited by educational attainments of five

'O' levels for candidates of 16 years, and by written examination for older candidates; and by internal departmental examination for clerical assistants.

Clerical Assistants are recruited similarly, the educational standards being lower.

Professional, Technical and Scientific Classes. These are recruited from candidates with specialist or professional qualifications, followed by an interview. Many are recruited on a temporary basis and are then offered permanent appointment later. For the higher posts in these classes a degree or diploma in technology is required; for the lower posts two 'A' levels and four 'O' level passes are required.

Salary and Conditions of Service

The machinery for negotiation on conditions of service affecting the Civil Service as a whole is provided by the **National Whitley Council**, first set up in 1921. The Council is composed of two sides: (i) the Official Side, and (ii) the Staff Side. The Official Side acts in co-operation with the Civil Service Department and is made up of senior Civil Service Department officials and the Establishment Officers from the main Departments. The Staff Side is made up of the various staff associations which civil servants are encouraged to join (e.g. Civil and Public Services Associations, the Society of Civil Servants, the Institution of Professional Civil Servants, and the Association of First Division Civil Servants). The Official Side and the Staff Side negotiate through the Whitley Council machinery. Where there is disagreement between the two sides on matters of pay, hours of service, and leave, provision is made for arbitration.

Salary. The salary which a civil servant receives is based on a fair comparison with that paid for similar work outside the service. Annual increments are usually paid until the civil servant reaches the maximum for the grade to which he belongs. Civil servants hold office 'at the pleasure of the Crown', subject to the *Trade Union and Labour Relations Act, 1974*. In practice, one of the attractions of civil service life is that of security of tenure of employment. Provided he is capable and efficient a civil servant may reasonably expect a full career in the public service and a pension on retirement.

As in most other employments a specified number of hours are laid down as the working week. Certain grades are paid overtime, but members of the higher grades are paid salaries on the assumption that, if need be, they will work long hours without additional pay.

The standard working week is forty-one hours in London and forty-two hours in the provinces. All civil servants receive annual leave, and sick leave on full pay may be granted to permanent civil servants up to six months in any twelve months. If a civil servant's health is permanently impaired he may be retired on medical grounds.

Characteristics of the Civil Service

The State is today the largest employer of labour, and Government touches almost every activity or aspect of life. Generalizations as to features and characteristics of the Civil Service may be misleading particularly where changes in the structure and operation of the service are continuously being made to enable the administrative machine to adapt to modern conditions.

E. N. Gladden states:

The requirements of the Civil Service are that it shall be impartially selected, administratively competent, politically neutral and imbued with the spirit of service to the community.

(i) *Impartial Selection.* Civil Servants are appointed by open competition (see p. 147) and there is no patronage.

(ii) *Permanence.* The Civil Service is permanent; its members continue in office notwithstanding changes of Government or Ministers. This permanence ensures continuity in Government administration. Ministers may come and go; civil servants continue, carrying on services vital to the community. Civil servants have a security of tenure of office and may look forward to a full and worthwhile career with reasonable pay and prospects.

(iii) *Neutrality.* Civil servants are non-political, i.e. they serve different Governments in power impartially and disinterestedly. Lord Attlee, Sir Winston Churchill, and Mr. Harold Wilson have all testified to the vigour of the Civil Service in applying policies. Thus in 1949 Labour proposed that the Iron and Steel Industry be nationalized. In 1951 the Conservatives proposed denationalization. Both policies were carried through by virtually the same officials.

In their relations with the public also civil servants must be impartial. This implies no discrimination, except so far as special circumstances justify this, between one member of the public and another. If Mrs. *A.* of Newcastle on Tyne, is entitled to a pension, Mrs. *B*, from Norwich, is entitled also, if the circumstances are similar.

(iv) *Anonymity.* This means that the Civil Service must work behind the scenes, without praise or blame. We have mentioned that a Minister is primarily concerned with policy. He runs his Department, and is politically responsible for its activities. He will, of course, consult his Permanent Under-Secretary on major policy decisions. The latter may suggest two or three alternative courses, pointing out the difficulties of each or the advantages and disadvantages. Finally the Minister must decide which course to follow. He alone will be answerable in Parliament for the results, good or bad which ensue, not the civil servant. Recently this tradition has been broken. Some civil servants have been named.

> When a Minister knows that he cannot put the blame on his civil servants he is stimulated to judge their advice independently and carefully, and to insist that they shall do their best. That he is answerable to Parliament causes him to insist that others shall be answerable to him. Further, the efficiency of representative government depends upon the use of the expert knowledge of the officials. (Finer: *Theory and Practice of Modern Government*.)

All civil servants within a Department are loyal to their political head and wish to avoid placing the Minister in an embarrassing position in Parliament or in public. They do this by carrying out the Minister's policy faithfully, by applying the appropriate administrative procedures as honestly and fairly as possible and by working efficiently. A good leader inspires confidence in the subordinate staff in the Department: there is mutual trust.

Mistakes and maladministration, however, occur from time to time. Where these happen and a civil servant is at fault he may be removed from the Department or his promotion prospects may be impaired or lost.

The question of Ministerial responsibility for the work of officials within a

Department was highlighted by the **Crichel Down case of 1954**. The facts of this case in brief were that farmland owned by Lt.-Com. Marten was compulsorily purchased by the Ministry of Agriculture in 1937. The land was used during World War II and, subsequently, as a bombing range. By 1952 Lt.-Com. Marten applied to buy back his former farmland which he proposed to use again as agricultural land. Meanwhile officials at the Ministry wanted to acquire the land for a model farm. Many difficulties were placed in the way of Lt.-Com. Marten's repurchase of the land. The former owner persisted in his endeavours and eventually (as a result of pressure in Parliament) the Minister (Sir Thomas Dugdale) agreed to a public inquiry, conducted by Sir Andrew Clark, Q.C. His report criticized the work of the officials of which the Minister had no knowledge and some of which had been performed before the Minister had taken office. A debate was subsequently held in the House of Commons, Sir Thomas Dugdale assumed moral responsibility and as a result of pressure from his own political backbenchers he resigned his office. It should be noted that Sir Thomas Dugdale had not forfeited the Prime Minister's confidence.

Sir David Maxwell Fyfe (later Lord Kilmuir), the Home Secretary in 1954, made the following statement during the debate:

> Where action has been taken by a civil servant of which the Minister disapproves and has no prior knowledge, and the conduct of the official is reprehensible, then there is no obligation on the part of the Minister to endorse what he believes to be wrong, or to defend what are clearly shown to be the errors of his officers. The Minister is not bound to approve an action of which he did not know, or of which he disapproves. But of course he remains constitutionally responsible to Parliament for the fact that something has gone wrong, and he alone can tell Parliament what has occurred and render an account of his stewardship.

By the very nature of the complexity of government work today a Minister cannot know all that goes on in his own Department, much less take all the decisions done in his name. The Crichel Down case alerted public attention to the difficulty of an individual in getting his case aired in public, and calling the decision-making civil servants to account for their actions where maladministration is alleged or prejudice occurs. This and similar cases showed the need for some machinery to enable grievances to be brought to light and the inadequacies or inefficiencies of public administration to be exposed. The *Parliamentary Commissioner Act, 1967*, was eventually passed into law and the office of **Parliamentary Commissioner for Administration** was created (see p. 266).

Criticism of Civil Servants

Bearing in mind that recruitment to the Civil Service is now by open competition; that candidates for the top positions must be highly qualified intellectually; show qualities of leadership; possess personal qualities of service and a capacity to work with others; what criticisms may be made of the service? The main standard of judgement is **efficiency**. The difficulty of measuring efficiency in public administration is great, mainly because the tasks of Government are so complex.

The general criticisms which are popularly made of the Civil Service are:

(i) Lack of vitality, absence of imagination, drive, and initiative.
(ii) Addiction to 'red-tape' and precedent, leading to inflexibility.

(iii) Bureaucracy.

(iv) The Administrative Class tends to be made up of persons of middle-class, and are therefore drawn from a narrow social background.

(v) Tendency to departmentalism, i.e. strong support for a civil servant's own Department, to the detriment of public administration as a whole.

(vi) Excessive caution and an unwillingness to admit mistakes.

(vii) Higher civil servants assume excessive self-importance, yet are protected by the anonymity of the Civil Service from criticism for errors.

Some of these criticisms may be true. Doubtless there are some members of the Administrative Class who lack vitality; some may have been worn out by the administrative machine. The same point may be made of those working in the lower clerical classes who can see no way to improve their lot by promotion. A civil servant who is expected to conform to tradition and the rules of the Service or his Departmental head is hardly likely to show initiative or drive if by so doing he will antagonize his superiors. Precedent and 'red-tape' are inherent in governments of all kind. Formal procedures must be laid down in all offices and these must be followed if chaos is to be avoided. Order is better than disorder. A file in writing is prepared and all applications from the public are dealt with in the same way. The simplest example is the income tax return. Documents have to be prepared, facts stated by the member of the public are recorded in the proper column, the formula of assessment is applied to each, and the amount due is notified. In unusual cases a civil servant will look for a precedent from past files to indicate how he is to deal with a problem. Precedents are useful guides. What was approved in the past will (one assumes) be applied in the future, unless there are contrary reasons. In law and public administration precedents are valuable in achieving certainty.

Bureaucracy is allied to the problem of precedent. Civil servants are trained in the methodical treatment of claims, petitions, applications, and complaints. This leads to officialism which in turn is criticized as inhumanity or indifference to individual and personal merits of the claimant. As we shall note later the Civil Service has its own Organization and Methods Branches (O. and M.) which reviews continuously the methods and procedures used in all departments.

The criticism that the Administrative Class largely emanates from the middle classes is no longer true. Changes in the educational system and particularly the more open entries to Oxford and Cambridge Universities has meant that candidates for the higher posts are drawn from a wider range of classes. Since 1964 there had been (according to the Fulton Report of 1968) 'a distinct and progressive change towards greater representation of people from less privileged backgrounds'. And, in its assessment of Method II procedure (see p. 144) the report stated:

> The principles on which it operates are sound and its duration is appropriate in the light of those principles; it provides equality of opportunity; it maintains a proper balance between the personal and intellectual qualities which are needed in the Administrative Class. It confers no advantage on those who merely have a small veneer of social graces, but it does give due weight to effectiveness in personal relations.

Departmentalism is inevitable in all organizations. It is known in colleges and schools, in industry and Government. It engenders pride in one's own

Ministry, loyalty between members, and a common ideal. It may stimulate competition between departments in service to the public. The difficulties may be overcome by proper and effective co-ordination, particularly by Ministers and the permanent heads of the Civil Service.

As to excessive caution in public affairs one has to bear in mind that any individual who is unjustly treated by a public official (civil servant, local government official, or the police) may complain to his Member of Parliament. The result may be a Parliamentary Question which exposes the Minister responsible to public attack, or, if the matter is serious enough, a public inquiry (see the Crichel Down Case). All civil servants are aware of the risk and tend to exercise that care which will avoid exposing the Minister (and indeed himself) to criticism. Moreover, the Press is always alert to maladministration and freely and openly attacks injustices arising from carelessness of public officials.

It is doubtful whether the higher civil servants are excessively self-important. Certainly they must have ability, exercise influence at the centre of government power, and are therefore important by right. It is their job to point out the snags of a Minister's policy, to act as a brake at times rather than a spur, to understand how the Minister thinks; to set aside their own vision on policy, and to be disinterested. The absolute 'non-entity' of the British administrator is, it has been said, his chief merit. The truth is that the main characteristic of the British Civil Service is that it is non-political, and successive Prime Ministers (Attlee, Churchill, and Wilson) have all paid tribute to the capacity of the Civil Service to serve Governments (Conservative and Labour) with equal vigour.

Training

Most civil servants on entry into the profession are untrained in the techniques of administration. Some entrants to the Professional and Technical classes must be professionally qualified before appointment, e.g. doctors, lawyers, and certain scientists and engineers.

Before 1943 civil servants who were appointed to administrative posts (at the top or bottom) 'learned by doing', performing the simpler tasks first and gradually moving on to the more complex and responsible. The method (or absence of method) was wasteful and uneconomical overall. Before 1943 the Civil Service gave little encouragement to those already established to prepare for degrees or diplomas in suitable subjects, e.g. public administration or political or government subjects. In 1943 a Committee on the Training of Civil Servants was set up under the chairmanship of Sir Ralph Assheton (a former Civil Servant). Its report criticized the lack of system and recommended a three-month course for new entrants to the Service on the general aspects of administration, periodic refresher courses, and up to twelve months' leave for members of the Administrative Class on reaching 30 years of age to carry out approved research. Financial restrictions in the 1950s prevented the full implementation of the Report.

The Fulton Report of 1968, however, gave added impetus to training and the position today is that full-time Training Officers and instructors are appointed to all the major Departments of Government. Their task is to state the training needs of the staff and to organize courses, general and technical, to provide for the varying requirements.

Civil servants under 18 are granted Day Release to attend local Technical

Colleges or Colleges of Further Education. Adult staff are assisted financially and by the giving of 'time off' to undertake private study to enable them to pursue studies leading to recognized educational or professional qualifications. Certain civil servants may be granted sabbatical leave to undertake research in areas of interest to themselves and their departments.

The co-ordination of training is carried out by the Training Requirements Division of the Civil Service Department which has central responsibility for personnel management, including training and career management, as well as manpower requirements and the development and dissemination of administrative and managerial techniques.

The main training centre is the Civil Service College, at Sunningdale Park, Berks. In addition there is a London Centre for training and a further centre in Edinburgh. Courses and seminars are run on a variety of subjects: management, economics, statistics, industrial growth, social administration, operational research, computers and information systems, and other specialized courses. Some civil servants are permitted to attend external management courses at Business Schools, the Administrative Staff College, and elsewhere.

Methods of training include lectures, closed-circuit television and video tape recordings, instructional films and programmed learning as well as 'on the job' training. Civil servants are regularly moved between the different branches of the Government Department to which they are attached, and sometimes between Departments to give wide experience of Civil Service work.

Generally, therefore, we may say that there has been a considerable expansion of training within the Service to enable personnel to keep abreast of the changes in society and to meet the demands for an efficient public service.

Political and Private Activities of Civil Servants

All Civil Servants enjoy the electoral franchise in common with all other adult citizens; they may vote in Parliamentary and local elections, but there are necessarily some restrictions on their activities.

The Masterman Committee on the Political Activities of Civil Servants in its report (Cmnd. 7718 of 1949) stated:

(i) In a democratic society it is desirable for all citizens to have a voice in the affairs of the State and for as many as possible to play an active part in public life.

(ii) The public interest demands the maintenance of political impartiality in the Civil Service and of confidence in that impartiality as an essential part of the structure of Government in this country.

The broad position is that industrial staff and the minor grades of the clerical class (numbering about 60 per cent of the service) are not restricted at all politically; they may stand for Parliament and represent a political party. Any such candidate must resign his appointment before nomination day on the understanding that if not elected he will be reinstated in his previous capacity within a week of the declaration of the election result. This group was categorized as 'below the line'.

Members of the Executive and Administrative classes are not allowed to participate in national politics at all. They must abstain from party office, speeches, canvassing, and public manifestations of views that might associate them with a political organization or political controversy. We have already noted that one of the leading characteristics of the British Civil Service is that it is 'non political', and it was noted by the Masterman Committee that 'any weakening of the existing tradition of political impartiality would be the first step in the creation of a "political" Civil Service . . .' Such a system would be contrary to the public interest and, in the long run, the Civil Service itself.'

In practice, few civil servants take an active part in politics. Entry to the Civil Service is a voluntary act, and those who cannot accept its conditions, particularly its neutrality in politics, can seek employment elsewhere.

Civil servants in all classes are subject to the very wide provisions of the *Official Secrets Acts, 1911–39*, which prohibit, for example, the making, obtaining, or communicating to any unauthorized person any sketch, plan, model, or other document or information which might be useful to an enemy for any purpose prejudicial to the safety of the State. The *Prevention of Corruption Act, 1906*, also contains wide provisions which are designed to protect the State against corruption by its officials, e.g. *A*, a civil servant, receives £1,000 from *B*, a public contractor, on condition that *B* is awarded a contract to build a Government office, bridge, etc.

A civil servant must not use his official position to further his private interests and is subject to certain restrictions in commerce and business. Thus, he may not hold private interests in public contracts, and he may not use official information in writing, broadcasting, or lecturing without the approval of his Department.

Security. The general rule is that the private political views of civil servants are not of official concern. But, there are some Civil Service duties, e.g. those connected with defence, foreign relations, the Armed Forces, in which secrecy is vital to State security. Civil servants employed on these matters must be reliable. Any civil servant who is known to be a member of, or actively associated with Communist or with Fascist organizations, or is known to be a 'security risk', will not, therefore, be employed on secret work. A 'screening' process known as the Positive Vetting System is operated to check the credentials of individuals before a civil servant undertakes secret work. Where a civil servant is found to have Communist or Fascist sympathies he may be dismissed or transferred to other work.

Each Government Department is responsible for its own internal security. The Security Service, under a Director-General, operates independently and is responsible to the Home Secretary. In addition to the above arrangements there is a Security Commission which may investigate and report on breaches of security in the public service. Such investigation may only be carried out if requested by the Prime Minister in consultation with the leader of the Opposition.

Crown Proceedings

The expression 'the Crown' may be used to describe (i) the Sovereign in her personal capacity, and (ii) the Sovereign as Head of State, in her corporate capacity. The Crown, in its corporate capacity, includes Her Majesty's Ministers, the Government Departments, and the Civil Service.

Two ancient maxims of the common law determined the relationship of the Crown to a subject: 'No action can be brought against the King personally, for he cannot be sued in his Courts'; and 'The King can do no wrong'. The Sovereign could not be sued personally for any alleged wrongs he may have committed in person. As a corporate body, the Crown was similarly immune from legal liability. The doctrine of vicarious liability (whereby at common law a master is liable for the wrongs of a servant committed in the course of his employment) did not apply to the Crown.

Petition of Right

The apparently harsh principle whereby the Crown escaped liability in contract and tort (a civil wrong) was mitigated, however, by an action known as the Petition of Right. This lay for the recovery of:

(a) Real or personal property in the possession of the Crown (the subject claiming restitution or compensation).
(b) Money due under contract made with the Crown by its servants.
(c) Unascertained damages for breach of contract.
(d) Sums payable to the petitioner under a grant from the Crown.

The *Petition of Right Act, 1860*, regulated the procedure to be followed by the applicant seeking redress in claims of a contractual nature mentioned above. However, it was first necessary to obtain the *fiat* (order) of the Attorney-General before proceedings could be commenced. There was no appeal against his refusal of the *fiat*, and the Act itself did not apply to claims in tort against the Crown.

Although the Crown itself was immune from legal action in respect of torts committed by a servant in the course of his duties, nevertheless it was possible to sue the Crown servant personally. For example, where a Ministry's van driver negligently knocked down a pedestrian, action could be taken against the 'tortfeasor' personally. In such cases the Government Department stood behind the civil servant and paid damages awarded against him. This protection was a matter of grace, and the claimant had no legal right to *enforce* payment from the Crown.

This action has been abolished, and is now subject to the *Trade Union and Labour Relations Act, 1974*.

The Crown as Employer

The Crown is now one of the largest employers of labour in the State. The legal relationship of master and servant in private life is governed by both the common law and statute. Each party has rights and duties in respect of the other, such rights and duties being enforceable in a court of law. In regard to Crown service, however, the position is somewhat different in that a civil servant holds office 'at the pleasure of the Crown'.

The phrase 'Crown employment' does not include employment in the police, the National Health Service or the local government service.

Generally British civil servants enjoy greater security of employment than most people. In fact, the Crown endeavours to act as a model employer, and internal Treasury regulations ensure just treatment of employees both during employment and on retirement. What it does mean is that the civil servant cannot sue the Crown at law to enforce 'rights' which apply in the normal relationship of master and servant.

The Crown Proceedings Act, 1947

This act was passed as a result of the unsatisfactory state of the law regarding legal proceedings against the Crown. The main object was to place the Crown in the same position, as far as possible, as a private person or employer;

i.e. able to sue and be sued for breaches of contracts or for torts committed by servants. The Act does not affect the Queen's personal immunity from legal proceedings.

Liability in Contract. The Act provides that actions for breach of contract may now be brought as of right against the Crown.

Liability in Tort. Section 2(1) of the Act provides that 'the Crown shall be subject to all those liabilities in tort to which, if it were a person of full age and capacity, it would be subject:

(a) In respect of torts committed by its servants or agents.
(b) In respect of any breach of those duties which a person owes to his servants or agents at common law by reason of being their employer.
(c) In respect of any breach of the duties attaching at common law to the ownership, occupation, possession or control of property'.

As an example of (b): A master is under a common law duty to provide reasonably safe plant and machinery for his employees. If, therefore, the Crown provides a faulty vehicle for use by its servant B, as a result of which C is injured, an action will lie against the Crown under s.2(1).

As an example of (c): A private person visits the local office of the Inspector of Taxes to discuss his income tax assessment. A defective electric light fitting falls from the ceiling and lacerates the caller's head. An action will lie for the tort at the instance of the injured person.

Procedure. Action is brought against the appropriate Government Department. The Treasury publishes a list of the Departments and names the solicitor to accept service of process on behalf of each Department. Where the Department is not named, or uncertainty exists as to the Department's identity, the Attorney-General may be made defendant.

The legal action then follows the usual procedure of a High Court or county court action. The Act provides, however, that:

(a) Judgement against the Department cannot be enforced by the ordinary methods of levying execution or attachment. The Department is required to pay the amount certified due as damages.
(b) An injunction and a decree of specific performance are inappropriate to the Crown. Instead, the court makes an order declaratory of the rights of the parties.
(c) No order for restitution of property will be made against the Crown. Instead, the court may declare the plaintiff entitled as against the Crown.

Special provision is made in the Act with regard to the Armed Forces of the Crown.

The Armed Forces. Nothing done or omitted by a member of the Armed Forces of the Crown while on duty shall subject him or the Crown to liability for inflicting death or personal injury on another member of the Armed Forces if (i) the latter is on duty or is on any land, premises, ship, aircraft, or vehicle used for the purposes of the Armed Forces, and if (ii) the Minister of Social Security certifies that the victim will receive an award.

Adams v. *War Office* (1955). *A* was killed on duty by a shell fired by other members of the Armed Forces on duty. The Minister certified that *A*'s death was attributable to service for the purpose of entitlement to an award, but it was also held that *A*'s father did not satisfy the conditions of the Royal Warrant under which parents might claim a pension in respect of the loss of a son.

Crown Servant. Section 2(6) of the Act defines the term 'officer' (in respect of whose actions the Crown now assumes liability in tort) as follows: the 'officer' shall (i) be appointed directly or indirectly by the Crown; and (ii) be paid in respect of his duties as an officer of the Crown at the material time *wholly* out of the Consolidated Fund, moneys provided by Parliament, the Road Fund, or a fund certified by the Treasury.

The police are not *wholly* paid out of such funds, hence the Crown is not subject to liability for torts committed by them.

Exercises.

1. 'The King', said Bagehot, 'has three rights: the right to be consulted; the right to encourage; and the right to warn. And a King of great sense and sagacity would want no others.' Discuss.

2. The Queen is said to be the 'fountain of justice' and the 'fountain of honour'. Explain.

3. 'Royal pageantry and pomp are significant features of the British way of life.' Discuss.

4. Name the main functions of a Prime Minister.

5. The power of a Prime Minister is not without limits. What are they?

6. Enumerate the qualities you consider most desirable in a Prime Minister.

7. Trace the history of the Cabinet.

8. What are the main functions of the Cabinet?

9. What is meant by the phrase 'Ministerial Responsibility'?

10. Describe the Cabinet Committees.

11. Describe briefly the organization of a Government Department.

12. What part is played by Advisory Committees in assisting a Minister to run his Department? Discuss the composition of some.

13. For what functions is the Civil Service Department responsible? Who controls this Department?

14. Who are Parliamentary Counsel to the Treasury?

15. What duties fall to be discharged by the Home Secretary?

16. Discuss the duties of the Minister of the Environment?

17. 'Road and Rail Transport are now so important to all of us that a Minister should be placed in sole charge answerable only to the Cabinet and Parliament.' Do you agree?

18. Outline the duties of Paymaster-General.

19. 'The Minister for Posts and Telecommunications has virtually nothing to do. The BBC, IBA, and the Post Office are all public corporations supposedly independent of Government.' Do you agree?

20. Outline the duties of the Lord Chancellor.

21. What duties are carried out by the Law Officers of the Crown?

22. Outline the history of the Civil Service.

23. How do candidates now qualify to enter the Administrative Class of the Civil Service?

24. Describe the characteristics of the Civil Service.

25. 'It is absurd that a Minister should have to resign over a dispute about a piece of farm land' (Crichel Down). Comment, and outline Sir David Maxwell Fyfe's views on the question of responsibility for administrative error.

26. 'The Civil Service is eaten out with red-tape, precedent, bureaucracy and dilatoriness.' Do you agree?

27. *A*, who is a clerical assistant in the Civil Service, wants to stand for Parliament as an anarchist. Advise him.

28. What provisions exist to maintain security within the section of the Civil Service handling specially secret matters?

CHAPTER FIVE

PUBLIC CORPORATIONS

Introduction

The basic functions of the State are (i) the maintenance of internal order and (ii) defence against external aggression. These duties remain today, but we have already noted that the State has increased the range of its functions, e.g. by creating social services of many kinds, so that we have today what is termed a Welfare State.

The main philosophy until the end of the nineteenth century was *laissez-faire* which implied that any goods or services required were best supplied by private enterprise. The Government ensured peace and good order, in which atmosphere private initiative and enterprise could flourish. This lasted until the Great War (1914–18) by which time the Government responsibilities were mainly limited to:

(i) Administration of Justice.
(ii) Defence (by maintaining Armed Forces).
(iii) Education (elementary).
(iv) Conducting foreign relations.
(v) Regulating conditions under which private enterprise could flourish, e.g. by administering Factory Acts, Weights and Measures Acts, and similar statutes.

These matters were dealt with by various Government Departments, the main ones being the Home Office, the War Office, the Admiralty, the Board of Education, the Foreign Office, the Board of Trade, and the Treasury.

The State itself did not initially carry on an industry; that was not its function. But, of course, there is no reason why a State should not do so. We may note the Communist States profess this to be one of their basic beliefs. We concede that a public service or an industry may be administered (i) by the State itself acting directly through a Government Department or indirectly through local government, or (ii) by private enterprise, acting through a public or private company, the main interest of which is profitability. In the first case the State owns and directs the service or industry and is accountable to Parliament, while in the second case private enterprise is not accountable to Parliament and must make a profit or go bankrupt.

In this chapter we are concerned with a third form or method, namely the public corporation, which is neither a Government Department nor a public or private company, but a semi-independent body which purports to combine the benefits or advantages of both forms.

The idea of the semi-independent body is not new. In Tudor times Parliament appointed **Commissioners of Sewers** to supervise the disposal of sewage (a basic health measure of great importance). In the eighteenth century **Turnpike Trusts** were set up to supervise the provision and maintenance of roads locally in the towns and counties. Commissions for local lighting and paving in towns, and Commissions to provide and supervise canals were also set up. The Commissioners were appointed to perform limited functions, each group of men being responsible for a particular job. It was the age of *ad hoc* authorities, for local government authorities did not exist to do the necessary work or provide the services.

The practice of appointing *ad hoc* authorities continued. School Boards were created by the *Elementary Education Act, 1870*. In 1834 **Poor Law Commissioners** were appointed to provide a public service to enforce the poor law throughout the country. Many of these powers were taken over by the local authorities created in the nineteenth century. The *Municipal Corporations Act, 1835*, gave corporate status to the towns; the *Local Government Act, 1888*, set up **County Councils** and **County Borough Councils**; in 1894 the **Urban District Councils** were created. All these authorities absorbed a number of the public services formerly carried on by the *ad hoc* Commissions and Boards (e.g. roads, sewers, canals, paving, lighting, and education.)

Other notable examples of semi-independent bodies performing public services were the Mersey Docks and Harbour Board (1857) and the Port of London Authority (1908) which administered the docks at Liverpool and London respectively; the Metropolitan Water Board (1902), and the London Passenger Transport Board (1933). Each of these authorities was created to bring order into the use and facilities of the ports or to create a unified system of passenger transport in London. These particular matters were important nationally and were considered to be outside the scope and function of local government, and the Boards continued their existence independently.

We note that the special bodies mentioned did not come directly under Government control, though some of the public corporations (as they became to be called), included representatives of a Government Department on their executive bodies (i.e. the Boards) in whom powers of management were vested.

Certain other bodies were created similarly constituted, notably the Forestry Commission (1919), the Central Electricity Board (1926), the British Broadcasting Corporation (1927), and the British Overseas Airways Corporation (1939), all following the same sort of pattern of previous bodies mentioned, i.e. the members of the corporations were appointed by the Government, but the bodies themselves had a degree of independence of the Government by which they were individually and collectively appointed.

Nationalized Industries and Services

Since its creation in 1900 the Labour Party has been committed to the policy of the nationalization or common ownership of the basic industries of the nation. When, therefore, the Labour Government came to power in 1945 under Mr. C. Attlee, it already had a definite programme of nationalization to carry through, and one of creating the Welfare State. The Port of London Authority, the London Passenger Transport Board and the other authorities already in existence were models on which the nationalization programme of the basic industries were built. Coal, electricity, gas, and transport industries were nationalized by means of statutes, and public corporations were created. These have been described as 'managerial–economic' bodies and are highly important in the nation's economy.

The Labour Government created the following:

(i) The National Coal Board (1946).
(ii) The British Electricity Authority (1947).

(iii) The Gas Council (1948).
(iv) The Transport Commission (1947).
(v) The Iron and Steel Corporation (1949).

The former owners and shareholders were divested of their ownership and were compensated by the Government for their properties which were then vested in the **Corporations** or **Boards** set up by the various statutes to manage and supervise the industries as efficiently as possible in the interest of the public. How far this has been achieved is always open to controversy.

The Conservative Party has traditionally opposed nationalization as ultimately leading to the totalitarian state and viewed the inroads of Government control of industry with suspicion. The outcome of the political clash between the main parties has been the creation of the **public corporations** of the twentieth century, some important examples of which we shall later consider in some detail.

Apart from the industrial corporations (sometimes called 'managerial–economic corporations') such as those created for coal, gas, electricity, transport, etc., there are also non-industrial corporations (sometimes called 'managerial social corporations') which were created shortly after World War II to provide social services such as the National Health Service, National Assistance, and new towns. The *National Health Service Act, 1946,* imposed on the Minister of Health a duty to create a comprehensive health service. The *New Towns Act, 1946* (now consolidated in Acts of 1965 and 1968) empowers a Minister to order the site of a new town to contain the overspill of city populations where these have become too crowded. Thirty-two new towns have been, or are being established in Britain, and their origin is due to the creation of a public corporation to initiate the acquisition of land and to develop the site for the new inhabitants. The **Development Corporations**, as they are called, produce a master plan, the capital cost is advanced from public funds, officials are appointed, houses, schools, etc., are built, and on completion the town becomes a local authority with powers similar to those possessed by all similar bodies.

The **Arts Council** was set up in 1946 and given a grant of money to encourage cultural life in Britain. Indeed the number of the corporations is too great for detailed account to be given here.

Government Department Form of Organization

Where a Government Department carries on a service or an industry, a Minister is appointed to be in charge of it and is politically responsible for its administration. His policy will be criticized in Parliamentary debates, for example, and he will be accountable to Parliament for the decisions of civil servants in the Department in the normal way (see p. 118 regarding Political Responsibility). Estimates will have to be submitted and approved by Parliament. The Department will be subject to close control by the Expenditure Committee, (see p. 100), the Public Accounts' Committee (see p. 102), and the Treasury.

It is argued that Parliament is not the place for debates on details of business or commercial administration. Its main function is the discussion of major political issues. M.P.s and Ministers lack the experience, technical knowledge, and skill to exercise proper control and management of an industry. Civil servants who are appointed to run or manage an industry frequently lack enterprise and initiative and the desire to make a profit—qualities which are the life-blood of successful commercial undertakings. Moreover, if they are subject to attack or criticism in or out of Parliament they will tend to play for safety, avoiding the risks which bold and imaginative policies entail. A cautious, middle-of-the-road approach ensures a more peaceful existence. Civil servants tend also to follow precedent, the usual procedures, and these tend to make for inefficiency and unprofitability. Each item of expenditure may be questioned and each item of service is provided at the lowest possible cost. **State-owned industries** are usually monopolies. This lack of competition is traditionally harmful and wasteful.

On the other hand efficient **private enterprise** is usually characterized by (i) the need for profit, (ii) speedy production of goods or services at the lowest cost and sale at the best price, (iii) all financial risk being taken by the owner, e.g. he invests his capital, in buildings, plant, or goods, provided the ultimate end is a potentially higher overall profit, (iv) competition, which ensures greater efficiency, since the owner who produces the best goods at the lowest price will command a market.

General Characteristics of Public Corporations

The following are the main features common to all public corporations:

(i) *Creation*. They are corporations created by statute.

(ii) *Ownership*. The corporations are publicly owned.

(iii) *Legal Capacity*. The corporations can sue and be sued in their corporate names.

(iv) *Employees*. They are not civil servants. Each corporation recruits its own staff and lays down its own conditions of service.

(v) *Profit*. The corporations are not solely profit-making, but each corporation must balance its accounts taking one year with another.

(vi) *Accountability*. The corporations are exempt from Parliamentary control of their day-to-day management but not policy.

(vii) *Finance*. The corporations obtain revenue from the goods and services they provide. They may borrow money from the Government (the Treasury) for long-term capital development. They do not submit estimates to Parliament.

Examples of Public Corporations

The following notes will be of assistance in showing the main features of a few of the public corporations prominent in national life today:

National Coal Board

This body was created by the *Coal Industry (Nationalization) Act, 1946*. The Board comprises a Chairman and eight to eleven members. The Board is appointed by the Minister of Power. Members must be paid and are selected from qualified persons. The Minister may give directions of a general character on matters appearing to affect the national interest, after consultation. The main function of the Board is to work and get coal, to secure the efficient development of coal-mining industry, and to make supplies of coal available. The Industrial Coal Users and Domestic Users Consumers' Councils exist to allow of official representation to the Board by the users. The NCB received heavy financial support (£47 million) under the *Coal Industry Act, 1967*, to relieve hardship caused by the diminution of the coal industry.

Electricity

The Central Electricity Generating Board was set up under the *Electricity Act, 1957*. It comprises a Chairman and seven to nine members, one of whom is Deputy Chairman. The Board members are appointed by the Minister of Power and must be chosen from qualified persons. The principal function of the Board is that it may give directions to the Area Boards (see below) and must co-ordinate the distribution of electricity. It may generate and acquire supplies of electricity.

The Electricity Council was constituted by the *Electricity Acts, 1947 and 1957*. The Council comprises a Chairman, two Deputy Chairmen, and three members, together with three members of the CEGB, and the Chairmen of the Area Boards. The Minister of Power appoints only the Chairman and the Deputy Chairmen, and he may give such directions of a general nature as seem to be in the national interest. The principal function of the Electricity Council is to advise the Minister and to promote and assist maintenance and development by Area Boards of 'an efficient, co-ordinated and economical system of electricity supply'.

The Area Boards. There are twelve Area Boards. All owe their existence to the Electricity Acts mentioned above. Each Area Board consists of a Chairman and five to seven members. One may be Deputy Chairman. The Minister of Power appoints from qualified persons, and may give similar directions as those to the Electricity Council. The Area Boards' function is to acquire bulk electricity, to carry out efficient and economical distribution in the Area for which each of the Boards operates. There is a Consumer Council attached to each Area Board.

Gas

The British Gas Corporation comprises a Chairman, Deputy, and the Chairmen of the Area Gas Boards (see below). The Minister of Power appoints the members who must be paid. The Chairman and the Deputy Chairman must be qualified persons. The Minister may give directions of a general character after consultation. The function and duty is to advise the Minister, to promote and assist the efficient exercise and performance by the Area Boards of their functions.

The Area Boards. There are twelve Area Boards. Each Board is made up of a Chairman, Deputy, and four to six members, plus the Chairman of the Area Consultative Council. The members must be paid, and the Chairman and Deputy Chairman must have had experience and shown capacity in gas supply. The Minister may give directions of a general character after consultation with the Gas Council and the Board. The duty of each Area Gas Board is to develop and maintain an efficient co-ordinated and economical system of gas supply for their area. There is a Gas Consultative Council attached to each Area Board through whom the public may make representations or complain.

Hospitals

The *National Health Service Act, 1946*, imposed on the Minister of Health a duty to create a comprehensive health service. Hospital and specialist services are administered on behalf of the Minister.

The *National Health Service* (*Reorganization*) *Act, 1973*, created a three-tier structure:

(i) Regional Health Authority (14);
(ii) Area Health Authority (90);
(iii) District Management teams.

The chain of responsibility moves upwards from district to area, to region, and finally to the Department of Health.

The Act specifies a number of bodies—e.g. local authorities, trade unions, and professional organizations—which the Secretary of State must consult before making appointments to the regional authorities. Local authorities nominate four members to area health authority, and the regional authorities must consult the appropriate bodies before making their nominations.

How far the reorganization brought about on 1 April 1974, at the same time as the local government reorganization, will promote democracy and efficiency within the hospital and medical services and the ancillary services is too early to judge. The reorganization aims at integration, which has meant the transfer of certain services (e.g. the ambulance service) from local government to the NHS.

In Wales, Scotland, and Northern Ireland there are no regional authorities; each area authority is directly responsible to the relevant Minister and central department. In Northern Ireland both health and personal social services are the responsibility of one authority in each area.

The British Broadcasting Corporation

The BBC was incorporated under Royal Charter as successor to the British Broadcasting Company, Ltd., whose licence expired in 1926. Then followed the grant of a Charter which expired in 1964. The present Charter expires in 1976. The BBC forms an exception to the general rule in that it owes its corporate status to the Charter and not statute.

The BBC was deliberately created in this form to avoid the possibility of political interference in so important a matter as broadcasting—radio or TV.

The Chairman, Vice-Chairman, and other Governors (ten) are appointed by the Crown. The Governors receive £1,000 per annum and serve part-time.

The BBC is financed by revenue from receiving licences for the Home Services and by a Grant in Aid from Parliament for External Services. The total number of television licences in force (1974) was 17,324,570 (11,766,424 monochrome, and 5,558,146 colour). Radio-only licences were abolished on 1 February, 1971.

The Independent Broadcasting Authority

This was created in 1954 to provide public television services of information, education, and entertainment. The *Television Act, 1954*, was renewed in 1964 for a further twelve years. The Chairman and members of the Authority are appointed by the Minister of Posts and Telecommunications.The programmes transmitted from the Authority's forty-five stations are provided by fifteen independent programme contractors whose revenue derives from the sale, subject to controls exercised by the Authority, of advertising time. The contractors pay a rent to the Authority to meet the IBA's own requirements and a levy based on net advertising revenue to the Exchequer.

There is a Chairman, a Deputy Chairman and nine Governors, and like the

BBC it has its Director-General with supporting staff. Its general role is that it acts as a competitor with the BBC but like the BBC is a public corporation and adopts similar standards of public responsibility.

Both the BBC and the IBA have a considerable degree of freedom in the programmes they produce, but where matters are raised in Parliament, the responsible Minister is the Minister of Posts and Communications.

Since 1972 the IBA's function has been extended to local radio.

Management

One problem facing the nationalized industries is the engagement of outstanding individuals to fill the management posts at the head of the important industries entrusted to their direction. As to salary, the nationalized industries stand half-way between private industry and the Civil Service. It is clear that unless attractive salaries are paid the best men will not accept the posts available. The Chairman of the NCB, the Chairman of the Gas Council and the Chairman of the Electricity Council each receives £22,500. The Chairmen of the twelve Electricity Boards each receives salaries of £12,000—17,000.

Some of the members of the corporations are part-time and others full-time. The constitution of each of the Boards varies widely. There are former senior civil servants, industrialists, professional men (lawyers, accountants, etc.) university professors, engineers, scientists, and senior personnel of the Armed Forces. Sometimes senior trade union leaders have been appointed to management posts. Engagements are offered for five years, on occasions, but at any time the Minister may dismiss a member or call upon a particular individual to resign.

Where part-time members are appointed they may continue other employment. Full-time members must devote their whole time to the particular corporation.

The selection of the best personnel is one of the current problems. The leadership of an industry is vital to its success; the increasing complexity of the technical aspects demands that the managers must know more of the detail of the industry and they must possess the personal qualities which command respect of the lower ranks of the industry and the public—the consumers or customers at large.

The tendency today is to appoint to the management career administrators or scientists already employed within the particular industry.

Personnel Policy

The efficiency of an industry depends on good management guiding the industry and efficient execution at all levels, from the top administrator or scientist to the newest recruit in the office or on the factory floor. Each corporation is responsible for salary policy and must compete for available men and women by offering a satisfactory and worthwhile career within its own industry. All public corporations must, therefore, adopt high standards in relation to employment policy. Thus they must provide good conditions of service, pension schemes, adequate holiday arrangements, sickness pay, and provide training schemes for staff.

Arrangements are made for workers' consultation with the management through consultative committees. Trade Unions negotiate at national, regional, or local level to ensure satisfactory wages and conditions of employment, including safety precautions, health measures, and amenities for staff.

Despite the *Trade Union and Labour Relations Act* strikes continue in the nationalised industries.

The Problem of Control

If we assume the public corporation is a semi-independent body, 'publicly owned', producing goods and services for the public generally, the questions arise as to who exercises control over it and as to how that control is exercised. The Electricity and the Gas Boards are obvious cases in point, though other corporations may be cited where the problem of political and managerial control and responsibility arises.

There are two opposite viewpoints: (i) a public service or industry may be managed and operated as a Government Department. The G.P.O. provided a service and until 1968 all the staff were civil servants with a Ministerial head, the Postmaster-General. From 1968 it became a public corporation; (ii) A public service may be managed in the same way as an efficient private enterprise, i.e. a private or public company.

If the corporations spend, or are financed by, public money and, if they administer services on behalf of the public, they ought in theory to be subject to public (i.e. Parliamentary) control through a Minister. The need for such control is undeniable. If all competition is eliminated (as it normally is) by the creation of a State-owned monopoly, periodic inquiries by the elected representatives of the people (i.e. Parliament) are necessary. The public are taxpayers and, in essence, replace the original shareholders (e.g. of the former gas companies existing before 1946) and they are entitled to know how their affairs are being run. The advocates of nationalization say that the nationalized industries are too important to be left in the hands of private individuals.

If, on the other hand, an industry or trading service is to operate on commercial or semi-commercial lines, it follows that good business management cannot be maintained by the appointment of elected members to run them. Elected members are not *ipso facto* good managers. Moreover, good management which is noted for its drive, initiative, inventiveness and similar qualities cannot thrive or survive if it is subject to detailed control by Parliament or by a Minister.

The art of government is the art of compromise. The result has been an attempt to combine the virtues of both forms, leading to the creation of the public corporations of today.

Ministerial Control

Most public corporations act today in association with or under the general surveillance of a Minister. The extent of a Minister's control can be ascertained only from the statute creating the corporation. Generally, Ministerial control is exercised in the following ways:

(i) *Appointment of Members.* The Minister appoints members of the corporation and may remove members if he is not satisfied with their work.

(ii) *Directions.* The statute usually authorises a Minister to give **general directions** where the national interest is involved, e.g. such as price restraint policy.

(iii) *Specific Controls.* A Minister may appoint auditors and approve programmes of reorganization or development involving capital expenditure and use of surplus revenues. The Minister controls borrowing powers (e.g. when money is required from the Government).

Where a corporation requires public money to meet losses or finance its investment or expand its building or machinery it is right that a Minister keeps a close watch on why the particular industry needs the money. How far a corporation should be aided is a matter of political controversy. Where public money is invested and a Minister begins to interfere in the management this may lead to inefficient operation. The closure of an uneconomic railway line may be justified on grounds of economy, but it may be attacked by those members of the public immediately affected by the loss of rail service and inconvenience.

Parliamentary Control

A Minister is now required to answer in Parliament only generally concerning the aims, activities, and problems of a particular corporation. Parliamentary controls operate in the following ways:

(i) *Annual Report.* Each public corporation is required by statute to submit an annual report. This is sent to the Minister who must lay it before Parliament, together with any report made by him.

(ii) *Annual Accounts.* A copy of the annual accounts is required to be submitted to the Minister. A copy is also laid before Parliament.

(iii) *Debates.* The annual report and the accounts may be the subject of debate. The House may debate the conduct of the public corporations on special motions and on Supply Days. The debates are limited to general issues of policy and have little value in practice.

(iv) *Finance.* The Financial Committees of the House of Commons have little influence over the public corporations. Each corporation is expected to pay its way, taking one year with another. But, sometimes a failure results, or money is asked for from Parliamentary funds. Parliament may then debate the motion for financial aid.

(v) *Parliamentary Questions.* Because the Minister is not wholly responsible for the work of the corporation he cannot be called to account for the administration of the industry. Parliamentary questions on the corporations may only be asked on matters for which the Minister is responsible, i.e. general directions, and matters of public importance.

We have noted the reasons for this already. Good management is hindered and harassed if it is subjected to scrutiny, controversy, and interference by Parliament. The opponents of this view stress that the object of creating the nationalized industries (usually a monopoly) was to make them subject to popular (i.e. Parliamentary) criticism and that real grievances of the public should be expressed in Parliament and that the corporations should not be protected from Parliamentary criticism. The Parliamentary Commissioner for Administration does not handle complaints against public corporations.

(iv) *Select Committee on Nationalized Industries.* Set up in 1956 this Committee (thirteen members) is required 'to examine the report and accounts of the nationalized industries' and 'to obtain further information about their current policy and practices'. The Committee has visited each industry, heard evidence, and produced useful reports. It has made recommendations many of which have been accepted by the Minister. The reports keep other M.P.s informed of what is happening, and is one of the most effective Parliamentary controls. The Committee is, through lack of time, limited to examining one industry a year. Its primary duty is to call the attention of Parliament to all matters that affect the efficiency of the nationalized industries. In this way Parliament can protect the public interest while not making the industries themselves accountable to the House for their routine or day to day administration.

Parliamentary control over the public corporations is not very effective. Having regard to the underlying dilemma of management (already discussed) this seems inevitable.

Consumer Protection and the Nationalized Industries

Consumers' Councils have been set up in relation to certain industries. Thus two Consumers' Councils exist in regard to the coal industry, namely, (i) the Industrial Consumers' Council, representing merchants and industrial users, to whom coal is supplied in bulk; and (ii) Domestic Coal Consumers' Council, which represents groups concerned with the domestic use of coal. These bodies report to the Minister. Their duties involve consideration of the commercial arrangements and activities of the National Coal Board (NCB) to ensure that regard is paid to consumers' interests.

Consultative Councils have also been appointed, and can be found, for example, in the gas and electricity industries. Each area of the country has its Consultative Council (twenty to thirty members) mainly nominated by local authority associations and by bodies representing industry, commerce, trade, and similar activities and associations. The duties of the Consultative Councils are to hear complaints from the public and to raise general matters affecting the rights of consumers. The object of the Councils was to act as bodies to which users could turn for defence and protection and to which management could turn for views of persons using the services, i.e. consumers.

Consultative councils are **advisory**, and although in theory are desirable vents for grievances, to reconcile the interests of producers and consumers, in practice they have been assessed as a rather ineffective link between the management and the consumers.

Conclusions

The public corporations are here to stay. They may be regarded as a new constitutional development of the twentieth century, and they are in process of evolution. There is no perfect form of administration or management of a basic or important nationalized industry. The most that can be hoped for is that the compromise which the public corporation represents will prove effective and convenient and manifest the best qualities of state ownership and private enterprise. Public corporations are found in the US (e.g. Niagara Falls Authority), W. Germany and Italy.

Exercises.

1. 'The idea that the public corporations were created in 1946–9 is untrue: they existed in the last century.' Do you agree? If so, trace their history.
2. Discuss the advantages and disadvantages of the concept of the public corporation.
3. 'The trouble is Parliament wants to control the public corporations but it does not want to be responsible for them.' Comment.
4. Explain the extent to which you consider consumer protection operates in regard to public corporations.
5. Describe the distinction between the BBC and IBA.

CHAPTER SIX

PUBLIC OPINION, PRESSURE GROUPS, AND THE MASS MEDIA

Public Opinion and the Government

Public opinion is a vague concept. All we may note is that it is the attitude of mind of most people. There are certain matters about which most people are commonly agreed. Most people in this country support the Monarchy; most people support Parliament and its institutions; most people support the judiciary and its traditional independence; most people support the police in their task to preserve public order. But, by the very nature of things, there is a division of opinion concerning politics, i.e. policies, leaders, and M.P.s.

Some of the problems facing Government today are highly controversial. For example: (i) the future of the House of Lords; (ii) Britain's entry into the European Economic Community; (iii) British action towards Southern Rhodesia; (iv) British intervention in Northern Ireland and the cure of the civil disturbances there, (v) the cure of unemployment involving 1 million; and (vi) the legal control of Trade Unions.

Most people do have views. Some think deeply about a problem; others accept what is printed in the Press or broadcast on radio or television. There are people, too, who do not bother to go beyond the headlines and have no opinion worthy of the name.

If a Government controls (i) the Press, and (ii) radio and television, it may control public opinion to a large extent. Totalitarian or authoritarian states like the U.S.S.R. do this. As everyone knows, the first requirement of a valid opinion is (i) the ascertainment of the true facts, (ii) the application of rational thought, to which may be added (iii) experience of life and judgement of the practicalities of the situation which enable a forecast of probabilities or possibilities. Mankind is, however, not gifted with foresight, and sometimes reaches conclusions by using false data and imperfect reasoning.

In wartime a democratic State through its Government is justified in suppressing information or controlling it, first because the release of vital information may be useful to the enemy, and secondly because a Government does not want to spread alarm or despondency or to disseminate false news or rumour which can be damaging to the war effort. The *Defence Regulations, 1939*, operated certain controls.

In peace-time no such controls operate. The Press is free **within the law**, the BBC and IBA are independent institutions and are not controlled by the Government as to what is transmitted by these powerful organs. Each body is controlled by Governors who, although appointed by the Minister of Posts and Telecommunications, have practically autonomous powers to administer the service. Both the BBC and IBA have resisted Government interference and notable figures, e.g. Lord Reith, a former Director-General, have withstood pressures from outside so that independence is assured (see pp. 161 and 172).

Public Opinion Polls

Formerly, public opinion was considered to be too vague to predict or to form a useful guide in politics. Politicians used to form their own idea of what public opinion felt. They had hunches and moved among the people to find out how they felt about policies and events. Many politicians still use this method.

Today public opinion or public reaction can be more accurately ascertained by **sampling** and **research** techniques. Broadly speaking, this involves making a sample survey of, say, one person in a 1,000, all over the country. Questions are asked, and answers are recorded. By this means a fairly accurate guide can be obtained of public reaction to a particular issue. For example, the popularity-rating of a Prime Minister, or Leader of the Opposition, can be assessed and charted on a graph which shows how people think over a period of months as a result of policies proposed or applied, or stemming from his personal impact on TV or radio. It has also been possible to forecast the result of an election with considerable accuracy.

This system of sampling and research was first introduced in America by **Dr. Gallup** in 1941. The techniques achieved a certain fame, and were introduced into this country later. The **National Opinion Poll** is another organization (privately financed) which also conducts surveys on similar lines. Similar methods are used by industry to forecast possible demands for certain goods. Politically, therefore, the surveys or polls are an important part of the present political scene and machinery. The five main 'public opinion' companies operating in the United Kingdom in 1972 are (i) Gallup, (ii) National Opinion Poll (NOP), (iii) Marplan, (iv) Harris, and (v) Opinion Research Centre. They are all independent of the Government. NOP, for example, is owned by Associated Newspapers, Ltd. But the forecasting or sampling of political views held by the public is merely one aspect of the research sampling undertaken by these groups.

Parliamentary By-Elections

Where a by-election is held for a Parliamentary seat, much attention will be paid by the Government and the Opposition to the result. Let us examine the following example for the 'Oxbridge' Constituency:

Party	1970 General Election	Party	1972 By Election
Cons.	20,000	Lab.	22,000
Lab.	15,000	Cons.	14,000
Lib.	5,000	Lib.	4,000
	40,000		40,000

If we assume the same number of people turned out for both elections (say eighty per cent), then we may conclude that there is evidence which indicates a large swing away from Conservative which lost 6,000 votes (20,000–14,000). Labour, on the other hand, increased its vote by 7,000 (from 15,000 to 22,000). The Liberal candidate lost 1,000 (5,000–4,000) votes. The change in representation may be due to various factors: (i) the unpopularity of present Government measures; (ii) increased activity of the local Labour organisation in getting voters out to the election booths; (iii) a change of candidate; (iv) local unemployment; or (v) a basic desire on the part of the voters to give the other fellow a chance to prove what he can do. There are many factors to consider. But, all parties will regard the by-election as significant, though by no means conclusive, that the same sort of result would be recorded all over the country if a general election were to be held in the next year.

Local Government Elections.

Local government seats are contested each year. The local authorities are usually composed of (i) Conservatives, (ii) Labour, and (iii) Independent candidates. Although only thirty to forty per cent of the electorate turn out for these elections, they do serve as a guide—but only a guide—as to what people in the constituencies feel and think about politics.

The above factors, namely Public Opinion polls, Parliamentary by-elections, and local government elections, are important indications of public feeling to which politicians of all parties pay heed.

The following list indicates some of the other sources available to Government and Opposition parties to gauge public opinion:

(i) Letters to Government Departments and Ministers.
(ii) Letters to M.P.s.
(iii) Letters in the Press.
(iv) Press comments.
(v) BBC and IBA broadcasts, showing how the 'man in the street' feels and thinks about persons and policies, or even politics in general.
(vi) Films such as 'Cathy Come Home' depicting the experiences of a family evicted from their home and the processes followed by local authorities, social services, the police, court officials and others.
(vii) Pressure Groups e.g. CBI, TUC, Local government representative organizations, and the other bodies referred to on page 169.

By tapping all these sources it is possible to build up a picture of public opinion on which, in the long run, a Government wins or loses.

As has been mentioned, a Government influences public opinion by means of policies, personalities, and events, and the people (the governed) in their turn influence their representatives. It is a case of action and reaction.

We may say, therefore, that today a Prime Minister will pay heed to all the above sources in fixing the date of the general election when he puts himself and his party to the test of public approval or rejection via the ballot box.

Pressure Groups

Pressure groups are groups of people who seek to change or influence the policy of a Government by persuasion, but without themselves assuming or usurping the power of Government.

The phrase 'pressure group' is not a term of art and may be misleading. All persons or groups have an inherent right in a civilized democratic society to approach or to try to influence an M.P. or a Government Minister. It is inevitable, therefore, that democratic legislatures must be subjected to 'lobbying'. The larger the number in a particular group the greater will be its persuasive force or pressure. There is strength in numbers. Generally, we may say also that the wealth of a group or its social or economic power increases its importance and the strength of its pressure.

Any persuasion or pressure applied must be lawful. Thus threats of personal violence to a M.P. or Minister constitute a crime; threats to Parliament as an institution could amount to sedition (the use of any form of physical force in any public matter connected with the State) and would be a breach of the privilege of either House. The forms of pressure usually include the following: (i) approach to M.P. or Minister personally or by letter; (ii) deputations to Parliament; (iii) mass meetings; (iv) Press propaganda, TV and radio interviews; (v) demonstrations and marching with banners through the streets.

Examples of Pressure Groups

In a complex society there are many varied interests and minority groups. In the past some have had worthy and beneficial ideals, notably the Anti-Slavery League, the Anti-Corn Law League, and the Suffragette Movement, to name but three. Their activities have resulted in enlightened and progressive changes in the law and in public attitudes. The various kinds of groups existing today may be listed as follows:

(i) *Economic.* A significant role is played by the Trade Unions. The Trade Union Congress (TUC) has a total membership of over 9 million members and maintains systematic relations with the Government and Government Departments. The Transport and General Workers Union has over 1½ million members, while the National Farmers Union represents over ninety per cent of the farmers in England and Wales. The Confederation of British Industry (CBI) represents the management side of industry in the United Kingdom and advises the Government on all aspects of Government policy which affect the interests of industry and business. Membership consists of 11,500 companies and over 200 trade associations and employers' organizations.

(ii) *Professional.* This group includes the British Medical Association (BMA) which protects the interests of doctors. The legal profession is represented by (*a*) the Law Society (solicitors), and (*b*) the Bar Council (barristers). The Church of England is itself a society, as are the Free Churches which may fall into this class. Teachers are represented by the National Union of Teachers (NUT). Local government officers are represented by the National Association of Local Government Officers (NALGO).

(iii) *Miscellaneous.* These include the following: The Lord's Day Observance Society; the Howard League for Penal Reform; the Campaign for Nuclear Disarmament; the National Council for Civil Liberties; the Association for Abortion Law Reform; Women's Institutes; the Humanist Society.

The Case For

(i) Pressure groups are natural and necessary in a democratic society. Men form groups through identity of interest, just as 'birds of a feather flock together'.

(ii) Groups educate (*a*) the public, and (*b*) their own members by clarifying the issues or moderating the extreme views of some members.

(iii) Minority views may be more effectively expressed through group pressure, and social justice more quickly and easily achieved. Old Age Pensioners unable to cope with the rise in the cost of living are examples of this.

(iv) Pressure groups may act as watchdogs in keeping track of issues that the general public might overlook.

(v) The Government is entitled to the best information available and habitually consults affected interests before proposed legislation. Thus the Minister of Transport Industries proposes to raise to 17 the age at which a person may ride a motor-cycle. He will consult the AA, the RAC, the police, vehicle manufacturers, RoSPA (Royal Society for the Prevention of Accidents), the medical profession, Road Research Laboratories and others. There are 7,500 deaths and 400,000 persons injured on the roads each year and the Minister's responsibility is to try to reduce this appalling number of deaths and injuries.

The Case Against

(i) Some groups are too powerful, e.g. the Confederation of British Industry (CBI), the Trade Unions, and the NFU.

(ii) The interests of consumers (i.e. the public) are not adequately protected, despite the existence of Consumer Associations. Producers organize themselves in their own economic interest.

(iii) Persons unable to organize themselves through illiteracy, lack of education, or ability are at a disadvantage in competition with those who can.

(iv) Poverty or the dispersal of a group frequently results in its ineffectiveness (contrast the CBI and the TUC and the Trade Unions which are financially powerful).

(v) Groups can sabotage or blackmail a Government. Thus if all doctors agreed to opt out of the National Health Service the service would be brought to a standstill; if all dockers refused to unload ships, or the police refused to enforce the law, or teachers refused to teach, or if all Trade Unions refused to co-operate in the administration of an Industrial Relations Act, the country could be brought to a standstill, and much damage could be done.

Resolving the Difficulties

Parliament is supreme and the elected Government must, in the final analysis, govern. It follows that a Government must reach decisions, impose legislation or issue its instructions only after it has weighed (i) the interest of the nation, and (ii) the interest of the minority group or factions which exert pressure. The over-riding duty of a Government is to safeguard the security and prosperity of the United Kingdom and its peoples, and to achieve that a Government must make decisions now for long-term as well as short-term benefits.

The Mass Media

We have already discussed the Press (see p. 17) and the BBC and IBA (see p. 161) and their place in the Constitution.

The law relating to the Press has also already been noted in broad outline. Under the terms of its Charter the BBC is a Broadcasting Service as 'a means of information, education and entertainment'.

Radio and Television

The BBC is required to broadcast any announcement when so requested by a Minister of Her Majesty's Government (Clause 13(3) of the BBC's licence). In practice, important Government announcements find their place in the regular news bulletins, but the Government may also from time to time require the BBC to make Special 'News Flash' announcements of items of pressing importance such as police messages or outbreaks of war or violence.

The BBC is also required to broadcast an impartial account day by day, prepared by professional reporters, of the proceedings in both Houses of Parliament (Clause 13(2)).

As has been noted, the Governors of the BBC have been granted practically autonomous powers of running the service. Nevertheless under Clause 13(4) the Minister of Posts and Telecommunications

> may from time to time by notice in writing require the Corporation to refrain at any specified time or at all times from sending any matter or matters of any class specified in such notice.

All former Ministers have respected this independence. Under clause 13(4) the Minister requires the Corporation to refrain from expressing in broadcasts its own opinion on current affairs or on matters of public policy. The BBC's policy in controversial matters must be one of impartiality.

Mass communication through radio, television, and the Press (which term includes newspapers, books, periodicals, magazines, comics, etc.) must influence the minds of recipients and, therefore, behaviour. The exact effect—whether for good or ill—is the subject of fierce debate. Strong views are often held by individual citizens, no less than by powerful group interests, as to what should or should not be printed in the Press or be broadcast in the way of 'information, education, and entertainment'. It is the duty of the BBC to keep in touch with public opinion and to weigh such representations as may be made to them. It maintains its own Audience Research and notes carefully what is said in Parliament, the Press, or elsewhere. The Press, too, maintains a close watch on public opinion, but unlike the BBC the Press is not a public corporation providing a public service. The Press exists to make a profit and need not be impartial.

Party Political Broadcasts

These need no description here for residents in the United Kingdom. The number of Party Political Broadcasts is normally settled for a period of twelve months in advance. After consultation between the Government, the opposition, and the broadcasting authorities (BBC and IBA) the following arrangements were made for party political broadcasting in 1969:

Television

Government (Lab.)	5 broadcasts	(2 of 15 min. and 3 of 10 min.)
Opposition (Con.)	5 broadcasts	(2 of 15 min. and 3 of 10 min.)
Liberal Party	2 broadcasts	2 of 10 min.

Radio

Government	9 broadcasts	6 of 5 min. (Radio 4) 3 of 5 min. (Radio 2 and 1)

Opposition (Con.)	9 broadcasts	6 of 5 min. (Radio 4) 3 of 5 min. (Radio 2 and 1)
Liberal Party	3 broadcasts	2 of 5 min. (Radio 4) 1 of 5 min. (Radio 2 and 1)

In addition the Scottish National Party and the Welsh National Party were each allowed one TV broadcast of five minutes and one radio broadcast of five minutes.

Since 1965 various Select Committees have given consideration to the question of broadcasting the actual proceedings of Parliament. Experiments have been carried out but, so far, no firm decision has been made to allow the proceedings to be broadcast.

How far, it may be asked, do pre-election party political broadcasts affect voting behaviour? The Television Research Unit at Leeds University, sponsored by Granada TV, carried out a survey covering a three-week period only during an electioneering programme. The study revealed that whilst viewers are not influenced significantly to change their attitudes, previously held views, opinions, or attitudes are reinforced.

Mass media is more likely to create opinion where the individual has no preconceived viewpoint or clear viewpoint.

This particular survey may have been too short for conclusions to be drawn as to the overall effects of mass media. Exposure to political broadcasts over a long period of time may produce different results. It appears that more research is needed into the whole question of the effects of mass media (particularly TV) on the population.

Statistics

Approximately ninety per cent of the people living in Great Britain have TV and of those with both BBC and ITV channels the average person watches ITV more than BBC.

Time spent per day. One-third of the viewers watch TV for one hour per day, one-third for two hours, and one-third for three to five hours.

During the year October 1968 to September 1969, the amount of time devoted to viewing BBC television amounted to 7·4 hours per week per head of population. On the average day over fifty-two per cent of the population viewed one or more of the BBC's programmes.

With regard to political broadcasts thirty per cent of the population (over the age of five) watched TV election broadcasts in 1966.

To sum up, the BBC and ITV are extending their programmes nationally and locally. Their effect cannot yet be gauged with accuracy. Lord Hill of Luton (Chairman of the Governors of the BBC) referring to the duty of **impartiality** said:

The BBC has no editorial opinion, and its reputation for impartiality is jealously guarded not only within the BBC but by people outside. That is why any critic with a suspicion that the Corporation is showing bias is liable to express shocked resentment—and the outcry is all the sharper when the matter of dispute arouses bitter personal feelings. One of the hardest tests in the history of the BBC came in 1969 when we were broadcasting to the people of Northern Ireland at a time when argument had burst into the violence of stones, petrol bombs and firearms. At such times, those who are most hotly partisan do not want impartiality; they want the

news and views that support their own fiercely held opinions. In this difficult
period the BBC was assailed by both sides, creating at least a presumption
that it had held the middle ground. Tempers were roused, too, though not
from such deep emotions, over the Nigerian Civil War and over the
attempts to break up the sporting fixtures of South African visitors to
Britain. Those who were angered by what they heard, or saw, in our broadcasts found it hard to believe that the BBC was not espousing the cause
they detested. But the BBC espouses no cause; it tries to hold the ring in
argument. The job of getting the facts right and holding the balance of
opinion fairly is a difficult one, and it requires constant vigilance. We may
err from time to time but impartiality remains our duty and our objective.
(BBC 1970 Handbook.)

Finally it must be noted that the BBC and IBA are subject to the law (see
p. 14) and may be prosecuted or sued in their corporate names. For
example, the BBC and IBA may be sued for defamation. Films, radio, and
television broadcasts which are defamatory are treated as libel (*Defamation
Act, 1952*).

The Press

The Press is a general term which includes daily and weekly newspapers, as
well as magazines and specialized papers which appear on the newstalls and in
the book shops of all towns in the United Kingdom. There are in fact 134
daily newspapers and Sunday newspapers, and 1,171 weekly newspapers
published in Britain.

So far as the British Constitution is concerned there is no special press law.
The State does not control the Press and does not impose censorship. The
Press is, of course, subject to the law. The editor or proprietor of a newspaper
or magazine or book may print or publish anything providing such publication
does not offend the law.

The main newspapers with their circulations are listed in Table 4. Some are
Conservative and some Labour but most are independent in outlook or
reporting slant. The effect of this is that although in general tone a paper may
be politically biased this does not prevent the paper from criticizing the
Government of the day whatever its political colour. A vigorous and free press
is, therefore, essential to a free society, speaking out clearly and strongly when
a policy is improper or when corruption is located in public affairs. On the
other hand, a newspaper may approve and congratulate Government leaders
or private citizens at will, providing the event, incident, or the individual is
newsworthy and interesting. The newspaper or magazine is a commercial
enterprise. It exists to make a profit, and if it fails to do so it risks bankruptcy
or liquidation and extinction.

The Press and the Law. In Britain the Press has the same freedom as the
individual. In other words it may print or say what it likes so long as it does
not transgress the law.

There are certain statutes which require the registration of newspapers for
postal purposes, but there are no specific press laws. There are, however,
clauses or sections in statutes which apply in particular to the Press. Thus, the
extent of newspaper ownership in television companies is limited and there are
restrictions on newspaper reporting of preliminary hearings of indictable
offences (in England, Wales, and Northern Ireland). The object of this is to

Table 4
The main newspapers and their circulations

TITLE	POLITICAL TENDENCY	AVERAGE CIRCULATION
DAILIES		
The Times (1785)	Ind.	345,044
The Daily Telegraph (1855)	Ind./Cons.	1,423,031
The Guardian (1821)	Ind.	344,356
Daily Express (1900)	Ind.	3,296,988
Daily Mail (1896)	Ind.	1,703,215
The Sun (1969)	Ind.	2,931,466
Morning Star (1966)	Official Communist	49,241
Daily Mirror (1903)	Left of centre	4,261,683
Financial Times (1888)	Ind.	194,651
LONDON EVENINGS		
Evening News (1881)	Ind.	861,453
Evening Standard (1827)	Ind.	680,407
SUNDAYS		
The Observer (1791)	Ind.	795,076
The Sunday Times (1822)	Ind.	1,504,515
The Sunday Telegraph (1961)	Ind./Cons.	755,326
News of the World (1843)	Ind.	5,950,645
The Sunday People (1881)	Ind.	4,428,598
Sunday Express (1918)	Ind.	4,086,482
Sunday Mirror (1963)	Left of centre	4,496,083

The above figures apply for the period Jan-June, 1973 (Britain: 1974, p.431)

preclude prejudice of the accused at his trial before a judge. The Press has the right to attend meetings of local authorities, although there is no general right to attend the committee or sub-committee meetings.

There are certain restrictions on the publication of the following:

(i) Divorce and domestic proceedings in courts of law.
(ii) Advertisement and investment circulars (certain Acts deal with the publication of false or misleading descriptions of goods and services and with fraud).
(iii) Advertisements of remedies for certain diseases which are covered by public health legislation.
(iv) Certain types of prize competitions.
(v) Copyrights (*Copyright Act, 1956*).

Of particular importance to the Press are the laws relating to defamation (see p. 228) or contempt of court. A newspaper may not publish comments on the conduct of judicial proceedings which are likely to prejudice their reputation for fairness before or during the legal proceedings. The Press may not, for example, publish before or during a trial anything which might tend to influence the result. The publication of seditious libel, incitement to disaffection, or of official secrets (see p. 229) is unlawful.

Libel actions (mostly brought by individuals) render the editor, proprietor, publisher, printer, and distributor liable. The author of any particular article which transgresses the law will, of course, also be held responsible.

The Press Council. In April 1947 a Royal Commission was appointed to inquire into the control, management, and ownership of the Press and news agencies, and to make recommendations thereon. The Commission, which reported in June 1949, recommended that a Press Council be formed.

A Press Council was established on 1 July 1953. This constitution was amended in 1963 by the introduction of an independent chairman and up to twenty per cent lay membership. The objects of the Council are:

   (i) To preserve the established freedom of the British Press.

   (ii) To maintain the character of the British Press in accordance with the highest professional and commercial standards.

  (iii) To consider complaints about the conduct of the Press or the conduct of persons and organizations towards the Press; to deal with these complaints in whatever manner might seem practical and appropriate and record resultant action.

  (iv) To keep under review developments likely to restrict the supply of information of public interest and importance.

   (v) To report publicly on developments that may tend towards greater concentration or monopoly in the Press (including changes in owner- ship, control and growth of Press undertakings) and to publish statistical information relating thereto.

  (vi) To make representations on appropriate occasions to the Government, organs of the United Nations and Press organizations abroad.

 (vii) To publish periodical reports recording the Council's work and to review, from time to time, developments in the Press and the factors affecting them.

The Press Council has a Chairman (Lord Shawcross), a Vice-Chairman, eighteen Professional members (representatives of Newspaper Publishers Associations and the National Union of Journalists and the Institute of Journalists), and nine lay members. Reports are published annually.

Exercises.

1. What are Public Opinion Polls?
2. How important are they to (i) a Prime Minister; and (ii) a backbencher?
3. What factors or agencies would you as an M.P. take into account in estimating public opinion in Britain?
4. Distinguish between (i) a political party, and (ii) a pressure group.
5. State (i) the case for, and (ii) the case against pressure groups.
6. What are the duties of the BBC under its charter?
7. What are party political broadcasts? What arrangements exist for these in the United Kingdom?
8. What controls operate on (i) the BBC and IBA; and (ii) the Press?
9. State the composition and functions of the Press Council.

CHAPTER SEVEN

THE LAW AND THE COURTS

The Nature of Law

The term 'law' is used in many senses: we may speak of the laws of physics, mathematics, science, or the laws of football or health. When we speak of the law of a State we use the term 'law' in a special and strict sense, and in that sense law may be defined as *a rule of human conduct, imposed upon and enforced among, the members of a given state.*

If a group or society is to continue, some form of social order is necessary. Rules or laws are, therefore, drawn up to ensure that members of the society may live and work together in an orderly and peaceable manner. The larger the community (or group or state), the more complex and numerous will be the rules.

If the rules or laws are broken, compulsion is used to enforce obedience. We may say, then, that two ideas underlie the concept of law:

(i) **Order,** in the sense of method or system.
(ii) **Compulsion,** i.e. the enforcement of obedience to the rules or laws laid down.

Custom, Morality, and Law

When we examine the definition of law given above we notice certain important points.

(i) *Law is a Body of Rules*

When we speak of 'the law' we usually imply the whole of the law however it may have been formed. As we shall see later, much of English law was formed out of the customs of the people, and our English 'common law' means the universal customs of the realm which are unwritten. But a great part of the law has been created by statute. Common law and statutory law together comprise what today we refer to as the 'Law of England'.

(ii) *Law is for the Guidance of Human Conduct*

Men resort to various kinds of rules to guide their lives. Thus moral rules and ethics remind us that it is immoral or wrong to covet, to tell lies, or to engage in private drunkenness. If we transgress these moral or ethical precepts we may lose our friends or their respect. The law, however, is not concerned with these matters and leaves them to the individual's conscience or moral choice and the pressure of public opinion: no legal action results (except where a person tells lies under oath in a court, when he may be prosecuted under the *Perjury Act, 1911*).

(iii) *Law is Imposed*

We sometimes think of laws as being laid down by some authority such as a King, dictator, or group of people in whom special power is vested. In Britain we can point to statute law for examples of law laid down by a sovereign body, namely Parliament. The jurist John Austin (1790–1859) asserted that law was

176

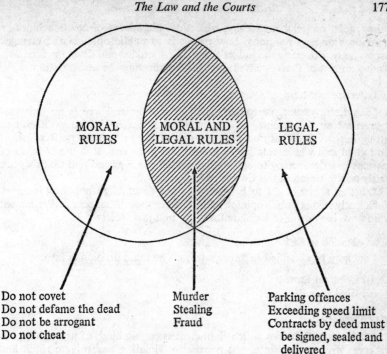

Do not covet	Murder	Parking offences
Do not defame the dead	Stealing	Exceeding speed limit
Do not be arrogant	Fraud	Contracts by deed must
Do not cheat		be signed, sealed and
		delivered

a command of a Sovereign and that citizens were under a duty to obey that command. Other writers say that men and women in primitive societies formed rules themselves, i.e. that the rules or laws sprang from within the group itself. Only later were such rules laid down by a Sovereign authority and imposed on the group or people subject to them.

(iv) *Enforcement*

Clearly unless a law is enforced it ceases to be a law and those persons subject to it will regard it as dead. The chief characteristic of law is that it is enforced, such enforcement being today carried out by the State. Thus if *A* steals a fountain-pen from *B*, *A* may be prosecuted before the court and may be punished. The court may then order the restitution of the pen to its rightful owner, *B*. The 'force' used is known as a **sanction** and it is this sanction which the State administers to secure obedience to its rules.

(v) *The State*

A State is a territorial division in which a community or people lives subject to a uniform system of law administered by a Sovereign authority, e.g. a Parliament.

The United Kingdom, which comprises a Parliamentary union of England, Wales, Scotland, and Northern Ireland, is for our purposes the State.

(vi) *Content of Law*

The law is a living thing and it changes throughout the course of history. Changes are brought about by various factors such as invasion, contact with other races, material prosperity, education, the advent of new machines or new ideas or new religions. Law responds to public opinion and changes accordingly. Formerly the judges themselves moulded and developed the law. Today an Act of Parliament may be passed affecting the whole nation.

(vii) *Justice and Law*

Men desire justice, personal, social, or economic. There is no universal agreement on the meaning of justice; ideal or perfect justice is difficult to attain in this life. What man strives for is relative justice, not perfect justice; and good and wholesome laws assist to that great end. It is the business of citizens in a democracy to ensure that wise laws are passed and that they are fairly administered in the Courts of Law.

Whether a law ought to be passed or not depends on public opinion. A sufficiently strong public opinion will influence those Members of Parliament who have the power to legislate for a fair and just society.

Classification of Law

Law may be classified in various ways. The main division is into:

(i) **Criminal Law.**
(ii) **Civil Law.**

(i) *Criminal Law*

Is that part of the law which characterizes certain kinds of wrongdoings as offences *against* the State, not necessarily violating any private right, and punishable *by* the State. Crime is defined as *an act of disobedience of the law forbidden under pain of punishment*. The punishment for crime ranges from death or imprisonment to a money penalty (fine) or absolute discharge.

The police are the public servants whose duty is the prevention and detection of crime and the prosecution of offenders before the Courts of Law. Private citizens may legally enforce the criminal law by beginning proceedings themselves, but, except in such minor cases of common assault where *A* may summon *B* to attend court, rarely do so in practice.

(ii) *Civil Law*

Is primarily concerned with the rights and duties of individuals towards each other. It includes the following:

(*a*) *Law of Contract*, dealing with that branch of the law which determines whether a promise is legally enforceable and what are its legal consequences.

(*b*) *Law of Tort*. A tort is a civil wrong for which the remedy is a common law action for damages. Examples of torts are: nuisance, negligence, defamation, and trespass.

(*c*) *Law of Property* is that part of the law which determines the nature and extent of the rights which people may enjoy over land and other property. For example, rights of 'ownership' of land, or rights under a lease of land.

(*d*) *Law of Succession* is that part of the law which determines the devolution of property on the death of the former owner and in certain other events. For example, the identity of persons and the rights of such persons who may succeed to property under a will.

(*e*) *Family Law* is that branch of the law which defines the rights, duties, and status of husband and wife, parent and child, and other members of a household.

The above are the major components of civil law. Its main distinction from criminal law is that in civil law the legal action is begun by the private citizen to establish rights (in which the State is not primarily concerned) against another citizen or group of citizens, whereas criminal law is enforced on behalf of or in the name of the State.

Characteristics of English Law

English law is one of the great legal systems of the world, and one-third of all mankind is today ruled by laws that came originally from this small island. What, then, are the characteristics of English law which give it this pre-eminence? The most important are these:

(i) *Age and Continuity*

English law is traceable to Anglo-Saxon times. The common law, which forms the basis of English law, has endured for 900 years and has continuously adapted itself to changing social and economic needs.

(ii) *Absence of Codification*

A legal code is a systematic collection of rules, laws, or statutes, so arranged as to avoid inconsistency and overlapping. Codification was a feature of Roman law and was adopted by certain continental countries, notably France, Germany, Austria, and Switzerland. The English common law was formed from the customs of the people through the practical experience of living and working together. Under the Norman kings these unwritten laws achieved a fairly uniform legal system. Certain parts only of English law have today been codified. The *Bills of Exchange Act, 1882*, and the *Sale of Goods Act, 1893*, are common examples, though we may bear in mind that a general codification is likely to be attempted in the future (*Law Commission Act, 1965*).

(iii) *Judicial Character of the Law*

The common law was largely 'judge-made' from the existing customary laws. It is from the records and reports of cases tried by the judges that we derive our knowledge of early case law. Judges formed or moulded the common law, and its growth and character can often be traced to outstanding men like Bracton, Coke, and Littleton. Although judges today may develop the common law within fairly narrow limits, they are mainly concerned with interpreting and applying statute law which is now the main source of legal development.

(iv) *Independence of Judiciary*

Justice requires that a judge be impartial and independent of either party to a particular legal dispute. The *Act of Settlement, 1701*, provided that judges of superior courts 'hold office during good behaviour, that their salaries be ascertained and established, and that they be removed only on the address of both Houses of Parliament'.

(v) *Independence of Lawyers*

The two branches of the legal profession comprise barristers and solicitors. Each branch is controlled by independent bodies which maintain high professional standards of education, training, and conduct. Lawyers are not appointed by the State and are not civil servants. They are not subject to direct political control, and, like the judges, are traditionally independent.

(vi) *Influence of Procedure*

Procedure has influenced substantive law. We shall see later that at one time the existence of a legal right depended on whether there was a suitable writ with which to begin the action. The writ system governed early law. Such procedural rules affected the law itself and they have left their imprint on the common law.

(vii) *No Reception of Roman Law*

Roman law had a great influence of continental countries. The English common law was of native growth, its rules being developed empirically (through trial and error) in the practical business of living and working.

Sources of English Law

In this context the word 'source' means the fountain-head from which the stream of law flows. Different meanings may be given to 'the sources of English law', but the three main ones are:

(i) **The Formal Source.** This refers to the Sovereign, the State, or the 'will of the people'. In other words it is the political power which gives the law its validity and force.

(ii) **Literary Sources.** These are the statutes, law reports, and written works of authority.

(iii) **Historical Sources.** These include religious beliefs, conscience, mercantile practices, theories of natural justice, human reason, and the opinions of jurists and legal philosophers. In modern times, they concern the opinions and reports of Royal Commissioners and research groups.

Some of these sources of English law are described as 'principal' and some as 'subsidiary'. The **principal sources** are (i) common law, (ii) equity, (iii) legislation. The **subsidiary sources** are (iv) mercantile law, (v) local custom, (vi) books of authority and treatises, (vii) European Economic Community Law since 1 January 1973.

The Common Law

In Anglo-Saxon times there existed three fairly distinct legal systems: *The Dane Law*, which had been adopted after the invasions and settlement of Danish and Scandinavian warriors in the coastal areas of northern and north-eastern England; *Mercian Law*, which bore traces of Germanic origin, following the Saxon invasions, and extended around the Midlands; *Wessex Law* which applied in southern and western England.

In each of the three systems the law was based on customs, and the customs varied from place to place and shire to shire. There was little distinction between criminal wrongs and civil wrongs at this time; the laws were generally primitive but nevertheless served to produce such good order as could be expected. But there were courts of law where cases were heard. The Anglo-Saxon courts before 1066 were:

(i) **The Shire Court** (or **Moot**), presided over by the sheriff, the bishop, and the ealdorman, and attended by the lords and freemen of the county, with the priest. This court sat twice a year.

(ii) **The Hundred Court** ('hundred' means a division of a shire), presided over by the hundredman, assisted by twelve senior thanes.

(iii) **The Franchise Courts,** granted to certain persons by the Monarch. The grantees were entitled to the profits, for the suitors or litigants who brought their cases to court for trial were required to pay fees. In Norman times the franchise courts were sometimes taken over by the lords of the manor who, in deciding disputes between tenants of land, continued the practice of charging fees.

Of these three courts the shire court was the most important, but all enforced the local laws and all had jurisdiction to deal with obvious criminal offences, such as murder, theft, violence to person and property, and also the civil claims concerning ownership or possession of land or cattle—both very important sources of wealth.

Before the Norman Conquest there was no strong central Government. The king with his council (or Witan) ruled loosely and controlled his Kingdom inefficiently. Royal justice was difficult to obtain.

The Norman Conquest

English legal development stems from 1066 when William of Normandy gained the Crown of England by right of battle. William and his Norman successors distinguished themselves in many ways. First, they possessed orderly minds and were efficient administrators. They crushed the rebellious English into submission and established a strong central Government.

William owned all England: all other persons possessed land either as tenants (not owners) or sub-tenants of the King himself. Feudalism, based on land tenure, was introduced into England. No immediate change was attempted in regard to the customary laws of the English, for this would have been an insuperable task. Primitive people do not take kindly to radical alterations in their way of living.

The changes made by William I include the following:

(i) The King's Council (*Magnum Concilium*) was set up. Here foregathered the barons, lords, bishops, and other important figures of the Kingdom on whose advice and wisdom the Monarch relied. Here was the strong central Government.

(ii) A new feudalism was introduced. The King owned (in theory) all the land, and the barons, lords, bishops, and freemen held of him as tenants or sub-tenants. All tenants, whether barons or freemen, were compelled to swear an oath of allegiance to the King himself. Freemen owed allegiance as sub-tenants not only to a lord of the manor but also to the King, an important fact making for closer Royal control.

(iii) The separation of lay courts and church (or clerical) courts, each with a definite jurisdiction. Bishops and clergy were henceforward to be tried in their own courts and Church (or canon) law was to be applied therein.

William and his successors achieved the uniformity of the law, making it the common law, by introducing the **general eyre**. This was a form of central control whereby representatives of the King were sent out from Westminster to all parts of the country to check the local administration in the shires. These representatives made records of the land and wealth of the country, they collected taxes and they adjudicated in disputes brought before them. In the course of time the general eyre became judicial rather than administrative. In the reign of Richard II the eyre was abolished, but the important practice of sending members of the Royal Council continued. These representatives of the King were the original **Royal judges** and derived their authority from the King's command by Royal Commissions, namely:

(i) **The Commission of Gaol Delivery,** empowering the judges to clear the gaols of untried prisoners.

(ii) **The Commission of Oyer and Terminer,** empowering the judges to hear (*oyer*) and determine (*terminer*) cases of serious crimes such as treason or felonies brought before them.

(iii) **The Commission of Assize,** which granted the judges jurisdiction over civil matters normally triable in the Royal courts at Westminster.

Whenever a plaintiff wished to bring an action in the Royal courts in a civil matter against another person he had to obtain a writ from the Lord Chancellor's writ office and serve it on his opponent. The writ commanded the defendant and the plaintiff to attend the Royal courts at Westminster on a certain date, unless before that date (*nisi prius*) the King's justices could hear the case locally, i.e. where the action arose. Attendance at Westminster was itself no easy matter in those days; journeys were long, delay in London was likely and witnesses could not always be found to attend. So a local hearing by the Royal judges was a useful and attractive expedient readily grasped by those who could not obtain justice in the manorial court or other local courts —which were frequently corrupt, partial, and unfair.

Here, then, were the Royal judges, known as **itinerant justices,** granting better justice which naturally proved popular with the people. Henry II (1154–89) reorganized the system by dividing the country into **circuits** and putting the excursions from Westminster on a regular basis.

We have seen that the judges were originally men appointed from the King's Council: they might be bishops, barons, or knights. Behind them stood the Royal power as evidenced by the King's Commissions.

The original justices were for the most part untrained in law. When they visited a county court (the shires became counties after the Normans) they had to ascertain the customs applicable to the local court. The Royal judges then applied the law thus discovered from the inhabitants. The twelfth and thirteenth centuries saw the introduction of **juries.** Juries were made up of local people who knew the facts of the local cases and the local customs relevant thereto, so that the justices could then enforce these customs in the name of the King.

On completing their circuits the justices returned to the Royal courts at Westminster. There they discussed together the customs ascertained in various parts of the country and their findings. By a process of sifting these customs, rejecting those which were unreasonable and accepting those which were not, and by the use of good sense and right reason, they formed a uniform pattern of customary law throughout England.

At the same time there grew up another important practice: the judges began to apply the principle of *stare decisis* ('let the decision stand'). Whenever a new problem of law came to be decided a rule was formed and this rule was followed subsequently by all other judges. By this means the law became more certain and predictable, and acquired the character of a legal system. So, out of the varied and different customs, there was formed what is now known as the common law of England, so called because it is the law common to all parts of England and Wales. Although unwritten it is the universal custom of the Realm.

It is estimated that the formation of the common law was complete by about 1250 when Bracton wrote his famous *Treatise on the Laws and Customs of England*, which was the first exposition of a part of the law that was destined to reach all parts of the world.

The Common Law Courts

The King's Council, sometimes called the *Curia Regis*, was the central Government of the Kingdom, performing legislative, executive, and judicial functions without distinction. From the King's Council special courts were instituted to deal with particular kinds of cases in which Royal justice was sought. The various courts staffed by Royal judges developed in the following order:

(i) **The Court of Exchequer.** This was formed during the reign of Henry I, and was primarily a Government Department concerned with national revenue. The Department split into two branches: one administrative, collecting taxes and dues; the other judicial, dealing with disputes over taxation. The court extended its jurisdiction to hear common law actions only remotely connected with the Royal revenue. The judges of the court were known as **Barons of the Exchequer.**

(ii) **The Court of Common Pleas.** The judges sat in the communal and feudal courts (e.g. manorial courts) and they claimed jurisdiction over disputes between persons, e.g. in relation to land. Their justice became popular and a special court called the **Court of Common Pleas** (so called because it dealt with pleas of the commoners as distinct from Royal pleas, i.e. criminal cases) was set up to decide disputes of a civil nature between subject and subject. In 1273 the first **Chief Justice** was appointed. This court administered the common law and survived until the *Judicature Acts, 1873–5.*

(iii) **The Court of King's Bench.** This was the youngest and the most durable of the courts to emerge from the *Curia Regis*. It owes its name to the close connection with the Monarch, for the King himself used to sit at a bench with the judges to decide disputes. This close connection with the *Curia Regis* and the King also gave it a unique importance. Its jurisdiction included criminal cases (in addition to those tried by the itinerant justices in the local courts), and also civil cases, concurrent with the jurisdiction of the Court of Common Pleas. But the King's Bench had a supervisory jurisdiction over the activities of all inferior courts, which it enforced by means of prerogative writs.

This court survives today with its civil, criminal and supervisory jurisdiction, and is under the control of the Lord Chief Justice who is assisted (as were former courts) by *puisne* (junior) judges.

At this stage some mention should be made of legal procedure. In medieval times criminals were arrested and placed in the gaols until they could be tried, either by the local manorial courts or by the Royal judges when they came to the district. In civil cases, however, procedure was more technical. The proceedings in the common law courts started with the issue of an 'original' writ (so named because it originated the proceedings), which was purchased from the main Royal office known as the **Chancery**.

The writ was a formal document addressed to the sheriff of the county where the defendant resided, commanding him to secure the presence of the defendant at the trial and setting out the cause of action or ground of claim of the plaintiff. For every civil wrong or cause of action there was a separate writ. Important examples were the writ of trespass, the writ of debt, and the writ of detinue (detinue alleged that the defendant detained an article or chattel from the plaintiff and would not return it). The plaintiff had to select the particular writ which he considered fitted the facts of his case.

The plaintiff attended the **Writ Office of the Chancery**, where a register of the various writs was kept, and applied for the writ most suitable to his claim. If there was no writ suitable to the civil claim made or the relief of the law, the plaintiff was at a severe disadvantage. We may say, therefore, that the writ system dominated the civil law: for where there was no remedy there was no right. Moreover, if the wrong kind of writ were selected by the plaintiff, the common law judges would throw out the case and refrain from inquiring into its merits. Under the rigid procedure of the writ system the remedy available to litigants became more important than the justice of the claim.

Some attempt to alleviate this system was made by the clerks in the Chancery. Where a writ was thrown out by the court, or where none existed to found the claim, the clerks endeavoured to accommodate litigants by issuing new writs, thus effectively expanding the rights available. At first the common law judges tolerated this procedure and accepted some new writs; but later their attitude stiffened and they refused to accept the new writs, since these amounted to new legislation.

The common law did not expand to meet the urgent and growing needs of the community. Suitors unable to get justice complained to the King and his Council regarding the inelasticity of the common law, which led to the emergence of the **Court of Chancery** and its special field known as **equity**.

Equity

In a general sense equity means fairness in the adjustment of conflicting interests, or the application of principles of good conscience to the settlement of controversies, i.e. natural justice. In the special sense adopted by English lawyers, equity means that portion of natural justice which, though capable of being enforced by the courts of common law, was originally enforced only by the Court of Chancery. Equity as thus understood had been described as 'a gloss (meaning a supplement) on the common law', filling in the gaps and making the English legal system more complete.

We have seen that petitions from persons unable to obtain justice in the common law courts were sent to the King as 'fountain of justice'. These petitions were sometimes examined by the King and his Council and the relief was granted or refused. Later, due to pressure of business in the Council, the petitions were sent to the Lord Chancellor, who as Chief Secretary of State and 'Keeper of the King's Conscience', dealt with them alone.

The petitions were usually in the form of allegations that:

(i) The common law was defective, e.g. the law of contract was undeveloped and inadequate to serve the growing needs of suitors.

(ii) The remedy of the common law courts, namely damages, was inadequate and not always a satisfactory relief.

(iii) The defendant was too powerful; men of wealth and power in a county could overawe a court and intimidate jurors.

(iv) The court lacked jurisdiction to decide certain cases, e.g. where foreign merchants were suitors.

By the end of the fifteenth century the Chancellor had set up his own court and was dealing with petitions for relief. The Chancellor was not bound by the writ system or the technical and formal rules of the common law, and he considered petitions on the basis of conscience and right.

At first the Chancellor used to consult the Council and sometimes the common law judges, but eventually it became his custom to summon the parties to the dispute to appear before him alone to answer 'interrogatories' (specific questions relevant to the issue) and to unburden their consciences so that the truth could be ascertained and justice done.

The Court of Equity (Chancery) proved popular with litigants and this caused some friction with the common law courts. Nevertheless, the Court survived enforcing Equity, which acted as an appendix to the sound common law enforced by the common law judges. The Chancery Court enforced mortgages, trusts, and offered its particular remedies of Specific Performance of contracts (an order to the suitors to carry out their promises when they had made a contract) and injunctions, which ordered a defendant not to do a certain act, e.g. prohibiting *A* from trespassing on *B*'s land in the future.

As a result of the reorganization of the structure of the courts which took place in 1873 (see p. 189) the Chancery Court was constituted as a Division of the High Court and remains such to this day. Its jurisdiction includes mortgages; administration of trusts; dissolution of partnerships; contentious probate matters (i.e. where two or more parties dispute the validity of a will); revenue matters (taxation); applications for specific performance of contracts and the granting of injunctions.

Technically, the Lord Chancellor is still the President of the Court. The administrative work is now performed by a Vice-Chancellor, a post newly created in 1970 (see p. 193).

Judicial Precedent

The essentials of good law are, on the one hand, certainty and, on the other hand, uniformity and consistency. Common law and equity are judge-made, i.e. the judges moulded or created out of the original customary rules the common law of England whose principles are today found in case law.

In both civil and criminal cases the early judges would announce not only their decisions in the particular cases but also the reasons for their decisions. Where cases involving similar facts or situations came before them, the judges would refer to the reasons given in previous cases. If the principle of law to be applied was the same the judges would follow the decision already announced. By this means the law became more certain and more uniform in its application. The practice of referring to previous decisions and arguing by analogy from them to the present case in order to arrive at a judgement is known as the application of **judicial precedent.**

Judgements in the highest courts of the land, e.g. the House of Lords and the various courts of appeal, have always commanded the greatest respect. The general rule established in the nineteenth century and consistently followed since is that decisions of the higher courts bind the lower. Thus decisions of the House of Lords bind all courts.

The order of precedence is shown in the following table:

Courts of Law binding others	Courts bound by those in first column
1. House of Lords	All courts
2. Court of Appeal: Civil Division	Itself and lower courts (4, 5, and 6)
3. Court of Appeal: Criminal Division	All lower courts (4, 5, and 6)
4. Divisional Court of the High Court	Itself and lower courts (5 and 6)
5. High Court (Queen's Bench Division, Chancery Division and Family Division).	All lower courts, but not itself
6. Crown Courts, County Courts and Magistrates' Courts	None

The two divisions of the Court of Appeal (2 and 3 above) are of equal status and are not strictly bound by each other's decisions, but in practice each does pay attention to the rulings of the other and each has a strong persuasive influence on the other to ensure certainty and uniformity of the law.

The House of Lords and Precedent. In 1966 the Lord Chancellor, on behalf of the Lords of Appeal in Ordinary, made the following pronouncement in the House of Lords:

Their Lordships regard the use of precedent as an indispensable foundation upon which to decide what is the law and its application to individual cases. It provides at least some degree of certainty upon which individuals can rely in the conduct of their affairs, as well as a basis for orderly development of legal rules.

Their Lordships nevertheless recognize that too rigid adherence to precedent may lead to injustice in a particular case and also unduly restrict the proper development of the law. They propose, therefore, to modify their present practice and, while treating former decisions of this House as normally binding, to depart from a previous decision when it appears right to do so.

In this connection they will bear in mind the danger of disturbing retrospectively the basis on which contracts, settlements of property and fiscal arrangements have been entered into and also the especial need for certainty as to the criminal law.

This announcement is not intended to affect the use of precedent elsewhere than in this House.

From this pronouncement we can pick out the following points concerning judicial precedent:

(*a*) It gives an indispensable foundation for deciding what the law is and what is its application.

(*b*) It provides reasonable certainty.

(*c*) It enables citizens to conduct their affairs with some assurance.

(*d*) It ensures orderly development of rules.

(*e*) It allows development of the law by the House of Lords.

(*f*) Other courts are bound by the decisions of superior courts in the usual way.

Legislation

Although common law provides the basis of the English legal system, since the end of the seventeenth century Parliament has been in the ascendancy, increasing in its power and the scope of its activities. Parliament can now make and unmake laws to any extent. It can, for example, change the religion of the land and even regulate the succession to the Throne (*Act of Settlement, 1701*).

Successive governments have interfered more and more positively with the social, economic, and industrial aspects of the nation. The Welfare State was brought about by legislation and many areas of the common law (civil and criminal) have been revoked or reformed. It follows, therefore, that the main source of law today is legislation, which may take the form of:

(i) Statutes or Acts of Parliament (see p. 89).

(ii) Delegated legislation, mainly in the form of Statutory Instruments (see p. 248).

Canon Law

After the Norman Conquest, William I separated the courts of law into (*a*) lay courts administering the common law, and (*b*) ecclesiastical (or Church) courts. In the early days the Church courts were very important and assumed a wide jurisdiction. They dealt with the discipline of the clergy; offences by clergy and laity against Church doctrine, faith, and morality. They had jurisdiction regarding the validity of marriage and administered what today would be called 'Family Law', and which included legitimacy. They also had jurisdiction in regard to wills of personal property (i.e. all property other than land which, according to feudal law, had to descend to the legitimate heir) and so inheritance to land was, therefore, decided in the lay courts. The Church courts continued their jurisdiction until 1857, when the jurisdiction in regard to divorce and wills was transferred to a Divorce Court and a Probate Court, respectively, staffed by civil (not ecclesiastical) lawyers.

The Church courts remaining today are (*a*) the **Provincial Courts** of the Archbishops of Canterbury and York, and (*b*) the **Consistory Courts** of the dioceses, each presided over by a Chancellor appointed by the Bishop of the diocese. Their jurisdiction is now practically confined to Church matters and the discipline of the clergy.

Mercantile Law

The **Law Merchant** (which is how this law is sometimes described) grew out of the customs of merchants, who travelled around England and originally attended the great local fairs, or who came from Europe and elsewhere to trade. They were concerned with buying and selling and gradually built up customary practices in commercial trading, which eventually became crystallized as law. That law was eventually enforced by the common law courts and ultimately became a part of the common law. Merchants grew to rely on it, the judges were fair, and this considerably increased the importance of London as the great commercial centre of the world. In the City were the great banks, insurance and commercial houses and close by were the Courts of Law to settle disputes. Today a **Commercial Court** has been created (as part of the Queen's Bench Division) and that jurisdiction is continued, based on the tradition of the past practices and law built up from the customary commercial code of the merchants.

Maritime Law

This law is closely allied to mercantile law and evolved out of the customary maritime or sea laws of the medieval era. Britain, once a great sea power, created courts to deal with maritime disputes. The jurisdiction achieved international repute for its fairness and efficiency and **Admiralty Courts** were set up at the important seaports to administer the law. Maritime Law was also absorbed into English law. Today the Admiralty Court is in the QBD of the High Court, and is carrying on the same sort of jurisdiction as its predecessors, e.g. in cases of prize jurisdiction (determining whether a ship and its cargo captured in time of war is 'Prize' and how the cargo is to be disposed).

Local Custom

Whereas the common law of the land is the customary law applying to all the people in the land, a local custom is merely a customary rule which applies within a defined locality, for example, a parish. Although the local custom may be special or particular to a defined area and may be at variance with the common law, it may nevertheless be enforced as of right in the Courts of Law. This is not an important source of law, but it is interesting that a local rule (observed by the inhabitants over the years) is enforceable in the Courts of Law, although certain conditions must be observed before a custom may be recognized and enforced.

Treatises.

This is another subsidiary source of law. From the twelfth century to the present day, important judges have written about the law of the land. The first was Glanvil's *Tractatus de Legibus et Consuetudinibus Angliae* and this was followed by a work by Bracton in the thirteenth century. Both these works described the law and made comments about it and were useful to succeeding judges for reference to the sources and precedents to be followed. Today there are works on the Law of Contract, the Law of Tort, and the Law of Crimes, by eminent authors. Judges are not bound to follow the views expressed in these authoritative works, but they may refer to them. Treatises are of persuasive value: jurists of high standing command respect and their views are likely to influence the individual judge and thus the law itself.

Courts of Law

History

In the nineteenth century the English Courts of Law were the subject of much criticism and it was an irrational system whereby many courts dealt with *ad hoc* matters and applied their own rules—the common law rules and remedies were administered only in common law courts and equity rules were administered only in Chancery. There was no rational appeal system and the administration of the law was itself inefficient, delays were frequent and costs high.

The *Supreme Court of Judicature Acts, 1873–75* remedied this state of affairs by creating a **Supreme Court of Judicature,** which was comprised of (i) the **Court of Appeal** and (ii) the **High Court of Justice.** The High Court of Justice was eventually divided into three Divisions, namely (*a*) the Queen's Bench Division, (*b*) the Chancery Division, and (*c*) the Probate, Divorce, and Admiralty Division. Above the Supreme Court of Judicature was the House of Lords to which a further appeal could be made from the Court of Appeal. From 1876, Lords of Appeal in Ordinary were appointed to hear appeals in the Lords, which was the final Court of Appeal in the land (see below). The formation of the Civil Courts is shown in the figure below.

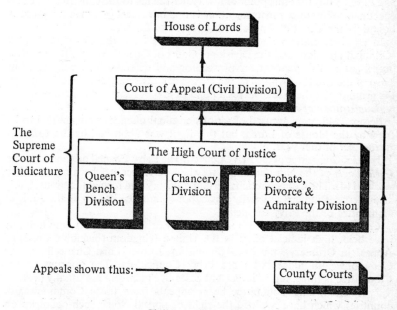

Civil courts until 1971

In 1846 the **County Courts** were established in the towns to give justice to the local people in small causes. County Court judges were appointed to dispense justice in regard to these small claims: debt, tort, breaches of contract, landlord and tenant claims, equity matters, dissolution of small partnerships and small companies. These courts proved popular and remain to this day, though the jurisdiction has been enlarged (see p. 193).

Civil Courts Today

The House of Lords stands at the apex of the judicial system, and is the final court of appeal in civil and criminal matters.

As a court of appeal, it is composed of the Lord Chancellor, the Lords of

Appeal in Ordinary, and other peers who have held high judicial office. A quorum of three is necessary to constitute the court. Each judge may deliver a separate judgement, the verdict being by majority.

Jurisdiction. In civil matters the court hears appeals from the Court of Session in Scotland, the Court of Appeal in Northern Ireland, and the Court of Appeal (Civil Division) in England. There is no general right of appeal: leave of the Court of Appeal or the House of Lords must first be obtained to appeal to the House of Lords.

The *Administration of Justice Act, 1969*, provides a new form of appeal in *civil* actions from the High Court (or Divisional Court) direct to the House of Lords, 'leap-frogging' the Court of Appeal. An appeal will lie only subject to the following conditions: (i) that, on application of any of the parties, the trial judge grants a certificate of appeal; (ii) that the certificate will only be granted if the judge's decision involves a point of law of *general public importance*; (iii) that this point of law either relates to the construction of an enactment or statutory instrument, *or* is one in respect of which the judge is bound by the Court of Appeal or the House of Lords.

In criminal matters the court hears appeals from the Court of Appeal (Criminal Division) and the Divisional Court of Queen's Bench. Both parties (appellant and respondent, or prosecutor and defendant) may appeal, but leave of the Court of Appeal or the House of Lords must first be obtained on the ground that the case involves a point of law of general public importance (*Administration of Justice Act, 1960*).

Before 1948 peers accused of serious criminal offences were entitled to be tried by the House of Lords, but this right was abolished by the *Criminal Justice Act* of that year.

Judicial Committee of the Privy Council. The Privy Council originated as the *Curia Regis* of the Norman kings, to which reference has been made earlier (see p. 114). The Council retains certain advisory and formal functions, but it also exercises judicial authority through a committee known as the Judicial Committee of the Privy Council.

Composition. The 'court' is made up of all Privy Councillors who hold, or have held, high judicial office in the United Kingdom (including Lords of Appeal in Ordinary), the Lord Chancellor, former Lord Chancellors, and Commonwealth judges who are Privy Councillors. The quorum of the Committee is three, but in important cases five members are usually present.

Jurisdiction. The Committee hears appeals from those Commonwealth countries which have retained the right of appeal (some such countries on acquiring independence abolished the right) and from colonial territories. More specifically the Committee hears appeals from:

(i) Prize courts. Jurisdiction extends over claims to captured ships during time of war.
(ii) Ecclesiastical courts.
(iii) Courts of the Isle of Man, the Channel Islands, British Colonies, British Protectorates and Trust Territories, and from Commonwealth countries retaining the right of appeal.
(iv) Tribunals of the medical, dental, and opticians' professions.

Procedure. The Committee sits as an advisory board and its procedure is informal. Judges, for example, are not robed. No judgement is given as in a Court of Law. The Committee tenders advice to the Monarch upon which an

Order in Council is made to dispose of the issue in question. No dissentient opinions are given.

The decisions of the Judicial Committee are not binding on itself or on the lower Courts of Law of the United Kingdom, but a decision on appeal from a colony is binding on the colonial courts of that territory. Generally and in practice the judicial strength of the Committee is such that its decisions are treated with great respect.

Court of Appeal (Civil Division). This court is composed of *ex officio* judges and other judges. *Ex officio* judges include the Lord Chancellor, the Lord Chief Justice, the President of the Family Division, the Lords of Appeal in

THE CIVIL COURTS

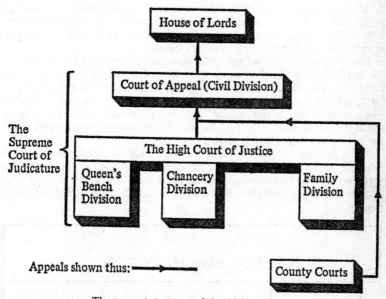

The present structure of the Civil Courts

Ordinary and the Master of the Rolls. In practice the Master of the Rolls is President of the court and he is assisted by a permanent staff of eight to eleven Lords Justices of Appeal. However, any High Court judge may be requested by the Lord Chancellor to sit. The quorum of the court is three and the court may sit in four Divisions at the same time.

The court may uphold, amend, or reverse the decision of a lower court, or order a new trial.

Jurisdiction. The court hears civil appeals from all Divisions of the High Court, from county courts and certain special courts.

The High Court of Justice. This court consists of:

    (i) The Queen's Bench Division (QBD).
    (ii) The Chancery Division (Ch. Div.).
    (iii) The Family Division (F. Div.).

The three Divisions are of equal competence, so each is empowered to try any action, but for administrative purposes and convenience specific matters are allocated to each Division as described below.

The Presidents of each of the respective Divisions are (i) QBD: The Lord Chief Justice; (ii) Ch. Div.: The Lord Chancellor (in practice the Vice-Chancellor presides); (iii) F. Div.: The President, Family Division. These are assisted by approximately 70 puisne (lesser) judges who are allocated to each Division. The Lord Chancellor may require any judge to sit in any Division.

(i) The **Queen's Bench Division** is composed of the Lord Chief Justice and approximately thirty puisne judges. It exercises three kinds of jurisdiction: (*a*) **original** (i.e. at first instance); (*b*) **appellate**; (*c*) **supervisory**.

(*a*) *Original Jurisdiction* is of three kinds. As a result of the *Administration of Justice Act, 1970*, the jurisdiction of the Admiralty Court has now been added to the Queen's Bench Division and a new Commercial Court has been added to deal with court cases involving traders and merchants. The characteristic of this court is that cases entered on the 'Commercial List' are tried in a simpler and quicker way than ordinary cases.

The effect of this is that the QBD jurisdiction comprises (i) all civil cases not specifically assigned to other Divisions of the High Court, such cases including tort cases, breaches of contract and actions for the recovery of land; (ii) Commercial Court cases as described above; and (iii) Admiralty cases, such as claims and actions involving ships with regard to collisions, salvage, towage, and prize jurisdiction. A diagrammatic representation of the functions of the QBD is shown below.

When hearing cases, the judges sit singly, but in exceptional cases (for example, defamation) a jury may be empanelled to assist the court. Jury verdicts may now be majority verdicts. There is no limit to the amount which may be claimed in the QBD. Some cases involve hundreds of thousands of pounds.

QUEEN'S BENCH DIVISION		
Q.B.D. cases (tort contract etc).	Commercial Division	Admiralty Division

(*b*) *Appellate Jurisdiction* is exercised by two or three judges sitting as a 'Divisional Court' to hear appeals from magistrates' courts and some Crown Courts by means of a process known as 'case stated'. These appeals are on points of law, the subordinate court setting out the facts of, and reasons for, the decision for solution by the Divisional Court.

(*c*) *Supervisory Jurisdiction* is exercised over inferior courts, tribunals, and administrative authorities 'acting judicially', by means of the writ of *habeas corpus* and the prerogative order of *certiorari, prohibition*, and *mandamus* (see p. 257).

(ii) The **Chancery Division** deals generally with matters which before 1873 fell within the jurisdiction of the old Court of Chancery. Certain other matters have, however, been added by statute, for example bankruptcy, claims, and company matters.

Composition. The court is composed of the Lord Chancellor, a Vice-Chancellor and seven puisne judges. The Lord Chancellor has, however, so many duties to perform as head of the judiciary, President of the House of Lords and member of the Cabinet, that he does not in practice take part in the work of the court, such duties falling to the Vice-Chancellor.

Jurisdiction of the division includes: (i) the administration of estates of deceased persons; (ii) the dissolution of partnerships and taking of partnership accounts; (iii) mortgages and charges on land; (iv) trusts, both private and public (or charitable); (v) the sale of property subject to a lien or charge; (vi) wardship of infants and care of infants' estates; (vii) company matters, e.g. dissolution and winding up; (viii) revenue matters, e.g. taxation; (ix) partition and sale of real estates; (x) rectification and setting aside of deeds or other written instruments of cancellation; (xi) bankruptcy matters; and (xii) specific performance of contracts.

(iii) The **Family Division** of the High Court deals mainly with the following matters: (*a*) divorce; (*b*) marriage of minors; (*c*) appeals from magistrates' courts on matrimonial matters, such as separation orders, maintenance, etc.; and (*d*) non-contentious probate business (probate means proving a will).

County Courts. These were first established by the *County Courts Act, 1846*, to provide cheap, speedy, and local justice—so obviating the need for bringing actions at Westminster or before the courts at *nisi prius*. The county courts proved efficient and their jurisdiction has been enlarged from time to time. The *County Courts Act, 1959* (a consolidating Act) now governs the composition and jurisdiction of these useful courts.

There are at present over four hundred such courts in England and Wales; and there are about ninety-eight county court judges, some of whom have charge of two or more courts. The number of cases dealt with annually amounts to over $1\frac{1}{2}$ million. Most actions are, however, disposed of or settled out of court before hearing.

Composition. The court is composed of one judge, known as a Circuit Judge (see p. 197), who sits singly. Circuit judges are appointed by the Lord Chancellor. They must be barristers of at least seven years' standing. In rare cases a jury of eight persons may be empanelled to assist the court.

The **registrar** of the court keeps the records of the court and performs the administrative work attached to it. He must be a solicitor of at least seven years' standing, and is appointed by the Lord Chancellor. A registrar may hear and adjudicate on certain small claims in place of the judge.

Jurisdiction. As a general rule the plaintiff must bring his claim or action in the court of the district where the defendant (or one of several defendants) dwells or carries on business. Actions relating to land must be brought in the court of the district wherein the land is situated.

Matters falling within the jurisdiction of the county courts include: (i) actions founded on contract or tort up to £1,000; (ii) equity matters (trusts, mortgages, etc.) up to £5,000; (iii) actions for the recovery of land, and questions of titles to land, where the net annual rateable value does not exceed £400; (iv) bankruptcies; (v) probate proceedings where the value of the deceased's estate is less than £1,000; (vi) winding up of companies with a paid-up capital of less than £10,000; (vii) supervision of the adoption of infants; (viii) Admiralty matters (in some courts only); and (ix) actions in relation to rent-restriction, hire-purchase, landlord-and-tenant, and similar matters as laid down by statute.

To relieve the burden of work falling on the Family Division of the High Court in regard to divorce petitions, and with a view to reducing legal costs, the county courts were given a limited divorce jurisdiction. The Lord Chancellor may designate any county court as a 'Divorce County Court' with power to hear and determine any *undefended* matrimonial cause.

Appeal from a county court lies to the Court of Appeal.

Since 1974 small claims—e.g. for debts, whether for goods sold, work done, or money lent, or for damages for negligence—where the amount in dispute does not exceed £100, may be dealt with **informally** before an arbitrator, who is usually the Registrar. The object is to enable persons to bring or defend actions without a solicitor, and perhaps running up costs and long delays. This court is in an experimental stage, but it may well meet a genuine need where people had been unjustly treated over small matters.

Criminal Courts Today

The courts in which criminal cases are tried are:

   (i) The House of Lords.
   (ii) The Court of Appeal (Criminal Division).
   (iii) Crown Courts.
   (iv) Magistrates' Courts.

In addition, the following court acts as an Appeal Court:

   (v) Divisional Court of Queen's Bench.

The House of Lords. This court hears appeals from the Court of Appeal (Criminal Division) and from the Divisional Court of Queen's Bench. Either prosecutor or defendant may appeal, but an important requirement is that leave of the Court of Appeal (Criminal Division) or the House of Lords must be obtained on the grounds that the case involves *a point of law of general public importance*. This is to prevent frivolous or minor cases going to this final court.

Composition. As already explained (p. 189), this court is composed of the Lord Chancellor, the Lords of Appeal in Ordinary, and other peers who have held high judicial office. The quorum is three, and each judge delivers a separate judgement, the verdict being by a majority.

Court of Appeal (Criminal Division). The *Criminal Appeal Act, 1966*, provides that the Court of Appeal shall consist of two divisions: one exercising civil jurisdiction and one criminal.

Composition. The court is composed of the Lord Chief Justice and the Lord Justices of Appeal. The Lord Chief Justice, or, in his absence, the Master of the Rolls, may require any judge of the Queen's Bench Division to sit. A quorum of three is necessary, and only one judgement is delivered except where the presiding judge permits separate verdicts to be pronounced on a question of law.

Jurisdiction. The court may dismiss the appeal or allow the appeal, and may order that any conviction recorded in a lower court shall be quashed. The court may order a new trial (*Administration of Justice Act, 1964*). The court may not increase the sentence against which appeal is being made. (Formerly a convicted person who wanted to appeal against what he considered too long a sentence ran the risk of having his sentence increased by the Court of Appeal, but this risk is now eliminated; the number of appeals on this ground has grown accordingly.)

To hear these appeals two courts sit full-time, while a third sits as and when required by the number of appeals listed.

Crown Courts. From medieval times the Royal judges went on circuit from Westminster administering justice in the provinces. They sat as **Courts of Assize** ('assize' means a 'sitting' or 'session') and had both a civil and criminal

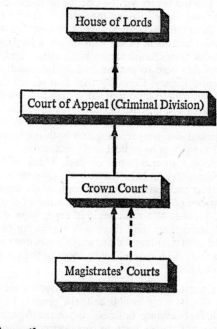

Appeals shown thus: ————→
Committals for trial: —— —→— —— —

The Criminal Courts

jurisdiction, although in modern times the criminal jurisdiction was the more important. The judges sat with juries and a Court of Assize could try, at first instance, any case in the criminal calendar, from treason and murder to simple theft. In practice, an Assize Court tried the serious crimes committed locally. If, therefore, *A* was brought before a magistrates' court charged with murder or some other serious offence, the magistrates would make a preliminary investigation and if the court decided that the prosecution had made out a *prima facie* case against *A*, the accused person would be committed to an Assize Court to stand trial.

Quarter Sessions Courts were also of medieval origin. These survived also until 1971. There were two kinds, namely a **County Quarter Sessions** and a **Borough Quarter Sessions Court.** The former was presided over by a chairman (who might be legally qualified or who might not, i.e. not a barrister or solicitor). The Chairman was assisted by magistrates drawn from the county. Most County Quarter Sessions in modern times had legally qualified chairmen. The Borough Quarter Sessions Court was presided over by a Recorder (usually a practising barrister who acted as a judge for the Borough). Their jurisdiction included less serious criminal cases than those reserved for the Courts of Assize. In addition, the Quarter Sessions court had an **appellate jurisdiction.** Thus if *A* were convicted of theft at a magistrates' court he could appeal to a Quarter Sessions Court against (*a*) his conviction, or (*b*) his sentence if it was too severe for the offence he had committed. Where *A* was prosecuted for an offence before a magistrates' court he had the option, if he was liable to three months' imprisonment or more, of (*a*) being dealt with by magistrates there and then, or (*b*) trial before a jury either at Assizes (if the offence was serious) or Quarter Sessions in other cases.

It is not possible here to outline in full the jurisdiction of each of these courts, or their efficiency. Certainly they had served their purpose well and were trusted. Nevertheless, no judicial system can stand still. A Royal Commission on Assizes and Quarter Sessions was appointed under the Chairmanship of Lord Beeching and the Commission reported in 1969 (*Cmnd. 4153* of 1969). It proposed sweeping reforms and both the Government and Opposition regarded the report as radical and spectacular.

The old circuit system was out of date. Many of the assize towns were situated in the country and the Assizes and Quarter Sessions Courts did not serve the interests and convenience of people in the large conurbations. There was inefficient use of judges, the administration of the judicial work needed rationalizing, so that the most serious cases were directed to those best qualified to handle them, and there was a growing back-log of appeals together with delay in handling the numerous cases due to the increase in crime.

The *Courts Act, 1971*, gave effect to most of the proposals. Only the main points are noted here:

(i) Assize Courts and Quarter Sessions Courts were abolished.

(ii) Crown Courts were established. (In general terms the Crown Court takes over all **first instance** business above magistrates' court level and all appeal business of Quarter Sessions, previously mentioned.)

The structure of the criminal courts from 1972 is as follows:

(i) House of Lords.
(ii) Court of Appeal (Criminal Division).
(iii) Crown Court.
(iv) Magistrates' Court.

Crown Court Jurisdiction. The Crown Court is a superior court, and it exercises original criminal jurisdiction. All proceedings on indictment must be brought in the Crown Court. (An indictment is merely a document which sets out the crime(s) with which a person is charged. Any offence punishable with three months' imprisonment or more is 'indictable', i.e. the accused may claim trial by jury—which will be in the Crown Court.)

The jurisdiction of a Crown Court will depend on how the Court is manned.

The broad principle is that the higher the status of the judge the more serious will be the cases he will try. So we must look at the judges of the Crown Court. They are:

(i) A judge of the High Court.

(ii) A circuit judge.

(iii) A Recorder.

(i) A **High Court judge** is a *puisne* (lesser) judge of the Queen's Bench Division. His position is similar to that of his predecessor (Assize Court Judge).

(ii) A **circuit judge** is a judge appointed by the Crown to serve in both (*a*) Crown Courts, and (*b*) County Courts. He must be a barrister of ten years' standing, or a person who has held the office of a Recorder (see p. 196) for five years. He must retire at 72 years of age, but may be allowed to extend his period of office until he is 75. All former county court judges (see p. 193), the Recorders of Liverpool and Manchester, a number of full-time Chairmen and Deputy Chairmen of Quarter Sessions, and certain other holders of judicial office become circuit judges.

(iii) A **Recorder** is a **part-time** judge of the Crown Court. He is appointed for a fixed term. Appointments are made from men of high professional standing, who are prepared to commit themselves to **not less than one month's work** on the bench each year.

The new Recorders must not be confused with those referred to on page 196 (Recorders of Boroughs whose office now lapses under the Act). The new Recorders are not associated with particular Boroughs.

The new system will give the authorities (e.g. the Lord Chancellor) the chance to assess the Recorders, as to their suitability for appointment to the High Court Bench, or to circuit judgeships.

The Division of Offences. Offences triable in Crown Courts are divided into four classes:

Class 1. Triable by High Court judge only.

(i) All offences punishable by death; (ii) misprision of treason and treason felony; (iii) murder; (iv) genocide; (v) offences under section 1 of the *Official Secrets Act, 1911*; (vi) incitement, attempt or conspiracy to commit any of the above offences.

Class 2. Triable by High Court judge only unless a particular case is released to be tried by a circuit judge, or Recorder.

(i) Manslaughter; (ii) infanticide; (iii) child murder; (iv) unlawful abortion; (v) rape; (vi) sexual intercourse with a girl under 13; (vii) incest with a girl under 13; (viii) sedition; (ix) mutiny; (x) piracy; (xi) offences under section 1 of the *Geneva Conventions Act, 1957*; (xii) incitement, attempt or conspiracy to commit any of the above offences.

Class 3. All indictable offences (i.e. triable before a jury) other than those in classes 1, 2 and 4).

Such offences may be tried (i) by a High Court judge, or (ii) a circuit judge or Recorder.

Class 4. Triable by a circuit judge or Recorder. (Sometimes by a High Court judge—see below.)

CROWN COURT

1. High Court Judge, Circuit Judge or Recorder
2. Justices of the Peace (not more than 4)
3. Clerk of the Court
4. Prosecuting Barrister (standing)
5. Defending Barrister (seated)
6. Solicitor or solicitor's clerk in attendance (Prosecution)
7. Solicitor or solicitor's clerk in attendance (Defence)
8. Probation Officer
9. Prisoner
10. Warder from prison
11. Police Officer (or Court Usher)
12. Witnesses who have given evidence
13. Jury
14. Press reporters
15. Public
16. Witnesses for Prosecution outside court waiting to give evidence
17. Witnesses for Defence outside court waiting to give evidence
18. Witness
19. Shorthand writer

(i) Indictable offences which may be tried summarily (i.e. before magistrates' court) or on indictment. For example, theft in a supermarket is indictable and may be tried (*a*) before magistrates' court, or (*b*) before the Crown Court. (ii) Causing death by reckless or dangerous driving; (iii) wounding or causing grievous bodily harm; (iv) burglary; (v) robbery, or assault with intent to rob; (vi) forgery; (vii) incitement, attempt or conspiracy to commit any of the above offences.

Considerable discretion is given to the presiding High Court judge responsible for a particular circuit, to allocate particular cases. For example, even if a substantive offence is not grave or serious in itself the circumstances or the points of law likely to arise may justify trial by a High Court judge rather than by a Recorder, who is a part-time judge and consequently has less experience.

Crown Courts and Justices of the Peace. The *Courts Act, 1971*, provides that the Crown Court shall consist of (*a*) a High Court judge, or (*b*) a circuit judge, or (*c*) a Recorder, sitting with not less than two nor more than four Justices of the peace:

(i) At the hearing of an appeal.
(ii) In cases where a defendant has been committed for sentence (for example, when a magistrates' court finds a man guilty, and that he should be sentenced by a Crown Court).

Furthermore, any jurisdiction (i.e. any case triable at a Crown Court) may be exercised by a court consisting of a professional judge and not more than four Justices. When they are members of a Crown Court, the Justices have one vote each and a decision is carried by a majority vote. The principle is that 'team effort' shall be fostered in the administration of justice.

Crown Courts and Solicitors. Solicitors of ten years' standing are eligible for appointment as **Recorders**. Moreover, if a solicitor holds the appointment of Recorder for five years, he is eligible for appointment as a **Circuit Judge**. This is the first breach in the monopoly exercised by the Bar.

Under the Act a provision has been made whereby solicitors can appear in court, and address the court in some proceedings in the Crown Courts. Hitherto the right to appear in the superior courts has been limited exclusively to barristers.

Appeal by Way of Case Stated. This form of appeal may be used in a magistrates' court and in a Crown Court, when the Crown Court re-hears a case on appeal from a magistrates' court. The court to which appeal is made is the Divisional Court of Queen's Bench, which is constituted by not less than two judges of that Division (the usual number sitting is three).

Where either party (prosecutor or defendant) is dissatisfied on a point of law with the decision of, for example, a Crown Court, that party may require the Crown Court to 'state a case' for the opinion of the Divisional Court of Queen's Bench. The Crown Court states the case in writing, giving the facts and the reasons for the decision. The Divisional Court then adjudicates on the written evidence submitted and gives its ruling.

There are two points to be noted: (i) the appeal must be on a point of law, not fact; (ii) both prosecutor and defendant may appeal. This is contrary to the general rule that where a charge is dismissed or the defendant is acquitted, the prosecution has no general right of appeal to a higher court. We should

Appeal by way of 'Case Stated'

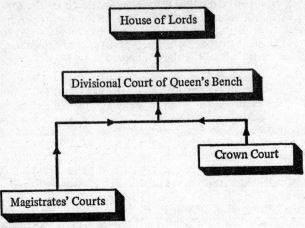

Points to note:
    Applies to magistrates' courts *and* Crown Courts.
    Defence *and* prosecution can appeal.
    Must be on *a point of law*.

further observe that this form of appeal applies to a magistrates' court as well as to a Crown Court when the latter sits in its appellate capacity (hearing a case from a magistrates' court).

Magistrates' Courts. The first Justices were appointed in 1327 as 'conservators of the peace'. For more than six hundred years their successors, now known as Justices of the Peace or magistrates, have performed the duties of enforcing the common law and statute law and of preserving locally the public peace and good order.

During the past fifty years Parliament has burdened magistrates' courts with enforcing increasing quantities of legislation, much of it highly complex. Magistrates' courts (or courts of petty sessions) today exercise wider jurisdiction and deal with more cases than any other court in the English legal system. For example, over ninety-eight per cent of all criminal prosecutions in England and Wales are dealt with by magistrates. Magistrates also deal with a wide variety of civil cases and perform certain administrative duties, particularly in licensing matters.

There are two kinds of Justices of the Peace: (i) County Justices and (ii) Stipendiary Magistrates.

(i) **County Justices** are appointed by the Lord Chancellor on the recommendation of the Lord Lieutenant of the county assisted by an advisory committee. They have jurisdiction throughout the county.

The important features of borough and county magistrates are that they are unpaid (though they may receive out-of-pocket expenses when adjudicating) and they are laymen. They number 21,000 in England and Wales.

Because of the importance of the work falling to magistrates, it is now ordained that all magistrates appointed after 1 January 1966, must undergo basic training in the duties of their office. They must understand the meaning

The Magistrates' Court

1. Chairman of Justices
2. Justices of the Peace
3. Clerk of Magistrates
4. Defending Lawyer (seated)
5. Prosecuting Lawyer (standing)
6. Probation Officers
7. Defendant
8. Police Officer
9. Witness
10. Other witnesses
11. Press
12. Public

of 'acting judicially', elementary legal procedure and sentencing policy, so as to preserve the highest standards of efficient judicial administration. The total number of lay magistrates in England and Wales is approximately 21,500.

(ii) **Stipendiary magistrates** are full-time paid magistrates. They are appointed by the Lord Chancellor and must be barristers or solicitors of at least seven years' standing. Stipendiary magistrates (eleven) are found in the larger cities, application for such appointments being made by the municipal corporations. A stipendiary magistrate can do alone any act which requires two or more lay Justices sitting in petty sessions.

Metropolitan magistrates are stipendiary magistrates appointed for the Metropolitan Area, which includes the City of London and the County of London, the latter being divided into court areas; there are 39 in all.

The Clerk to the Justices is the official attached to each magistrates' court who advises the Justices on points of law and procedure, makes a record of evidence and prepares depositions (i.e. statements sworn on oath in the presence of an accused person) made by witnesses in those cases sent forward for trial at a Crown Court. He also performs the administrative work of the court such as preparing informations, summonses and warrants granted by the magistrates, and collecting fines.

The *Justices of the Peace Act, 1949*, provides that a clerk must be a barrister or solicitor of at least five years' standing. The Act also provides for the setting up in the counties of committees to supervise the administrative work of the magistrates' courts.

A clerk to the Justices must not retire with the Justices to consider their verdict, such matters being solely for the magistrates.

Jurisdiction of Magistrates' Courts. The jurisdiction of these courts falls under three main headings: (*a*) as a court of trial; (*b*) as a court of preliminary investigation; (*c*) miscellaneous.

(*a*) *Court of Trial.* The jurisdiction is exercised by from two to seven justices, and the maximum punishment that may be imposed for any one offence is six months' imprisonment or a fine of £400. A single Justice in petty sessions may try trivial cases such as simple drunkenness.

Criminal offences can be divided into three classes:

(i) Indictable offences, i.e. those triable on indictment at a Crown Court. All offences punishable with three months' imprisonment or more are indictable. The magistrates must ask any person accused of such an offence whether he wishes to be tried on indictment or to be tried summarily (see below). An indictment is simply the document used in jury trials which names the offence(s).

(ii) Offences triable summarily, i.e. there and then in a magistrates' court. Offences which can only be tried summarily include riding a pedal cycle at night without lights, begging in a public place, and being found drunk and incapable on the highway.

(iii) Indictable offences triable summarily in the magistrates' court if the accused so elects. Let us take by way of example a case where the accused is alleged to have stolen a penknife. Since theft is an indictable offence (it is punishable by seven years' imprisonment), the accused may claim trial before a jury. However, the magistrates will offer him the choice of either trial at a Crown Court or trial by the magistrates. If he chooses the latter, the magistrates will try the case there and then, i.e. summarily. If he chooses to be tried at a Crown Court, the magistrates will sit as a court of preliminary investigation.

The agenda of a typical magistrates' court reveals a wide variety of offences: petty theft, wilful damage, common assault, drunkenness, driving a motor-car without a driving licence, driving without insurance, failing to obey traffic signs, parking offences, driving without due care and attention, and similar road-traffic offences. Some offenders will be dealt with then and there (even though they qualify for trial by a Crown Court), while defendants who elect for trial by jury will be committed for trial if the prosecution makes out a *prima facie* case in respect of each. (A *prima facie* case is one which appears 'at first sight' or 'from the first impression' to be an offence.)

(*b*) *Court of Preliminary Investigation.* In this capacity the magistrates' court is called upon to determine whether an accused person, who is brought before it by means of a summons or by arrest, shall be committed to stand trial at a Crown Court.

The prosecution calls its witnesses and produces exhibits (e.g. a gun or knife). The evidence of the prosecution witnesses is taken down in writing in the presence of the accused, and the document (called a deposition) is signed by the witness (called a deponent) and by the Justice present at the hearing. After all the evidence for the prosecution is heard, the accused is charged with the alleged offence. He may plead 'guilty' or 'not guilty'; he may give evidence himself and call witnesses in his support, or he may reserve his defence until the actual trial. Usually an accused reserves his defence.

After hearing the evidence the magistrates decide whether the prosecution has made out a *prima facie* case. If it has, the accused and the witnesses are bound over to attend the trial at a Crown Court. These proceedings are known as **committal proceedings**, and although they may be taken before one Justice, in practice two or more lay magistrates usually preside over this important step in the judicial process.

If the prosecution has not made out a *prima facie* case against the accused, the magistrates must release him. When an accused is committed for trial he may be either remanded in custody (i.e. to a prison to await trial) or remanded on bail (i.e. liberated from the magistrates' court on condition that he turns up at the trial at a later date when his case will be heard).

The *Criminal Justice Act, 1967*, provides that, in certain circumstances, an accused person may be committed for trial on **written** evidence alone instead of oral evidence taken down in the form of depositions.

The Act also restricts the publication of reports of committal proceedings to purely formal matters, i.e. the identity of the court and magistrates, the names of the parties, and the nature of the charges. The object is to avoid prejudicing the accused by pre-trial publicity.

(c) *Miscellaneous Jurisdiction.* In addition to the foregoing duties, the magistrates perform administrative functions in regard to liquor licensing (approving applicants and premises), betting licensing, theatre and cinematograph licensing, and have a limited jurisdiction in regard to civil debts (e.g. unpaid income tax where the amount due is less than £30).

Other important duties include: (i) making matrimonial orders for separation and maintenance of spouses; (ii) affiliation orders; (iii) consent to marriage; (iv) guardianship of infants; (v) adoption of children; (vi) orders under the Mental Health Act, 1959; and (vii) orders in regard to children and young persons in need of care, protection or control.

Juvenile Courts. Certain magistrates attached to a petty-sessional division form a special panel to deal with offences committed by children (i.e. persons under 14) and young persons (i.e. over 14 and under 17). The juvenile court is formed by three lay Justices, one of whom must be a woman. All such Justices retire at 65 years of age. A stipendiary magistrate may sit in this court.

The juvenile court sits separately from the adult court: if it cannot sit in a different room it must sit on a different day. Proceedings in juvenile courts are shielded from publicity. The Press must not disclose the identity of the child or young person unless the court, in exceptional cases, permits.

Where a child or young person is charged jointly with an adult the case is dealt with in an adult court, i.e. the usual magistrates' court.

Appeals from magistrates' courts are organized as follows:

(*a*) Where the defendant wishes to appeal against (i) conviction and/or (ii) sentence, appeal lies to the Crown Court.

(*b*) Where the defendant wishes to appeal against conviction or sentence on a point of law, appeal lies to the Divisional Court of Queen's Bench by way of 'case stated'.

(*c*) Appeals concerning separation and maintenance orders, affiliation, adoption, and consent to marry lie to the Family Division of the High Court.

Special Courts

Central Criminal Court. This famous court, commonly known as the Old Bailey, was set up by the *Central Criminal Court Act, 1834*. It exercises the criminal jurisdiction of a Crown Court and hears cases on indictment committed from the City of London and the Greater London area. In addition, the Central Criminal Court may try any crime committed at sea. Proceedings may be removed into the Central Criminal Court from a provincial court if there is a risk that strong local feelings might otherwise prejudice the accused's case.

The court is held at least twelve times a year and is, in practice, very busy and is in almost continuous session.

Composition. The judges of the court are the Lord Chancellor; the judges of the Queen's Bench Division; the Lord Mayor, Aldermen, Recorder, and Common Serjeant of the City of London; and the judge of the City of London Court. In practice, the judges are those of the Queen's Bench Division and judges appointed by commission.

The court is constituted by a single judge who sits with a jury.

Restrictive Practices Court. This court was set up by the *Restrictive Trade Practices Act, 1956*, and is a new superior court of record. Its purpose is to consider and adjudicate on agreements entered into between firms, suppliers, or buyers, in which restrictions are imposed on the price, quantity, quality, or method of distribution of goods.

Restrictive agreements must be registered with the Director-General of Fair Trading, whose duty it is to refer to the court any agreement deemed to offend against the public interest.

Composition. The court is equal in standing to the High Court, and consists of three judges of the High Court, a judge of the Court of Session of Scotland, and a judge of the Supreme Court of Northern Ireland. In addition there are ten lay members experienced in industry, commerce or public affairs, two of whom with one presiding judge form a quorum. The court may sit in two or more Divisions. Appeal lies to the Court of Appeal.

Coroners' Courts. The office of coroner and the coroner's inquest (or inquiry) are of ancient origin. The first coroners were appointed in the reign of Richard I in 1194. Originally they had wide powers concerning local administration and the criminal law, but these have now been shed and the coroner of today carries out those duties laid down in the *Coroners Acts, 1887 and 1954*, and rules made thereunder.

The main duties of the coroner are to investigate the death of any person which has been (i) sudden, (ii) violent, or (iii) unnatural (i.e. against the course of nature), (iv) deaths of prisoners, and (v) deaths of persons in mental institutions where there is no satisfactory medical evidence as to the cause of death. The coroner may, however, hold an inquest into *any* case of death.

A coroner *must* summon a jury when there is reason to suspect that death is due to murder, manslaughter, infanticide, a road accident, poisoning, or notifiable disease. An inquest may be held in any place (e.g. a court or a private house). Proceedings are carried out in a formal manner. The public are admitted to the court except when this would be prejudicial to national security.

The purpose of the inquest is to enable the coroner, with the aid of a jury when so required, to ascertain the identity of the deceased person and the place and cause of death. If the jury find that the cause of death is murder, manslaughter, or infanticide they may name the person responsible, and the coroner must then issue a warrant of arrest. However, if some person has already been arrested and charged with the murder, manslaughter, or infanticide of the subject of the inquest, the coroner must adjourn his inquiry until the criminal proceedings are ended.

Money, coin, gold, silver, plate, or bullion found hidden in the earth or a private place, the owner of which is unknown, is called **treasure trove** and belongs to the Crown. When such articles are uncovered, the coroner holds an inquest to establish whether they are in fact treasure trove. If so, the finder and the owner of the land on which they were found are customarily recompensed by the Treasury.

A coroner must be a barrister, solicitor, or medical practitioner of at least five years' standing. He is appointed by a county council or a borough council having a separate commission of the peace. The Lord Chancellor may dismiss a coroner for inability or misbehaviour amounting to misconduct.

Law Reform

The law is open to the criticism that in general it is conservative. Many statutes are ancient, appertaining to a bygone age and feudal system; some common law offences are inappropriate today. For example, the offences of challenging to fight, eavesdropping, being a common barrator, a common scold or common night walker were abolished only in 1967 by the Criminal Justice Act of that year. Furthermore, it is argued that legal procedures are unduly formal and slow, and that the system of courts needs overhaul and remodelling.

Some of these criticisms may seem fair and reasonable; but it is clear that reform of the law and the machinery of the courts are matters which cannot be approached carelessly, irresponsibly, or hurriedly. Nevertheless, law is a living thing and reform is continual. The agencies through which reform is effected include the following:

(*a*) Law Reform Committee.
(*b*) Criminal Law Revision Committee.
(*c*) Law Commission.
(*d*) Royal Commissions.
(*e*) Government Legislation (Public Bills).
(*f*) Private Members' Bills.

(*a*) *The Law Reform Committee* began in 1952 and took over the work of the Law Revision Committee set up in 1934. It is made up of judges and practising and academic lawyers, and deals with civil-law matters referred to it by the Lord Chancellor. Members of the committee, and the general public also, may raise matters and suggest subjects for consideration. The following statutes reformed parts of the civil law and were passed as a result of the recommendations of the committee:

The *Limitation Act, 1939*.
The *Law Reform (Contributory Negligence) Act, 1945*.
The *Occupiers' Liability Act, 1957*.
The *Law Reform (Husband and Wife) Act, 1962*.

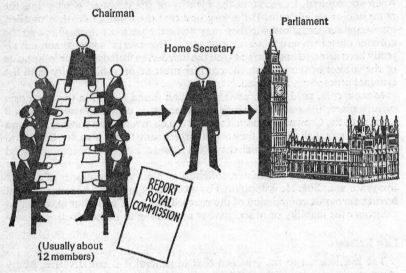

Chairman

Home Secretary

Parliament

REPORT ROYAL COMMISSION

(Usually about 12 members)

A Royal Commission

(b) *The Criminal Law Revision Committee*. While the Lord Chancellor is concerned with the Law Reform Committee and the reform of the civil law, the Home Secretary is primarily concerned with the administration of the criminal law. The Criminal Law Revision Committee (a Standing Committee) was set up in 1959 to examine aspects of the criminal law, to consider whether the law requires revision, and to make recommendations.

The Committee has issued several reports; the seventh (Felonies and Misdemeanours) and eighth (Theft and Related Offences) have resulted in the *Criminal Law Act, 1967*, and the *Theft Act, 1968*, respectively.

(c) *The Law Commission*. The *Law Commissions Act, 1965*, set up a full-time Commission whose duty is to keep under review the English law as a whole with a view to its systematic development and reform, including, in particular, its codification, the elimination of anomalies, the repeal of obsolete and unnecessary enactments, the reduction of the number of separate enactments, and, generally, the simplification and modernization of the law. Pursuant to programmes approved by the Lord Chancellor, the Commission undertakes the examination of particular branches of the law and the formulation, by means of draft Bills, of proposals for reform. It is responsible for the consolidation and revision of statute law.

The five commissioners and a legal staff are appointed by the Lord Chancellor. The Commission issues an annual report which is laid before Parliament.

(d) *Royal Commissions* are appointed by the Crown on the advice of a Minister who names a Chairman. The membership of each Royal Commission varies, but it usually reflects expert, professional, and lay opinion. The duty of a Royal Commission is to investigate some matter of public importance, to take evidence and to make recommendations. On receipt of its report, the Government may give legislative effect to the recommendations. For example the main recommendations of the Royal Commission on Tribunals and Inquiries appointed in 1955 found expression in the *Tribunals and Inquiries Act, 1958*.

The Royal Commission on Local Government Reform (1966–9) resulted in the *Local Government Act, 1972*.

(*e*) *Government Legislation.* A Government's legislative programme varies with the political party in power. Some Bills may inaugurate entirely new services, e.g. the National Health Service legislation of 1946, but some legislation may aim at tidying up, consolidating, or reforming the law in a particular respect. The *Road Traffic Act, 1972*, and the *Town and Country Planning Act, 1971*, consolidated and reformed existing law in these two matters. Moreover, delegated legislation may be passed into law by Ministers to whom Parliament has entrusted its power. Thus many statutory instruments amend, reform, or consolidate existing rules.

(*f*) *Private Members' Bills* (see p. 90) may reform existing law in important respects. Examples include the *Inheritance (Family Provision) Act, 1938*, the *Matrimonial Causes Act, 1937*, and the *Defamation Act, 1952*. Parliamentary time is, however, limited, and Government Bills must come first. Hence the Private Members' Bill is not the most important medium of reform.

Juries

(*a*) *The Criminal Jury* comprises twelve persons of either sex and is found in the Central Criminal Court and the Crown Courts. Juries are not used in magistrates' courts, juvenile courts, the Court of Appeal or the House of Lords. The sworn duty of the jury is 'to well and truly try the case and give a true verdict according to the evidence'.

The defence and the prosecution have a right of challenge to the array of jurors or to individual jurors. Those jurors objected to will be asked to stand down and others will be empanelled to take their places.

Formerly the verdict of a jury had to be unanimous. Now, the *Juries Act, 1974*, provides that a majority verdict may be allowed. The court cannot, however, accept a majority verdict unless the jury has been deliberating for not less than two hours, when the verdict need not then be unanimous if (i) in a case where there are not less than eleven jurors, ten of them agree; or (ii) in a case where there are ten jurors, nine of them agree.

Where a juror dies or is ill, provided that both sides agree and the number of jurors is not reduced below ten, the case may continue and a verdict may be given.

(*b*) *The Civil Jury* is not used as frequently as its criminal counterpart. Certain civil actions are unsuitable for trial by juries, e.g. taxation cases and company matters involving detailed examination of accounts. The general rule following the *Administration of Justice (Miscellaneous Provision) Act, 1933*, is that the civil court has a discretion in its use of a jury. A jury may, however, be ordered on the application of either party in cases of defamation, malicious prosecution, false imprisonment and fraud, unless the court considers that, for example, the trial will involve prolonged examination of documents or accounts.

In actions in the Chancery Division juries are used only rarely. In defended divorce cases or contested probate actions a jury may be applied for.

In High Court cases the jury comprises twelve persons. A majority verdict is now accepted. In county court actions the jury numbers eight. In coroners' courts the jury comprises from seven to eleven persons; the coroner may accept a majority verdict, provided that the number of dissentients does not exceed two.

When a judge sits without a jury, he determines questions of law and fact.

Qualifications of Jurymen

The *Criminal Justice Act, 1972*, abolished the former property qualification for jury service in England and Wales. The basic qualification is that of **citizenship** as evidenced by inclusion in the Electoral Register. Anyone between the ages of 18 and 65 registered as an elector who has lived here for five years or more since the age of 13 becomes liable for jury service.

Payments in respect of jury service for travelling, subsistence, and financial loss are made to jurors.

Ex-prisoners are disqualified from serving on a jury. Mentally ill persons are ineligible. Sick, blind, and deaf persons may be excused on compassionate grounds.

Peers, judges, M.P.s, clergymen, barristers, solicitors, medical practitioners, members of H.M. Forces and police officers are among the more notable persons exempt from jury service. The *Juries Act, 1974*, consolidates the law.

The **advantages** of trial by jury are:

(*a*) Jurors are independent of the parties to a trial.

(*b*) Juries represent the verdict of ordinary people of common sense, and this fact can act as a corrective to the harshness of the law.

(*c*) There is public confidence in jury trials.

(*d*) In jury trials the judge explains the facts to be proved and the law to be applied, which tends to clarify the issues verbally. The public thus sees that justice is done.

(*e*) The English jury trial has been copied by other countries (e.g. the United States) and is found satisfactory.

The **disadvantages** of trial by jury are:

(*a*) Complicated financial frauds may be incomprehensible to ordinary folk.

(*b*) Jurors have no physical or educational test for their task.

(*c*) Jurors may be too easily impressed and swayed by advocacy of experienced counsel.

(*d*) Juries are too prone to leniency to an accused or defendant in criminal trials.

(*e*) Local prejudice may exist in certain trials, and this may be reflected in local jurors.

(*f*) Jurors are susceptible to corrupt influences, threats, and intimidation from outside parties.

(*g*) Some trials are long and, as a consequence, cause inconvenience to jurors; self-employed jurors may suffer financially. Hence the jury system is expensive.

(*h*) Persons at 18 may be considered too inexperienced.

Legal Aid and Advice

Free legal assistance to persons of limited means has existed at least in a few courts since the thirteenth century. Such schemes were run by unofficial voluntary organizations known as the Poor Man's Lawyers. Apart from such schemes, the general situation before 1949 was that legal aid and advice were available only to those who had the money to pay for them.

The *Legal Aid and Advice Act, 1949*, revised existing schemes and expanded them into a service covering the full range of needs and providing (i) free, or assisted, representation for all who require it; and (ii) virtually free legal advice on matters unconnected with court proceedings (known as non-litigious matters). The *Legal Aid Act, 1974*, consolidates the law on this matter.

Legal Aid in Civil Proceedings

Legal aid is available for proceedings in the House of Lords, Court of Appeal, High Court, county courts, coroners' courts, and certain other tribunals, and to civil proceedings in magistrates' courts.

Proceedings wholly or partly in respect of defamation, breach of promise of marriage, and proceedings by way of Judgement Summons in a county court are excepted from the scheme. All other civil proceedings, including matrimonial causes, qualify for legal aid.

Eligibility for legal aid in civil proceedings depends on an applicant's 'disposable income' and 'disposable capital'.

In practice a 'means test' is operated thus:

(*a*) *Free* legal aid is available to those with a disposable income not exceeding £570 per annum and whose disposable capital is £250 or less.

(*b*) *Contributory* legal aid is available to those with a disposable income which does not exceed £1,790 and whose disposable capital is less than £1,200 or such larger figure as may be prescribed.

Aid is now available for persons of average income. The 'disposable income' and 'disposable capital' are assessed by the Supplementary Benefits Commission of the Ministry for Social Services in accordance with regulations, taking into account any maintenance expense of dependants, interests on loans, income tax, rent, etc., as well as the value of an applicant's house, furniture, and household effects.

The Legal Aid Scheme is run by the Law Society under the general guidance of the Lord Chancellor. There are twelve area committees and a network of local committees composed of barristers and solicitors (who may be paid a fee) with a salaried staff. The cost of operating the scheme is met by (i) contributions from assisted persons; (ii) costs recovered from opposite parties in litigation; and (iii) grants from the Exchequer.

Procedure. An applicant for legal aid must approach the local committee and show that he has reasonable grounds for his claim. If successful he is entitled to select from a panel a solicitor, who, if necessary, will instruct a barrister. The case then proceeds in the normal way, payments being made into and out of the Legal Aid Fund. The costs of an action which an assisted litigant loses to an unassisted opponent may also, if the court so orders, be met out of the Legal Aid Fund (*Legal Aid Act, 1974*). For example, let us suppose that *A*, an assisted person, sued *B*, an unassisted person, in negligence. *A* loses his case against *B* who is now faced with paying his solicitor's fee and other incidental expenses arising from his successful defence. The court may, at its discretion, order that *B*'s costs be paid out of the Legal Aid Fund.

Legal Advice. Anyone over 16 may obtain legal advice under the 'Green Form Scheme'. This includes letter-writing but *not* representation in court. The service is free for those with disposable income less than £16 per week. Those with disposable income over £30 per week must pay for the advice, etc. Those between £16 and £30 pay on a sliding scale.

Legal Aid in Criminal Proceedings

A criminal court, e.g. magistrates' court, or Crown Court, has power to order legal aid to be granted where it appears desirable to do so in the interests of justice. Trivial cases, e.g. simple drunkenness, do not qualify. The court *must* make an order in cases where a person of limited means is committed for trial on a charge of murder.

The court will not make an order for legal aid unless it is satisfied that the person's means are such that he requires assistance in meeting the cost of the proceedings in question.

Application for legal aid should be made to the appropriate court where proceedings are to take place. An applicant may be required to make a contribution towards the costs of the action. To ascertain the amount of this contribution he will be required to produce written evidence of means. An assessment of means will be carried out by the Supplementary Benefits Commission, which reports to the court. No contribution is required from a person who has insufficient means. Any doubt which exists as to the means of the defendant is resolved in his favour. The court has power to amend or revoke a legal-aid order.

As a general rule, legal aid in criminal cases includes representation by counsel and solicitor. In magistrates' courts, however, representation will be by solicitor alone unless the offence is serious.

Legal aid may also be granted in connection with appellate proceedings, e.g. on appeal to the Court of Appeal (Criminal Division), and, if need be, to the House of Lords.

Dock Briefs

Where a person is committed for trial from a magistrates' court he will, should his means be insufficient, be granted facilities for legal aid in the form of advice and representation of his case in court during the committal proceedings. Arrangements will then be made for a barrister to represent him at a Crown Court.

If, however, a prisoner has no barrister to represent him at a Crown Court, he may (irrespective of his means) choose any counsel, robed and in court, to defend him. By tradition the barrister selected will never refuse to take his 'dock brief', and will defend the prisoner to the best of his ability for a very small fee. This customary aid has fallen into disuse because of the statutory provisions, i.e. *Legal Aid Act, 1974*.

Law and Laymen

The making of law, the administration of law, and the administration of justice in the courts and tribunals are matters of supreme importance to civilized men everywhere.

Laymen in Anglo-Saxon and Norman times participated closely in making and administering the law. They were, as we have noted, responsible for keeping the King's Peace. If crimes were committed they had forthwith to raise the 'hue and cry' and to surrender the criminal (if known) to the Courts of Law; for failing to do so they were collectively held responsible and fined. The laymen or their representatives attended the Anglo-Saxon dooms; they attended the hundred court, the shire court, the manorial court, and the Royal court. They adjudged, as jurymen, in disputes as to ownership and possession of land and cattle and goods, and they pronounced on innocence or guilt— giving the verdict of the country. They petitioned successive Monarchs to change the laws and to grant remedies or relief when the laws pressed heavily upon themselves. Ultimately they achieved a great constitutional reform of Parliament in 1689, which ensured that the will of the people (laymen) should prevail against the supreme might and power of a despotic King. Such, in broad outline, were some of the reforms by laymen who played their part— sometimes at great personal risk—in the creation of the English legal system we now enjoy.

Today in a free society the will of the people finds its highest democratic expression in a Parliament composed of representatives of all classes, elected by popular vote of laymen who hold universal franchise.

As to making the law, we may note that a layman can offer himself as a Parliamentary candidate; he can, as of right, make representations to change the law to his M.P., to a Minister of a Government Department, to the Prime Minister, if need be. He can offer advice and evidence to Royal Commissions set up to inquire into a matter of immediate public importance, and he can suggest reform or improvement of the law itself, e.g. to the Law Commission (see p. 207).

As to administration of the law today, we may note particularly the part played by laymen (*a*) as Justices of the Peace, (*b*) as jurors, and (*c*) as lay assessors who assist a professional judge or lawyer acting judicially in the special courts and administrative tribunals already described.

(*a*) *Justices of the Peace.* A description of the composition and jurisdiction of the magistrates' courts has already been given. All we need to note here is that there are some 21,500 lay Justices regularly adjudicating on a wide variety of matters and performing numerous administrative duties. These Justices deal with more than ninety-eight per cent of the criminal cases in Britain, and they may now sit in the Crown Courts.

Lay Justices appointed after 1 January 1966, are required to undergo train- ing in the basic duties of their office. This does not render them professional lawyers, but assists them in understanding the meaning of 'acting judicially' so that they may more efficiently administer justice to the local people, from whose numbers they are drawn and whose public interests they serve.

(*b*) *Juries.* A detailed description of the different kinds of juries is given on p. 207. We should bear in mind that juries are composed of laymen on whose shoulders rests the final determination of verdicts in civil and criminal cases in a wide variety of courts.

(*c*) *Lay Assessors in Special Courts.* Examples of this form of participation are found in:

(i) *The Admiralty Court.* This is presided over by a High Court judge with jurisdiction to decide cases involving ships, shipping disputes, collisions at sea, etc. There is no jury, but in suitable cases (e.g. negligent navigation) the judge may call on the assistance of two nautical assessors (Elder Brethren of Trinity House) who are competent to advise on technical maritime matters.

(ii) *The Restrictive Practices Court.* The jurisdiction of this court has been dealt with on p. 204. It is a superior Court of Record and is composed of professional judges and men experienced in commerce and business. Each court sits with a High Court judge and two laymen.

(iii) *Administrative Tribunals.* These have an increasingly important part to play in the lives of all people, and mention may be made of Rent Tribunals, National Insurance Tribunals, National Insurance Industrial Injuries Tribunals, Pensions Tribunals, National Health Service Tribunals, Transport Tribunals, and those of the Area Traffic Commissioners.

Although the constitution of each may vary in detail, the common factor is the presence of laymen, usually representing interests or bodies such as local authorities, employers' organizations, and employees' organizations. Usually the Chairmen are legally qualified persons (*Tribunals and Inquiries Act, 1971*), but the presence of the laymen ensures that tribunals display the characteristics of 'openness, fairness, and impartiality' and helps to achieve a just and proper balance of opinion on the tribunal bench.

Administrative Personnel

The distinction between laymen and professional lawyers is not always clear. The Welfare State has enormously increased the number of local and central Government servants and has introduced a whole range of enforcement officers who must specialize in and enforce certain parts of the law. Pre-eminently, the police must know the criminal law and the powers of arrest and procedure very well indeed if they are to enforce its detailed and complicated provisions. They receive special training throughout their careers to equip them to discharge their duties efficiently. Many legal battles in the criminal courts revolve around whether the particular police officer has, or has not, acted in accordance with the law (common law or statute law), all of whose precepts he is presumed to know.

Other officials include probation officers, children's officers, mental-health officers, inspectors of factories, and inspectors of weights and measures. Like the police, these officials who execute or administer the law may lay information for summonses, may prosecute cases before the magistrates' courts, and in some cases may detain persons. They are therefore in a special class and do not strictly fall under the headings of laymen or professional lawyers.

For some nine hundred years laymen have played their part in the creation of the legal system and the constitution which we inherit. The word 'justice' appeals to the idealism in men the world over. Laymen have seen to it that it is much too important a matter to be left to professionals or to be dispensed in secret. 'Every court of justice is open to every subject of the King', said Lord Halsbury in *Scott* v. *Scott* (1913). The public, or laymen collectively, recognize the truth of the following utterance in a court of law: 'Justice is not a cloistered virtue; she must be allowed to suffer the scrutiny and respectful, even though outspoken, comments of ordinary men' (*Ambard* v. *Attorney-General of Trinidad and Tobago*, 1936).

All laymen, whether officiating as magistrates, assessors, jurors, witnesses, or merely spectators in the public gallery, ought to ensure that full and positive meaning is given to the words of Lord Chief Justice Hewart: 'It is not only necessary that justice should be done, but also that it should manifestly be seen to be done.'

Exercises

1. Define 'Law'. Distinguish between a law and rule of morality.
2. What are the main characteristics of English law?
3. What are the main sources of English law? What subsidiary sources are there?
4. What were the effects of the Norman Conquest on English law?
5. What do you understand by Equity? Trace its development to the present time.
6. What do you understand by the doctrine of Judicial Precedent? Distinguish between *ratio decidendi* and *obiter dicta*.
7. What is the composition and jurisdiction of the House of Lords when sitting as a Court of Appeal?
8. Outline the composition and jurisdiction of the Judicial Committee of the Privy Council.
9. The Queen's Bench Division of the High Court exercises (i) an original jurisdiction, and (ii) an appellate jurisdiction. Describe its jurisdiction carefully.
10. What is the composition and jurisdiction of the Court of Appeal, Criminal Division?
11. Describe the composition of the Crown Courts, and give an outline of their jurisdiction.
12. Distinguish between (*a*) a High Court judge; (*b*) a circuit judge; and (*c*) a Recorder.
13. What is meant by 'an appeal by way of Case Stated'?
14. Distinguish between a stipendiary magistrate and a county magistrate.
15. Outline the jurisdiction of a magistrates' court.
16. What is a court of preliminary investigation?
17. Indicate the main agencies responsible for Law Reform.
18. What qualifications have jury members? Outline the arguments (*a*) for, and (*b*) against the jury system.
19. What are the main provisions of the *Legal Aid Act, 1974*?
20. What part do laymen play in the administration of English law?

CHAPTER EIGHT

JUDICIAL OFFICERS, LAW OFFICERS, AND THE LEGAL PROFESSION

The Lord Chancellor

The Lord High Chancellor of Great Britain, more usually known as the Lord Chancellor, ranks eighth in order of precedence in England after the Queen: a status which reflects his importance as a Minister of the Crown chiefly responsible for the administration of justice.

The Lord Chancellor is appointed by the Crown on the advice of the Prime Minister. His position combines duties which are legislative, executive, and judicial: it is therefore an exception to the constitutional doctrine of the 'separation of powers'.

In his legislative capacity the Lord Chancellor presides over the House of Lords. He may take part in its debates and can vote in all of its divisions.

As an executive or administrative officer he is a member of the Cabinet, its chief legal and constitutional adviser and one of its representatives in the House of Lords. He is the Ministerial head of the Land Registry, the Public Record Office and the Public Trustee, and provides advice and assistance in cases of difficulty in the administration of these departments. He is also responsible for the custody and use of the Great Seal, which authenticates important legal documents such as Letters Patent.

In his judicial capacity the Lord Chancellor is head of the Judiciary, President of the House of Lords (in its appellate capacity) and President of the Supreme Court. He is the most important member of the Judicial Committee of the Privy Council, and is head of the Chancery Division of the High Court. However, he rarely sits as a judge other than in the House of Lords and the Judicial Committee of the Privy Council. He appoints, in the name of the Crown, the following judicial officers: puisne judges of the High Court; Recorders; Circuit judges, and magistrates. The appointments of legally qualified chairmen of certain administrative tribunals are subject to his approval.

The Lord Chancellor is served by a staff of professional assistants and his office is in the House of Lords.

Judges

(i) *The Lord Chief Justice* (L.C.J.) is appointed by the Crown on the advice of the Prime Minister. He is head of the Court of Appeal (Criminal Division) and of the Queen's Bench Division. He is also a member of the House of Lords.

(ii) *The Master of the Rolls* (M.R.) is appointed by the Crown on the advice of the Prime Minister. He is deputy to the Lord Chancellor and is head of the Court of Appeal (Civil Division). He supervises the admission of solicitors to the Rolls of the Supreme Court.

(iii) *The President of the Family Division* is appointed by the Crown on the advice of the Prime Minister, and is responsible for the work of this Division of the High Court.

(iv) *The Vice-Chancellor of the Chancery Division.* This post was recreated in 1971 after one hundred years. The Vice-Chancellor is head of the Chancery Division under the Lord Chancellor (the official President).

(v) *The Lords of Appeal in Ordinary* are known as Law Lords and are appointed by the Crown on the advice of the Prime Minister from among existing judges or barristers of at least fifteen years' standing. They are life peers and can adjudicate in appeal cases heard in the House of Lords. They are also *ex officio* members of the Judicial Committee of the Privy Council. There are eleven Law Lords.

(vi) *Lords Justices of Appeal* are appointed by the Crown on the advice of the Prime Minister from among existing judges or barristers of at least fifteen years' standing. They are judges of the Court of Appeal. They are twelve in number.

(vii) *Judges of the High Court* are known as puisne judges and are appointed by the Crown on the recommendation of the Lord Chancellor from among barristers of at least ten years' standing. Nine judges are assigned to the Chancery Division, forty-four to the Queen's Bench Division and seventeen to the Family Division of the High Court.

Each of the above judges receives a substantial salary which ensures independence and reflects the importance of judges in society.

All the judges referred to above hold office 'during good behaviour' and may be removed by the Crown on an address presented by both Houses of Parliament. Their salaries are fixed by statute and form a charge on the Consolidated Fund. The effect of these two important provisions is to ensure judicial independence: a vital feature in the administration of law and justice within the State.

Judges of the High Court retire at the age of 75, and are eligible for pensions granted by statute. Today judges hold exercises and conferences in penology and sentencing policy to ensure uniformity in judicial administration.

(viii) *Circuit judges* are judges appointed by the Crown on the advice of the Lord Chancellor to serve in both (i) Crown Courts, and (ii) county courts. A circuit judge must be a barrister of 10 years' standing or a person who has held the office of a recorder for five years. The retiring age is 72, with the possibility of extension to 75. All existing (1971) county court judges become circuit judges, as do the Recorders of Liverpool and Manchester, a number of whole-time Chairmen and Deputy Chairmen of Quarter Sessions and certain other holders of judicial offices. (*Courts Act, 1971.*)

(ix) *Recorders.* Under the *Courts Act, 1971* (see p. 196) these are part-time judges of the Crown Court. Appointments are made to men of high professional standing who are prepared to commit themselves to not less than one month's work on the bench each year. Solicitors of 10 years' standing (as well as barristers) are eligible for appointment to this office. If a solicitor holds the appointment of Recorder for five years he may then be appointed a circuit judge (see above).

Attorney-General and Solicitor-General

Together these are known as Law Officers. Both are appointed by the Crown on the advice of the Prime Minister. They are political appointments, and the holders are precluded from private practice.

(*a*) *The Attorney-General* is usually a member of the House of Commons. His duties comprise the following:

(i) He represents the Crown in the courts in civil matters, and may prosecute in important and difficult cases in the criminal courts.

(ii) He advises Government departments on important legal matters and may take part in many judicial and quasi-judicial proceedings affecting the public interest, e.g. the administration of charities and patent law.

(iii) Certain criminal offences must be reported to the Attorney-General, and his consent is necessary before criminal proceedings may be taken in certain cases, e.g. bribery, incest, corrupt practices, and offences against the *Official Secrets Acts, 1911 and 1939*, the *Dangerous Drugs Act, 1951*, the *Public Order Act, 1936*, the *Prevention of Violence (Temporary Provisions) Act 1939*, and various other Acts.

The Attorney-General superintends the work of the Director of Public Prosecutions. He is head of the English Bar, and points of professional etiquette may be referred to him.

(b) *The Solicitor-General* is deputy to the Attorney-General and his duties are similar. He is a barrister and is usually a member of the House of Commons. By the *Law Officers Act, 1944*, any functions authorized or required to be discharged by the Attorney-General may, unless expressly excluded, be discharged by the Solicitor-General if the Office of Attorney-General is vacant, if the Attorney-General is absent or ill, or if the Attorney-General authorizes his deputy to act in any particular case.

Director of Public Prosecutions

The office of Director of Public Prosecutions was created by the *Prosecution of Offences Act, 1879*. The Director must be a barrister or solicitor of at least 10 years' standing. He is a civil servant who has had wide experience of the criminal law in the courts. He acts under the superintendence of the Attorney-General, and is assisted in his work by a staff of professional barristers.

The Director and his staff advise the police, clerks to magistrates, and other persons enforcing the criminal law on prosecutions in serious or difficult cases. He must prosecute in offences punishable by death (e.g. treason), and in cases of murder and manslaughter. He may also prosecute in any case referred to him by a Government Department or in any case which, because of its importance or difficulty, requires his intervention. Chief officers of police must report to him all offences formerly punishable by death, offences under the *Incitement of Disaffection Act, 1934*, the *Official Secrets Acts, 1911 to 1939*, the *Forgery Act, 1913*, *Punishment of Incest Act, 1908*, and other enactments. The Director appears for the Crown in every appeal to the Court of Appeal (Criminal Division).

The Legal Profession

There are two branches of the legal profession in Britain: barristers-at-law and solicitors of the Supreme Court. In most other countries, including some parts of the Commonwealth, there is no such division.

Solicitors

The modern solicitor is the successor of three former ancient professions known as attorney (or representative), solicitor, and proctor. These assisted judges in the King's Bench in the early stages of litigation or carried out the less skilled work in the ecclesiastical and Admiralty courts. By a succession of *Solicitors Acts, 1839* to *1974*, the profession has been unified and regulated.

The regulations of the Law Society provide for:

(i) The scales of remuneration and fees of solicitors.
(ii) The terms and conditions of articles of clerkship for new entrants.
(iii) Courses for the education and training of students.
(iv) The conduct of examinations.
(v) The discipline of all solicitors.

A person who has served articles (from $2\frac{1}{2}$ to 5 years) to a solicitor, and who passes the examinations of the Law Society, may be admitted a solicitor by having his name enrolled. He thereby becomes an officer of the Supreme Court, and receives his Certificate to Practise which is renewable annually. There are some 26,000 solicitors in England and Wales.

Duties of a Solicitor. Most solicitors are employed in private practice, either alone or in a partnership firm. Others are employed in the public service, industry, and commerce.

Practising solicitors are consulted by, and receive instructions from, lay clients on a wide variety of matters both civil and criminal, e.g. the making of wills, administration of estates, family matters, the formation of companies, drawing up of documents, conveyancing, and criminal offences of all kinds. In cases of unusual difficulty or where a trial is to take place in the superior courts, the solicitor takes his instructions from the client, prepares briefs and approaches a barrister (counsel) who thereupon gives an 'opinion' or represents the client at the trial.

Solicitors have a right of audience only in certain courts, e.g. Magistrates' Courts, County Courts, and Crown Courts (if the solicitor defended the accused in the Magistrates Court) (see p. 200).

The relationship between solicitor and client is based on professional confidence, and a solicitor cannot be compelled to disclose in court communications made in a professional relationship. Nor is a solicitor liable for defamation in respect of statements made in court during the course of a trial. A solicitor is, however, liable to be sued for damages for negligence in the conduct of his profession: e.g. where he has carelessly lost documents entrusted to him.

Solicitors may now be appointed as Recorders in Crown Courts (see p. 197).

Barristers

Anyone wishing to become a barrister must join one of the four Inns of Court: Gray's Inn, Lincoln's Inn, Inner Temple, and Middle Temple. These four Inns of Court are unincorporated bodies of medieval origin, owned and controlled by their senior members called the Masters of the Bench.

In 1966 a Senate of the Inns of Court was created to take over the functions previously exercised by each of the four Inns. The Senate deals generally with conditions for the admission of students, legal education and welfare; a Disciplinary Committee has been established.

Each intending barrister must make a certain number of attendances (known as 'keeping terms') at his Inn, and to qualify for Call to the Bar he must pass the examinations conducted by the Council of Legal Education. After passing the examinations a barrister intending to practise must undertake one year's pupillage in chambers, following which he has the right of audience in any court of law in England and Wales. As noted above, he may take instructions only from a solicitor, not from a lay client direct. Unlike the solicitor, he may not sue for his fees and is not liable in negligence in the conduct of a case.

Duties of a Barrister. Many barristers take positions in industry, commerce, the universities, and the public service. A barrister intending to practise must choose in which part of the law he intends to specialize. A barrister is essentially an advocate whose task is to present his client's case effectively in court. To be successful he must possess certain personal and intellectual qualities and, above all, a capacity for hard work. A portion of his work includes the drafting of opinions on difficult points of law, the settling of pleadings and advice on evidence and procedural matters.

The difference between the two branches of the profession may be summarized as follows:

(*a*) Solicitors have a right of audience in inferior and Crown Courts; barristers may appear in all courts.

(*b*) Solicitors are liable for negligence in the conduct of a case; barristers are not so liable (*Rondel* v. *Worsley*, 1967).

(*c*) Solicitors are agents for their clients and can bind them by what they say; barristers cannot so bind their clients.

(*d*) Solicitors may make binding contracts with clients; barristers cannot make such contracts with clients.

(*e*) Solicitors deal with clients direct; barristers deal with clients only through the medium of a solicitor, as a matter of professional etiquette.

(*f*) Solicitors are in close touch with the community and are to some extent businessmen; barristers are less so, and need a specialized knowledge of law and skill in forensic advocacy, i.e. in presenting a case in court.

(*g*) Solicitors are controlled by statute (*Solicitors Acts, 1839–1974*); barristers are controlled by their Inns of Court and the recently established Senate, non-statutory bodies.

When a barrister has acquired practical experience, skill, and distinction in his profession, he may apply to the Lord Chancellor to 'take silk', i.e. become a Queen's Counsel. If the applicant's request is granted, Letters Patent are issued and he will then be called by his Inn of Court 'within the bar' thus relinquishing his former status of 'outer' or 'utter' barrister.

By his new status the successful applicant will expect to attract more difficult cases and to command higher fees. He will no longer draft pleadings, conveyances, or similar documents. Thenceforward he will have the assistance of junior counsel who will be briefed with him and who will receive a proportion of his fee. A Queen's Counsel is distinguished by the letters Q.C. after his name, and is referred to as a 'Leader'.

A Minister of Justice

The question whether there should be a Minister of Justice in the Government has agitated the minds of some people for years past. Jeremy Bentham urged this over a century ago. France, West Germany, Switzerland and Italy each has a Minister of Justice who holds one of the most important posts in the respective Governments.

In the United Kingdom the functions performed by such a Minister are distributed among:

(i) The Lord Chancellor.
(ii) The Home Secretary.
(iii) The Attorney-General.

In 1918 Lord Haldane, Chairman of 'The Machinery of Government Committee' recommended to Parliament that the Home Secretary should be 'Minister of Justice' under the Lord Chancellor. Nothing has been done since, though the functions and powers of each of the three officers of State have widened considerably during the years since 1918.

The Arguments For

The following are some of the points which may have advanced in favour of such an appointment:

(i) The administration of justice is one of the most important of the social services. A senior Minister should be appointed to the post and should be a member of the House of Commons responsible to that Chamber. The Lord Chancellor sits in the Lords and cannot answer in the Commons.
(ii) A Minister of Justice should be responsible for:

(*a*) The appointment of all judges.
(*b*) The legal profession (barristers and solicitors).
(*c*) The administrative arrangements by Circuit Administrators, Clerks of Courts (County Courts and Magistrates' Courts) and recording judgements.
(*d*) The police and criminal law enforcement.
(*e*) The prisons, detention centres, borstals, and similar institutions, and the after-care of prisoners.

(iii) Reform of the Law has traditionally been slow. The reform of the legal system, particularly the courts has also been slow. A Minister with political drive would ensure that the administration of justice would keep pace with the needs of the times. These are constantly changing and will continue to change at an increasing rate, hence the need for constant review by one person specially charged with responsibility.
(iv) The growth of Administrative Tribunals (see p. 251) and Industrial Courts itself imposes an increasing responsibility. These tribunals proliferate with no single Minister in charge of them. The tribunals represent almost another legal system dispensing 'administrative justice', and their numbers will increase as the State intervenes in the private lives of subjects more and more.
(v) A Minister or Justice should recommend appointments to the office of Parliamentary Commissioner for Administration. More commissioners are now created, e.g. for complaints against local government authorities (see p. 321) and the Health Service and hospitals (see p. 270). A Minister could co-ordinate in this field.
(vi) The post is a logical one. If such Ministers are found satisfactory and compatible with liberal democracy in the main European countries there is no reason why a similar post may not be created in the United Kingdom. The responsibilities and powers are essentially the same.

The Arguments Against

The following are some of the arguments against such an appointment:

(i) The appointment of a Minister of Justice would violate the doctrine of the separation of powers (see p. 10), in that he would purport to combine (i) executive and (ii) judicial duties in one office. His roles must inevitably conflict.

(ii) English law is different from the European systems and the United Kingdom has one of the finest legal systems in the world. The main characteristics are (i) its age and continuity; (ii) an independent judiciary; and (iii) an independent legal profession.

(iii) A Minister of Justice may not be a trained lawyer who is familiar with the problems inherent in law and the administration of justice. If a Minister is not himself a lawyer he would be 'in the hands of' the higher civil servants.

(iv) The police are traditionally independent, and it would be wrong in principle if a Minister were directly responsible for police and police action. In the hands of the Executive the police service is a powerful weapon.

(v) The judges in the past have stood against the Executive and guarded individual private rights, and declared as wrongful and illegal 'Acts of State' (see p. 223) and Ministerial orders, (e.g. Regulation 18B, Defence Regulations, 1939: (*Liversedge* v. *Anderson* (1942)).

(vi) The 'administration of justice' itself is too vast a subject for one Minister effectively to control. It is better that the responsibilities be shared so that each of the present officers of State can act as a check on the other(s).

(vii) The division of responsibility: The Lord Chancellor, responsible for the administration of the civil law, with the Home Secretary, responsible for the administration of the criminal law, is a partnership which works well. Each has a Law Reform or Law Revision Committees (see p. 206) under his surveillance, and the Law Commission is effectively working through the law with a view to its eventual codification. Law Reform does keep pace; see the *Courts Act, 1971*, the *Administration of Justice Act, 1970*, which have inaugurated changes in the criminal courts (see p. 195) and the High Court (see p. 192).

(viii) There is public faith in the present office holders and, although change inevitably takes place, the law and its administration is one subject where changes and modifications ought to be made slowly. It is better that law be certain even if there are occasional injustices. A reformist zeal is inappropriate in a Court of Law. The wheels of the law grind slowly—and not without purpose.

Conclusion

There is no absolute conclusion here. There are views for and views against, and there are many other implications which would have to be weighed in the balance.

The prime duty of any Government is the preservation of law and order. That is the basic duty which must be discharged. Only an independent and disinterested stranger can properly evaluate the freedoms which we enjoy within the law. Although there are inevitably strains on the forces of law and order and the administration of justice, ordinary citizens may live out their lives in reasonable safety and peace. Any disturbance of the delicate 'checks and balances' which operate on the constitution must be measured with care. It is no justification to say that if other countries have Ministers of Justice we must follow suit. It may well be that British people like British justice as it is, which is justification enough for Parliament to be satisfied with the present arrangements and its present officers.

Exercises

1. Describe the office and functions of the Lord Chancellor.

2. What is meant by the phrase 'The Law Officers of the Crown'? What are their duties?

3. Describe the office held by the Director of Public Prosecutions and indicate his duties.

4. Describe the duties of a solicitor, and indicate the functions of the Law Society.

5. Describe the profession of barrister, and distinguish it from that of a solicitor.

6. Who are Queen's Counsel?

7. There is no Minister of Justice in Britain. How are the functions performed by such a Minister in other countries distributed in Britain?

8. What are the main arguments for and against the creation of the post of Minister of Justice?

CHAPTER NINE

LIBERTIES OF THE SUBJECT

Personal liberty, freedom of thought and freedom of speech are familiar to British people. We accept them as part of the British way of life, the British tradition, yet it is unwise to take them for granted. Their safeguard today lies in representative government, in the power of the body of citizens to express their will through their Government, in the use they make of that power, and in an independent judiciary.

Freedom is dear to the hearts of most people; men have given their lives for it and will doubtless do so again. Yet freedom is by no means a simple conception. It may take many forms: national, political, religious, economic, and personal.

There is no formal guarantee under the British constitution that all subjects shall be free. Magna Carta, 1215, (Art. 39), which is still the law of the land, lays down:

> No free man shall be taken or imprisoned or dispossessed or outlawed or in any way destroyed ... unless by the lawful judgment of his peers (equals) or the law of the land.

Outlawry is no longer permitted, and a man may no longer be 'destroyed' (killed). The main point of this provision is the declaration that there shall not be arbitrary or illegal arrests, in other words it was an early manifestation of the 'Rule of Law'. There are, however, declarations of rights in the Bill of Rights, 1689, and the Act of Settlement, 1701, but there is no written statement by Parliament or the law that I have a legal right to my freedom. Under the American Constitution (a written constitution) we see:

> Congress shall make no law respecting an establishment of religion, or prohibiting the free exercise thereof; or of abridging the freedom of speech or of the Press; or the right of the people peaceably to assemble, and to petition the Government for a redress of grievances.

These rights, and others, have been incorporated as fundamental rights, but they have necessarily been curtailed or qualified by law, making the fundamental rights not absolute but relative.

What English law says is not 'You can do this' but 'You cannot do this.' I am free within the limits of the law; I can do what I please so long as I do nothing prohibited by law. For example, if I trespass on your land the law gives you a legal remedy against me for my wrong to your rights of possession. If I drive a car dangerously down the road a police prosecution may follow whereupon a court of law may punish me for my offence.

Freedom of the Person

Briefly, therefore, we may say that *A* can do anything or go wheresoever he wishes in this country so long as he does not offend the law. If therefore

A does not trespass on another's property or commit nuisance, and behaves as a rational civilized being he will not be interfered with by the Government or its agents (the police) responsible for maintaining the law.

Under the Rule of Law (discussed on p. 14) we mentioned that no one, not even a Secretary of State acting in the name of the Crown, may interfere with my personal freedom by arresting me unless he has legal power so to do. Governments have in the past, in moments of crisis and emergency, tried to arrest those of whom they were suspicious or did not like. Secretaries of State have tried to act under the authority of 'Act of State' and have issued general warrants which purport to authorize the arrest of *unnamed persons* and search *unnamed premises*. Such documents virtually authorize officials (e.g. police) to search any house or building or arrest any person.

By a series of cases in the eighteenth century these warrants were declared illegal by the courts. Thus in *Leach* v. *Money* (1765) a general warrant to arrest unnamed printers and publishers of the 'North Briton' (a journal), which the Government sought to suppress, was declared illegal. In *Entick* v. *Carrington* (1765), it was held that there was no inherent power in a Secretary of State (i.e. the Home Secretary) to order arrest except in cases of treason.

Where it is necessary for the police to obtain a warrant of arrest or search they will (on sworn information in writing) obtain a warrant from a J.P. (or a judge). The person to be arrested is named (or identified) in the warrant and the premises to be searched are described. Search warrants are necessary for a number of offences, e.g. stolen property, possessing explosives, dangerous drugs, firearms, and the law authorizes their issue to enable search to be made. Any stolen articles, drugs, firearms, etc., discovered will be seized in accordance with the warrant and brought before a court of law, together with the alleged culprit.

An interesting case arose in 1968:

> *Chic Fashions* (*West Wales*) *Ltd.* v. *Jones* (1968). The police, under a search warrant which referred to clothing stolen from a particular manufacturer, searched the Chic Fashion shop. During the search the police seized other items of clothing which they believed to have been stolen, although made by another manufacturer. None of the clothing was, in fact, stolen. The company sued the police. *Held*: (by the Court of Appeal) that the police have power under a search warrant to seize *any* goods which they believe to have been stolen.

Lawful Imprisonment

A person may be lawfully arrested either under the common law or under powers granted by statute. For example at common law a police officer or a private person may arrest any person found committing treason, murder, theft, or dangerous wounding, or a breach of the peace. There are numerous statutes which give legal power of arrest to (*a*) a private person, and (*b*) a police officer. These will be referred to later. A police officer has wider powers of arrest than a private citizen.

The following are the occasions when **lawful** imprisonment is permitted:

(i) By arrest pending trial (e.g. for murder, arson, burglary, theft, breach of the peace, and many other offences).

(ii) By sentence of imprisonment or detention after trial by a court, e.g. a judge or magistrate may issue a warrant of commitment to a prison.

(iii) By detention of a mentally sick patient or lunatic. (*Mental Health Act, 1959.*)

(iv) By detention of a child (i.e. a person under 14), or a young person (14–17 years) where such person is found by a court as being in need of care, protection, or control. (*Children and Young Persons Acts, 1933 and 1963.*)

(v) By parental authority, as where a parent detains his child in a room (technically an imprisonment).

We have mentioned that a person may lawfully be arrested by (*a*) a police officer, and (*b*) a private person, and that there are two types of arrest: (i) by a warrant, and (ii) without a warrant. Moreover, a person may be arrested under **common law powers** and by **statute**.

Warrant. First, what is a warrant? It is, of course, a legal document authorizing some act to be done, and has been defined thus:

A warrant is a written authority signed by a Justice (or a judge) directing the person or persons to whom it is addressed to (*a*) arrest an offender to be dealt with according to law, (*b*) to take a person to prison, (*c*) to search premises, or (*d*) to levy distress for the non-payment of a legal penalty.

Where a constable sees *A* committing a serious offence (e.g. murder or theft) the constable may arrest *A* immediately. He does not need a warrant at all. But suppose *A* commits a theft and absconds from the district. A constable will make inquiries and ascertain that *A* is the probable culprit. The constable may then lay his information before a magistrate, giving details of the alleged offence and the name or identification of the alleged culprit, upon which information the magistrate may then issue a warrant which authorizes the arrest of *A*.

We have mentioned that there are several statutes which give powers to police and private persons to arrest another. The common law and the statutory powers of arrest before 1967 were confusing mainly because of the medieval distinction between felonies (serious offences such as murder, manslaughter, and theft), and misdemeanours (i.e. all other offences, except treason which was in a special category of offences altogether). The misdemeanours included certain offences such as fraud which could be very serious indeed but in respect of which the power of arrest was circumscribed. There were some anomalies in this part of the law and as a result the *Criminal Justice Act, 1967*, was passed which clarified the position and created what is called an **arrestable offence.** This phrase, arrestable offence, means—

(i) an offence for which the sentence is fixed by law (i.e. the magistrates or judges have no discretion as to the penalty on a finding of guilt); and

(ii) an offence for which a person may be sentenced to five years' imprisonment on *first* conviction.

There are very few offences under the heading (i) above. Murder was formerly punishable by death, the judge having no discretion once a person was found guilty of that offence. But now, of course, the death penalty for murder has been abolished. As regards (ii), the following are the main arrestable offences:

Assault causing bodily harm.	Possessing firearms with intent to endanger life.
Assault with intent to rob.	
Indecent assault on a girl under 13.	Using firearms to resist arrest.
Armed assault.	Assisting prisoners to escape.
Burglary.	Criminal damage.
Conspiracy to murder.	Living off immoral earnings.
Causing death by dangerous or reckless driving.	Manslaughter.
	Murder.
Drug offences.	Piracy.
Using explosives with intent to grievous bodily harm, or causing injury by using explosives.	Rape.
	Theft.
	Treason.
Obtaining property by deception.	Wounding causing bodily harm.
Possessing firearms while committing another offence.	Wounding with intent to murder or maim.

All the above are punishable with imprisonment for five years. Some, e.g. murder, manslaughter, piracy, and rape are punishable with life imprisonment.

The *Criminal Justice Act*, 1967, lays down the following:

Arrest by any Person.

(i) Any person may arrest without warrant anyone who is or whom he, with reasonable cause, suspects to be in the act of committing an arrestable offence. (s. 2(2).)

(ii) Where an arrestable offence has been committed any person may arrest without warrant anyone who is, or whom he, with reasonable cause, suspects to be guilty of the offence.

Arrest by a Constable.

(i) Where a constable, with reasonable cause, suspects that an arrestable offence has been committed, he may arrest without warrant anyone whom he, with reasonable cause, suspects to be guilty of the offence.

(ii) A constable may arrest without warrant any person who is, or whom he, with reasonable cause, suspects to be, about to commit an arrestable offence.

To arrest any such person, under the powers noted above, a police officer may **enter** (if need be, by force) and **search any place** where that person is or where the constable, with reasonable cause, suspects him to be.

A word of warning is necessary in regard to the use by a private citizen of the powers of arrest. Although there may be, for example, legal power to arrest another for 'breach of the peace' (which can be a fight or the use of insulting words or behaviour) a private citizen is ill advised to use it, since if he interferes unlawfully, he may be sued or prosecuted for assault or false imprisonment by the supposed culprit.

Remedies for Infringement of Personal Freedom

We have seen that any interference with the personal freedom of another, whether by assault, removal from premises, or arrest is unjustified unless there is some lawful authority for that interference.

The person interfered with is not without remedy, and he may look for protection in the following:

   (i) Self-defence.
   (ii) Prosecution or civil action for assault.
   (iii) An action for wrongful arrest (false imprisonment).
   (iv) Right of bail, if arrested.
   (v) Habeas Corpus.

(i) **Self-defence.** If a man is attacked by an assailant in such a manner as to cause him reasonable fear of danger to himself, his wife or child, he is justified in adopting **proportionate** means to ward it off; and if, having retreated as far as he can, until he has no means left of escaping from the attack, he turns upon his assailant and kills him in order to avoid his own death, he will not be guilty of murder. For example, if *A*, *B*, and *C* come towards *D* at the top of a cliff intent on killing *D*, the latter may have no means of escape, and is entitled to kill *A*, *B*, and *C*.

What the law permits is a reasonable or proportionate degree of force, and it is not reasonable if it is either (i) unnecessary (i.e. greater than is requisite for the purpose); or (ii) disproportionate to the evil to be prevented. Thus if *A* throws a tennis ball at *B* (technically an assault and battery), *B* cannot turn round and shoot *A*.

The use of self-defence against the police is a dangerous expedient. It is an offence to assault or resist or wilfully obstruct a constable in the execution of his duty, or to assault, resist, or wilfully obstruct a person assisting a constable in the execution of his duty:

   Donnelly v. *Jackson* (*1970*). A constable approached Donnelly as he was walking along a road to enquire about an offence which he suspected Donnelly to have committed. Donnelly ignored requests to stop, and the police officer touched him on the shoulder intending to stop him and speak to him, but not to arrest him. Donnelly then struck the constable. Donnelly was convicted of assault, but he appealed to the Court of Appeal: *Held*: a constable is acting in the execution of his duty when, if he wishes to speak to someone, he touches them on the shoulder to attract attention. Accordingly Donnelly's appeal was dismissed.

(ii) **Action for Assault.** An assault is some act accompanied by such circumstances as indicate an intention of using actual violence against the person of another, providing the attacker has the means of carrying out his intention. A battery is the actual application of unlawful force to another. Any hostile touching, however slight, is a battery. Every battery, therefore, includes an assault.

Where, therefore, an assault or battery is committed an aggrieved party may take civil action in a county court or a prosecution in a magistrates' court for redress of the wrong done. If the attack is a serious one the police will undertake the prosecution, otherwise the matter will be left to the injured party to pursue in his own way.

(iii) **Action for False Imprisonment.** False imprisonment is any unjustified act of arresting, imprisoning, or otherwise preventing a person from exercising his right of leaving the place in which he is. To constitute imprisonment actual force is unnecessary; threats procuring submission are sufficient. Actual imprisonment in a room or cell is unnecessary, but the deprivation of liberty must be complete, as e.g. by putting handcuffs on another or merely holding his arm so that he cannot leave. No imprisonment arises by preventing a man's going in some direction while leaving him free to go in others, as by blocking a path or roadway against him. (*Bird* v. *Jones* (1845).)

Because the police must arrest persons they are particularly exposed to the risk of legal actions for false imprisonment. A constable who, let us say, arrests *A* must inform *A* of the true grounds for the arrest in accordance with rules laid down in *Christie* v. *Leachinsky* (1947).

(iv) **Right of Bail.** Where *A* is arrested without warrant by the police, the officer in charge of the police station to which *A* is taken *may* grant bail to *A*. If no bail is granted (*A* being placed in police cells), then *A* must be brought before a magistrates' court within twenty-four hours of the arrest.

When before the court *A* may apply for bail to the magistrate who will hear what the police say and will then make up his mind, having regard to all the circumstances, and grant or refuse bail. If bail is refused the magistrate must inform *A* that he (*A*) may apply to a judge of the High Court or Crown Court for bail.

The police may have very good reason for refusing or opposing bail by the court, e.g. the seriousness of the offence, fear that the prisoner on release will interfere with witnesses, or will abscond overseas, etc. On the other hand it is clearly wrong to imprison a man for a long time awaiting trial. Good justice is speedy justice; but, on occasion, the police cannot complete their inquiries to proceed with the prosecution and must, consequently, ask for further remands in custody.

Where bail is granted, the *Bill of Rights, 1689*, states that excessive sums cannot be imposed, as, for example, where *A* is released from custody and bailed in the sum of £250,000. If *A* does not turn up at court on the day named for trial the rule is that the sum named is forfeited to the Crown unless the court otherwise directs.

(v) **Habeas Corpus.** This is the name given to a writ of the Queen's Bench Division addressed to the person who holds another in custody, directing him to produce the body (corpus) of the prisoner and show cause for his detention. The writ first appeared in the reign of Edward I (1272–1307), and was issued under the common law. Habeas corpus is now governed mainly by two Acts, the *Habeas Corpus Act, 1679* (which applies to criminal matters) and the *Habeas Corpus Act, 1816* (which applies to detainees under the civil law, e.g. an inmate of a Mental Hospital).

The procedure for grant of the writ is as follows: an application is made by **affidavit** (sworn statement) to the Divisional Court of the Queen's Bench Division, (if in vacation, to a judge in chambers) by the prisoner, his lawyer or friend, setting out the reason why the detention is unlawful. The court may then grant the application immediately if urgent, but may, of course, hear the other side (e.g. the Governor of the prison who may have very good reason for the detention). Where the Divisional Court makes an order, either party (i.e. the prisoner and the person or body imprisoning) may appeal to the House of Lords with leave of either Court.

Where a writ is granted the prisoner must be released forthwith; otherwise the refusal so to do would amount to contempt of court, a punishable offence.

Freedom of Speech.

As with personal freedom, there is no constitutional or positive right to say or write whatsoever one wills. The right is residual. In effect, *A* may say or write anything so long as he does not offend the law. Although we shall consider the legal limitations on the freedom of speech, in practice we know that this liberty is one of the most precious in the land. Indeed, were it otherwise there would be an end of democracy itself. Small wonder, therefore, that there are few prosecutions, say, for sedition, if enforcing that law entails the sacrifice of democracy.

The main restrictions on freedom of speech are found in the law relating to: (i) defamation, (ii) sedition, (iii) blasphemy, (iv) obscenity; (v) *Official Secrets Acts, (1911–1939)*, (vi) *Incitement to Disaffection Act, 1934*, (vii) *Public Order Act, 1936*.

We shall deal with these in order, although space will not permit a full account of these detailed subjects.

(i) **Defamation.** Defamation is 'the publication of a statement which tends to lower a person in the estimation of right-thinking members of society generally; or which tends to make then shun or avoid that person' (per Professor Winfield)

There are two forms of defamation: (i) **libel**; and (ii) **slander.** Libel is defamation in some **permanent** (usually written) form, while slander is defamation in some **transitory** form, such as speech. What the law does here is to provide the machinery to enable a person to protect his good name. If, therefore, *A* writes to *B*'s employer falsely describing *B* as a rogue who has been guilty of theft, great harm and mischief can be done. This is clearly a defamatory statement, and since *A* has published the statement to the employer the law allows *B* to sue *A* in defamation (libel) to recover damages.

We have all seen caricatures of politicians and statesmen. Some of these are defamatory from a legal standpoint, but the politician may do nothing about it, letting the 'dirty water' splash off his shoulders. That is all part of politics. If, of course, the cartoon or the statement goes too far, then a politician may have recourse to the law and sue the artist or author and publisher. The usual remedies available are (i) damages, and (ii) an injunction against repetition of the libel or slander.

Some statements are protected by what is known as **Absolute Privilege.** Thus, it is not possible to sue in respect of statements, however defamatory they may be, in the following cases:

(i) Statements made in the course of judicial proceedings.
(ii) Statements made in either House by a member of either House. (Parliamentary Privilege.)
(iii) Statements made in Parliamentary papers and published by the order of either House of Parliament. (*Parliamentary Papers Act, 1840*.)
(iv) Statements made by one officer of State to another in the course of their official duty.

Qualified Privilege is something different again. The main examples of this are statements made in pursuance of a legal, moral or social duty to a person who has an interest in receiving them. For example, *A*, an employee of *B* applies for a post with *C*. *C* writes to enquire of *B* as to *A*'s character. *B* may give an honest reply or he may write a dishonest assessment of *A* (to prevent *A* leaving his employment or merely out of spite). In the latter case, if *A* knows of the defamatory statement he may sue *B* and the Qualified Privilege is withdrawn with the possibility of damages being awarded to *A*. Qualified Privilege extends to all such statements, but they will be protected only where there is no malice, ill-will, fraud or other motive of which the law disapproves.

(ii) **Sedition.** This usually takes the form of a seditious libel which is the publication of something with intent to excite disaffection against the Sovereign, the Government or the administration of justice, or to incite crime or disaffection. Thus advocating rebellions, insurrections, assassinations, outrages, or physical force or violence of any kind may be held seditious (*R.* v. *Aldred* (1909)). In practice, very few prosecutions of this nature occur, and the consent of the Director of Public Prosecutions (see p. 216) must first be obtained.

(iii) **Blasphemy.** This is committed *where a person denies and ridicules the Christian religion in a scandalous or scurrilous manner* (Blackstone). Prosecutions for this offence are rarely undertaken. In practice, there is freedom of religion and anyone may practise any form of religion (or no religion) as he pleases.

(iv) **Obscenity.** This, in the context of freedom of speech, means the publication of matter which has a tendency to deprave and corrupt those into whose hands it might fall. As we all know, greater freedom in literature and the Press is now permitted, yet the law must still be upheld. The most recent trial was that in 1971 involving the publishers of *Oz*. This case illustrated the fact that the line between licence and liberty is always very difficult to draw.

(v) **Official Secrets.** The *Official Secrets Acts, 1911–1939*, are the main statutes dealing with spying and other practices prejudicial to the safety and interests of the State. The statute is very widely drawn and makes it an offence:

> to make, obtain or communicate to any other person, any sketch, plan, model, or *other document or information* which might be useful to an enemy for any purpose prejudicial to the safety of the State (1911 Act. s. 1).

It is, for example, an offence for an officer of the Board of Inland Revenue to disclose information on an income tax return form to an unauthorized person.

Recently there has been some concern about the way in which the statutes were drafted. The safeguard against over-zealous enforcement of this part of the law is that the consent of the Attorney-General is required to any prosecution under the Acts, and all offences must be reported by the police to the Director of Public Prosecutions. Clearly, spies must be brought to trial, and the prosecution of such persons is the real purpose of this legislation. It should be noted that Ministers, civil servants, members of the Armed Forces, and the police are all restricted by the Acts in the giving of confidential information to unauthorized persons.

(vi) **Incitement to Disaffection.** The *Incitement to Disaffection Act, 1934*, makes it an offence to seduce any member of H.M. Forces from his duty or allegiance to Her Majesty, and to have for a person in his possession or under his control any document of such a nature that the dissemination of copies thereof among members of H.M. Forces constitutes an offence. Similarly, it is an offence to cause disaffection among members of the police (*Police Act, 1964*, s. 53).

The Act of 1934 has also been the subject of attack since, due to its wide provisions, it is regarded as striking at the liberty of the subject. The safeguard here is that no prosecutions under the 1934 Act may be undertaken without the consent of the Director of Public Prosecutions.

(vii) **Public Order Act, 1936.** This Act makes it a summary offence:

> for any person in a public place or meeting to use threatening, abusive or insulting words or behaviour with intent to provoke a breach of the peace or whereby a breach of the peace is likely to be occasioned. s. 5.

This section is not confined to a meeting. The police often invoke the provisions of the Act where a person uses abusive or threatening or insulting words in a street, road or highway.

> In *Jordan* v. *Burgoyne* (1963): *J* (a teacher) addressed a meeting in Trafalgar Square, London, of 5,000 people. *J* said: 'Hitler was right. Our real enemies—the people we should have fought—were not the National Socialists of Germany, but World Jewry and its associates.' *J* was convicted at a magistrates' court and appealed to Quarter Sessions which allowed the appeal. The prosecution then appealed (by way of case stated) to the Divisional Court of the Q.B.D. *Held*: *J* should be convicted: It was said: 'a speaker must take his audience as he finds it. If those words to that audience are likely to provoke a breach of the peace the speaker is guilty of an offence. The right of free speech is not in question: he may express his views as strongly as he likes, but he must not threaten, abuse or insult that audience.'

General. In addition to the above restrictions, we may note also the *Race Relations Act, 1968,* which makes it an offence to publish and distribute any written matter, or to use insulting or abusive words at any public meeting, which is likely to stir up hatred against a section of the community on grounds of colour, race, ethnic or national origins. s. 6.

We may note also that it is a tort to publish an **injurious falsehood,** i.e. an oral or written statement which is maliciously published and calculated to injure some interest of the plaintiff other than his reputation.

Censorship

The *Theatres Act, 1968,* repeals the *Theatres Act, 1843,* and abolishes the Lord Chamberlain's powers of censorship in regard to films, plays and similar productions intended for public performance. The new Act of 1968 makes it an offence 'publicly to perform plays which tend to deprave and corrupt the audience, or are intended or likely to incite racial hatred, or are intended or likely to cause a breach of the peace'. It is a defence to a charge of 'depravity and corruption' that performance is for the public good as being in the interests of art or learning. No prosecutions may take place without the consent of the Attorney-General.

The State takes no part in the censorship of films. The British Board of Film Censors (set up in 1912) grades films into four categories:

'U' suitable to be seen by any person not less than five years.
'A' for persons of not less than five years, but containing material that some parents might prefer their children not to see.
'AA' for persons of not less than fourteen years.
'X' for persons of not less than 18 years.

The local authority has powers under the *Cinematograph Acts, 1909–1952*, to license the showing of films and may prevent the showing of any particular film. Generally, however, the local authorities rely on the gradings of the Board of Film Censors referred to above.

Freedom of Association and Assembly

Association

The right to associate is the freedom of two or more to combine or meet together providing such combination or meeting does not infringe the common law or statute. The right is clearly supremely important, for only by securing the support of others in a common purpose can political objects normally be achieved or meet with success.

The right of association and the right of assembly or meeting are closely allied. A meeting or an assembly may amount to a conspiracy.

Conspiracy. The crime of conspiracy is defined as the 'agreement of two or more persons to do some *unlawful* act or to do some lawful act in an *unlawful* manner'. Everything said, written or done by any one of the conspirators in furtherance of their common purpose will be evidence against the other conspirators. Thus it is a conspiracy for '*A*' and '*B*' to agree to steal another's property, to injure another by blackmail or to corrupt public morals.

But, in addition to the **crime** of conspiracy, there is also the **tort** of conspiracy which is committed where there is a combination of two or more persons to effect an unlawful purpose resulting in damage to a plaintiff.

In the early days of their history, trade unions were looked upon as criminal conspiracies, and we recall the Tolpuddle martyrs. Since 1871 various Trade Unions Acts have legalized their activities. The *Trade Union and Labour Relations Act, 1974*, inaugurated a new era with regard to employer–employee relations. The act recognizes the legality of trade unions and requires that all such bodies be registered. Industrial disputes will be resolved in the Q.B.D. and by tribunals set up under this very important Act. Today the legal control of trade unions is a sensitive political issue.

Picketing, which means setting or posting persons round a place, is a form of activity commonly used to draw public attention to a grievance and to persuade fellow-workers or the public to adopt a course of action in industrial disputes. Peaceful picketing is lawful, but where it is accompanied by violence or intimidation, the law gives protection to the person whose freedom of action is violated. There are many provisions to ensure that no undue pressure is placed upon a worker, and a criminal prosecution may follow if the law is broken. You will see in the Press or on the television that the police are usually present at strikes to ensure the rule of law prevails and that public peace is preserved.

Assembly

The law recognizes no legal right of public meeting. But this does not mean of course, that public meetings are never held. They occur everywhere—in the smallest parish or hamlet, at the Royal Albert Hall, London or at the Central Hall, Westminster, where hundreds of people may foregather at one time. As with other forms of freedom, a public meeting may be held in any place and at any time so long as it does not offend the law.

For example, there is no right of public meeting on a highway. Any interference with the right of passengers to pass and re-pass on the highway is an obstruction. That is an offence against the criminal law and those holding such a meeting may be prosecuted: (*R.* v. *Cunninghame, Graham and Burns* (1888).) The holding of a meeting on occasions in a place of public resort (e.g. a public park) without protest does not confer a right to do so in the future. In other words one cannot acquire a *legal* right to hold meetings by *long usage* or **prescription** under the *Prescription Act, 1832*.

Where a meeting is held on *private* premises, the law as to trespass and nuisance applies, as well as the general law affecting property.

The law as to public meetings is usually dealt with under headings:

  (i) Unlawful assembly.
  (ii) Rout.
  (iii) Riot.

(i) **Unlawful Assembly.** An assembly of persons is unlawful when it is composed of three or more persons who have met together to carry into effect some illegal purpose or who have met in such numbers or under such circumstances as to endanger the public peace or cause alarm and apprehension to Her Majesty's subjects.

A lawful assembly is not rendered unlawful merely because those taking part are aware that *other* persons, hostile to the assembly, will probably cause a breach of the peace. The following case illustrates the point:

  Beatty v. *Gilbanks* (*1882*). The Salvation Army assembled at Weston-super-Mare and marched through the town. Opponents (called the Skeleton Army) interfered with them violently on several occasions. The police, to maintain the peace, reported the Salvationists for unlawful assembly. The Justices thereupon bound the Salvationists over to keep the peace and took sureties from them. The Salvationists appealed by 'case stated' to the Q.B.D. on the ground that as they had not committed any offence they could not lawfully be 'bound over' to keep the peace. *Held*: the disturbances were caused by the opponents. The Salvationists had not committed acts of violence and therefore could not be convicted of unlawful assembly or be bound over to keep the peace.

If a meeting is constituted in such numbers or under such circumstances so as to endanger the public peace it is an offence. If, therefore, a constable (or indeed any other person) of reasonable firmness and courage fears a breach of the peace, the meeting *prima facie* becomes unlawful and is an unlawful assembly.

  Wise v. *Dunning*. (1902). A protestant crusader held meetings in a public place in Liverpool and, when addressing the assembly used words and gestures highly insulting to Roman Catholics of whom a number were present. *Held*: the meeting was unlawful and the speaker could be bound over to keep the peace.

All persons who join an unlawful assembly and all who give support to it are liable to prosecution. If the circumstances are likely to endanger the public peace it is immaterial that the purpose of the meeting is lawful.

It is the duty of the police to disperse an unlawful assembly and to prosecute those responsible for holding the meeting and those who offer resistance by obstruction of the police.

Duncan v. *Jones* (1936). Mrs. D. held a meeting near the entrance to a training centre for unemployed. No obstruction of the highway was alleged, the purpose of the meeting was lawful and its conduct orderly and peaceable. Mrs. D. was ordered by a police officer to stop the meeting, but she continued it. She was arrested and convicted of obstructing the police in the execution of their duty. The police stated that disturbances had occurred at a previous meeting held by Mrs. D. at the same place, and the police feared a breach of the peace if a further meeting were held. *Held*: The police had a duty to stop the meeting.

A public meeting may be held on private premises. The question of police power to enter such premises was dealt with in the following case:

Thomas v. *Sawkins* (1935). A meeting was held in a Welsh town to protest against a Parliamentary Bill and to demand the dismissal of the Chief Constable of Glamorgan. Admission to the meeting was open to the public free of charge. Police attended and were requested to leave. Proceedings were taken before the magistrates' court where it was found that the police had reasonable grounds for believing that seditious speeches would be made and that incitement to violence and breaches of the peace would occur. Appeal was made (by case stated) to Q.B.D. *Held*: Police had power to enter and remain on the private premises when they had reasonable grounds for believing that the commission of an offence was imminent even though not accompanied by a breach of the peace.

The effect of this case is therefore that police may **enter private premises** when they have reasonable suspicion that seditious speeches will be made or a breach of the peace may occur. The police have no right to enter private premises (e.g. a garage) in connection with a summary offence (e.g. parking a car on highway) not involving a breach of the peace (*Davis* v. *Lisle* (1936)). Where a police officer enters on private premises, e.g. to make an enquiry, and is then requested to leave by the occupier, the police officer should leave. He becomes a trespasser if he remains (*Bailey* v. *Wilson* (1968)).

(ii) **Rout.** This is an unlawful assembly and is committed when three or more persons assemble with a common purpose to do an *unlawful* act and make some *advance* towards doing it. A rout is the step just before a riot. It is an offence at common law. Prosecutions for this offence are rare.

(iii) **Riot.** A riot is defined as:

a tumultuous disturbance of the peace by three persons or more, assembling together of their own authority, with an intent mutually to assist one another against anyone who shall oppose them in the execution of some enterprise of a private nature, and afterwards actually executing the same in a violent and turbulent manner, to the terror of the people, whether the act intended was of itself lawful or unlawful (Archbold).

The following are the essential elements:

(*a*) Three or more persons assembled together.
(*b*) With a common purpose.

(c) Execution or inception of the common purpose.
(d) Intent to help one another by force if necessary against any person who may oppose them in the execution of their common purpose.
(e) Force or violence used or displayed in such a manner as to alarm at least one person of reasonable firmness and courage.

Under the *Riot (Damages) Act, 1886*, as amended by the *Police Act, 1964*, where a house, shop or building, in any police district, or the property therein, has been injured, destroyed or stolen owing to a riot, compensation to the person(s) aggrieved is to be paid out of the police fund.

> *Munday* v. *Metropolitan Police District Receiver* (1949). A large crowd invaded the plaintiff's premises in order to see a football match on an adjoining ground after the gates to the ground were closed. Plaintiff's daughter and gardener were assaulted during the invasion, and damage was done to plaintiff's premises. *Held*: Plaintiff could recover from the police rate for damage done by the crowd.

The *Riot Act, 1714*, which empowered a magistrate (or sheriff, or a mayor) to read the Riot Act, calling upon a riotous assembly to disperse and peaceably to 'depart to their habitations or to their lawful business' has now been repealed. The police are the responsible authority to suppress a riot, and may use force if need be. Moreover, a police officer is empowered to call upon all other subjects of the Queen to assist him, and it is the duty of every citizen (whether called upon or not) to assist in suppressing a riot. If a person refuses to assist a constable in the execution of his duty when called upon to do so, and such person is capable of doing so and has no lawful excuse, he commits an offence.

Disturbances at Public Meetings. The *Public Meetings Act, 1908*, as amended by the *Public Order Act, 1936*, makes it an offence, punishable summarily (i.e. before a magistrates' court) or on indictment (i.e. before a Crown Court) for any person at a lawful public meeting to act in a disorderly manner for the purpose of preventing the transaction of the business for which the meeting was called.

The *Representation of the People Act, 1949*, makes it an offence to incite disorder at a Parliamentary or a local government election meeting.

The Public Order Act, 1936, is the main act under which most prosecutions are taken today, although the common law as to unlawful assembly, rout and riot still exists. The Act of 1936 contains important powers in regard to political uniforms, quasi-military organizations and processions:

Thus the following acts are prohibited:

(i) *Wearing Uniforms.* The wearing in a public place of a uniform signifying association with a political organization or with the promotion of any political object. s. 1.
(ii) *Quasi-Military Organizations.* Taking part in the control or management, organizing, or training of any association (a) for the purpose of enabling the members to be employed in usurping the functions of the police or Armed Forces of the Crown; or (b) organized to use or display force in promoting any political object. s. 2.
(iii) *Processions.* A chief officer of police may give directions to organizers

and prescribe the route to be taken, and he has power to prevent entry of any place specified. s. 3.

(iv) *Offensive Weapons.* It is an offence for any person while present at any public meeting or procession to be in possession of any offensive weapon, otherwise than by lawful authority (e.g. rifle club, cadet corps, and similar bodies). s. 4.

We have already mentioned the frequently used provision under s. 5 which makes it an offence for any person in a **public place** or **meeting** to use threatening, abusive or insulting words or behaviour with intent to provoke a breach of the peace, or whereby a breach of the peace is likely to be occasioned.

The general effect of all these provisions in practical terms is that although there is no constitutional right to hold meetings or take part in processions, meetings do, of course, take place both on private premises and in public places. Moreover, everyone is aware that processions are today part of the common scene. The law does not generally prevent meetings or processions, but it does ensure that both are held peaceably and in good order. So one sees a police officer accompanying a group to Westminster to petition M.P.s. The procession is orderly, the peace is kept and the petition reaches its destination, i.e. Parliament. That is the civilized form of protest. Where the forces of law and order break down, the foundations of democracy crumble.

Freedom of Religion

Many times in the course of history, Kings, rulers, and dictators have tried to impose particular religious beliefs on their subjects. Rulers have repeatedly gone to the extremes of war against infidels (e.g. The Crusades) and neighbouring states with the avowed object of converting others to their particular beliefs. In medieval times the Church, through its bishops and clergy, maintained a strict discipline over the religious beliefs of the people, and punished members of the flock for heresy or unorthodox beliefs.

For centuries there was no freedom of religion in Britain. The main division was between the Roman Catholics and the Protestants. Henry VIII (1509–47) broke from Rome and declared himself to be Head of the Church of England. Those who were Royalists adhered to the newly established Church. The *Test Act, 1673*, was passed which prevented Catholic and Protestant-Non-Conformists from holding State or municipal office. Life for the Catholics and Protestant dissenters, who did not support the Established Church, was very difficult. Eventually, in 1828, the *Test Act* and the *Corporation Act* (which also prevented those not of the Established Church from election to the municipal authorities) were repealed, and in 1829 the *Catholic Emancipation Act* removed the disabilities imposed on Roman Catholic believers. The only real survival today is the prohibition excluding a Roman Catholic from accession to the Throne of the Kingdom. (*Act of Settlement, 1701.*)

The Queen is Head of the English Church, and the Archbishops and certain bishops have seats in the House of Lords. There has, however, been a decline in Christian belief and in Church membership in modern times.

The position today, therefore, is that any person may practise any religion he pleases providing that in so doing he does not infringe the general law of the land. Blasphemy, which is the offence of vilifying the Christian religion or bringing its beliefs into contempt, is still a common law offence, though in practice no prosecutions are brought mainly because of the tolerance and restraint observed by most members of society.

In the United States *Bill of Rights* we note in Article I:

> Congress shall make no law respecting an establishment of religion, or prohibiting the free exercise thereof; of abridging speech, or of the Press or the right of the people to assemble, and to petition the Government for a redress of grievances.

There is under the British Constitution no guarantee of freedom of religion since we have no written constitution. Here we may say there is freedom of religion—within the law. Though nominally Christian, the country contains adherents of practically every world religion who are free to practise their particular beliefs in a tolerant and free society.

Detention by the Police

The Rule of Law applies to the police just as it does to other officials purporting to exercise legal powers. A constable who trespasses on the lands or goods of another or arrests another person must, if sued, be prepared to justify his action in a Court of Law.

Mr. Justice Devlin (now Lord Devlin) stated:

> You may sometimes read in novels and detective stories, perhaps written by people not familiar with police procedure, that persons are sometimes taken into custody for questioning. There is no such power in this country. A man cannot be detained unless he is arrested.

This does not mean that the police cannot arrest on suspicion—but that they have no power to detain a person merely for questioning. If, for example, P.C. X has reasonable suspicion that Y has committed an arrestable offence he may arrest Y. If P.C. X later discovers that Y is innocent Y must be released forthwith. If Y thereupon decides to sue P.C. X he may do so (he may also sue the Chief Constable of the force—see p. 243). If the case proceeds to trial it will be for the judge (not the jury) to say whether P.C. X had reasonable suspicion that Y had committed the offence mentioned. *McArdle* v. *Egan* (1933).

Much depends on the words 'reasonable suspicion'. Clearly, if A is discovered at midnight emerging furtively through the front window of a house, he should not be surprised if he is arrested by a constable who sees him. There is reasonable suspicion. It is one of the risks which everyone is exposed to. The only true safeguard lies in trusting that the police will be adequately trained to know their wide powers and to use them with discretion and tact. This they do, and the public considers the police to be efficient and fair and carry out their duties honestly. The relations between the police and the public are generally good. Where, however, a police officer oversteps the bounds of his authority and makes a wrongful arrest (there being no 'reasonable suspicion') or where he has no statutory authority so to do a civil action in tort may be brought against him and his chief officer for assault, battery (if he is manhandled) and false imprisonment. (*Police Act, 1964.*)

Police Interrogation and 'The Judges' Rules'

The primary duty of the police is the prevention and detection of crime. The police are also responsible for the maintenance of peace and good order within our society. One of the main tasks of any Home Secretary is to ensure that the police are efficient in the discharge of their important duties which increase in range and scope year by year.

When a crime is reported to the police, an inquiry is made (*a*) to ascertain the facts, and (*b*) to detect the author of the crime from the available evidence. Once the preliminary inquiries are completed, a police officer will have to decide whether he has sufficient evidence to justify proceedings against the suspect. If so, the police officer may interview the suspect and report him for summons, or he may arrest the suspect. In either case the suspect will be interviewed and a statement may be obtained in accordance with the rules mentioned below.

Sometimes the police will have insufficient evidence to justify arrest or summons, but the evidence may suggest that *A* could be the culprit. *A* may be interviewed by the police. If he satisfies the police that he is innocent he will hear no more about it. *A* may know (if he is guilty) that the police have insufficient evidence to charge him with the offence. He may lie to the police and may decline to make any statement to them.

The cardinal rule of English law is that a confession made to a person in authority such as a police officer will only be admitted in evidence at the trial when such confession has been made freely and voluntarily, i.e. without constraint, force, or as a result of inducement held out by the officer (*Ibrahim* v. *R.* (1914)). A valid confession is itself sufficient to enable a Court of Law to convict an accused person, without corroborative evidence (*R.* v. *White* (1823)).

Confessions obtained by threats of physical punishment, or promises of favour, e.g. 'If you tell me where the goods are I will be favourable to you' (*R.* v. *Cass* (*1784*)) have been held inadmissible. Similarly, in *Regina* v. *Richards* (1967) when a police officer was questioning a suspect (Richards) concerning a housebreaking the police officer said: 'I think it might be better if you made a statement', it was held that the officer's remark was clearly capable of constituting an inducement, and the statement made was held inadmissible.

What are sometimes called 'third degree' methods are clearly wrong and unlawful. Any officer using threats or violence against a suspected person or a prisoner is liable (*a*) to disciplinary proceedings under the Police Discipline Regulations, and (*b*) to civil or criminal actions at the instance of the person injured.

The origin of the Judges' Rules (see below) is traceable to an approach made by the police themselves to the Lord Chief Justice in 1906, requesting guidance in the correct police procedure in the interrogation of suspects and the obtaining of statements of confessions of guilt. Certain rules were formulated in 1912 and these were approved by the judges of the King's Bench Division. Further rules were added in 1918 and in 1964. The present Judges' Rules are as follows:

1. When a police officer is trying to discover whether, or by whom, an offence has been committed he is entitled to question any person, whether suspected or not, from whom he thinks that useful information may be obtained. This is so whether or not the person in question has been taken into custody so long as he has not been charged with the offence or informed that he may be prosecuted for it.
2. As soon as a police officer has evidence which would afford reasonable

grounds for suspecting that a person has committed an offence, he shall caution that person or cause him to be cautioned before putting to him any questions, or further questions relating to that offence.

The caution shall be in the following terms: 'You are not obliged to say anything unless you wish to do so but what you say may be put into writing and given in evidence.'

When after being cautioned a person is being questioned, or elects to make a statement, a record shall be kept of the time and place at which any such questioning or statement began and ended and of the persons present.

3. Where a person is charged with or informed that he may be prosecuted for an offence he shall be cautioned in the following terms: 'Do you wish to say anything? You are not obliged to say anything unless you wish to do so but whatever you say will be taken down in writing and may be given in evidence.'

There are three additional rules. Thus, where two or more persons are charged with the same offence and statements are taken separately from the persons charged each person should be furnished with a copy of such statements. If the person charged desires to make a statement in reply the usual caution should be administered.

Any statement made in accordance with the above rules should, whenever possible, be taken down *in writing and signed by the person making it* after it has been read to him and he has been invited to make any corrections he may wish.

A record should be kept by the police officer of the times at which the taking of the statement started and finished, and of any intervals and refreshments.

It is for the judge at the court of trial to say whether a statement obtained by the police shall be admitted in evidence.

The Police Service

The first duty of any government is to maintain peace and promote good order within the State. The preservation of the peace is supremely important to ourselves as citizens, to Parliament and, indeed, all branches of the Executive. We cannot go about our work or perform our functions as citizens unless we have a reasonable assurance that we shall not be molested in what we do, and that our property will be reasonably secure.

The agents appointed to ensure the peace is preserved and that crimes are prevented and detected are the police. The advent of the Welfare State has not, alas, resulted in a reduction in crime. On the contrary, crime has increased since the second World War. This has meant increasing burdens on the forces of law and order, in particular the police.

Organization

The police service of Great Britain is organised in a number of large forces (i) linked with local government, and (ii) subject to the influence and final control of the Home Secretary in England and Wales. In Scotland the final responsible authority is the Secretary of State for Scotland. In Northern Ireland there is one police force only (the Royal Ulster Constabulary) the final responsibility resting in normal times with the Minister of Home Affairs at Stormont.

The number of regular police forces in 1974 was sixty, comprising forty in England and Wales and twenty in Scotland.

In England and Wales the forces are defined according to the area of responsibility: following the reorganization of local government the areas correspond to counties or cities.

Combined forces are forces whose area of responsibility extends over two or more counties or county boroughs. In addition to the above there is the Metropolitan Police Force which is responsible for an area within a radius of approximately fifteen miles from Charing Cross. Within this area (separate from the Metropolitan Police Force) is the City of London Force which operates within the one square mile of the City of London. In Scotland there are four burgh forces, fifteen combined forces, and one county force.

The strength of the regular police force in Great Britain is approximately 114,000, of which number there are 102,000 in England and Wales. The size of each force depends on (*a*) area, and (*b*) population within a police area. The Metropolitan Police Force has a strength of 21,000, and outside this force the establishments range from 700 to 7,000. Most forces are within the range 1,000 to 2,500. In Scotland the forces range from 300 to 3,000.

Note that the police service is not a 'national' service directly controlled by and responsible to a Secretary of State. Each force is headed by a Chief Constable who is appointed by and dismissible by a police authority (see next paragraph). This arrangement disperses police power amongst a number of local bodies (Police Committees) who supervise the administration of each separate police force.

Police Authorities

Each police force is maintained by a police authority. In the counties of England and Wales the authority is the Police Committee. Committees of the local council consist of (*a*) councillors, and (*b*) magistrates, in the proportion of two to one. Combined police authorities (which arise as the result of the amalgamation of small forces into large police forces) consist of councillors and magistrates from each constituent area covered by the amalgamation scheme.

The police authority for the Metropolitan Police Force is the **Home Secretary**. In the City of London the Court of Common Council is the police authority. A Standing Committee is appointed to deal with all police matters.

In Scotland the police authority is the county council. Here too we find combined police authorities in the same way as in England and Wales.

Duties of the Police Authority

The duties of the police authority are:

(*a*) To maintain an adequate and efficient force for the area.
(*b*) To appoint the Chief Constable, and any deputy or assistant chief constable (in each case subject to the approval of the Home Secretary).
(*c*) To determine the establishment of the force.
(*d*) To provide premises and equipment.
(*e*) To require the officers referred to at (*b*) above to retire in the interests of efficiency (again subject to the approval in each case of the Home Secretary).
(*f*) To appoint a member of the police authority to answer questions on

the discharge of the functions of the police authority put to him by the county or county borough councils.

(g) Reports. The chief constable is required to submit an annual report in writing. The police authority can require a Chief Constable to submit a report on policing of the area. The Chief Constable may, if the matter required by the police authority to be reported on is against the public interest, refuse until permission is granted by the Secretary of State.

The duties of the Chief Constable are to see that the force under his control is used efficiently. The Home Secretary is responsible for ensuring that the police authority and the Chief Constable are enabled to exercise their powers and do so. This redefinition of function of the police authority means that the Home Secretary is answerable in Parliament for the efficient policing of the country as a whole rather for the defaults of a particular force. In the first half of the nineteenth century when police forces were originally founded, their control was deliberately vested in the local authorities so as to ensure that there would be no authoritarian use of police forces by the central Government which could, were a Government so minded, be dangerous. There is a tendency now against the diffusion of power to the smaller authorities; the forces are becoming larger (as combined forces) and there is a lobby for the whole of the police forces to be nationalized on the grounds of efficiency, e.g. in the C.I.D., where some benefits might accrue. The problem is a difficult one, but the *Local Government Act, 1972,* has caused the areas and authorities to be redefined.

Central Control of Police Forces

Co-ordination in the administration of the police forces is ensured through powers granted by Parliament to (i) the Home Secretary in respect of England and Wales, and (ii) the Secretary of State for Scotland in respect of the Scottish forces. Each Minister has power under the *Police Act, 1964,* to:

(a) Make regulations as to the government, administration and conditions of service throughout the police service.

(b) Approve voluntary or initiate compulsory schemes for the amalgamation of police forces.

(c) Recommend the appointment of inspectors to inspect and inquire into the efficiency of the police forces outside the Metropolitan Police Area.

(d) Withhold the whole or part of the police grant.

(e) Approve the appointment of Chief Constables, Deputy and Assistant Chief Constables.

(f) Adjudicate on appeals in disciplinary matters.

(g) Require co-operation between forces, and to supply police to another force.

(h) Order a local inquiry into a police matter.

(i) Obtain any report he wants from the Chief Constable.

(j) Retire a Chief Constable in the interests of efficiency.

The police regulations cover such matters as ranks; qualifications for appointment; promotion and retirement; discipline; hours of duty, leave, pay, and allowances, and uniform and equipment. Some of these (e.g. pay, allowances, and leave.) are first negotiable with the **Police Council for Great Britain** which is the negotiating body for the police. It is constituted on

Whitley Council lines with representatives from the Home Office, Scottish Office, local authorities, and all ranks of the police service. Other matters are discussed by the Home Secretary (or his representative) with representative advisory bodies. Thus before making regulations under certain sections of the *Police Act, 1964*, the Minister shall furnish a draft to the Police Advisory Board.

The Home Secretary is advised on all matters concerning police efficiency by Her Majesty's Chief Inspector of Constabulary and nine Inspectors of Constabulary. Two of the latter are concerned with crime and traffic respectively; one is concerned with Police Planning Organization and six are individually responsible for the inspection of a number of forces. They also deal with individual forces and their Chief Constables when particular problems arise. The inspectors report annually to the Home Secretary on the state of efficiency of all forces except the Metropolitan Police Force. Similar administrative arrangements are made for the inspection of Scottish forces, reports being made to the Secretary of State for Scotland.

All police authorities receive a grant of one-half of their net expenditure. (The Common Council for the City of London Force receives one-third.) Both the Home Secretary and the Secretary of State are empowered to withhold the grant, in whole or in part, permanently or for such time as they may determine, if they are not satisfied that a police area is efficiently policed, that a police force is not maintained and administered, or that the rates of pay or allowances are as prescribed or approved by them.

Police Officers

Entry to the regular police force is open to both men and women. The usual recruitment ages are between 19 and 30 years (men) and 19 and 35 (women), subject to extension in special circumstances. The examination for entry is of modest standard, but in recent years there has been a drive to recruit graduates, and there are now over two hundred serving in the police forces in the United Kingdom. Moreover, certain candidates are selected to pursue courses at universities to read for degrees.

The ranks of the police forces are: Chief Constable, Superintendent, Inspector, Sergeant, and Constable. Most forces now have intermediate ranks (e.g. Chief Superintendent and Chief Inspector). In the Metropolitan Police the chief officer is known as the Commissioner of Police of the Metropolis who is assisted by a Deputy Commissioner and four Assistant Commissioners. Below these are Commanders responsible for a specific area of the Metropolis. The City of London has its own Commissioner of Police who has an Assistant Commissioner.

Police officers may not belong to a trade union. It is a basic principle of the police service that there shall be no political bias in the discharge of their duties. The various ranks have their representative organizations, the most important being the **Police Federation**. This body has a central committee which is able to negotiate with the Home Secretary and the police authorities. It has been the practice to engage as a consultant an M.P. to represent the police service point of view in Parliament. Mr. James L. Callaghan and Mr. Eldon Griffiths were formerly consultants and advisers to the Police Federation.

In addition to the main body of police there are Police Cadets. These are young persons aged between 16 and 18 who are given training in preparation for entry to the force on reaching the minimum age. In addition there is a considerable civilian staff performing the clerical work associated with the police function.

All police forces have special constables who assist the regular police in their spare time. They act as auxiliaries and perform their duties as volunteers without pay. They have similar powers, however, to the regular police.

Traffic wardens are also employed to deal with traffic duties and offences, and they may serve fixed penalty notices for minor traffic offences. The traffic wardens remain under the control of the Chief Constable of the force to which they are attached, whatever duties they perform.

Police Duties.

The main duties of the police are:
(a) To preserve the peace.
(b) To prevent crime.
(c) To protect life and property.
(d) To maintain public order.

There are many other duties. For example, the police are the main service to organize emergency aid schemes in case of local disasters such as train crashes. They also attend road accidents, give first-aid to the injured, and have the duty to enforce many regulations governing road vehicles, licensed houses, and many other matters.

Status

The office of constable has been in existence since the eleventh century. Between the eleventh and fourteenth centuries a constable was the executive agent and representative of the village or township, the local keeper of the peace, exercising his powers under the common law as 'a person paid to perform, as a matter of duty, acts which if he were so minded he might have done voluntarily'. Thus he kept the peace, arrested felons (i.e. criminals suspected of murder, housebreaking, theft, or other crimes), and brought them to justice before the magistrates of his area. As with other services of medieval origin, the industrial revolution and the changes in society generally imposed too heavy a burden on the old system, and a reorganization took place in the early nineteenth century, inaugurated by Sir Robert Peel. It was Peel who in 1829 introduced the modern police in London at first as an experiment. This was successful and eventually civilian police forces were established in all areas during the middle of the nineteenth century.

In modern times their duties have become increasingly complex and responsible, demanding physical fitness, courage, discretion, and tact, as well as initiative of a high order.

The exact legal and constitutional status of a police officer is unique, and one must look to both the common law and numerous statutes to ascertain his powers. A constable is not a Crown servant, and the Crown is not liable for his acts or omissions during his employment. The *Crown Proceedings Act, 1947,* does not apply to a police officer. Nevertheless a constable is a person who 'holds office under Her Majesty' for the purpose of the *Official Secrets Acts, 1911* to *1939,* and may be prosecuted if he commits any offence under these statutes. On joining the police, a constable makes a solemn attestation, declaring that he will 'well and truly serve Our Sovereign Lady the Queen in the office of constable, without favour or affection, malice or ill will', and that he will to the best of his power cause the peace to be kept and preserved and prevent all offences against the persons and properties of Her Majesty's subjects. (*Police Act, 1964*, s. 18.)

A constable is not a 'local government servant'. In *Fisher* v. *Oldham Corporation (1930)* it was held that a police constable is not the servant of the borough. He is a servant of the State, a ministerial officer of the central power, though subject, in some respects, to local supervision and local regulation. In another case, *Att.-General for New South Wales* v. *Perpetual Trustee Co.* (1955) Viscount Simond said:

> His authority is original, not delegated, and is exercised at his own discretion by virtue of his office: he is a ministerial officer exercising statutory rights independently of contract. . . . His relationship to the Government is not in common parlance described as that of servant and master.

Under the *Police Act, 1964*, a chief officer of police has vicarious liability for any wrongful act a constable may commit in the performance of his functions as a constable. A constable is himself also liable and may be sued in respect of his wrongful act. This creates by statute the same sort of relationship as applies in the general law of master and servant. A constable has a certain independence in enforcing the law. Thus he, and he alone, must make up his mind whether to arrest for a suspected offence. Although a constable must obey the **lawful** orders of a Chief Constable and is liable for disciplinary proceedings if he does not, a constable is not bound even if ordered by a Chief Constable to make an arrest which is manifestly illegal. (*Keighley* v. *Bell* (1866).)

The main departments in all police forces are: (i) Uniform department; (ii) C.I.D., (iii) Road Traffic Department. Specialized departments include the River Police (e.g. in London for the River Thames), the Mounted Branch, the Training Branch, and certain others with particular functions such as the use of police dogs.

The use of scientific aids in the prevention and detection of crime has grown increasingly in recent years: £12 million is spent annually on police equipment, including £2 million on radio-communications. A national computer is used for the keeping of records and dissemination of information.

The Home Office has introduced a **Police Planning Organization**, staffed by senior police officers, scientists, and accountancy and management experts. Its duty is to study police methods and the development of new equipment and new techniques throughout Great Britain, so that the police service generally will be able to match the increasing demands made upon them by the increase in crime and by the use of more sophisticated methods on the part of criminals.

New Scotland Yard, the Headquarters of the Metropolitan Police, performs special duties on behalf of all police forces, such as the publication of the *Police Gazette* (for wanted criminals, etc.), the investigation of company frauds (by the Fraud Squad), the execution of extradition orders made by the courts, and it also maintains relations with the **International Criminal Police Organization** (Interpol) on behalf of all forces in Great Britain.

Nationality and Domicile

By a person's nationality we mean his status as a citizen or member of a particular state to which he owes allegiance. Everyone is the subject of some state to which he owes political allegiance and loyalty, for which he may be called upon to fight, pay taxes and support, and from which he may expect protection. These are broad general statements only. For instance, although we say that all persons must be national subjects of some state or other, we know that due to upheavals of war there are some unfortunate 'stateless' persons who have been disowned by, or expelled from, their country of birth and origin.

Nationality is of great importance in the field of public law. Thus, British subjects enjoy universal franchise, i.e. the right to vote at local and Parliamentary elections. Aliens in Great Britain have no such right. Some aliens disapprove of all that is fundamental to the British way of life, and it would be highly irregular for them to be accorded the rights which have been won by hard struggles in the past to create this way of life. Aliens, therefore, are subject to certain restrictions concerning entry into the United Kingdom and employment after entry; furthermore they must register certain particulars with the police.

Apart from these requirements, English law treats aliens in much the same way as ordinary British subjects: for example, they are subject to the same rules of criminal law and the same laws of tort and contract. Some special disabilities or restrictions apply. Thus an alien may not own, or become part-owner of, a British ship registered at a British port and sailing under the British flag.

In the following pages we shall deal with the acquisition of British nationality and the allied question of domicile, which is becoming increasingly important as travel makes it easier for people to move from one country to another.

British Nationality.

The *British Nationality Act, 1948*, as amended, divides 'British subjects' into two classes:

(*a*) Citizens of the independent nations of the British Commonwealth. Into this class fall citizens of Canada, Australia, New Zealand, India, Pakistan, Ceylon, Ghana, Nigeria and the other twenty independent Commonwealth countries. These persons are known as 'Commonwealth citizens'.

(*b*) Citizens of the United Kingdom and Colonies. This type of citizenship may be acquired in the following ways:

(i) *By Birth*. As a general rule, every child born within the United Kingdom or the Colonies (or on a British ship or British aircraft) acquires British citizenship automatically, irrespective of the nationality of his parents. Exceptions are children of foreign Sovereigns, ambassadors and diplomatic staff.

(ii) *By Descent*. Any child, wherever born, whose father is at that date a citizen of the United Kingdom and Colonies, acquires citizenship by descent at his birth.

(iii) *By Registration*. A citizen of one of the Dominions (independent states of the Commonwealth) may, if of full age and capacity, apply to the Secretary of State for registration as a British citizen, provided that he has satisfied certain requirements as to residence or is in Crown service in the United Kingdom.

(iv) *By Naturalization*. Aliens and British Protected Persons (see below) may apply to the Secretary of State for a certificate of naturalization. The conditions of grant (which is at the discretion of the Home Secretary) are that the applicant must be of full age and capacity, of good character, have sufficient knowledge of the English language, and have been resident within the United Kingdom for five out of the previous seven years.

(v) *By Marriage*. An alien woman who marries a citizen of the United Kingdom and Colonies will acquire citizenship of the United Kingdom and Colonies if she chooses to do so by registration as in (iii) above.

(vi) *By Incorporation of Territory*. The Sovereign may, by Order in Council, direct that all, or specified classes of, persons within a newly acquired territory shall be British subjects.

Loss of Nationality

Citizenship of the United Kingdom and Colonies may be lost by:

(i) *Renunciation*. This is effected by a person making a declaration of renunciation, which must be registered with the Home Secretary.

(ii) *Deprivation*. This applies *only* to citizens who acquired citizenship by naturalization or by registration, and may be ordered by the Home Secretary for serious misconduct, e.g. criminal acts.

Where a female citizen of the United Kingdom and Colonies marries an alien under whose national law she acquires her husband's nationality, she does not automatically lose her citizenship of the United Kingdom and Colonies. In all such cases her British citizenship is retained unless she expressly renounces it.

British Protected Persons

So far we have been dealing with British subjects and aliens. A third group of persons, known as British Protected Persons, must be mentioned. These are members of those territories described as Protectorates, Protected States or Mandated or Trust Territories and declared as such by an Order in Council.

Aliens

All persons other than British subjects and British Protected Persons are aliens. The following general restrictions apply to an alien:

(i) He may not vote at local or Parliamentary elections.
(ii) He may not become a Member of Parliament.
(iii) He may not work in the United Kingdom unless specially permitted.
(iv) He must register with the police and notify changes of address to them.
(v) He is liable to deportation if he engages in crime.

Domicile

Most persons make their homes permanently within the state of which they are subjects. Danes live in Denmark, Dutchmen in the Netherlands, and so on, each national being subject to his own country's laws. Some members, however, uproot themselves and decide to make their permanent homes outside their own country. For example, an Italian may decide to live permanently in England, a Frenchman may decide to live permanently in Italy. In such cases, under English law, the Italian and the Frenchmen are held to have acquired domiciles in the countries where they intend permanently to reside.

The concept of domicile, under English law, involves two elements: (i) actual residence; and (ii) *animus manendi*, i.e. the intention to remain in that place or country. Where these two elements co-exist a person is said to have a domicile in that country.

Whereas nationality implies a political relation existing between a person and the state to which he owes allegiance, domicile determines important civil rights and obligations which will be discussed later.

First we must note that under English law it is an inflexible rule that (i) every person must possess a domicile, and (ii) no person can have more than one domicile.

There are three classes of domicile:

(*a*) *Domicile of Origin*. This domicile attaches at birth. A legitimate child takes the domicile of the father; an illegitimate child that of its mother. A foundling (deserted infant without known parents) acquires the domicile of the place where found.

A domicile of origin cannot be entirely lost or extinguished. If a person with a 'domicile of choice' (see later) abandons his present domicile. the domicile or origin revives and attaches to him until he acquires a new domicile.

(*b*) *Domicile of Choice*. Where a person sixteen or over establishes his home permanently in a country with the intention of remaining there permanently (such country being different from his last domicile), he is regarded as acquiring a domicile of choice.

(*c*) *Domicile of Dependent Persons*. (i) A minor takes the domicile of his parent as at (*a*) above. He may take his mother's domicile. however, where the spouses are separated and the child makes his home with his mother. (ii) Since 1974 a married woman is capable of acquiring a domicile independent of her husband. The *Domicile and Matrimonial Proceedings Act, 1973*, states that a person is capable of acquiring an independent domicile when he reaches sixteen.

The above represent the main rules regarding the concept of domicile in English law. The law of domicile is important in regard to the following matters:

(*a*) *Jurisdiction in Divorce*. For example, Atkins, a British subject domiciled in Nevada, U.S.A., is granted a divorce by the Divorce Court of Nevada on the grounds of 'incompatibility of temperament'. The divorce is recognized in English law even though the grounds are much less than those required to sustain a divorce in England.

(*b*) *Validity of Wills of Movable Property and the distribution of such property on an intestacy*. For example, Brown, a British subject domiciled in Ruritania, makes a will attested by one witness. English law requires two witnesses to a will, whereas the law of Ruritania requires one witness only. Brown's will is regarded as valid in English law because it complies with the law of the domicile.

(*c*) *Legitimation*. The law which gives legal status to children born before marriage.

(*d*) *The Essential Validity of Marriage*. The 'essential validity' includes the form of celebration, age of parties, etc. It is possible for an English court to decide that a marriage contracted without the form required in England is valid because it complies with the law of the domicile.

English law takes the view that a person who establishes a domicile in a country attracts to himself the rights, duties, and obligations of that country; he therefore assumes the law of the domicile.

Proof of Domicile. Although long residence in a country affords strong proof that a person has acquired a domicile in that country, we must note that residence and domicile are not the same thing. The English court decides the question of domicile by applying English law, taking account of the *intention* of the party. Evidence of intention may include correspondence, oral or written declarations, the purchase of a house, or even a grave. Inquiry by the English court may range over the whole of a person's life to enable the court to establish where a domicile has been acquired.

Exercises

1. When may a person be lawfully imprisoned?
2. Define a warrant.
3. What remedies are available for the infringement of personal freedom?
4. What is meant by Bail? Who may grant it and when?
5. What do you understand by the writ of *Habeas Corpus*? To whom must application be made for this writ?
6. Define defamation. Distinguish libel from slander.
7. Distinguish between Absolute Privilege and Qualified Privilege in the law of defamation.
8. What do you understand by (*a*) sedition, (*b*) obscenity, and (*c*) blasphemy?
9. What are the main provisions of (*a*) the *Incitement to Disaffection Act, 1934*; and (*b*) the *Public Order Act, 1936*?
10. What rules exist in regard to censorship of films and plays today?
11. Explain the main rules of law relating to public meeting in Britain.
12. Distinguish between (*a*) an unlawful assembly, (*b*) a rout, and (*c*) a riot.
13. Describe the main rules relating to detention by police.
14. What are 'The Judges' Rules' in regard to interrogation by police.
15. Discuss 'Freedom of religion' with respect to its application in the United Kingdom.
16. Who are the Police Authorities in England and Wales? What are the duties of a Police Authority?
17. How does the Government control the police?
18. What are the main duties of a police officer? Discuss his constitutional position in the United Kingdom.

CHAPTER TEN

ADMINISTRATIVE LAW AND JUSTICE

Delegated Legislation

Parliament can grant to some other person or body the power to make orders, regulations, or rules which have the force of law. In strict legal theory, Parliament ought to retain in its own hands the power and duty to enact all the laws and rules affecting the State and its peoples. In practice, Parliament cannot discharge this duty mainly because it has so much to do and so little time in which to do it. To overcome this difficulty it resorts to **delegated legislation**, sometimes called subordinate legislation or indirect legislation.

Statutes nowadays tend to lay down general principles or policy and to leave the working out of the administrative details to subordinate authorities who are responsible for carrying the statutes into effect. For example, the *Road Traffic Act, 1972*, empowers the Minister for Transport to make regulations in respect of road traffic matters by means of statutory instruments; the Home Secretary may make orders and regulations under the *Police Act, 1964*, in relation to the government, administration, and conditions of service of police; and the Secretary of State for Education and Science may make orders under the *Education Act, 1944*.

Forms of Delegated Legislation.

Delegated legislation is comprised of:

(*a*) **Orders in Council** are Orders made by the Queen in Council and have been described as the most dignified form of subordinate legislation. In practice, the Minister of a Government Department usually drafts and makes the Order in the name of the Queen, whose approval 'in Council' is a formality. They may be issued (i) under statute, or (ii) under power of the Royal Prerogative.

(*b*) **Statutory Instruments, Rules and Orders** are normally made by Ministers in charge of Government Departments, but such rules must be submitted to Parliament either before or after they come into force.

(*c*) **Bye-Laws** are made by local authorities, railways, water boards, and similar bodies and, like statutory instruments, derive their authority from Acts of Parliament. Bye-laws require the approval of the appropriate Minister before they have legislative force.

All the forms of subordinate legislation noted above are enforced equally with statutes. For example, infringements of bye-laws, such as misconduct of some kind on a railway platform or damage to trees or seats in a public park, are enforced equally with offences such as simple theft, in the magistrates' courts. Appeal lies to higher courts against conviction or sentence imposed by the lower court.

The Government of a country of fifty-five million people is a highly complex matter. The most that Parliament can get through in the legislative field in one session (one year) is between sixty and seventy Acts of Parliament.

On the other hand more than two thousand statutory instruments are issued each year and, in addition, bye-laws increase annually.

Growth of Delegated Legislation

The following reasons are advanced for the growth of delegated legislation:

(*a*) **Lack of Parliamentary time.** The Legislature has insufficient time to deal with and debate all the measures necessary for efficient government.

(*b*) **Urgency.** Parliament is not always in session, and its legislative procedures are slow. Emergencies and urgent problems arise, and delegated legislation is the best means of meeting the situation.

(*c*) **Flexibility.** A statute requires elaborate and cumbersome procedures for its enactment and can be revoked or amended only by another statute. A Ministerial order or statutory instrument can be made speedily and if it proves unworkable or impracticable, it can be quickly revoked.

(*d*) **Technicality of subject-matter.** Modern legislation tends to be technical and detailed, e.g. road traffic matters which may deal with 'special type' vehicles; building regulations; dangerous drugs regulations. Such legislation is best dealt with by Ministers, advised by experts familiar with the technical or scientific problem, rather than M.P.s who may be unfamiliar with the technicalities involved and who do not have access to experts.

(*e*) **Future needs.** Parliament cannot foresee the difficulties which may arise when new major schemes like the National Health Service or National Insurance are launched. Unforeseen difficulties are better dealt with by delegated legislation rather than statutes.

Criticisms of Delegated Legislation

The processes of Government and, in particular, the making of statutes are continuously subject to critical examination and analysis. Among the criticisms frequently levelled at delegated or subordinate legislation are:

(*a*) **Matters of Principle.** These are the primary concern of Parliament and Ministers ought not to be empowered or entitled to legislate by means of orders in respect of matters of principle.

(*b*) **Delegation of Taxing Power.** Parliament fought for years for the sole and exclusive right to impose taxes. History shows that the right can be abused and should not be yielded to subordinate authorities or Ministers. The *Import Duties Act, 1932*, gave the Treasury the power to legislate on taxation by fixing import duties and altering the 'free list', which usurped the sole right of the House of Commons to levy taxes.

(*c*) **Sub-delegation.** The *Emergency Powers* (*Defence*) *Act, 1939*, provides a clear example of five-tier legislation as it embraces: (i) the parent statute (made by Parliament); (ii) regulations made under the statute; (iii) orders made under the regulations; (iv) directions made under the orders; and (v) licences issued under the directions.

In its Report of 1946, the Select Committee on Statutory Instrument condemned the practice of delegation at four removes from Parliament of the power to make subordinate legislation.

(*d*) **Exclusion of the Jurisdiction of Courts.** The power of the courts to declare the regulations void on the ground of *ultra vires* ought not to be excluded either in the parent Act or the delegated legislation.

(*e*) **Authority to Modify an Act of Parliament.** This power, known as 'the

Henry VIII clause', enables a Minister to modify the Act itself and thus usurp the essential function and duty of Parliament.

(*f*) **Inadequate Publicity.** The Press usually reports the purpose and effect of new statutes, but there is frequently inadequate publicity given to the numerous statutory instruments (over 2,000 annually) made by Ministers. A citizen reported for an offence against a statutory instrument of whose existence he was unaware, cannot plead in court that he did not know of it: ignorance of the law is no excuse (*ignorantia juris non excusat*).

Control of Delegated Legislation

The main forms of control over the power of a Minister to make delegated legislation are:

(*a*) Consultation of interests.
(*b*) Control by the courts.
(*c*) Control by Parliament.
(*d*) Publication.

(*a*) **Consultation of Interests.** In practice Ministers consult experts both within their own Departments and outside, and take the advice of various interests and bodies likely to be affected by proposed legislation. Thus road traffic legislation would involve consultation with local authorities, the police, the A.A., the R.A.C., motor manufacturers, and others likely to be intimately affected. Sometimes a Minister must, as set down in a statute, consult an advisory body or submit a draft of any statutory instrument to it for approval. For example, under the *National Insurance Act, 1946*, regulations proposed by the Secretary of State for Social Services must be submitted in draft to the National Insurance Advisory Committee. When a Minister proposes to make rules of procedure for tribunals set up within his own Department, he must consult the Council on Tribunals (*Tribunals and Inquiries Act, 1971*).

(*b*) **Control by the Courts.** Rules and regulations made by Ministers and other administrative bodies under statutory authority are liable to be subject to challenge in the courts on two grounds: (*i*) *ultra vires* and (ii) unreasonableness. While a court cannot invalidate an Act of Parliament, it may declare that statutory instruments, rules or bye-laws are void on the ground that they are *ultra vires*, i.e. beyond the powers conferred by the Act under which they were made. In practice, Ministerial rules and orders are only rarely challenged on this ground because great care is taken by the legal advisers of the Minister on such procedural matters.

Bye-laws may be challenged on the grounds of **unreasonableness** which means that they are partial and unequal in their operation as between different people. If rules are manifestly unjust, if they disclose bad faith, or they involve 'such oppressive or gratuitous interference with the rights of those subject to them as can find no justification in the minds of reasonable men, the court might well say Parliament never intended to give authority to make such rules; they are unreasonable and *ultra vires*' (Lord Russell in *Kruse* v. *Johnson*, 1898).

(*b*) **Control by Parliament.** (i) Parliament may revoke or vary the delegated power. (ii) Certain Acts require that regulations made under them shall be laid before Parliament. This is to enable M.P.s to know what has been done by a Minister, or what he proposes to do. (iii) A Select Committee on Statutory

Instruments was set up in 1944 to consider every statutory instrument, rule or order laid before the Commons. A Special Orders Committee exists in the Lords to do similar work. In 1974, to avoid duplication in the two Houses, a Statutory Instruments (Joint) Committee was created, comprising members of a Select Committee from the Commons and members of the corresponding committee in the Lords. The Joint Committee, which replaces the two former committees in their consideration of S.I.s, reports to the House on any order or regulation deserving special attention on the following grounds:

(i) That it imposes a charge on the public revenue, or imposes or prescribes charges for any licence or consent or for any services from a public authority.

(ii) That it is made under an Act which precludes challenge in the courts.

(iii) That it appears to make some unusual or unexpected use of the powers conferred by the statute under which it is made.

(iv) That there appears to have been unjustifiable delay in publication or laying before Parliament.

(v) That for any special reason its form or purpose calls for elucidation.

(vi) That the drafting is defective.

(vii) That it purports to have retrospective effect.

The Joint Committee may require a Department to submit a memorandum or explanatory note on any instrument, and may request a representative of the Government Department to appear and explain a document personally. Before the Committee reports that the special attention of the House should be drawn to an instrument, it gives the Department concerned the opportunity to furnish an explanation.

(*d*) **Publication.** H.M. Stationery Office publishes lists showing dates of issue of statutory instruments, and the *Statutory Instruments Act, 1946*, provides that 'it shall be a defence to prove that the instrument had not been issued by H.M.S.O. at the date of the alleged contravention, unless it is proved that at that date reasonable steps had been taken for the purpose of bringing the purport of the instrument to the notice of the public or of persons likely to be affected by it, or of the person charged.'

Administrative Tribunals

From early times special courts of local or limited jurisdiction have been set up apart from the main Courts of Law forming the English judicial system (see p. 188). The Tolzey Court of Bristol, the Piepowder courts (from *pieds poudrés* Fr. = dusty feet) set up to administer mercantile and commercial law for merchants attending local fairs in the Middle Ages, and the early Church Courts which dealt with disciplinary offences by the clergy and offences by the laity, such as blasphemy, heresy, and similar matters were some examples of the early tribunals.

For the past fifty years, successive Governments have been concerned with regulating the social life of the people and social legislation to improve the general well-being of the country has included the *National Health Service Act; National Insurance Act; Education Act; Housing Acts; Town and Country Planning Acts; Rent Restriction Acts;* and other Statutes. Although the collective good and the welfare of the community are admirable aims, the effect of much of the legislation is that, while promoting the public interest, it also circumscribes the rights of private individuals.

For example, Adams owns a field which the local education authority proposes to purchase compulsorily as a site for a technical college. Adams wishes to retain his valuable field for grazing and to contest the right of the education authority to acquire it. If the field is compulsorily acquired, Adams may further dispute the amount payable to compensate him for the loss of his land. Tribunals decide (i) whether the field may be acquired, and (ii) the amount of compensation if the field is taken by the authority.

Similarly, Black receives an injury at work which disables him from continuing his employment. He can claim a pension under the *National Insurance Industrial Injuries Acts*, but his claim may be repudiated by the National Insurance Officer on the ground that the injury is not within the Act: it was sustained after working hours or not 'during the course of employment'.

Many such disputes occur between a private individual seeking to protect his own private rights and a Minister, Government Department, local authority or other body, or person to whom authority has been given by law to administer a particular Act. In 1970 it was estimated that more than 150,000 people in Britain had their lives affected by Government-sponsored tribunals of one kind and another.

There are now some forty-five different types of tribunals dealing with a variety of cases ranging from mental health review boards (e.g. where *A* wishes to obtain his release from a mental institution) to air transport licensing boards. Each tribunal has its own jurisdiction and rules, and in many cases they either overlap or are confusingly different.

It may be argued that disputes of the kind mentioned ought to be decided in the traditionally impartial and fair atmosphere of a Court of Law which follows a known procedure and applies a known system of law—common law or statute. In practice the disputes are frequently decided by special tribunals, not on the basis of law, but on grounds of policy and discretion. The difficulty faced by the tribunals lies in trying to reconcile the rights of the individual with those of the general public in whose interest the particular legislation may have been passed.

The position occupied by administrative tribunals in the Constitution and the type of law applied therein, known as **administrative law,** is a matter of great importance. Administrative law is defined as *that body of legal principles which concerns the rights and duties arising from the impact upon the individual of the actual functioning of the executive instruments of Government*. (C. K. Allen, *Law and Order*.)

Types of Tribunals

There are three main types of administrative tribunals dealing with three different areas of jurisdiction:

(i) Deals with disputes in which a Government Department or a public authority is involved. These tribunals hear, and usually decide, appeals from the decisions or proposed decisions of Government Departments. The decision may be made either by a tribunal (e.g. a local valuation court on rating) or by the relevant Minister after an inquiry.

(ii) Deals with disputes between individual and individual. These are concerned with disputes between private persons and interests which result from attempts by the Government to regulate a particular aspect of the economy (e.g. rents and roads) or the functioning of a particular service (e.g. the National Health Service).

(iii) Deals with the enforcement of professional discipline such as the General Medical Council for doctors, the Law Society for solicitors. The constitution and procedure to be followed by these tribunals are determined by the respective professional body. They have no jurisdiction over the general public.

At this stage we may conveniently examine some of the reasons advanced for the creation of tribunals and the advantages and disadvantages which administrative tribunals display.

The reasons usually given for the establishment of administrative tribunals are:

(*a*) Ordinary courts are already overburdened with work, and additional jurisdiction would cause a breakdown.

(*b*) The costs of judicial proceedings in ordinary courts would be heavy.

(*c*) The Courts of Law are slow and the procedure is too elaborate.

(*d*) Matters involving a public service are best administered by specialists in that service.

(*e*) Policy decisions are best settled by an administrative authority, e.g. a Minister.

The advantages of administrative tribunals are:

(i) Decisions are quick and delays are avoided.

(ii) The procedure is cheap; no fees are payable usually.

(iii) The informal atmosphere and less rigid procedure suit the litigant.

(iv) They have wide discretionary power. This avoids the rigidity which the doctrine of judicial precedent imposes on Courts of Law.

(v) Tribunals are often staffed by experts: e.g. doctors on Pensions or Injuries Tribunals determine disability or extent of injury.

(vi) Tribunals aim for efficient administration of social or economic policies found in statutes; while Courts of Law sift facts and decide on the basis of established rules of law different in character from social policy.

The disadvantages are:

(i) Administrative tribunals are sometimes held in private and lack publicity. Suspicion may therefore be aroused as to 'administrative justice'.

(ii) The parties are sometimes prohibited from being represented by lawyers. The inarticulate person is therefore at a disadvantage in explaining his case. Legal aid is not generally available.

(iii) Reasons for decisions are not always published.

(iv) Technical experts and administrators are not always capable of acting impartially or of sifting the facts accurately. The lawyer-chairman is more suitable and qualified in this field.

(v) Tribunals sometimes include a civil servant of the Ministry directly involved in a dispute. He is, therefore, not sufficiently independent or impartial to give a just decision.

(vi) Rights of appeal are limited in some cases, and they differ as between tribunals.

(vii) Discretion of a tribunal is sometimes so wide as to make decisions inconsistent and unpredictable.

Examples of Tribunals

National Insurance. Claims for benefits under the *National Insurance Act, 1965*, are dealt with locally by an insurance officer. If disagreement arises the applicant for benefit has a right of appeal to a local tribunal composed of a Chairman, who is a lawyer, and two lay members, one representing employers' organizations and one representing employees' organizations. From the tribunal's decision appeal lies to the National Insurance Commissioner, a senior barrister appointed by the Crown.

There is no right of appeal either on a point of law or on a matter of fact from the Commissioner's finding. Some technical questions are reserved for decision by the Minister who may refer the matter to a judge of the High Court. From the Minister's decision on such question, there is a right of appeal to the High Court whose decision is final.

Industrial Injuries. There is a similar system of adjudication in respect of industrial-injuries claims under the *National Insurance (Industrial Injuries) Act, 1965* (as amended). The insured person must establish that his injury arose during the course of his employment. If the insurance officer disallows the claim the applicant may appeal to the tribunal applicable to National Insurance (see above).

If the applicant establishes that his injury did arise in the course of his employment, the next question to consider is the extent of the disablement. This claim is decided first by a medical board of two doctors. Further appeal lies to a medical appeal tribunal made up of two doctors with a lawyer as Chairman. From the medical appeal tribunal appeal lies to the National Insurance Commissioner.

Decisions of the Commissioner in national insurance and industrial injuries cases are published officially, and such decisions bind insurance officers and local tribunals.

Industrial Tribunals: Redundancy Payments. The *Redundancy Payments Act, 1965*, created an obligation on employers to make payments to employees who have been dismissed, laid off or kept on short time, by reason of redundancy. The Act established a Redundancy Fund, to which employers must contribute, and from which payments are made to redundant employees according to their lengths of continuous employment.

Where an employee disputes the redundancy payment (e.g. as to amount) he has the right to appeal to an industrial tribunal. This consists of a Chairman (legally qualified) and two lay members representing (*a*) employers' organizations and (*b*) employees' organizations, respectively. The tribunal sits in various parts of the country as required.

The appellant may be legally represented or may be represented by a trade union official; send written representations setting out the facts and arguments; require the production of documents, and request the tribunal to order the attendance of any person to give evidence or to produce documents.

The decision of the tribunal is given in writing with reasons. The decision is final, subject to a right of appeal to the High Court on a point of law.

Rent Tribunals. Under the *Rent Act, 1965,* restrictions are placed on the rent payable for 'regulated' tenancies, i.e. lettings of unfurnished dwellings with a rateable value on 23 March 1965, not exceeding £400 in Greater London, and £200 elsewhere in England and Wales.

Disputes may arise between landlord and tenant over the assessment of a fair rent. If the assessment of the rent officer (an official appointed for an area) is disputed, a party may appeal to a rent tribunal (or rent assessment committee).

Members of the panel of adjudicators are appointed by the Minister of Local Government and Development and the Lord Chancellor, and are comprised of one-third lawyers; one-third valuers or surveyors; and one-third lay people. Rent Assessment Committees are appointed from the panel and have three members and the Chairman is usually a lawyer. Each Committee is served by a clerk who is a civil servant.

Legal representation is allowed, hearings are open to the public and the Press, and evidence is never taken on oath. If requested, reasons for the decisions of the Rent Assessment Committee may be given in writing or orally. Appeal, on a point of law only, lies to the High Court.

Domestic Tribunals. Domestic tribunals exist to determine questions, decide disputes and maintain discipline among members of a particular trade or profession. Thus a trade union or a professional body may lay down its set of rules governing membership and conduct. If the rules are infringed a tribunal may be set up to deal with the incident, and it may punish or expel an offender.

Three important examples of domestic tribunals are:

(*a*) **Trade Unions.** The disciplinary tribunals of trade unions are created by members themselves. A governing committee frames the rules of membership, the rules constituting a tribunal, rules of procedure and the forms of punishment. Members who violate the rules may be expelled or fined. Expulsion from a union could mean that an individual member is prevented from following his former trade. Such powers are, however, controlled by the Courts of Law and a member may claim the protection of the law if the union acts unlawfully. In *Bonsor* v. *Musicians Union* (1955) it was held that a musician who had been wrongly expelled by his union could obtain damages to compensate him for his financial loss resulting from the expulsion.

The *Trade Union and Labour Relations Act, 1974,* altered the law relating to trade unions, and protects employees against unfair dismissal. Its provisions are too detailed for consideration here (see p. 231).

(*b*) **Solicitors.** The *Solicitors Act, 1957,* provides for the setting up of a committee to exercise disciplinary powers over solicitors. The disciplinary committee sits as a board with a minimum of three members, and follows the usual legal procedure of a Court of Law. The Board may strike a solicitor off the roll, suspend him from practice, impose a fine of up to £500, or order the payment of costs. Appeal from the committee lies to the High Court.

(*c*) **Doctors.** The General Medical Council has power under the *Medical Act, 1956,* to strike a doctor off the Medical Register for infamous conduct in his profession, and he can be barred from further practice. Appeal against the decision of the General Medical Council lies to the Judicial Committee of the Privy Council.

The General Dental Council has similar powers under the *Dentists Act, 1957*, concerning dentists, and the Central Midwives Board has similar authority over midwives. There are, however, many more tribunals (forty-five different types) but lack of space prevents their description here.

Judicial Control of Administrative Tribunals

A tribunal is another name for a court, but to avoid confusion the term is applied here to those bodies possessing judicial power which operate outside the traditional Courts of Law described on page 188.

The essential purpose of a tribunal is adjudication in a particular type of dispute; to follow proper procedures; to act fairly and impartially, and finally to reach a decision. Many of the tribunals today have very wide powers indeed, therefore, their judgements and decisions must be subject to the supervisory control of the Courts of Law. Such control is exercised mainly by the Queen's Bench Division which continues the ancient jurisdiction of the original Royal court of King's Bench, in seeing that justice is done by a tribunal, local authority or other body acting judicially.

As a rule Parliament leaves the professional organizations to form their own rules and procedures and to discipline their membership. Only in exceptional cases will the Courts of Law interfere with these. But, where the administration of a statute, the exercise of powers under it, and the setting up of tribunals to decide disputes are entrusted to a Minister, Parliament generally requires that certain rules be framed to ensure fairness in the administration of the statute and of any tribunals set up, (cf. the National Insurance Tribunals on p. 254). Nevertheless injustice does sometimes occur and the purpose of this section is to examine the grounds on which the Courts of Law exercise their supervisory jurisdiction, and the procedures that are followed.

Where a tribunal acts **judicially** it must follow certain unwritten rules of common law known as **natural justice**. Natural justice embraces two main rules:

(*a*) The rule against bias ('no man may be a judge in his own cause').

(*b*) *Audi alteram partem* ('hear the other side').

(*a*) **The Rule against Bias.** A true judicial decision can be reached only if the judge himself is impartial. This is an obvious requirement in a Court of Law or a tribunal. It was held in *R.* v. *Rand* (1866) that a judge is disqualified where (i) he has a direct pecuniary interest, however small, in the subject matter in dispute; or (ii) there is a real likelihood that the judge would have a bias in favour of one of the parties.

For example, if a judge is related to, or is a friend of, one of the parties to a dispute there would be a real likelihood of bias. It is immaterial whether a judicial decision was **in fact** biased, for as was said by Lord Chief Justice Hewart in *R.* v. *Sussex Justices, ex parte McCarthy* (1924): 'Justice should not only be done, but should manifestly and undoubtedly be seen to be done.'

As an example of pecuniary bias we may note:

Dimes v. *Grand Junction Canal* (1852). Lord Chancellor Cottenham made judicial decrees in a Chancery suit in favour of a canal company. Lord

Cottenham held several shares in the company. *Held* (by the House of Lords): that the decrees be set aside on the ground of pecuniary interest. No bias was proved in fact, nor could it be shown that Lord Cottenham was in any way influenced by his own shareholding.

(*b*) **Audi Alteram Partem.** The second rule of natural justice is that a man has the right to be heard in his own defence. 'It is contrary to the spirit of our laws that anyone should be convicted without having an opportunity of being heard in his own defence,' said one judge in 1795, and that principle still holds good.

The rule embraces the propositions that a party sued or prosecuted should have the opportunity to:

(i) Know the case against him.
(ii) State his case (orally or in writing).
(iii) Make submissions on relevant rules of law.
(iv) Comment on all material considered by the judge.

Ridge v. *Baldwin* (1964). The Chief Constable of Brighton was dismissed from his post by the local Watch Committee for certain acts of misconduct (alleged). The Chief Constable was not present at the meeting of the Watch Committee, nor given the grounds of the proposal to dismiss him nor any particulars of the facts alleged. The Chief Constable appealed to the Courts of Law and eventually in the House of Lords it was held: that the rules of natural justice required that a hearing should have been given to the Chief Constable before the Watch Committee exercised its power of dismissal. Failure to give a hearing invalidated the dismissal.

The above basic rules of natural justice, together with the further rule that neither side may communicate with the judge behind the other's back, are in truth elementary and procedural. The courts follow strict procedural rules which have been hammered out over the centuries to ensure fairness. Administrative tribunals, however, are not bound to follow exactly the same rules which are applied by the courts, but they must apply the general basic principles of justice as noted above.

Supervision by the Queen's Bench Division

The Monarch is 'the fountain of justice' and the Queen's Bench Division of the High Court, acting for the Crown, supervises the administration of justice by inferior courts (e.g. magistrates' courts, administrative tribunals and subordinate tribunals) throughout the Kingdom. Moreover the Q.B.D. exercises supervisory control over Ministers of the Crown, civil servants, local authorities, or other authorities purporting to exercise statutory powers. If such authorities act *ultra vires* (i.e. beyond the powers conferred on them by law) the Q.B.D. may declare such excess of power to be void.

Control is exercised by the Q.B.D. by means of prerogative orders of (*a*) **mandamus**, (*b*) **prohibitition**; (*c*) **certiorari**; and (*d*) **declaratory judgement**.

(*a*) **Mandamus** is an order issuing out of the Q.B.D. commanding (*mandamus*: we command) a person or body to perform a duty imposed by common law or statute. The order is available to enforce administrative duties, e.g. to compel a local authority to produce its accounts for inspection by a ratepayer; to enforce judicial duties, e.g. to compel a housing tribunal to hear and determine an appeal, or magistrates to decide a case in petty sessions.

(*b*) **Prohibition** is an order issuing out of the Q.B.D. to prohibit an inferior court or tribunals from continuing to exceed, or threatening to exceed, its jurisdiction. The order may be directed to magistrates, coroners, and all statutory tribunals.

(*c*) **Certiorari** is an order removing the decision of an inferior judicial body into the Q.B.D. to have its legality enquired into. The word *certiorari* means 'to be informed'; in effect the Q.B.D. reviews the decision. The order may be used (i) to secure an impartial trial; (ii) to review an excess of jurisdiction; (iii) to challenge an *ultra vires* act; (iv) to quash a judicial decision made contrary to natural justice (see above); and (v) to correct errors of law on the face of the record of the lower court or tribunal.

An order of *certiorari* will lie 'whenever any body of persons having legal authority to determine questions affecting the rights of subjects, and having the duty to act judicially, act in excess of their legal authority'. Again the order can be issued to magistrates' courts, administrative tribunals, disciplinary tribunals of, e.g. the police and fire service, and to arbitrators.

(*d*) **Declaratory Judgements.** These are simply judgements which declare what the law is on a particular point and are not accompanied by any sanction or means of enforcement. The Rules of the Supreme Court, Order 25, r. 5 provides:

> No action or proceeding shall be open to objection on the ground that a merely declaratory judgment or order is sought thereby, and the Court may make binding declarations of right whether any consequential relief is or could be claimed, or not.

The remedy is particularly useful where a local authority or public body (or a private person) proposes to spend a large sum of money and is unsure of the law. To forestall subsequent proceedings which may invalidate the project (and cost the local authority much to defend), the local authority may apply to the High Court for a Declaration as to what the law is.

The Court will not adjudicate on hypothetical issues. A concrete case must have arisen.

The Law Commission has proposed (Working Paper No. 40) that there should be a single remedy for judicial review of administrative action and orders, and should be called 'the application for review'.

Tribunals and Inquiries Act, 1971

The wide powers granted to tribunals and the varied procedures which each followed in determining the private rights of individuals caused considerable disquiet in the period following World War II. This came to a head in the Crichel Down case in 1954, concerning the acquisition by a Government Department of privately owned land, which eventually resulted in a special inquiry by the Government. This inquiry revealed inefficient administrative procedures by the Civil Service and apparent injustices to the person whose land was taken and who wanted it back. As a result, a committee was set up in 1955 by the Government under Sir Oliver Franks (now Lord Franks). Its terms of reference were to examine and make recommendations on (i) the constitution and working of tribunals set up by statute; and (ii) the working of administrative procedures, e.g. the holding of an official inquiry or the hearing of appeals by a Minister as the result of objections, particularly in relation to the compulsory purchase of land.

The difference between a tribunal and an inquiry is that a tribunal is, in general, constituted under statutory authority; it has a regular or permanent existence; a defined jurisdiction to hear and determine disputes; and resembles a judicial body such as a court in reaching a decision or finding. An inquiry, on the other hand, is set up at the instance of Parliament, the Government, or a Minister, to hear and receive evidence concerning a matter and to report the facts to some other body, e.g. Parliament, a Minister, or some other body, or to make recommendations. Important inquiries are those like the Aberfan Disaster Inquiry of 1966, and the Inquiry regarding the Third London Airport. An inquiry is most frequently employed in disputes over the compulsory purchase of land by a Government Department or a local authority and in appeals against refusal of planning permission by a planning authority. The Minister appoints an inspector to hold an inquiry the purpose of which is to ascertain the facts and details from the parties, the local authority, the public. The inspector submits his report to the Minister who comes to a decision.

The Franks Committee reported in 1957 and some of its main recommendations passed into law in the *Tribunals and Inquiries Act, 1958*.

The general provisions of the *Tribunals and Inquiries Act, 1971* (a consolidating statute), include:

(*a*) **A Council on Tribunals** shall be formed of ten to fifteen members appointed by the Lord Chancellor. (A Scottish committee is appointed to deal with Scottish matters, the members being appointed by the Secretary of State for Scotland.)

(*b*) **Duties of the Council** are to keep under review the constitution and working of the tribunals listed in a schedule to the *Act of 1958*. The Council acts in an advisory capacity and does not itself hear appeals.

(*c*) **Reports** of the Council are made annually to Parliament.

(*d*) **Chairmen** of the various tribunals to which the Act applies are selected by the appropriate Ministers from a panel of names suggested by the Lord Chancellor. This ensures that nominees have the qualifications, legal or otherwise, for appointment.

(*e*) **Membership** of tribunals can be terminated only with the consent of the Lord Chancellor.

(*f*) **Reasons for decisions** made by tribunals must be given in writing or orally, if the tribunal is requested by a party, even before the decision itself has been announced.

(*g*) **Appeal** on a point of law to the High Court is given in the case of a number of tribunals (e.g. rent, schools, and employment tribunals) where the right had not existed before the Act.

(*h*) **Prerogative Orders**; judicial control by resort to *certiorari*, *mandamus*, and prohibition is safeguarded.

Tribunals of Inquiry (Evidence) Act (1921)

Under this Act both Houses of Parliament may resolve that it is expedient that a tribunal be appointed to inquire into 'a matter of urgent public importance'. Since 1921 there have been seventeen such tribunals dealing with various matters: allegations of bribery of Ministers and public servants over the issue of licences; disclosure of Budget secrets; the loss of a submarine during diving trials; corruption in municipal offices; complaints against police; a spy (Vassall) at the Admiralty; Aberfan disaster (144 children and adults killed) in 1966; civil disturbance in Ulster (13 deaths) in 1972—the Widgery Tribunal.

The instrument appointing the tribunal may confer on it all the powers of the High Court in regard to examination of witness, production of documents, etc. Usually a High Court judge is appointed to preside, and he is assisted by two independent members who may or may not be lawyers. There is no accused person. The case is presented by a Law Officer of the Crown or counsel who may call witnesses. Legal representation is allowed to witnesses whose interests might need to be protected.

The purpose of the inquiry is to ascertain the truth of a particular matter. At the end of the inquiry the President of the court submits his report to the Home Secretary.

A Royal Commission on Tribunals reported in November, 1966, that 'there is need for standing legislation to permit the setting up whenever necessary of an inquisitorial tribunal and for this purpose the *Tribunals of Inquiry* (*Evidence*) *Act* (*1921*) subject to certain amendments and safeguards should be retained'.

Statutory Inquiries

Efficient decision-making involves, as a first step (1) an inquiry to ascertain the facts of a situation; (2) reasonable thought and judgement; and (3) the actual decision. This is prudent whenever an important action is proposed both in private or public life. Administrative authorities are expected to act responsibly in public affairs and it follows that many inquiries must be made in a wide variety of matters, before a final decision is arrived at.

These inquiries range from the preliminary investigation of an executive of a local authority—e.g. a sanitary inspector or public health inspector, or a police officer before a summons is issued or an arrest is made—to the full-scale inquiry presided over by a judge and (say) two independent members forming a tribunal.

Ministerial Statutory Inquiries

In some cases a statute imposes a *duty* on the Minister to hold an inquiry. This form of inquiry has been defined by section 14(1) of the *Tribunals and Inquiries Act, 1958*, thus: 'an inquiry or hearing held or to be held in pursuance of a duty imposed by any statutory provision . . .'. Examples of statutes requiring such an inquiry are: the *Town and Country Planning Act, 1971*; and the *Housing Act, 1957*.

In other cases a statute gives a *power* to a Minister to hold an inquiry. Thus under the *Police Act* (*1964*), s. 32(1), we find 'The Secretary of State *may* cause a local inquiry to be held by a person appointed by him into any matter connected with the policing of any area'.

For the rules as to the procedure to be followed at the inquiry one must look to the statute itself.

In addition to inquiries initiated under a power given or a duty imposed by statute, a Minister may order an inquiry on his own volition. Such an inquiry may be called an extra-legal inquiry—e.g. the Crichel Down Inquiry of 1954, the Mountbatten inquiry into Prison Administration following the escape of Blake (a spy) in 1967.

Generally, therefore, although inquiries may be held for any purpose whatsoever, the term 'statutory inquiry' is used to refer to the obligatory inquiry to enable objections to be made to some scheme, for example, the siting of a New Town, the compulsory purchase of land, before a final decision is made by the Minister. It is a useful administrative device to that end.

Compulsory Acquisition of Land

Government Departments and local authorities may purchase or acquire land by agreement. The normal rules of contract generally apply to these. Authorities may also purchase land *compulsorily*—for, e.g. airfields, fire-stations, cemeteries, children's homes, drainage schemes, police-stations, markets, swimming-baths, and so on. The local authority may wish to clear an area of bad housing (slum clearance) or to pull down a single house as unfit for human habitation.

Statutory authority for such schemes is found in various acts: the *Housing Act (1957)*, which prescribes the procedure to be followed in the Inquiry. The *Acquisition of Land (Authorization Procedure) Act, 1946*, is a general act which may be applied whenever land is to be compulsorily acquired, and lays down the procedure to be followed.

Thus, the steps to be followed in the compulsory acquisition of, say, a portion of land known as Blackacre are:

1. Resolution of the local authority to purchase Blackacre.
2. Compulsory purchase order made by the local authority.
3. Advertisement of the order in local Press.
4. Notices served on every owner, lessee, and occupier of Blackacre.
5. Objections to the proposal may be made by any person within time permitted (must be not less than twenty-one days from notice).
6. If an objection is made the Ministry may:
   (a) hold an Inquiry; or
   (b) give objector right to be heard in private.
7. Inquiry is held. (If objector pursues his rights).
8. Assuming objections are over-ruled, the Minister may make a confirmation order.
9. Minister publicizes the making of the compulsory purchase order.
10. Within six weeks of confirmation order an objector may apply to the High Court for the order to be quashed on two grounds:
    (1) that the order is *ultra vires*; or
    (2) that the interests of applicant were substantially prejudiced by failure to observe proper procedure.
11. If no proceedings under '10' are taken within the six-week period the order 'may not be questioned in any legal proceedings whatsoever'.

No. 10 is described as 'the standard form of challenge' and applies in other statutes where compulsory powers of acquisition are given to administrative authorities. In practice the land or house is usually acquired by agreement before the complete procedure is gone through.

Town and Country Planning

Under the *Town and Country Planning Act (1971)*, the 'responsible authorities' are (1) the Minister for the Environment; and (2) County Councils and District Councils who are designated 'local planning authorities'.

The main duties of the local planning authority are to (1) submit planning proposals for the area to the Minister; and (2) control local 'development' by owners, occupiers, etc. Under (1) the local authority must submit to the Minister a 'development' plan allocating areas for residential, agricultural, or industrial purposes. Notice of the submission of the plan to the Minister must be published in the *London Gazette* and local Press. Objections may be sent to the Minister within a specified period. The Minister must consider all objections either at (1) a public local inquiry; or (2) private hearing. The procedure follows that outlined in previous paragraph. The Minister may approve the plan with or without modifications. The 'standard form of challenge' within six weeks applies in this case.

Where a person wishes to 'develop' his land he must obtain planning permission from the local planning authority. 'Development' means:

the carrying out of building, engineering, mining, or other operations in, on, over or under land, or the making of any material change in the use of any buildings or other land.

If the planning authority refuses permission or permission is granted subject to conditions, the applicant may appeal to the Minister who may (i) dismiss the appeal; (ii) allow the appeal; (iii) reverse or vary any part of the authority's decision.

Before determining the appeal the Minister must, at the request of either the applicant or the planning authority hold an inquiry. Both the applicant and the authority will have an opportunity to be heard. The inquiry is held by an inspector appointed by the Minister, and the report of the inquiry is sent forward for decision by the Minister. Subject again to the standard form of challenge, the Minister's decision 'shall not be questioned in any legal proceedings whatsoever'.

The holding of a 'local inquiry' or 'statutory inquiry' is required under various acts—e.g.:

1. *New Towns Act, 1946.* A site is chosen to build a new town—e.g. Stevenage; a 'development corporation' is constituted, and the plan is publicized. Objections may be made at the statutory inquiry; a confirmation order is made with the standard form of challenge.

2. *Pipe Lines Act, 1962.* This act empowers the Ministry of Power to control the construction of cross-country pipe-lines (e.g. for oil, gas). Again objections are heard at the statutory inquiry and the standard form of challenge applies also in this case.

3. *Local Government Act, 1972.* Two local government commissions (one for England, and one for Wales) were set up to review the organization of local government, and to make proposals for the alteration, amalgamation, and extinction of certain existing local authority areas. A statutory inquiry may be held in some cases to consider objections. Otherwise a local conference will be held.

Accident Inquiries

Where a serious railway accident occurs or where, for example, there has been serious loss of life at sea, the Minister for Transport is responsible for ascertaining the cause and circumstances. To do this an inquiry is set up, evidence is taken and a report is made to him officially. We may note the following inquiries.

1. Shipping Casualties. The Minister of Transport Industries is empowered under the *Merchant Shipping Act (1894)* to hold an inquiry into the loss, stranding or abandoning of a ship and other shipping casualties, whether or not there is loss of life. Where a formal investigation is made a court of inquiry is set up presided over by a Wreck Commissioner, who is assisted by two expert assessors. Such a court has all the powers of a court of summary jurisdiction. The findings are announced in public, they may recommend or stipulate the suspension or revocation of the certificate of the ship's officers. They may also recommend the substitution of a certificate of lesser competence as—e.g. a mate's certificate for a master's. Copies of the findings of the court are printed by H.M. Stationery Office and made available to the public.

2. Railway Accidents. The Minister has statutory powers to order inquiries into train accidents and other accidents involving railway personnel. Train accident inquiries are investigated by the Inspecting Officers of Railways.

The object of the inquiry is to ascertain the cause of the accident and to make recommendations to prevent recurrence. The rules of evidence are relaxed, and the inspecting officer may in his discretion take any part of the evidence in private, an expedient which is adopted where there is a possibility of criminal proceedings—e.g. manslaughter involving a train-driver or signalman. Trade union representatives and railway officers may put questions to witnesses on points relevant to the purpose of the inquiry.

On completion the inspector's report is sent to the Minister indicating the circumstances of the accident, its cause, and any observations arising out of the investigation. The report is printed by H.M. Stationery Office and made available to the public. In some cases where proceedings are pending against a person (e.g. a train-driver) the report is withheld until the judicial proceedings are concluded.

3. Air Accidents. The Civil Aviation (Investigation of Accidents) Regulations (1951) direct that when an accident occurs to a civil aircraft involving death or serious injury to any person, or serious damage to an aircraft, particulars should be notified to the Minister of the Department of Trade and Industry.

An inspector of accidents will be required to investigate the accident and a special court will be appointed to hold a public inquiry, the findings of which will be reported to the Minister.

Extra-legal Inquiries

Non-statutory or extra-legal inquiries may be held at the initiative of the the Minister and are therefore discretionary. The Crichel Down case of 1954 is an example.

Comment

A statutory inquiry is not an engine of bureaucracy designed to over-ride private interests in any event. It is an administrative process. The judicial procedure is ordered by Parliament to deal with objections, to assuage the mind of the objector, to enable him 'to blow off steam' in the hope of rallying public support to his view, but primarily to enable the facts to be brought to the mind of the Minister. He is responsible to Parliament, must carry out the policy of the Government—e.g. to create the new town, clear slums, eliminate bad housing, build schools, prisons, a new airport and the like, and must have first regard for the public interest and welfare generally. The evidence produced by one objector is part only of the facts, pressures and responsibilities to which he must pay attention. Administrative justice is difficult to attain and there is no ideal solution. Lawyers have not always understood the problem clearly and the distinction between an 'administrative decision' and a 'judicial decision' is not helpful.

As a result of these and other criticisms two committees were set up: (1) The Committee on Ministers' Powers in 1932, which made a report, but little action was taken; and (2) the Franks' Committee (chairman Sir Oliver Franks, now Lord Franks) in 1955 (following the Crichel Down case of 1954) which made its report in 1957. The *Tribunals and Inquiries Act (1958)* followed upon the Report (see p. 259).

Redress of Grievances

Introduction

In all civilized states injustices occur from time to time. The Cabinet Ministers, the Civil Service, local authorities, police, public corporations, and other bodies have enormous powers to regulate the lives of us all. Despite the fact that the authorities purport to act 'in the best interests of the community' or for the common good, somewhere there will be a person who has been unjustly treated.

The Crichel Down affair, which arose out of the acquisition of land in Dorset in 1937, and finally resulted in an independent inquiry and a Report to Parliament in 1954 (*Cmnd. 9176, 1954*) brought into focus some of the problems facing administration today, including ministerial responsibility and the techniques of administration in the Civil Service. The report disclosed an apparent injustice to a citizen who persisted in securing his private rights to property he formerly owned and of which he was dispossessed (see p. 147).

Following the report the Government appointed the Franks Committee in 1955 to consider the working of statutory tribunals and the administrative procedures followed in holding an inquiry on an appeal or as a result of objections or representations. Where a citizen's rights are prejudiced there may, in some cases, be formal procedures laid down by statute to be followed whereby the decisions questioned can be pursued or appealed against. The Courts of Law may also control the actions of administrative authorities (see p. 256), but there are limitations to those controls. The Franks Committee observed:

> Over most of the field of public administration no formal procedure is provided for objecting or deciding on questions. For example, when foreign currency or a scarce commodity such as petrol or coal is rationed or allocated, there is no other body to which an individual applicant can appeal if the responsible administrative authority decides to allow him less than he has requested. Of course the aggrieved individual can always complain to the appropriate administrative authority, to his Member of Parliament, to a representative organisation or to the Press. But there is no formal procedure on which he can insist.

Channels of Complaint

These are some of the channels through which a citizen may complain:

(i) A statutory inquiry (e.g. compulsory acquisition of land).
(ii) Statutory tribunals (e.g. National Insurance Tribunal).

(iii) Parliamentary Inquiry (*ad hoc*, e.g. Crichel Down Inquiry).

(iv) Courts of Law.

(v) Consumer Council (e.g. gas, electricity, etc.)

(vi) Representative Organisations (e.g. TUC., NALGO, to act as a pressure group or for remedy).

(vii) The Press.

In 1960 the British section of the International Commission of Jurists ('Justice' for short) initiated an inquiry into the problem of the redress of grievances against administrative authorities such as the Civil Service and others, and produced a report in 1961 called *The Citizen and the Administration: the Redress of Grievances*. It became known as the Whyatt Report, Sir John Whyatt being the Chairman of the committee initiating the inquiry.

The reported mentioned two types of complaint: (i) those alleging that a decision affecting the individual was wrong; and (ii) those alleging maladministration.

Examples of complaints. The following are some of the many instances in which there was no effective machinery for securing redress to the person aggrieved:

(*a*) **Education.** The selection of a child for a particular school following an '11-plus' examination. The local education authority decides, and the parent has no right of appeal.

A parent may wish his child to attend school *X* near his home, but the local education authority may direct that the child attend school *Y* at a distance from the home or 'for the child's good'.

(*b*) **Health Service.** 'Marginal benefits', e.g. a mechanically propelled invalid chair is granted or withheld at the discretion of civil servants in the Ministry, or a hospital authority. There is no formal machinery for review of a disappointed applicant's case.

(*c*) **Telephones.** The allocation or refusal of a telephone to a would-be subscriber is a matter for a local Telephone Manager. An applicant who is refused may appeal only to a higher official in the Post Office.

(*d*) **Farmers' Subsidy.** The amount of agricultural subsidy to be paid to individual farmers is decided by officials. No statutory right of appeal exists but a farmer may complain to an agricultural executive committee, a body independent of the Ministry. In practice the decisions of the committee are almost always accepted by the Minister.

In these types of cases the Whyatt Report suggested that 'the guiding principle should be that the individual is entitled to have an impartial adjudication of his dispute with authority'. It was acknowledged that in some cases the Minister should, in the public interest, retain responsibility for the final decision.

The Report suggested that a **general tribunal** should be set up to deal with miscellaneous appeals from discretionary decisions made by authorities. It was also recommended that the Council on Tribunals should be empowered to keep this aspect of public administration under review, and to make proposals for new tribunals.

After reviewing the remedies and procedures available and the channels through which an aggrieved citizen might pursue his complaint the Report noted:

a continuous flow of relatively minor complaints, not sufficient in themselves to attract public interest, but nevertheless of great importance to the individuals concerned, which give rise to feelings of frustration and resentment because of the inadequacy of the existing means of seeking redress.

The Parliamentary Commissioner for Administration

The 'Justice' Report then examined the office and function of the **Ombudsman** which has existed in Sweden for 150 years, and in more recent years is found in Denmark, Norway, Finland, and New Zealand.

The function and powers of each Ombudsman vary, but the common characteristics are that the Ombudsman is:

(i) An impartial person.
(ii) Independent of the Government of the country, although appointed by and acting on behalf of the Parliament of his country.

His main duty is to investigate complaints of **maladministration** made to him by members of the public against any person acting in the service of the State.

In October 1965 the Government produced a White Paper *The Parliamentary Commissioner for Administration* (Cmnd. 2767). In 1967 the *Parliamentary Commissioner Act* was passed which created the post of **Ombudsman** and Sir Edmund Compton was duly appointed to discharge the duties laid down.

Appointment

The Commissioner is appointed by Letters Patent. He may be removed from office by an Address from both Houses of Parliament and shall vacate this office on reaching 65 years of age.

The Commissioner shall not be a member of the House of Commons or of the Senate or House of Commons of Northern Ireland. He shall be an *ex officio* member of the Council on Tribunals and of the Scottish Committee of that Council (see p. 259).

The Commissioner's salary is £14,000 a year, the appointment carries a pension and the salary and pension are paid out of the Consolidated Fund.

Departments and Authorities Subject to Investigation

A schedule to the Act lists the Departments and authorities subject to investigation. Broadly these include all the Government Departments (listed on p. 127) and the other 'authorities' include, the Public Trustee, the Public Records Office, Registry of Friendly Societies, the Royal Mint, bodies ancillary to or under the supervision of a Government Department or Minister. The Departments and bodies must exercise functions 'on behalf of the Crown'.

How may a Complaint be made?

A has a complaint of maladministration in respect of some act or omission by the Ministry of Social Security. *A* now wishes to complain to the Parliamentary Commissioner for Administration.

(*a*) *A* makes a **written** complaint to an M.P.

(*b*) The complaint must amount to **maladministration.**

(*c*) *A* **consents** to the reference to the Commissioner.

(*d*) The **M.P. refers complaint** to the Commissioner.

(*e*) **M.P. requests investigation** into the complaint.

Matters not Subject to Investigation

The Commission will not investigate any matter where *A*, the aggrieved person, has a right of appeal or review before a statutory tribunal (e.g. National Insurance Tribunal), or where *A* has a remedy in a court, unless in the latter case *A* has a reasonable excuse for not taking proceedings.

The following matters are specifically excluded:

(*a*) **Foreign relations.** Dealings between Governments or international organizations.

(*b*) **Ambassadors, Consuls.** Action by, outside the U.K.

(*c*) **H.M. Dominions.** Action by Dominion Governments outside the United Kingdom.

(*d*) **Extradition and Fugitive Offenders.** Action taken to retrieve offenders who escape from the United Kingdom to other countries.

(*e*) **Criminal Investigation.** Action taken by the Home Secretary for the security of the state, and respecting passports.

(*f*) **Legal Proceedings.** Commencement or conduct of civil or criminal proceedings before the courts or the Navy, Army, or Air Force tribunals (Military Tribunals).

(*g*) **Prerogative of Mercy.** Action taken by the Home Secretary respecting the prerogative of mercy.

(*h*) **Contracts and Commercial Transactions.** Action taken in contracts, etc., made in the United Kingdom or elsewhere by a Government Department or authority to which the act applies.

The following, however, are **within the jurisdiction of** the Commissioner:

(i) Transactions for or relating to the acquisition of land compulsorily or in circumstances in which it could be acquired compulsorily.

(ii) The disposal of surplus land acquired compulsorily or in such circumstances as described at (i) above.

(*i*) **Personnel Matters re Armed Forces, Crown Servants.** Action taken in respect of appointments, removals, pay, discipline, superannuation or other personnel matters in relation to (*a*) Armed Forces and their auxiliary forces; (*b*) civil servants.

(*j*) **Honours.** The grant of honours, awards, or privileges within the gift of the Crown, including the grant of Royal Charters.

Who May Complain?

The broad rule is that any individual, including a body corporate, such as a company, may complain through the proper channels to the Commissioner.

Who may not Complain?

Local authorities, nationalized corporations, and any other authority or body, whose members are appointed by Her Majesty or any Minister of the Crown or Government Department, or whose revenues consist wholly or mainly of money provided by Parliament, may not complain.

Where *A* an aggrieved person, had a complaint but dies, provision is made for the complaint to be made by *A*'s personal representatives (i.e. the executor of his will, or the administrators of his estate if he left no will), or a member of *A*'s family.

Time Limit for Complaints

The broad rule is that a complaint must be sent to an M.P. within one year of the time when the aggrieved party had notice of the matters alleged in the complaint. Where special circumstances apply the Commissioner may extend the period.

A complaint shall not be entertained unless the aggrieved person is resident in the United Kingdom or the complaint relates to action taken in relation to him while he was present in the United Kingdom.

Procedure in respect of Investigations

The main points to be observed in regard to procedure are the following:

(*a*) **Audi Alteram partem** ('Hear the other side'). The Commissioner will hear views expressed by the Government Department against whom complaint is made.

(*b*) **Privacy.** Proceedings may be conducted in private. The Commissioner has a discretion to order otherwise.

(*c*) **Legal Representation.** The Commissioner decides whether any person may be represented by a lawyer.

(*d*) **Information.** The Commissioner may obtain information from such persons, in such manner and may make such inquiries as he thinks fit.

(*e*) **Expenses.** The Commissioner may pay reasonable expenses to persons who attend or furnish information for investigation, and may make compensation for loss of time.

(*f*) **Evidence.** The Commissioner may require any Minister, officer, or member of the Department or authority concerned, or any person who is able to furnish information or produce documents relevant to the investigation to furnish any such information or produce such document.

(*g*) **Attendance of Witnesses.** Witnesses may be compelled to attend and/or to produce documents. The Commissioner has virtually the same powers as a Court of Law in this respect.

(*h*) **Secrecy or Claim of Privilege.** In effect this means that a witness (e.g. a member of a Government Department) may not claim that his information is secret. Nor may such person claim 'privilege' and refuse to disclose information. The broad rule here is that the same procedure applies as that followed in a Court of Law.

(*i*) **Cabinet Proceedings.** Information concerning Cabinet matters are secret and may not be disclosed.

(*j*) **Obstruction and Contempt.** Obstruction of the Commissioner or a member of his staff in the execution of their duties amounts to contempt. Where the Commissioner certifies that an offence has been committed the matter is referred to a Court of Law which will deal with the matter.

Reports

The first duty is to notify the M.P. who forwarded the complaint whether the Commissioner has decided to investigate the complaint or not. Many complaints are received which do not warrant any action at all. If the Commissioner conducts an inquiry he notifies the result to the M.P. sending the complaint: where he makes no inquiry the Commissioner states his reasons for not proceeding.

Annual Report. The Commissioner shall annually lay before the House of Commons a general report on the performance of his functions under the Act.

Special Reports. The Commissioner may lay a special report before the House of Commons where the Commissioner believes that an injustice has not been, or will not be, remedied.

The reports are specially protected from action for defamation, and they are protected by the rule of absolute privilege.

Special provision is made in regard to the disclosure by a Minister of documents which would be prejudicial to the safety of the State or contrary to the public interest. In these cases the Commissioner is not authorized to communicate to any person the contents of the document or the information referred to.

Limitations

There are certain important fields of public service which are immune from investigation. The most important of these are: (i) the Police and (ii) nationalized industries.

In regard to the local authorities, local government commissioners are appointed each working independently in a particular part of the country. Complaints are routed through councillors (see p. 321).

As for the police, the Prime Minister in July 1969 assured the House of Commons that the Home Secretary was keeping procedures for investigating complaints against the police under review. This is a very sensitive area, and the police are in a particularly exposed position from the very nature of the work which they must undertake (see p. 237). The procedure at present adopted is outlined on page 271.

The nationalized industries are in a somewhat different position since they are in fact hybrid bodies. Nevertheless there ought, in principle, to be some method whereby maladministration can be complained about and injustices prevented or rectified.

The term 'maladministration' is nowhere defined in the 1967 Act. The Commissioner initially limited the definition to the 'process' of decision-making, but it appears that the meaning may best be quoted: 'The test of maladministration is whether proper consideration was given before the decision was made'.

In May 1968 the Parliamentary Commissioner issued a Special Report on the *Sachsenhausen Case*. Certain British ex-prisoners of war (Servicemen) claimed compensation from the Foreign Office for exclusion from the Anglo-German relief fund set up for victims of the Nazis. The Foreign Secretary ruled that the claim was made too late and that no further money was available for the claimants. They complained through an M.P. who passed the application to the Commissioner for investigation. The Commissioner found there had been maladministration and submitted that funds should be provided to compensate the complainants. The Special Report was debated in the House of Commons and the Foreign Secretary said that although he did not accept the findings of the Commissioner as regards maladministration by the Foreign Office, he would act on the Commissioner's Report and make financial awards to the claimants.

The general evaluation since the 1967 Act is that the Parliamentary Commissioner for Administration is an important office in the Constitution, that Sir Edmund Compton (Sir Alan Marre held office from 1974 to 1976, when Sir Idwal Pugh was appointed) performed his duties efficiently and well and that on balance the inquiries so far conducted have not revealed serious maladministration in the Government Departments with which he was dealing. In other words the Ministers and the Civil Service have vindicated the belief that they are efficient and fair in the discharge of their duties.

Table 5

Annual number of cases referred to the Parliamentary Commissioner 1967–1972

Year	Cases referred	Cases outside jurisdiction	Cases fully investigated	Maladministration
1967	1,069	561	188	19
1968	1,120	727	374	38
1969	761	445	302	48
1970	645	362	259	59
1971	548	295	182	67
1972	573	318	261	79

The statistics in tables 5 and 6 show (i) the number of cases referred annually to the Parliamentary Commissioner for the period 1967–72, and (ii) the particular Government Departments where maladministration was found during the same period.

Table 6

Maladministration by Department

DEPARTMENT	1967	1968	1969	1970	1971
Inland Revenue	6	13	26	32	39
Social Security	5	7	6	6	11
Home Office	—	4	2	—	3
Employment	3	1	1	3	2
Housing	2	1	2	—	—
Transport	1	2	2	—	—
Foreign Office	1	3	—	1	—
Customs and Excise	1	—	3	1	—
Defence	—	1	1	—	1
Education	—	—	1	1	3
Board of Trade	—	1	1	—	—
Public Building and Works	—	—	2	—	—
Agriculture, Fisheries and Food	—	1	—	3	1
Technology	—	—	1	—	—
Scottish Office	—	1	—	1	—
Land Commission	—	1	—	1	—
*Environment	—	—	—	5	2
*Trade and Industry	—	—	—	2	3
Public Trustee	—	—	—	1	1

*New Departments from 1970.

Every year it may be assumed that about half the cases referred to the Commissioner are outside his jurisdiction. As will be seen most complaints each year have been in respect of the Inland Revenue.

The Health Service Commissioners

The *National Health Service (Reorganization) Act, 1973*, makes provision for the appointment of Health Service Commissioners for (1) England, and (2) Wales, and (3) Scotland (a separate Act applies to Scotland). The three offices are held by the Parliamentary Commissioner, Sir Idwal Pugh, who started his duties following the resignation of his predecessor, Sir Alan Marre, on 1 April 1976.

The Health Service Commissioner will be responsible for investigating complaints against the National Health Service authorities that are not dealt with by those authorities to the satisfaction of the complainant.

Complainants will have **direct access** to the commissioner, but he will not investigate a complaint until he is satisfied that the Health authority concerned has had a reasonable opportunity to investigate it and to make a reply. If the complainant is still dissatisfied the Ombudsman will take up the case.

When the patient is unable to act for himself in pursuit of his rights, another person can lay the complaint for him.

1. The Ombudsman will not investigate complaints that in his opinion relate to the exercise of **clinical judgement** by doctors and other staff.

2. He will not study complaints for which statutory procedures already exist—e.g. those about general medical practitioners, dentists, pharmacists, and opticians—which will continue to be dealt with under the service procedure.

3. He will not study complaints which he thinks could reasonably be pursued through the courts or before a tribunal.

Complaints against the Police

Complaints against a police officer by a member of the public may allege (*a*) a crime, or (*b*) incivility or other impropriety which may be an offence against the Police Discipline Code. The *Police Act, 1964* (s. 49), applies.

All complaints are recorded and all are investigated by the Deputy Chief Constable of the force concerned. Where a crime is alleged to have been committed, a report of the evidence is submitted to the Director of Public Prosecutions (see p. 216), who decides whether or not to prosecute the officer before the courts in the normal way.

Where following an investigation by the Deputy Chief Constable it appears that an offence against the police regulations may have been committed he may decide to take no action (the matter being trivial or unfounded) or he may recommend that the officer be dealt with before a police disciplinary tribunal. In any case, the matter will be submitted to a Complaints' Board, comprising two commissioners, who may agree with the D.C.C. that no action be taken or that the matter be dealt with by the Chief Constable of the force, who himself will hold a disciplinary tribunal.

The commissioners (the lay element) may sit with the chief constable when he hears the charge and the evidence. The lay commissioners will thus ensure that justice is done and that the complaint has been determined fairly.

Where an officer is found guilty, the Chief Constable may order dismissal, reduction in rank, fine, reprimand or caution. In certain cases (e.g. dismissal) the officer has a right of appeal to the Home Secretary whose determination is final.

At the time of writing a Bill is before the Commons to permit the appointment of Commissioners to the Board and the tribunal. The police are in an exposed position in society, subject to a stringent code, and it is hoped that the procedure will allay any disquiet over maladministration.

Exercises

1. What are the main forms of delegated legislation?

2. What reasons are advanced for the growth in this form of legislation?

3. What criticisms may be aimed at delegated legislation?

4. What controls are exercised (*a*) by the courts, and (*b*) by Parliament over delegated legislation?

5. What are 'Administrative Tribunals'? Describe the three main types which exist.

6. What reasons are usually given for their creation?

7. Discuss (*a*) the advantages, and (*b*) the disadvantages of Administrative Tribunals.

8. By what means may a Court of Law control Administrative Tribunals?

9. What are the Prerogative Orders issued by the Q.B.D. of the High Court?

10. What is a Declaratory Judgement? What is its practical value to, say, a local authority?

11. What do you know of the *Tribunals and Inquiries Acts, 1958–71*?

12. What are the main provisions of the *Tribunals of Inquiry* (*Evidence*) *Act, 1921*?

13. Name some of the main channels of complaint through which a citizen may air a grievance against authority.

14. Discuss the origin of the office of the Parliamentary Commissioner for Administration.

15. How may a complaint be made to him?

16. Discuss the procedure adopted by the Parliamentary Commissioner for Administration in the investigation of complaints.

17. What limitations exist in regard to the investigations able to be undertaken by the Parliamentary Commissioner for Administration? Adduce reasons, for and against, a similar appointment to investigate complaints against local government maladministration.

CHAPTER ELEVEN

LOCAL GOVERNMENT

Introduction

Most civilized states have some form of local government, although theoretically it is possible for a central Government to administer all public services in the regions and in the local areas. In the United Kingdom there are local authorities (Councils) which are not part of the Civil Service but are local bodies which work in partnership with the central Government.

The structure of local government broadly is the same for England, Wales, and Scotland, the minor differences in regard to Scotland being due to historical reasons.

History of Local Government in England and Wales

It is important to know something of the history of local government in order to understand the present composition and the functions it performs in the British Constitution. There are four main periods of development of local government in the United Kingdom: local government before 1830; local government from 1830 to 1880; local government from 1880 to 1945; and local government from 1945 to the present.

Local Government before 1830

Before 1066 there were regional Kings, such as Alfred the Great (849–99), King of Wessex. In Anglo-Saxon times the country was divided into shires which were ruled or presided over by the sheriff who was the King's outpost officer or agent.

William I (1027–87) invaded the country in 1066, defeated the English, proclaimed himself King at Westminster and set up a strong central Government and unified the Kingdom. William I retained the office of sheriff which was useful in curbing the rebellious English feudal barons. The sheriff was appointed by the King and presided over the shire court, which was primarily an administrative body, maintaining local control, collecting the Royal revenues and paying these taxes over to the Monarch. The sheriff was also a judicial officer who decided civil and criminal disputes in the shire court where he was assisted by the bishop and the ealdormen. The sheriff was also responsible for military organization; for keeping the King's peace and arresting those persons accused of crime; justice being administered according to the customary law of the English people. The sheriff in Norman times was a powerful figure, deriving authority from the Monarch himself.

The shires were divided into **hundreds** (an area of land) each under the control of the medieval hundredman. Below the hundred was the manor, the vill or small township.

The Boroughs. There were in Anglo-Saxon and Norman times certain Roman cities still inhabited; York, Chester, Winchester, and London, to name a few, and some new towns which sprang up as a defence against the Danes. Until the beginning of the twelfth century there was no separate form of government for these. The Monarch then began the practice of granting

273

charters to the boroughs (townships), giving some of them corporate status which enabled them to organize some form of local government. The rights in the charters varied from borough to borough. Some boroughs were governed by guilds or companies of merchants (a comparison exists in the City of London today) and some were granted a special 'court' composed of favoured persons of the King, the privilege of attending court passing lineally from father to son. Sometimes a borough was honoured by having its own sheriff. Elsewhere in the shires the sheriff was the important figure.

The Decline of the Sheriff. In many areas the sheriffs were oppressive, which caused disquiet and unrest, and in 1327 Edward II created **Conservators of the Peace** (Justices of the Peace) from among the knights of the shires. Their duties were to preserve the peace and to administer a primitive police system by the appointment of a Constable or Head Constable to act as the executive officer of the Justices, arresting those people accused of a crime, and executing the Justices' warrants and orders.

The Justices of the Peace, as they came to be called, grew in importance and power as the local controllers and judicial officers primarily responsible for maintaining peace and good order. They were leaders in the localities, were efficient and as their power and prestige grew that of the sheriffs declined. The office of sheriff still exists today, but the holders of this ancient office now carry out only formal and nominal duties.

The Justices of the Peace. The feudal system began to decay in the thirteenth and fourteenth centuries and the changes in the social structure caused labour troubles and much poverty. The magistrates were empowered by law to regulate wages. Where the highways fell into disrepair the magistrates were empowered to maintain them and the *Statute of Bridges, 1530*, authorized J.P.s to compel landowners or corporations to repair them. At the same time, the *Highways Act* empowered the J.P.s to appoint surveyors to each parish to ensure that the inhabitants repaired the roads and bridges.

In 1563 the first Poor Law made contributions for the relief of the poor compulsory. In 1601, the *Poor Law Act* made each parish responsible for providing work for the unemployed and for giving poor relief. The officials responsible for seeing that the law was carried out were the churchwardens and the **Overseers of the Poor**, who were given the power to tax all the inhabitants of the parishes for the relief of the poor. These officials acted under the control of the J.P.s, who were authorized by statute to levy a 'poor rate' (tax). The Parish Vestry was the meeting place of the local leaders responsible for the elementary and basic duties of local government.

In the boroughs control was vested in the corporations. J.P.s were nominated to their posts by the corporations, but the appointments were made by the Crown. Their responsibilities were the same as those of the county J.P.s, i.e. local order, highways, and relief of the poor.

The Industrial Revolution. From 1750 the Industrial Revolution changed the country from an agricultural to an industrial society. Large urban areas grew apace as people left the land and their agricultural work for industry and the industrial towns of the midlands and the north. The existing local government in the towns, operated by the J.P.s and the corporations, was quite inadequate to cope with the bad social conditions which industrialization brought in its train: the factories were insanitary; there was poor housing, unemployment, and poverty.

Some boroughs obtained local Acts to ensure the towns were paved, lit, and policed, sometimes a local Act empowered a corporation to build a hospital; but, generally, the local services were quite inadequate to cope with the problems of ill health, poverty, and the high death rate among young people which resulted from the industrial changes taking place. In the early nineteenth century there were no local services for public health; no arrangement for the care and needs of special groups such as children, the sick and the elderly, no adequate police to cope with the prevalent crime and there were no fire-brigades.

Local Government: 1830–1880

The Change in Thinking. Robert Owen (1771–1858) and Thomas Paine (1737–1809) preached against the existing conditions in society. Later Thomas Carlyle (the writer); Benjamin Disraeli (the politician); John and Charles Wesley (the religious leaders) and members of the Established Church agitated with Lord Shaftesbury for legislation to reduce the misery of the Industrial Revolution.

Jeremy Bentham (1748–1832) also advocated changes in the law and the Government and preached to doctrine of **Utilitarianism,** i.e. that the test of good law was whether that law promoted the greatest happiness of the greatest number of people. If laws or government (central or local) failed in that test they were not good. Edwin Chadwick (1800–90) became a follower of Bentham and adopted utilitarianism as a philosophy. Chadwick held important Government posts and tried to improve conditions, particularly by changing the Poor Law. A Poor Law Commission was set up by the Government in 1831 which included Chadwick. The Report of the Commission resulted in the *Poor Law Act, 1834*. This Act provided:

(i) The Poor Law was to be administered by Local Boards of Guardians, elected by the local people. This was an important step forward in that local people (householders) elected local representatives.
(ii) The area of the Board was a 'union' of parishes, i.e. a convenient and efficient local area (several parishes joined or united) to serve the needs of people within that area.
(iii) The Board employed paid officials to do the work, who were controlled by the Guardians.
(iv) Poor Law Commissioners were appointed to ensure central control (i.e. from the central Government).

The Poor Law Commissioners could make orders, appoint paid officials, and inspect local administration. In effect, therefore, the Commission was the forerunner of the Ministries of the present century, responsible for the vast services administered by local government. The Commission was followed by (i) the Poor Law Board which in time became; (ii) the Local Government Board which subsequently became; (iii) the Ministry of Health which was succeeded by (iv) the Ministry of Housing and Local Government and now; (v) the Department of the Environment.

At the same time that the Poor Law Commission was set up in 1831, the great *Reform Act of 1832* was passed, which greatly altered the political representation in Parliament (see p. 25).

The *Municipal Corporations Act, 1835*. This Act, the result of another Commission, introduced certain important changes in the boroughs, which were now agitating for reform:

(i) A municipal corporation was defined as a 'legal personification of the local community, represented by an elected council, and acting for, and responsible to, the inhabitants of the district'.

(ii) The vote was given to all rate-payers who resided within the area of the corporation for three years.

(iii) Council meetings were to be open to the public.

(iv) The council was empowered to appoint paid officials.

(v) Provision was made for levying a rate.

(vi) An annual audit of accounts was provided for.

(vii) Three-quarters of the council were elected by the householders and one quarter were nominated and elected by the councillors and were called **aldermen**.

The 1835 Act deprived the municipal council of the power to nominate the Justices: from that time the J.P.s of the boroughs were solely concerned with judicial work; while the councillors and aldermen performed the administrative work of local government. In 1888 the county justices were similarly deprived of their administrative functions in the local government of the counties and from then onwards they devoted themselves to judicial work in the county magistrates' courts and Quarter Sessions.

The defects of the *Municipal Corporations Act, 1835,* were that it did not apply to all urban areas; London was too large to be subject to the Act, and there was still left in the country 'a chaos of areas and a chaos of authorities'. If a borough wanted to extend its powers it had to promote a private Bill in Parliament. Central control was also defective and inadequate, except in the auditing of accounts.

In 1872 the corporations became Public Health Authorities, and in 1882 they were given powers to regulate roads and streets; drainage and sewage; public health; gas and water supply. In addition, some of the larger boroughs (such as Liverpool and Manchester), secured the passing of special statutes to enable them to deal with sanitation and unfit housing.

The Development of the Public Health Movement. In 1850 half the population of the country lived in towns, but by 1880 this number had increased to two-thirds. The early pioneering work of Edwin Chadwick, who was secretary of the Poor Law Commissioners, showed up the many defects in urban living and the inadequacies of local administration and the local authorities. He advocated enlarging the areas and authorities and granting increased powers to the local bodies. The *Public Health Act, 1848,* set up the General Health Board and local health boards in areas with high death rates. Some 670 of these local boards were established and designated as urban and rural sanitary authorities.

In 1868 the Royal Sanitary Commission was set up. This body reported in 1871, and recommended:

(i) That the numerous existing laws on public health matters should be consolidated in one or more Public Health Acts.

(ii) That the administration of the law be made uniform throughout the country, instead of depending on local initiative. The operation of the main powers should be compulsory, so that all areas should reach minimum standards in street cleansing, water supply and similar matters.

(iii) All local health powers should be the responsibility of one authority in each area, instead of being spread over several sets of authorities. The local authorities should be supervised by a central Government Department, on the lines of the Poor Law Board.

This Report was followed by the *Local Government Act of 1871*, which set up the central authority, the Local Government Board, and took over the powers of the other Government agencies. In 1872 the *Public Health Act* of that year set up local sanitary authorities for the whole country. The law was consolidated by the *Public Health Act, 1875*, which dealt with public health generally and also highways.

Under this revised system England and Wales were divided into sanitary districts: urban sanitary districts for the boroughs and rural sanitary districts for the Poor Law Unions. The authority, responsible for the administration of these local bodies, was the elected representatives in the urban districts, and the Poor Law Guardians in the rural districts. In the urban areas the sanitary authority was also responsible for highways.

Education was another service which needed attention. The Government took the view that education of the masses was not their responsibility. There were voluntary and religious bodies which ran schools and to which the Government made grants, but only a small number of children received any form of education, and it was not till the *Education Act, 1870*, that a move was made. The Act provided for the setting up of School Boards to provide education. The Boards were under the control of the Privy Council and were required to provide education of an elementary kind.

Local Government, 1880–1945

Between 1835 and 1888 there was a confusing number of authorities, each with their own separate power and function. It is true that in urban districts the health authority was also the highway authority and that the guardians of the poor were also responsible for public health in rural districts. Generally, however, the pattern was 'one service, one authority', and local government powers were distributed among various authorities: the Justices of the Peace, borough councils, sanitary authorities, poor law guardians, improvement commissioners, vestries and similar bodies. The areas for which each body was responsible varied and the consequence was a confusion in which order had to be restored. The first important change was brought about by the *Local Government Act, 1888*.

The *Local Government Act, 1888*. This important Act set up the county councils as elected bodies, applying the same kind of local self government as that found in the boroughs. The principal features of the Act were:

(i) **Transfer of Powers.** The powers of the J.P.s in Quarter Sessions were transferred to county councils, which were directly elected by the people.

(ii) **Areas.** The county councils were responsible for county areas which were retained.

(iii) **London.** A new London County was created from three geographical counties adjoining the Metropolis.

(iv) **Boroughs.** The largest boroughs, with populations of 150,000 and over, were excluded from the county council structure. These boroughs were called 'county boroughs' and became (like the county councils) multi-purpose authorities exercising all the local government functions for their areas, independent of the county. Some older boroughs with smaller populations than 150,000 agitated against the loss of borough status and against their being incorporated within the county councils. These boroughs were allowed to become 'county boroughs'. Altogether there were fifty-seven, and four of which had populations of less than 50,000.

The *Local Government Act, 1894*. This Act completed the programme of local government reform by renaming the urban and rural sanitary districts, within the counties, 'urban districts' and 'rural districts', and by putting them under the control of elected councils. There are no aldermen found in these elected councils. The district councils were given the powers of the former sanitary authorities (urban and district). The newly created urban and district councils took over the function of the highway boards which were then abolished.

The position of the parishes in the structure of local government declined after the loss of their poor law functions in 1834. The new 1894 Act created within the rural districts (i) parish councils, and (ii) parish meetings, both with limited powers.

With the passing of the 1894 Act, the pattern of local government was complete and the system has lasted till 1972. The reformed system was based on elected councils, to which the responsibility of administering public services was entrusted. It was, however, impossible to remove all the *ad hoc* authorities at one sweep and a few remain even today. However, the functions of most of them were gradually taken over by the local councils. The last important one to disappear was the Poor Law Guardians, a body which was finally abolished by the *Local Government Act, 1929*, which transferred the duties to the county councils or county borough councils.

From 1894, therefore, there was a general enlargement of local services and responsibility transferred to the general-purpose or all-purpose authorities, e.g. the county councils, the county borough councils. The *Education Act, 1902*, enlarged the scope of the system of education in the United Kingdom and transferred responsibility from the School Boards, which were then abolished, to the county councils and county borough councils. Certain large urban districts within counties were, however, enabled to be an educational authority separate from the county.

The *Housing Act, 1919*, imposed on county district and county borough councils a duty to provide new houses for the working classes and, at the same time, the Act gave generous financial assistance fot this purpose. Subsequent Housing Acts continued this principle, although the Government grants were restricted.

The *Housing and Town Planning Act, 1909*, gave urban local authorities an optional power to control town planning. From 1919 town planning became compulsory and today this aspect of local government work is very important indeed.

The *Rating and Valuation Act, 1925*. Rating, which was formerly dealt with by the Overseers, as a heritage of the Poor Law, was taken over by the borough, urban and rural district councils under the *Rating and Valuation Act, 1925*. The various rates, which had been levied, were consolidated in one general rate and this simplified financial procedure.

The *Local Government Act, 1933*. This Act was passed to consolidate the law relating to local government and was the first Act to contain all the provisions regarding the structure and constitution of local authorities outside London. Previous legislation passed in the 1880s was repealed.

Other important Acts passed around the same time were the *Housing Act, 1936*, the *Public Health Act, 1936*, and the *Food and Drugs Act, 1938*.

The structure, as noted in the diagram (on page 282) exists, in broad outline, now, but the complex and confusing system of *ad hoc* authorities gave way to the general-purpose or multi-purpose authorities of today.

During World War II the United Kingdom was divided into regions for civil defence purposes, each under a Civil Defence Regional Commissioner responsible for co-ordination of the civil defence arrangements organized by individual local authorities. The fire service was nationalized during the war, but afterwards the counties and county boroughs were made responsible for the administration of the fire service.

Local Government, 1945–58

In 1944 the *Education Act* was passed which made provision for wider educational facilities ranging from nursery schools to colleges of further education and colleges of advanced technology.

In 1945 the Labour Government came to power and the nationalization measures then enacted removed from local authority control the utilities, for example, gas and electricity.

The main aspects to be considered are: (1) the transfer of certain functions from the smaller local authorities to the larger; and (2) the transfer of functions away from local government to central Government Departments or new *ad hoc* bodies, and the preference for larger units for the new functions.

(1) *Transfer of Functions to Major Authorities.*

The *Education Act of 1944* made the county councils and the county borough councils the educational authorities for the country. County districts lost their duties in relation to education, except that some were made **agents** of the county council. The reason for this transfer of duty was the knowledge that the provision of a wide range of schools, from nursery schools to Colleges of advanced technology, could only be undertaken by the larger authorities. A major service ought to be administered by major authorities. Moreover it was administratively more convenient to deal with only 140 education authorities rather than the many hundreds which existed independently before the 1944 Act.

The *National Health Service Act, 1946*, introduced a new set of local health services: home helps, vaccination and immunization, health centres, and ambulances. Some of these services had previously been run in another form by the district councils, while others were new. The county councils and the county borough councils were made responsible for the services.

The National Fire Service was disbanded after the war, and, by the *Fire Services Act of 1947*, services were returned to the county councils' or county borough councils' control.

Similarly the *Police Act, 1946*, abolished some separate small police forces and absorbed them into the larger forces: examples of this were Penzance (Cornwall) and Tiverton (Devon), small towns with their own forces, which were incorporated into the forces of Cornwall and Devon respectively.

The *Town and Country Planning Act, 1947*, made county borough councils and county councils the planning authorities, but enabled the county councils to delegate power to county district councils, if they so wished.

The *Children Act, 1948*, placed on the county councils and the county boroughs responsibilities under this Act and, at the same time, deprived the county district authorities of their powers.

Similarly the *National Assistance Act, 1948*, more or less abolished the old Poor Law, leaving the few remaining local assistance services with the county borough councils.

(2) *Transfer of Functions from Local Government.*

After World War II it was felt that county councils and county boroughs were too small to administer certain services. Consequently the Government reverted to *ad hoc* authorities and transferred responsibility for certain services away from local government control.

(i) **Hospitals.** The hospital service was, under the *National Health Service Act, 1946*, transferred to Regional Hospital Boards, below which were the local Hospital Management Committees, both bodies being appointed by the Minister. A few services (e.g. the ambulance service) were left with local government.

(ii) **National Assistance.** The *National Assistance Act, 1948*, placed responsibility for public assistance on the National Assistance Board (below which were regional offices and local offices), which was controlled by the Minister. The Act took away from the local authorities the responsibilities for poor relief.

(iii) **Trading Undertakings.** Certain local authorities operated gas and electricity services for their areas. The *Electricity Act, 1947*, and the *Gas Act, 1948*, nationalized both industries and created public corporations with responsibility allocated to Area Boards (see Public Corporations, p. 156).

(iv) **New Towns.** Most towns in the past grew up spontaneously for geographical or industrial reasons. The *New Towns Act, 1946*, provided for the establishment of new towns to relieve the congestion in certain overpopulated urban areas. The Minister appoints members of a Development Corporation to start the work and when the town is built and completed it is transferred to local authority control.

(v) **Valuation for Rating.** The valuation of property for rating purposes has since 1601 been undertaken by the local authorities. The *Local Government Act, 1949*, transferred from local authorities to the Inland Revenue Department the duty of valuation of property and premises.

Therefore, after 1945 there was a conscious reduction in the functions traditionally performed by the local authorities by transferring certain of those duties to *ad hoc* authorities, by appropriating them to Government Departments, or Boards acting as agents of Government Departments.

At the same time, however, the local authorities enlarged certain of their services, particularly social services and the expansion of those services retained by local authorities involved closer central control by Ministers, operated mainly through:

(i) **Inspection.** For example, the educational service is a wide and important one. H.M. Inspectors are appointed at the Ministry whose task is to ensure uniformity of standards and efficiency in the expanded educational services.

(ii) **Appeals**. When decisions made by local authorities adversely affect the rights of citizens, provision is made for statutory appeals to be made to the Minister, for example, planning appeals. Similarly if a local authority wishes to clear slum dwellings or make new roads, a scheme is prepared, published locally and an appeal against this may be made to the Minister, who makes the final decision.

(iii) **Finance.** If local authorities wish to engage in capital projects, e.g. buildings, houses, and schools they must if they have insufficient finance, apply for loans or grants of money from the central Government. There is a great deal of dependence therefore, by local authorities on the central Government for grant aid for new projects, improvement of existing projects, buildings, services, etc. This dependence on central Government aid means that a closer watch, in the interests of national economy, must be kept on the local authorities to ensure that national policy, national planning and national standards are maintained. Ministry supervision by this budgetary control extends into the field of policy and administration. Inevitably, conflict arises between local authorities, who wish to initiate new schemes and the central Government, which must take account of its national, or regional, plan and the economy of the country as a whole. Tensions between the local authorities at the periphery and the central Government are endemic in all Governments.

Reversion. Whereas in the early nineteenth century this country had a range of *ad hoc* authorities dealing with specific services, by the end of the century there were a series of local authorities which took over practically all the *ad hoc* bodies and became **compendious** authorities. Since 1945, however, there has been a return to the idea of creating *ad hoc* bodies as the best means of administering certain functions (e.g. gas, electricity, hospitals) on a national or regional basis, by using the concept of the public corporation, agencies of Ministries, or by the Ministries taking over the functions themselves.

Changes. Apart altogether from changes which any Government may initiate there are social and economic forces operating on local authorities continuously. There are increases in population, for example. In 1871 the population of England and Wales was 23 million; in 1901, 31 million; in 1931, 40 million, and in 1961 there were 46 million people. Moreover, people have tended to move from the country to the towns. As a consequence urban areas have grown and increased their revenue; rural areas have declined and correspondingly lost their revenue from the ratepayers, who left for the larger towns. The cities and larger towns have extended their boundaries into the counties.

The advent of the motor-car during the past fifty years has increased the ease of transport, communications and quicker supervision by central authorities of outlying authorities. It has also meant more pollution (a pressing problem) and road accidents on an increasing scale (7,000 killed per annum, and 400,000 injured).

Post-war measures of reform have included the establishment of the Local Boundary Commission set up in 1945; Local Government Commissions for England and Wales, set up in 1958; and the Royal Commission on Local Government in the Greater London Area, set up in 1957, which resulted in the *London Government Act, 1963*, and set up the new authorities (see p. 287).

Principal Types of Local Authority: *1972*

The main pattern of local government organization in England and Wales will continue in existence until 1 April 1974.

The Greater London Area will be discussed later (see p. 287) The rest of the country is divided into: (i) **county boroughs;** and (ii) **administrative counties.**

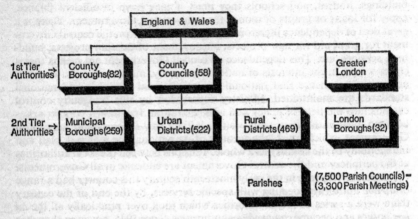

Local government structure (until 1974)

The above diagram may appear to indicate a fairly straightforward and rational organization. However, in 1966 a Royal Commission was set up (see p. 284), and reported in 1969. Eventually the *Local Government Act, 1972* (running to some 450 pages), was passed which brought about far-reaching reforms. We shall consider in the following pages the structure and functions of local government as it applies today. The effective date for the change-over from the former authorities to the present was 1 April 1974, a landmark in the history of the country.

London Government

The administration of local government in London differs from other parts of England and Wales, partly for historic reasons, but mainly because London is the capital city, the centre of trade and commerce and is such a large unit.

Briefly the London County Council (which ceased to exist on 1 April 1965) was established, with other county councils, by the *Local Government Act, 1888.* Its constitution, powers and duties were consolidated in the *London Government Act, 1939.* A Royal Commission was set up to review the system and working of local government in London and its Report (*Cmnd. 1164*) was issued in October 1960. A White Paper (London Government Proposals for Reorganization (*Cmnd. 1562*)) was published in 1961, which endorsed the Commission's overall design and subsequently the *London Government Act, 1963,* was passed which provided the present structure.

The Greater London Council

The Greater London Council and thirty-two London Borough Councils were constituted under the Act of 1963. They replaced on 1 April 1965 the London County Council, the Middlesex County Council, the County Borough Councils of Croydon, East Ham and West Ham, twenty-eight metropolitan boroughs, thirty-nine non-county boroughs and fifteen urban district councils. The boundaries and constitution of the Corporation of the City of London were not affected.

Under the Act, Greater London became for the first time a clearly defined local government area. Greater London had a population estimated in 1969 at 7,703,410, and an area of 610 square miles, including, in addition to the former counties of London and the greater part of Middlesex, parts of Metropolitan Essex, Kent, Surrey and Hertfordshire.

Composition. The Greater London Council consists of one hundred councillors and sixteen aldermen. Elections are held every third year and for the first three elections in April 1964, 1967, and 1970, the electoral areas were the thirty-two London boroughs, each returning two, three or four councillors, according to the size of the electorate.

Aldermen are chosen by the councillors and hold office for six years, half their number retiring every third year. These will continue to serve on the GLC till 1976. The Chairman, Vice-Chairman, and Deputy Chairman are elected annually by the councillors and aldermen. The political head of the administration is the Leader of the Council, elected by the majority party.

Meetings. The Council meets fortnightly at 2.30 p.m. on Tuesdays except in holiday periods. Out of the thirteen standing and two special committees, one meets fortnightly, ten monthly and the others, as required.

London Borough Councils. Each of the thirty-two London Borough Councils consists of a mayor, a varying number of councillors and aldermen (till 1977) to the total of one-sixth of the councillors for the borough.

Distribution of Functions. The functions of (i) the Greater London Council, and (ii) the thirty-two London Borough Councils were redistributed and it will be helpful if we note the following summary which indicates the body responsible for the main services:

Greater London Council	*London Borough Council*
Ambulance Service.	Housing.
Fire Service.	Lighting.
Housing (major projects and estates inherited from LCC).	Libraries.
Main highways (metropolitan roads).	Highways (other than metropolitan roads).
Main sewers and disposal works.	Child Care.
Planning (overall development plan).	Local Health Service.
Certain parks, ultimately to be transferred to boroughs.	Parks.
Traffic Control.	Planning (subordinate to overall planning of GLC).
Vehicle licensing.	Education.
	Public Health including refuse collection and street cleansing.
	Sewers (except main sewers).
	Welfare.

Two-tier System

Broadly, therefore, there is a two-tier system, but there is no clear division of responsibility in all services. Housing, for example, is shared between the

GLC and the London Boroughs. The GLC accommodates 15,000 families a year, more than 5,000 of them in expanding towns many miles from London. The GLC building programme in London is 7,500 a year.

Planning must be co-ordinated between the GLC and the London Boroughs. The GLC has prepared a Development Plan which, if approved by the Minister, will be the overall plan within which the London Borough Councils will make their own plans. Town planning control of private development proposals is mainly the concern of the London boroughs, but the GLC has some responsibilities in this field.

Education. The local education authority for an area corresponding with the area of the twelve inner London boroughs and the City of London is the Inner London Education Authority. The ILEA consists of the GLC representatives for the boroughs concerned, plus one nominee from each of their borough councils. Elsewhere the borough councils are the responsible education authorities.

The City Corporation

Lying at the very heart of the metropolis occupying one square mile is the City of London (the centre of the financial world, banking interests, Fleet St., St. Paul's, the Law Courts). It has a unique place in the constitution, mainly due to its history and is unlike any other local authority in England and Wales. The full title of the City Corporation is **Mayor and Commonalty and Citizens of the City of London.**

The City Corporation acts through three courts: (i) The Court of Common Hall, consisting of the Lord Mayor, the sheriffs, the aldermen, and such of the liverymen of the City Companies (of which there are seventy) as are freemen of the City; (ii) the Court of Aldermen, consisting of the twenty-five aldermen, and (iii) the Court of Common Council, which is a legislative and deliberative assembly, consists of the Lord Mayor, the aldermen, and the common councilmen.

The Lord Mayor is nominated by the liverymen of the City Companies and is elected by the Court of Aldermen to hold office for one year. During his term of office, he is, **ex officio,** a member of the Privy Council. He presides over the meetings of the Corporation, attends to the civic and ceremonial duties and dispenses hospitality on behalf of the City Corporation. The Lord Mayor receives a salary of £12,500 a year, but this by no means covers his expenses.

The aldermen are elected for life by the ratepayers and inhabitants of the twenty-five wards in the City. The common councilmen are elected annually by the same voters who elect the aldermen, in different proportions for each ward. There are now 159 councilmen.

The City Corporation is not affected by the reorganization of the GLC and the London Boroughs or by the 1972 Act.

Local Government Reform 1969–72

Introduction

In 1966 a Royal Commission on Local Government Reform was set up under the Chairmanship of Lord Redcliffe-Maud. The Commission comprised eleven members and its terms of reference were:

To consider the structure of local government in England, outside Greater London, in relation to its existing functions; and to make recommendations for authorities and boundaries, and for functions and their division, having regard to the size and character of areas in which these can be most effectively exercised and the need to sustain a viable system of local democracy; and to report.

The Commission presented its report to Parliament in June 1969. The Commission took written and oral evidence from over 2,000 witnesses and its published report ran to two volumes and contained 650 pages.

In February 1970 the Labour Government having accepted and studied it then made its proposals in a White Paper *Reform of Local Government in England (Cmnd. 4276)*. This broadly accepted the conclusions of the Royal Commission's Report, subject to a number of minor exceptions. The Labour Government reserved its position on the idea of Provincial Councils until the Report of the Royal Commission on the Constitution had been received. The Chairman of this Commission was the late Lord Crowther.

In June 1970 the Conservative Government came to power having pledged itself to 'a sensible measure of local government reform, which will involve a genuine devolution of power from the central Government and will provide for the existence of a two-tier structure'.

In February 1971 the Conservative Government presented its White Paper *Local Government in England (Cmnd. 4584)*. In October 1971 the Conservative Government introduced a Local Government Bill which finds expression in the *Local Government Act, 1972*, the main provision of which will be considered later at page 291.

The Redcliffe-Maud Proposals

Only the briefest outline can be given here of the Report:

(1) Main Recommendations

The Royal Commission recommended replacing the present structure of local government. Its main proposals were:

(a) There should be sixty-one new local government areas.

(b) Fifty-eight of these areas should be governed by single-tier authorities, called unitary authorities.

(c) In the three areas surrounding (1) Birmingham, (2) Liverpool, and (3) Manchester, there should be a two-tier system, divided between major or metropolitan authorities, and second-tier metropolitan districts. There should be twenty metropolitan districts: seven for Birmingham, four for Liverpool, and nine for Manchester.

(d) The sixty-one new areas (see (a) above), together with Greater London, should be formed into eight provinces, each with a provincial council. These provincial councils would be in part elected by the unitary and metropolitan authorities (and in the S.E. province by the Greater London Council) and in part co-opted. The functions of provincial councils would be concerned with provincial strategy, economic planning, and economic and social development in co-operation with the central Government. They would replace the existing regional economic planning councils.

(*e*) Within the unitary areas, local councils should be elected to represent the areas of the existing county and non-county borough, urban district and parish councils (in metropolitan districts local councils would be elected where the inhabitants wanted them). Their duty would be to represent local opinion; they would have the right to be consulted on matters of special and local interest; and they would have powers to do a number of things best done locally. Subject to agreement of the major authorities, it should be possible for local councils to play some part in major services.

(2) Ideas Underlying Recommendations

(*a*) *Defects of Existing Structure*

The Commission suggested there were four basic faults in the existing structure (i.e. before 1971):

   (i) The failure of the existing areas to meet the present needs of the country.

   (ii) The impracticability of separating town and country when planning development and transportation.

   (iii) The present fragmentation of the administration of services.

   (iv) The small size of many authorities, which prevents them employing the more highly qualified manpower and technical equipment which a modern world calls for.

Because of these faults the Commission were of the opinion that few people bother to vote at local elections (thirty to forty per cent on average).

(*b*) *The Purpose of Local Government*

The Commission stated that the purpose of local government is fourfold:

   (i) To perform efficiently a wide range of profoundly important tasks concerned with the safety, health and well-being of people in different localities.

   (ii) To attract and hold the interest of its citizens.

   (iii) To deal with national government in a valid partnership.

   (iv) To adapt itself continuously to changes in the way people live, work, move, shop and enjoy themselves.

(*c*) *How New Areas Were Determined*

The Commission tried to achieve a balance between a number of considerations in recommending their areas. It followed a number of general principles:

   (i) The areas should be so formed that within them there is a community of interest.

   (ii) There must be interdependence between town and country.

   (iii) All environmental services must be the responsibility of one authority. The same applies to personal services (as recommended by the Seebohm Committee). Wherever possible, these authorities should be the same.

   (iv) To have the resources and manpower needed to meet the requirements of modern living, authorities must be bigger. To operate satisfactory personal services a local authority would require a population of between 250,000 and 1,000,000.

(v) Where it is impracticable for environmental and personal services to be in the hands of one authority, there must be a clear division of responsibility and related matters must be dealt with by the same authority.

(d) *Advantages of Proposed System*

The Commission believed their proposed new system of local government would provide four main advantages:

(i) Better services would be available.
(ii) Better use of resources.
(iii) New authorities would be more adaptable to the changing needs of society.
(iv) With a shift of power from central Government to the new local authorities there would be a strengthening of democracy.

(e) *Local Democracy*

On this question the Commission said:

If we are not willing to face the pains involved the prospect for local government is bleak. Local governors under the present system, we are convinced, cannot grapple effectively with their problems; this indeed was generally admitted to us. Already the odds against success are heavy, but present problems are not going to stand still. Their weight gathers momentum every year. During the next decade, unless the system is reformed, local government will be increasingly discredited and will gradually be replaced by agencies of central Government.

Reorganization of the system will make heavy demands on present local governors, both council members and their officers. Many of them, while accepting that some reorganization is needed, will disagree with our particular proposals. Most of them will regret disturbance of their own local authority. But if they believe that local government should have a long and fruitful future, can they resist the logic of the need for drastic and immediate change? Will not such change give them a better chance of serving effectively as local governors in years to come? There is room, of course, for endless argument about **what** change; no one knows that better than we do. But we believe that our analysis points conclusively to the new system we propose.

Throughout the course of our enquiry we have become steadily more convinced that a powerful system of local government can in some crucial ways enhance the quality of English national life. The whole Commission is unanimous in its conviction that, if the present local government system is drastically reformed, its scope extended to include functions now in the hands of nominated bodies, and the grip of central Government relaxed, England can become a more efficient, democratic and humane society.

The Commission then made recommendations on (*a*) the functions of major authorities (metropolitan authorities and metropolitan district councils); (*b*) the administration of the major authorities, and their relationship to local councils and provincial councils, whose powers were also described; (*c*) finance; (*d*) electoral system; (*e*) the mechanics of reorganization.

One member of the Commission, Mr. Derek Senior, disagreed with the recommendations in certain major respects, and his report with his counter-proposals appeared at the end of the main report. Its details cannot be examined here.

The foregoing comments apply only to England. But Wales and Northern Ireland are similar to England in respect of local government. It follows that each of these countries must also follow suit if the Government of the day is insistent (as it is) that there shall be a reform of the whole of local government now. Scotland has certain radical differences which will be respected and accommodated into the new structure proposed.

The Government White Paper: Government Proposals for Reorganization. (Cmnd. 4584), 1971

The structure of local government in England is that which was bequeathed to us by the legislation of 1888 and 1894. Then there were no motor-cars on our roads; no electricity in our homes; and the population of England was less than 28 millions. Reorganization of local government has been under discussion for the past twenty-five years. Reorganization is now urgent.

We have already referred to the reform of London Government and to the Royal Commission under Lord Redcliffe-Maud. The Government (and the other two major parties) pledged themselves to reform. The Conservative Party pledged themselves to introduce a system of two-tier government rationalizing the operation of the various functions. Local government provides vital services on which the quality of social and economic life depends. It is an essential part of the whole democratic framework of Government. Naturally the findings of the Redcliffe-Maud Commission's Report were carefully considered together with Mr. Senior's dissenting memorandum.

The pace of change and the scale of technological control over that change is such that men and women in local government can influence the environment in which they and their children will live in a way that has never been open to previous generations. The Conservative Government were determined to return power to those people who should exercise decisions locally, and to ensure that local government is given every opportunity to take that initiative and responsibility effectively, speedily and with vigour.

The Government recognized that the areas of many of the existing authorities were outdated. The division between counties and county boroughs had prolonged an artificial separation of big towns from surrounding hinterlands for functions whose planning and administration need to embrace both town and country. It recognized:

   (i) There were too many authorities.
  (ii) Many were too small in area and too small in resources to support the operation of services to the standards which people expect today.
 (iii) The division of responsibilities between authorities is, in some fields, confusing and illogical.

The Government recognized that 'local democracy' meant that authorities must be given real functions—with powers of decision and the ability to take action without being subjected to excessive regulation by central Government through financial and other controls.

Local authority areas should be related to areas within which people had a common interest—through living in a recognizable community, through the links of employment, shopping or social activities, or through history and tradition.

The Government recognized there were advantages in simplicity and intelligibility in making the structure of local government uniform throughout the country. No one structure can be suitable equally for the densely and sparsely populated areas.

Concentrating authority for all services in the hands of one authority in each area has similar advantages and makes for coherence of administration. But it carries the grave penalty that if such areas are to be large enough for some services they will be too large for others. The theoretical advantages of radical restructuring must be weighed against the advantages of building on the existing well-established organizations and minimizing the disorganization of services during the period of transition.

Constitution of Local Authorities

All local authorities are, or act on behalf of, corporate bodies; that is, they are corporations or legal persons in their own right. They may, for example, own property, enter into contracts and sue or be sued in their legal corporate name. Another distinctive feature of the corporation is that it continues to exist independently of the persons who for the time being compose it. A corporation never dies, it has been said; it must be killed—usually by the revocation of the charter which created it or by Act of Parliament.

For every county and for every district there shall be a council consisting of the chairman and councillors; and the council shall have all such functions as are vested in them by the *Local Government Act, 1972* (s. 21). Each council is a body corporate by the name 'The County Council' or 'The District Council' with the addition of the name of the particular county or district, e.g. The Avon County Council, The Taunton Deane District Council.

The first duty of the council on election is the election of a Chairman and a Vice-Chairman. Each may be paid sums of money enabling him to meet the expenses of his office. The amount is such allowance as the council thinks reasonable. In the event of an equality of votes in a council meeting the chairman shall give a casting vote in addition to any other vote he may have.

Who are the Councillors?

Most readers do not know the names of the local councillors representing them, such is the lack of interest in local government. In 1965 a Government Social Survey for the Maud Committee showed that the average age of the 40,000 councillors then in office was 55. The average of women councillors and that of the county and rural district councillors was higher than the average age of all councillors. Only 5 per cent of male councillors were below 35 and only 12 per cent of councillors were female. Twenty per cent of councillors were retired. The occupations of councillors varied, but employers, managers, professional workers, and farmers predominated. Councillors were immobile, nearly two-thirds having lived in the area they represented for 25 years. Generally councillors were better educated than the average of the total population, and the youngest councillors had obtained most academic qualifications. Most councillors were active in community affairs and were members of political parties and other representative local bodies.

New counties for England and Wales
(as from 1st April 1974)

County ————————
Metropolitan County ▨
Region ——————————
Island authority —·—·—·—

Local authority areas in Great Britain (*Crown Copyright*)

Whether the new arrangements ensuing from the *Local Government Act, 1972,* which took effect on 1 April 1974, will result in a different constitution remains to be proved. The retirement of aldermen from the council chambers will reduce the average age, but whether the other changes will induce those best able to serve the community to make local government efficient and convenient also remains to be seen.

Allowances for Members

The new Act contains a code permitting county councillors and district councillors to claim a flat rate attendance allowance as of right in the performance of council business, without proof of loss of earnings. The allowance is taxable. Travelling and subsistence allowances on a reimbursement (non-taxable) basis are available. The amounts of the allowances are decided by each local authority within maxima to be prescribed by the Secretary of State.

Aldermen. All members of county councils and district councils are now directly elected. Aldermen who were formerly elected by the councillors from among their number occupied a special historic position in the council; but although many aldermen had served their communities well, they were not directly elected by the people themselves and to that extent their position was undemocratic in the opinion of many. The aldermen, who were usually over 65, hung on to office, reluctant to resign despite advancing years and declining powers, and were often elected in a 'party context'.

The *Local Government Act, 1972,* states that all county councils and all district councils are entitled to elect, as an honorary alderman, anyone who has given eminent service as a member of the authority or as a member of an existing authority superseded on reorganization. The honour of 'honorary alderman' does not give the recipient any local government responsibilities or powers.

Aldermen will continue to serve on the GLC until 1976 and on the London borough councils until 1977.

Structure of the Local Authorities in England and Wales from 1974

1. Principal Councils

(*a*) From 1 April 1974, England (outside Greater London, see p. 292) is divided into local government areas to be known as **counties**. Within these counties there are local government areas known as districts.

The new counties are largely based on the areas of the 1972 counties, but they absorb the areas of the former county boroughs. The new counties bind together all of the urban and rural districts within their boundaries and, where possible, the former county boundaries have been retained to preserve existing loyalties and to lessen the administrative probems of transition. Some of the former names have disappeared from the list, e.g. Westmorland, and some new ones have been added, e.g. Avon, Cleveland, Cumbria.

Although there are two tiers—counties and districts—the Act does not intend that one shall be answerable to the other. Each is independent with its own statutory functions.

(*b*) There are now 39 county councils in England (plus 8 county councils in Wales) and 296 district councils (together with 37 in Wales).

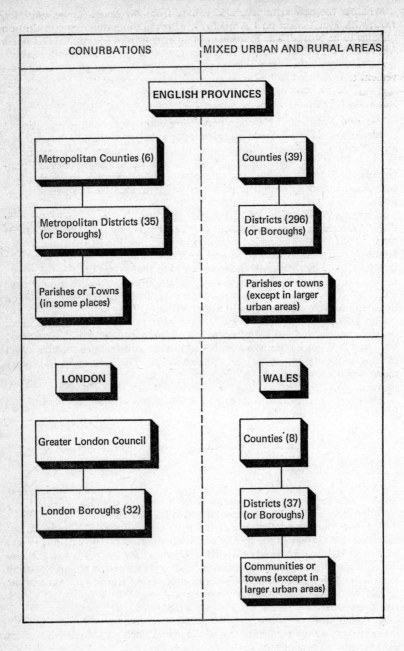

Structure of new local authorities: 1974

In addition there are 6 **metropolitan counties.** Within these metropolitan counties, listed below, are 36 **metropolitan districts.**

Metropolitan Counties

Greater Manchester	(10)	Tyne and Wear	(5)
Merseyside	(5)	West Midlands	(7)
South Yorkshire	(4)	West Yorkshire	(5)

The figures in brackets indicate the number of Metropolitan Districts within each metropolitan county.

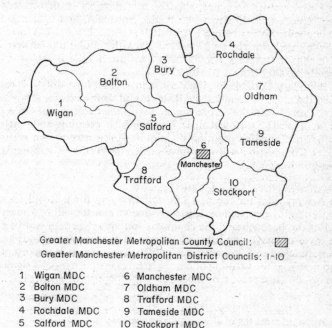

Greater Manchester Metropolitan County Council: ▨

Greater Manchester Metropolitan District Councils: 1-10

1 Wigan MDC	6 Manchester MDC
2 Bolton MDC	7 Oldham MDC
3 Bury MDC	8 Trafford MDC
4 Rochdale MDC	9 Tameside MDC
5 Salford MDC	10 Stockport MDC

Structure of a metropolitan county council showing metropolitan district councils

2. *Parishes*

Rural parishes existing immediately before 1 April 1974 will continue to exist and will continue to be known as parishes. Provision is made under the Act (s. 47) for the creation of new parishes in urban areas and the abolition of former parishes. The parishes may have either parish councils or parish meetings, and may deal with local matters, maintenance of burial grounds, footpaths, and discussion of matters as they affect the parish.

3. *Local Government Boundary Commission for England*

A Boundary Commission is established under the Act (s. 46). It began its work in 1971, under the chairmanship of Sir Edmund Compton. The Department of Environment invited local authorities to make representations or proposals on the future pattern of districts. Guidelines for the Boundary

Commission were laid down stating that district populations should preferably be in the range 75,000–100,000. However, it was accepted that in sparsely populated areas populations might fall to 40,000 or fewer. The Commission was advised that where possible the identity of large towns should be retained.

The question of boundaries almost always gives rise to controversy. The Commissioners had, therefore, to hear the evidence, assess its worth, and try to persuade local authorities to reach local agreement. If that failed the Commission would offer its advice to the Secretary of State for decision.

The Commissioners' recommendations on the new boundaries were accepted by the Government. As noted, the 296 new districts in non-metropolitan counties replace the 953 county boroughs, boroughs, and urban and rural district councils existing before 1 April 1974. Of the 296 districts there are 14 which have populations below 40,000 and 104 with populations between 75,000 and 100,000. The average population of a district now is 90,000 as compared with 28,000 before 1 April 1974.

The Boundary Commission is a permanent body whose duty it is regularly to review the areas of counties and districts and their electoral arrangements. It is empowered to make recommendations to the Secretary of State for the alteration of local government areas, for abolishing, creating, and amalgamating authorities and for granting or withdrawing metropolitan status. The Boundary Commission will also have power to consider the boundaries in Greater London (s. 48).

4. *Borough Status and Civic Dignities*

The Act provides for the new Districts to apply for a Royal Charter of incorporation. The council of districts granted a charter will be known as the council of the borough and the chairman and vice-chairman will be entitled to the style of mayor and deputy mayor of the borough. Thus the civic dignities attached to borough status will be preserved. It is important, however, to note that the granting of borough status is of ceremonial significance; it does not create a second or more privileged council at district level.

5. *The Advantages of New Structure*

The main advantages of the new structure are:

(i) The reduction in the number of English local authorities from over 1200 to 411 (including Greater London and the six new metropolitan counties).

(ii) Local government areas will be larger in size, resources and population. The average population of the new districts will be 90,000 compared with 28,000 before 1 April 1974.

(iii) The vast conurbations (six at present outside London) have special problems. The metropolitan counties with the 36 metropolitan districts have been created to meet those problems and needs.

(iv) The interdependence of town and country is acknowledged and the disadvantages of the former dual (urban and rural) system eradicated.

(v) The areas have been rationalized in the light of the realities of modern living, e.g. roads, cars, mobility.

Parishes

The *Local Government Act, 1972*, lays down that a district council *must* establish a separate parish council if either:

(*a*) the parish has 200 or more local government electors; or
(*b*) there are 150 or more but less than 200 electors and the parish meeting so resolve.

If there are less than 150 electors, the district council *may* establish a parish council following a resolution of the parish meeting.

The minimum number of parish councillors (to constitute a parish council) is five and there is no upper limit. The number is fixed 'from time to time' by the district council within which the parish lies.

A parish council or a parish meeting may make a request for boundary review direct to the Boundary Commission (see p. 293) and it may also ask for the electoral arrangements to be reviewed.

Parish councils must hold at least four meetings a year, one being the Annual Meeting. The council may authorize committees or officers to discharge their functions and may appoint committees jointly with other local authorities. Members of the public and Press are entitled to be present at both council and committee meetings, but may be excluded by resolution if their presence would prejudice the public interest. The council may no longer exclude the public by simply going 'into committee'.

General responsibilities include maintenance of burial grounds, footpaths, bridle-paths, and similar matters of local importance.

Wales and the Local Government Act, 1972

As we have noted from the diagram on p. 292 there are now 8 counties and 37 districts, replacing the former 181 local authorities.

The division of functions between Welsh county and district authorities is broadly the same as that which operates outside the metropolitan counties in England. The main exceptions are that: (1) Welsh district councils are responsible for refuse disposal as well as refuse collection; (2) district councils may be designated to exercise library, weights and measures, trade descriptions, and food and drugs functions; (3) county councils will have no reserve powers over housing; (4) with county approval, Welsh districts have powers to provide car parks (English districts do not have such powers).

Communities. At a more local level than the districts, 'communities' are created throughout Wales, many of which have councils with powers broadly equivalent to those of former parish councils. Community councils also have concurrent powers with the districts relating to allotments, cemeteries and crematoria, public baths, swimming baths and washhouses. They also have powers relating to museums and art galleries, parks and playing fields.

The main differences between England and Wales are in the allocation of functions and in the introduction of communities in Wales, instead of parishes.

Northern Ireland

In Northern Ireland the former 66 local authorities are now replaced by a new single-tier structure of 26 district authorities. At the same time, responsibility for administering many of the more important services formerly provided by local authorities is transferred to ministries of the Northern Ireland Government at Stormont; their administration will be carried out either through local offices of the Ministries concerned, or through area boards responsible to them.

Responsibility for the municipal functions at present exercised by two of the development commissions will also be transferred to the new district authorities or, where appropriate, to the Northern Ireland Ministries.

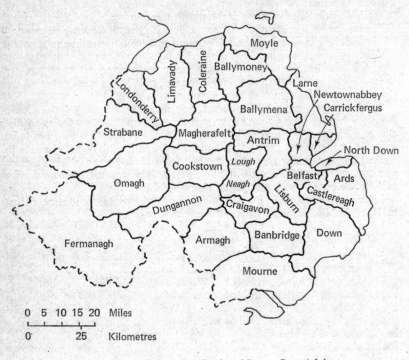

Northern Ireland: new districts (*Crown Copyright*)

Local Government Electoral System

By the *Representation of the People Acts, 1949 and 1969*, any person is entitled to vote at a local government election provided that he or she is over 18 years of age, is a British subject or a citizen of the Irish Republic and is registered as a local government elector for the area for which the election is being held.

An officer of the district council (usually the Chief Executive Officer) is responsible for registration of electors and the conduct of both parliamentary and district council elections.

Electors

A person qualifies for registration as a local government elector if, on the qualifying date for the register, which is compiled annually, he or she is resident in the council area.

Voting takes place at polling stations arranged by the returning officer concerned and under the supervision of a presiding officer appointed for the purpose. The procedure for local government voting in the UK is similar to that of Parliamentary elections. Postal voting, however, is more restricted. Each elector has one vote for each seat contested in the electoral area. He need not record all his votes, but must not give more than one vote for each candidate.

Candidates

A candidate for election as councillor normally stands as a representative of one of the national political parties, as a member of an association representing some local interest, or as an independent. He must be of British nationality and aged 21 years or over. He must also be registered as a local government elector in the register of electors for the area of the local authority to which he seeks election, or have resided within that area (or within three miles of it) during the whole of the twelve months preceding the day on which he is nominated as a candidate.

Local authority areas are divided into electoral areas. Counties are divided into electoral divisions in accordance with orders made by the Home Secretary, the Minister for the Environment and the Secretary of State for Scotland. District councils are divided into wards. For district council elections or parish council elections, each ward or parish (sometimes a combination of parishes) forms an electoral area, which returns one or more members.

Under the 1972 Act, county councillors are elected on the basis of single-member electoral divisions. They will retire together every fourth year. District councillors are elected on the basis of wards, each returning three, or a multiple of three, members. One third of the councillors will retire at a time and there will be district elections in three years out of four—in those years when there are no county elections. From 1975 onwards all local government elections will be held on the same day. This is a notable improvement since all electors should be aware of the date, and it is hoped that this simplification will encourage a higher poll. Only about forty per cent of voters normally make use of their democratic right.

Parish councillors will all retire together every fourth year. Parish elections will be held on the same date as the district elections.

For the purposes of elections to the Greater London Council, each London borough forms an electoral area returning, two, three, or four councillors, depending on the size of the area.

Disqualifications. The *Local Government Act, 1972*, lays down certain disqualifications for election as councillor. These include:

(i) A candidate must not be a paid employee of the council.

(ii) He must not be a bankrupt.

(iii) He must not have been found guilty of corrupt or illegal practices at a previous election: e.g. bribery (gifts, loans or promises of money to a voter to influence his vote); treating (e.g. to food and drink); undue influence; impersonation of another voter; making a false declaration of election expenditure.

(iv) A candidate must not have been convicted of an offence punishable with three months' imprisonment or more without the option of a fine, during the last five years before the election.

(v) A candidate must not have been surcharged by a District Auditor for more than £500 during the five years before the election.

Where a serving councillor incurs any of these disqualifications he can no longer serve on the council. The vacancy is then filled by holding a by-election.

Functions of New Authorities

Allocation of Main Functions between County and District Councils

County councils	Metropolitan county councils
Education	As for county councils, *plus* passenger transport
Personal Social Services	Not responsible for education, libraries or Social Services (see below)
Libraries	
Planning:	
Structure plans	
Development control (strategic and reserve decisions)	
Acquisition and disposal of land for planning purposes, development and redevelopment	
Highway authorities, Traffic and Transport co-ordination	
Housing (certain reserve powers, e.g. for overspill)	
Consumer protection:	
Weights and measures	
Food and drugs	
Refuse disposal	
Museums and art galleries[1]	
Parks and open spaces[1]	
Playing fields and swimming baths[1]	
Police[2]	
Fire[2]	

District councils	Metropolitan district councils
Passenger Transport	As for district councils, *plus* Education, libraries, and Personal Social Services (see above)
Planning (local plans and control)	
Road maintenance (urban unclassified)	
Housing (including clearance and improvement)	
Building regulations	
Environmental health (clean air, food, safety, nuisance, slaughterhouses, shops and offices legislation, port health, refuse collection and sewers)	
Museums and galleries[1]	
Parks and open spaces[1]	
Playing fields and swimming baths[1]	
Cemeteries and crematoria	

Note on the Allocation of Functions

The new district councils describe areas within counties outside the conurbations. Their powers are different from the metropolitan district councils (like

[1] Concurrent powers exercisable by county councils and district councils.
[2] Some counties are amalgamated for police purposes (e.g. Somerset and Avon) and some for fire services.

Birmingham) also introduced by the Act. In the conurbations, the metropolitan districts have more functions; outside the conurbations the counties have more functions.

There is within the new framework a greater flexibility for the authorities, e.g. for sharing operations differently, by mutual 'agency' agreements. The Act does not apply to London or Scotland.

Education. Includes the provision of nursery, primary and secondary education; further education (including technical and art colleges); adult education; school meals; pupils' transport; award of student grants; education of handicapped children.

Education is the responsibility of county councils and metropolitan district councils. Joint committees covering facilities like polytechnics which serve adjoining local authority areas are allowed (e.g. under the *Education Act, 1944*).

Town and Country Planning. Preparation of development plans, indicating land use (for housing, industry, recreation, open spaces, agriculture, roads); control of development; applications for planning permission; tree preservation; control of outdoor advertising.

Major planning (structure plans) are undertaken by counties and metropolitan counties; local planning (including planning applications) by districts and metropolitan districts.

Housing. Includes provision and management of local authority housing, housing improvement grants and schemes for 'general improvement areas' (that is, improvement of environment as well as houses); housing for the homeless; slum clearance.

Districts and metropolitan districts will run local authority housing and take over responsibility for housing homeless people. Special housing for staff remains with the employing authority. Counties and metropolitan counties provide rent officer service and rent assessment.

Personal Social Services. Includes domiciliary services; services for mentally ill and handicapped; services for physically handicapped (including social work support, domiciliary services, employment assistance, and transport); residential homes (for children in care, at special schools and community homes); residential accommodation for the elderly; provision of housing for the homeless. Here counties and metropolitan districts take on responsibility.

Where delegation to subcommittees applies, powers may be varied (e.g. decisions on the siting of buildings may be made at subcommittee meetings). Management of gipsy caravan sites is a district and metropolitan district council responsibility, but county or metropolitan county councils can act as agents. District councils and counties consult about housing for the infirm and disabled and provision for homeless falls to district councils.

Environmental Health. Includes food safety and hygiene; communicable diseases; refuse collection and disposal; clean air; home safety; conditions in offices, shops, and factories; diseases of animals; slaughterhouses; public lavatories. These are retained by districts and metropolitan districts. Animal diseases are the responsibility of counties and metropolitan counties. Refuse functions, formerly within the districts, are now divided: districts and metropolitan districts being responsible for collection of refuse, and counties and metropolitan counties for its disposal. Any local authority may sort and bale waste paper collected separately from other refuse. Subject to consent of the appropriate highway authority, all local authorities may provide public lavatories.

Traffic, Transport, Highways. Includes new roads and improvements to existing ones; traffic regulations (e.g. waiting restrictions and pedestrian crossings); rights of way; highway maintenance; road safety; parking; street lighting.

The highway authority is the county or metropolitan county council. Districts and metropolitan districts may opt for agency functions on certain urban roads (carrying out certain responsibilities as agents of the county) or partnership arrangement (acting within an area on decisions jointly taken). All districts' basic powers are limited: maintenance of footpaths; bridleways and urban roads other than trunk or classified roads. Disposal and removal of abandoned vehicles is the responsibility in England of county and district councils, and in Wales that of district councils.

Consumer Protection. Includes weights and measures responsibilities, such as checking goods sold in shops; testing weighbridges and petrol pumps; test weighing bagged fuel such as coal; trade descriptions in respect of goods and services; provision of advice to shoppers; sampling for analysis of foods, drinks, and drugs.

County and metropolitan county authorities are responsible in England; district councils (where orders are made by the Secretary of State) or counties in Wales. Consumer advice services may be set up by the appropriate authority. Arrangements for food and drugs services are rationalized with counties and metropolitan counties responsible for questions of quality; districts and metropolitan districts for matters relating to hygiene, food, conditions in shops, etc.

Police and Fire. Includes local police and fire brigade functions. Counties and metropolitan counties are responsible, with an increasing tendency towards combinations with neighbours in joint forces (e.g. Thames Valley Police Force), responsible to joint committees comprising local authority representatives (two thirds) and magistrates (one third), to use manpower and technical resources more effectively.

Libraries. County councils and metropolitan districts will run libraries. Some district councils in Wales may be designated to do so.

Museums and Art Galleries. County and/or district councils are able to provide these facilities.

Youth Employment. Service taken over by local education authorities (counties and metropolitan districts).

Swimming Baths, Parks, Open Spaces and Recreational Training. Can be provided by county and district authorities as the need arises. Basically these services are the responsibility of districts and metropolitan districts.

Coast Protection. Responsibility of district councils.

Cemeteries and Crematoria. Responsibility of district councils.

Emergencies. County councils and district councils have a new general power enabling them to take immediate action to avert or cope with an emergency or disaster in their area, e.g. an aircraft crash on a town, a railway disaster, a reservoir bursting banks, severe flooding involving loss of life and homes. The Police Service is the co-ordinating service in these cases where immediate action of rescue and preservation of life and property is concerned.

The explosion at a chemical plant making caprolactam (an ingredient of nylon) at Flixborough, near Scunthorpe, on 1 June 1974, in which 29 lives were lost, emphasizes the need for a general power to meet emergencies of this kind.

Loss of Functions

Health Services. From 1 April 1974, the local health services formerly provided by local government—for example, the general supportive services such as home nursing, home helps, health visiting, and the ambulance service —will be transferred to the new Area Health Authorities (90) in the United Kingdom. These authorities will not therefore be part of local government.

The advantage of bringing together the whole of the fragmented field of health care under the responsibility of one authority is obvious to all. The area health authority is now able to define priorities and organize its responsibilities in the way best suited to its particular area.

There is a close link between the social services of local government and the health services, and it is fortunate that the boundaries of the new health authorities (outside the GLC) now coincide with the local authority areas.

Water Services. The Government has replaced former joint water boards and sewerage boards by 10 regional water authorities. These authorities are now responsible for water conservation, water quality control, navigation and recreation functions of the former river authorities. The regional authorities are also responsible for the water supply and sewage disposal functions of local authorities in England and Wales (*Water Act, 1973*).

Internal Organization of Local Authorities

Local authorities are free to a large extent to make their own internal arrangements and to choose the means and methods by which they perform their duties and responsibilities.

Committee System

All councils (except perhaps some parish councils) use the committee system. The range of services administered by a local authority is too wide for a full council to deal with the entire work. The council resorts to committees to carry out or administer the various services, e.g. highways, planning, environmental health, estates, markets, and so on. Most councils now establish a Policy and Resources Committee (or its equivalent) which operates as a management committee (see p. 320).

Most councils have adopted the concept of a number of committees responsible for groups of functions of the council or 'programme areas' as they are called in the Bains' Report on Management (see p. 318). Some committees may be purely advisory committees or co-ordinating committees.

We shall deal later with the various kinds of committees. In general there has been a substantial reduction in their number as a result of the reorganization in April 1974.

Whatever re-structuring may take place, the fact remains that committees tend to be overburdened and any committee of the council may itself form sub-committees for particular purposes. The subcommittee stands to the parent committee in a relationship similar to that of the main committee to the full council.

Powers and Duties of Committees

The powers and duties of local authority committees are usually laid down in Statutes (e.g. Education Committee under the *Education Act, 1944*) or more usually in the appointing council's standing orders. A council is free to delegate all its powers to committees, subcommittees or officers (s. 101, *Local Government Act, 1972*). Certain powers in connection with (i) raising loans, (ii) levying rates, or (iii) making financial demands on other authorities (known as raising precepts in England and Wales) are excepted; these powers are reserved to the council as a whole.

Kinds of Committees

These are various kinds of committees detailed below.

Standing Committee. This type of committee is appointed each year for a particular service. Thus a district council may choose the title of Housing Committee or Development Committee, Policy and Resources Committee, etc. Such committees are permanent (hence standing) committees. However, this is entirely within the discretion of the authority.

Special Committee. This committee is appointed *ad hoc*, i.e. to perform a special task, such as to make arrangements for a Royal visit or centenary celebrations of a borough. Once the task allocated to the committee is accomplished the committee dissolves.

Statutory Committee. Certain Statutes make the appointment of some committees obligatory. These are:

  (i) The *Education Act, 1944*, requires every county council to appoint an Education Committee.
 (ii) The *Local Authorities Social Services Act, 1970*, requires every County Council to appoint a Social Services Committee.
(iii) The *Police Act, 1964*, requires the appointment of a Police Committee. This applies to county councils who may be amalgamated for police purposes (e.g. Thames Valley Police Force).

Under the *Local Government Act, 1972*, local authorities may appoint such committees as they think fit.

Optional Committees. It follows from the above that much depends on the type of local authority, the area it services and the needs of the people. Although the intention is that the structure of committees will be on Programme Areas, there is bound to be devolution of power and function to subcommittees which will deal with special matters appertaining to that authority, e.g. Parks Committee, Markets Committee, Entertainments Committee. Such are optional committees set up at the discretion of the council.

Admission of Public and Press to Committee Meetings

Under the *Local Government Act, 1972* (s. 100), the public, including the Press, have a right to attend all committee meetings and to meetings of the local authorities themselves. *The Public Bodies (Admission to Meetings) Act, 1960*, applies and the right to attend is subject to the qualification that the local authority or the committee may exclude the public and the Press on a specific occasion, e.g. for the discussion of confidential matters, staff promotions or defaults, property transactions of a confidential nature.

The Necessity of the Committee

The committee system is one of the chief characteristics of local government. It is difficult to see how a local authority could function without such a system. Parliament itself makes increasing use of the device.

The **advantages** of the committee system are:

Saving time. The setting up of a committee saves the time of the full council and it saves the time of individual councillors.

Specialization. Councillors prefer the work of some committees to others. They become interested in special aspects (e.g. social services, education, amenities, etc.) and then tend to specialize. This imparts a degree of professionalism and skill in administration. A councillor gets to know the duties imposed by the council and by law, the resources of the local authority, the area affected and the people living there.

Atmosphere. Full council meetings tend to be unduly formal and stiff. Committees, which usually sit in an informal atmosphere, encourage a freer exchange of views that makes for more efficient administration.

Smaller Numbers. Committees of twelve or fewer are found, in practice, to be more efficient and deal with more business than large, unwieldy groups.

Contact with Officials. A relaxed atmosphere and informality tend to make for easier relations with officials. Fruitful and beneficial administration is brought about when there is full co-operation between the councillors and the professional local government officer or specialist.

To the above advantages may be added the following which the Maud Committee considered:

(i) They lead to a better chance of the right decision being taken.
(ii) They lead to wider participation in the work of the authority.
(iii) They represent wider interests.
(iv) They are a safeguard against bureaucracy and unresponsive administration.
(v) They keep officers in close touch with political and public opinion.

The **disadvantages** of the committee system are summarised below.

Critics of the system point to the delays in getting people together; to the proliferation of subcommittees; to the encouragement of paper work; 'red tape' and bureaucracy—all of which tend to slow down the machine. They contrasted the business world where quick decisions, some vital, had to be made at once and 'red tape' eliminated. There is also the danger that the chairmanships of committees are awarded for party political reasons rather than on grounds of merit and personal ability and integrity. Co-option can be operated to the disadvantage of the local authority and the public.

Officers and Employees

The *Local Government Act, 1972*, s. 112, states that local authorities are permitted to appoint 'such officers as they think necessary' for the proper discharge of their functions.

Formerly, certain statutes laid down that local authorities had to appoint specified officers (e.g. Medical Officers of Health). Those statutes cease to have effect from 1 April 1974, with the following exceptions, who must be appointed by law:

(i) Chief Education Officers (s. 88, *Education Act, 1944*) and the Chief Education Officer of the Inner London Authority.

(ii) Chief Officers and other members of fire brigades (*Fire Services Act, 1947*).

(iii) Directors of Social Services (s. 6, *Local Authority Social Services Act, 1970*).

(iv) Public Analysts (*Food and Drugs Act, 1955*).

(v) Agricultural Analysts and Deputy Agricultural Analysts (*Agriculture Act, 1970*).

(vi) Inspectors of Weights and Measures (s. 41, *Weights and Measures Act, 1963*).

(vii) District Surveyors and Deputy District Surveyors of the GLC, appointed under the London Building Acts.

In respect of all the above a Minister is concerned with the appointments and dismissals. He is concerned to ensure that in each case a suitably qualified person is appointed, and in the fields of education and the social services the central government oversees the administration of these two services, which occupy a vital part in the lives of all. The central government ensures that counties appoint statutory committees for both education and social services.

The Bains Working Group argued against the compulsion of local authorities to appoint specified officers. It was felt that this militated against the introduction of the most suitable management structures. Local authorities were now encouraged to be independent and as the councils were composed of men and women of responsibility, they should be given the power to hire and fire similar to that of other independent organizations. The Bains Working Group did not see the need to obtain Ministerial approval for the appointment of certain officers, e.g. the Chief Education Officer, Director of Social Services. The local authorities were capable of selecting persons of the right qualifications and calibre and the approval of the Minister was superfluous.

The contrary view, however, is that in some authorities there had been an element of prejudice or nepotism, and it is right that central control or approval of the appointment and dismissal of certain vital officers be retained (see p. 314). In practice, the Minister rarely interferes with the appointment made locally unless there is something obviously amiss.

Employees of the council fall into three main classes: (i) heads of department or chief officers: (ii) professional, clerical or technical; and (iii) manual workers who perform the physical work for which the council is responsible, e.g. roadsweepers, gardeners, park keepers, etc.

The appointments of senior staff are usually made by the committee particularly concerned. Junior appointments may be made by heads of departments either alone or in consultation with a personnel officer. Methods vary between councils, but control is maintained by a local authority committee and all appointments and engagements are made in conformity with the council's agreed establishment.

Rates of pay and conditions of service for local authority staff are within the jurisdiction of the employing council. The pay and conditions are based on recommendations made by Whitley Councils, of which the largest is the National Joint Council for Local Authorities' Administrators, Professional, Technical and Clerical Services and the National Joint Council for Local Authorities' Services (Manual Workers). Conditions of service and salary scales for senior local government officers are determined by separate joint committees for England and Wales, and for Scotland. Northern Ireland has its own joint negotiating machinery at various levels.

All local government officers are expected to maintain a high standard of conduct. As public servants they 'must be honest in fact, but must be beyond the reach of the suspicion of dishonesty'. Like the Civil Service, the local authorities' staffs are not corrupt in the main, despite the instances which were widely broadcast in relation to contracts in the North-East in 1974. There are few criminal charges brought against officials whether of high or low rank, and the public generally has confidence in local administration.

Staff Commission. Under the *Local Government Act, 1972*, a Staff Commission is established to consider and keep under review arrangements both for the transfer of staff and for recruitment of staff for the new authorities.

The Commission also considers staffing problems that arise as a result of reorganization and advises the Secretary of State on steps needed to safeguard the interests of staff affected. The Commission plays no part in regard to matters concerning salaries, gradings, or other conditions of service. It will not be involved with terms of compensation. There are separate Commissions for England and Wales.

As regards staff prejudicially affected by the reorganization on 1 April 1974, provision was made for safeguarding superannuation rights and for payment of compensation to local government employees who suffered by loss of office or reduction in pay. In June, 1975, there was a total of 1,500,000 full-time employees and 915,000 part-time employees in local government in England and Wales.

Delegation to Officers. Under s. 101 of the *Local Government Act, 1972*, local authorities have the right to delegate: 'A local authority may arrange for the discharge of any of their functions (a) by a committee, a sub-committee or an officer of the authority; or (b) by any other authority.'

The local authority itself remains liable for any wrongs committed by the committee, officer or other authority to whom the power to act has been given. This provision merely legalizes what had been the practice in the past. Clearly certain decisions, issue of licences, grant of planning approval for minor development, should be within the province of competent staff who can apply formal procedures. It is for the council itself to determine what matters should be delegated to the staff of all ranks. As the work of local authorities becomes more complex and far-reaching the delegation to officers will inevitably increase, though the responsibility remains with the council.

Personnel Management. Because local authorities are now one of the largest employers in any area it follows that the greatest use should be made of one of their major resources, namely manpower. The Bains Working Group suggested that the 'Establishment' title should give way to the more widely accepted and used 'Personnel Management'.

The working group recommended that the head of personnel should be given the status of a chief officer, and that other chief officers should accept and act on his advice in matters of personnel management, in the same way that they (other chief officers) acted upon the advice of the Treasurer in finance matters. Moreover the Personnel Officer should have direct access to the Chief Executive Officer.

Chief Executive. The Chief Officer of a Ministry of the Central Government is the Permanent Under-Secretary of State. The chief officer of a local authority is now known as the Chief Executive Officer, whether of a county or district council, and he is head of the authority's paid service. The Bains Working Group recommended that he be free of departmental responsibilities, that he lead a team of chief officers and that he secure the overall co-ordination and control at officer level.

Job specification. As chief executive officer he would

1. Have authority over all other officers so far as this is needed for the efficient management and execution of the council's functions. He is, in short, *the chief*.

2. Be *leader* of the officers' *management team*, and through the Policy and Resources Committee, be the *principal adviser* on matters of *general policy*.

3. Be responsible for securing the best advice on the *forward planning of objectives and services*, and to lead the management team in securing a *corporate approach* to the local authority's affairs generally.

4. Secure efficient and effective *implementation* of the council's *programme* and policies and secure that the *resources* of the authority are most *efficiently deployed* to those ends.

5. Keep under *review the organization and administration* of the authority itself; *make recommendations* (through the Policy and Resources Committee) to the Council if major changes are required *for effective management*.

6. Be responsible to ensure *manpower policies* are developed and implemented in all departments of the authority in the interests of (a) the authority, and (b) the staff.

7. Be responsible for good *internal and external relations*.

It follows from the above that any such appointee should possess outstanding managerial ability, skills, and personality.

Chief Officers management team (for average non-metropolitan district)

Members of Staff

The relationship between members of a council and the staff is crucial to the working of the new authorities. The Bains Working Group stated that 'neither members nor officers can regard any area of the authority's work and administration as exclusively theirs'. The Group confirmed the view of the Maud Committee on Management, which exploded as a myth the belief that policy was a matter solely for elected representatives and administration a matter for officers. The Bains group pleaded for a corporate approach. It added that a 'them and us' attitude between members and officers fostered distrust and dissipated effectiveness.

The question of who runs whom, and the role of the elected member *vis-à-vis* the officers and staff is a perennial one. Mr. R. G. E. Peggie, in a paper to the Local Authorities Management Services' Advisory Committee (LAMSAC) in 1971, stated that the elected member '. . . should be concerned to ensure that the machine works, but he should not be required to operate it himself.'

The rôle of the elected member can be described as:

(i) *deliberative*. As a member of the council he should have the opportunity to discuss and decide policy and priorities.

(ii) *control*. As part of the council he should have effective control of the organization carrying out the work of that body.

(iii) *representative*. As an elected member for an area he is concerned with the affairs of the people he represents.

Clearly the object of becoming a councillor is to achieve power, to exercise it in the interest of the community and to get things done. A councillor may be a director or manager of a company; he may run his own business skilfully and well; he may be more efficient than any local government officer could hope to be. Such a person will not readily subserve an official of a local authority by whatever name called. He may argue that either the council member is in charge (and responsible to his electors) or the official is. The same problem applies to an M.P. translated to a Ministry. Who runs whom?

There is no perfect system of management, and the problem of reconciling efficiency with democracy is a baffling one. The question resolves itself into a sensible compromise between members on the one hand and the officers on the other to achieve the best results for the locality and its citizenry, whose welfare and interests both should seek to promote.

Local Government Finance

The sources of local authority income are: **government grants** (about two-fifths); **local rates** (about two-fifths); and **rents** from municipal houses, **dividends** and **interest** (about one-fifth).

Government Grants

The first grants were made to local authorities in 1835 by the central Government on a percentage basis, whereby the local authority paid one-half of the service and the central Government paid one-half. Under the *Local Government Act, 1929*, grants were made on a block basis. In order to assess the amount to be allocated to a local authority, the Government took into account (i) the size of the population of a district, weighted by the number of children under 5; (ii) a low rateable value; (iii) abnormal unemployment; and (iv) sparsity of population. *The Local Government Act, 1948*, brought back the percentage grant, and the *Local Government Act, 1958*, restored the block grant system except in regard to certain special services, e.g. the police service where the percentage grant was retained.

The case for the block grant is that it gives a council a greater scope to make the best use of its money. The council which wishes to devote more to housing than to roads or health measures may do so. The advocates of the percentage grant argue that this system ensures that a hesitant unimaginative and frugal council cannot cut a service too low and that this ensures the maintenance of all services at a high level of efficiency and quality. Both methods have merit, but the subject is very much a matter of party politics.

Today capital investment is, for the most part, financed by borrowing. On occasion, however, Government grants take the form of capital grants, paid on approval of claims to the Government and made by the local authorities for specific services, e.g. roads and public lighting, and annual subsidies payable for local authority housing (council houses and flats, etc.).

Most Government grants are, however, revenue grants, which are related to local authority revenue expenditure, other than towards deficits on housing and trading accounts. These particular Government grants are payable, both in aid of revenues generally (hence they are called **rate support** grants) and for specific services. In 1973/74 the rate support grants to local authorities in England and Wales amounted to £2904 million, and the grant for specific services was approximately £255 million; the figures for Scotland amounted to £362 million and £33 million respectively.

The rate support grants are distributed among the various local authorities. The amount allocated to each authority is based on three points: (i) the needs element, which takes account of the total population and, in particular, the number of children of school age, together with supplementary payments which take account of the numbers of children under 5 and of adults over 65 years of age, the cost of various stages of education, the density of population and road mileage; (ii) the **resources** element, which is paid to authorities whose rateable resources are below the average for all authorities in relation to population; and (iii) the **domestic** element which compensates rating authorities for loss of rate income from reductions in rate poundage, which they are required to give to householders: in England and Wales £0·06 in 1973/74 and in Scotland £0·15.

Services which qualify for specific grants are the police and comprehensive building schemes.

Grants are also made towards the cost of rate rebates for people with low incomes. The aggregate revenue grants are estimated to shift the balance from rates to taxes on revenue account by about one-half per cent per annum.

Rates

Rates are a local tax paid by the occupiers of land and buildings, as a contribution towards the cost of local services provided by the local authority. The only main class of property which is exempt from rates is agricultural land and agricultural buildings.

How, then, does one calculate the rate of a householder? The amount of each payment is calculated by multiplying the rate poundage (say 60p in the £), determined by the rating authority, which assesses the rateable value of the property. The rateable value is based on or reflects the rental value of the property in the open market. It is assessed in respect of land and buildings by Valuation Officers of the Board of Inland Revenue, who are independent of the local authorities. The last valuation lists were compiled in 1964, when assessments of all classes of property were made and new valuation lists came into force in 1973. Where a tenant wishes to dispute the assessment of his house, building or land, he applies to have his case heard by a local valuation court. The court consists of three members of an independent local valuation panel. If he is not satisfied then a tenant may appeal to the Lands Tribunal.

Rate Rebates. Where householders have small incomes, they may apply to the local authority for rate rebates, and if their application is successful they will pay less than the normal rate, whereas commercial and industrial properties are assessed higher than ordinary householders. Charities pay only half the full rate on their property which is used for charitable purposes, but further reliefs may be allowed by the rating authority. A rating authority also has the power to reduce or remit the rates for a wide range of non-profit-making bodies. Half the rates may be levied on the owners of all empty premises. Where a tenant so wishes, he may pay his rates in ten instalments a year.

A similar system of rate and rate-assessment is carried out in Scotland and in Northern Ireland, though there are differences in the names of assessors and courts.

Levying and Collection of Rates. In England and Wales the responsibility for levying and collecting rates lies with the district councils. In the metropolis the London Borough Councils are responsible and, in the City of London, the Common Council is the responsible authority.

The rate poundage for each county district consists mainly of a district rate and a county rate, calculated in accordance with the requirements of the two authorities (i.e. the county council and the district council). The county rate is passed on to the county council following collection. In districts the rate levied in each parish takes into account precepts issued by the parish council or parish meeting.

In the metropolis the Greater London Council raises revenue by precepting on the London boroughs and the City.

The same broad principles also apply in Scotland and Northern Ireland.

Control by Central Government

Reasons for Control

'The interests of the local areas must be subservient to the interests of the nation as a whole, and so there must be control from the centre to achieve the dominance of this interest' (Jeremy Bentham). Central control by the Government over local authorities may be justified on the following grounds:

(i) *Minimum Standards.* Certain essential services, such as health, education, police, fire service, cannot be allowed to fall below a certain minimum standard in the public interest.

(ii) *Finance.* Local services are costly, and where the central Government provides grants or financial aid it is justified in expecting the local authorities to provide satisfactory services. Moreover, the central Government bears a responsibility to the taxpayer who ultimately 'foots the bill'.

(iii) *Providing Expertise.* The central Government has greater technical resources, more knowledge and data, and a greater number of specialist and technical advisers. Local authorities are encouraged to take advantage of these resources in providing the public services for which they are responsible.

(iv) *Preventing Corruption.* Central control assists in the prevention of corruption, e.g. fraud by councillors or officials, or the misuse of powers which are vested in such officials as chief officers of police. Audit of accounts, Government inquiries and inspection by H.M. Inspectors assist in preventing illegal or corrupt practices by local authorities, their officials, or their members.

Forms of Control

Central control over local authorities assumes three forms: **legislative, administrative,** and **judicial.**

Legislative Control. All local authorities are created by statute. They owe their existence to statute (*Local Government Act, 1972*) and as corporate bodies they may act only under powers given by law, i.e. statute law made by Parliament. So where a local authority provides any of the essential services, such as housing, refuse collection, public health services, police and fire services, it must do so under authority of a statute. It must also ensure that it acts within the powers granted. Otherwise, it infringes the *ultra vires* rule. These statutes providing the services mentioned are known as *Public General Acts* which Parliament passes in the interest of the whole nation. The *Local Government Act, 1972*, is an important one in this regard.

The *Public General Acts* may (i) impose a **duty** on a local authority, or (ii) give it **permissive** power. The essential difference between these is that in (i) a local authority **must comply** with the law imposed by statute, whereas in (ii) a local authority may use its discretion, whether to adopt the power or provide the service which the particular Act permits.

Adoptive Acts is the name given to those statutes which are passed by Parliament but which permit the local authority to adopt at its discretion. In general Adoptive Acts enable progressive authorities which want to provide some extra service for their inhabitants to do so. Essential services, i.e. those which all local authorities must provide, are called **mandatory.**

Certain authorities find that existing legislation is, nevertheless, inadequate for them. Any such authority may seek to promote a Private Local Bill to obtain the necessary legal authority for its particular purpose. Private Bill procedure follows a special course in the legislative process and has been described on page 91. The procedure to promote a Private Bill is laid down in the *Local Government Act, 1972*. Certain preliminary steps must be taken: (i) a resolution must be passed by the whole council; (ii) the approval of the Minister for the Environment must be obtained; (iii) the Bill must be deposited at the House of Commons; (iv) in the case of a district council a public meeting of all the electors must be held to consider the promotion of the Bill. If the electors vote against the Bill it must be withdrawn. If the Bill proceeds to the Commons the procedure follows that described on page 91.

An alternative means of acquiring legislative powers for a proposal by a local authority is to apply for a **Provisional Order**. This is a simpler and less expensive method and involves an application to the Minister for an Order. The Minister holds an inquiry and, if satisfied that it is in the public interest of the locality, may make an Order, which must be confirmed by Parliament before it takes effect. Usually several Provisional Orders, from various authorities, are presented together to Parliament in a Provisional Orders Confirmation Bill which passes through Parliament in the usual way. As it has the approval of the Minister before inclusion in the Confirmation Bill its passage is normally assured without undue difficulty. A Parliamentary Committee considers the Bill, similar to the committee which adjudicates on a Private Bill.

Statutory Instruments are important means of control. Certain statutes empower a Minister to make regulations (see p. 248). These regulations are made on grounds of urgency and technicality of subject-matter to carry into effect a service, which the central Government places on local authorities. The statutory instruments are enforceable in the courts equally with statutes.

Administrative Control. Granted there is justification for central control over local authorities, the question arises how that control is carried out.

Statutory Control. Certain statutes impose a duty on a Minister. The

Education Act, 1944, imposes a duty on the Minister of Education and Science of promoting:

> the education of the people of England and Wales and the progressive development of institutions devoted to that purpose, and to secure the effective execution by local authorities under his control and direction, of the national policy for providing a varied and comprehensive educational service in every area.

Similar powers and duties are imposed on the Home Secretary under the *Police Act, 1964,* to ensure that the Police Committees, on which local authorities are represented, provide an adequate police force for their areas (see p. 240).

The Minister of the Department responsible for a particular service writes circulars of advice (e.g. explaining legislation), to local authorities indicating how the rules should be interpreted and the spirit in which they should be enforced. These circulars sometimes contain indications of policy. The Minister from time to time requires from local authorities returns, indicating e.g. the number of houses being built, the number of teachers employed in particular types of schools, the cost of school meals, the details of fire brigade equipment owned, the number of police recruits enrolled and the number of resignations, retirements, etc., from various services. These circulars keep the Government Department in touch with the local authorities who, for their part, may request information and advice from the Ministry. The general atmosphere, in which this relationship is carried on, is courteous and polite and a spirit of partnership is engendered.

Financial Control. Loans may be raised by local authorities to finance capital expenditure. They may do this under powers of a general statute or of a Private Act having local application. Expenditure in key sectors such as education, housing and roads, local authorities in England and Wales must obtain approval from the government department concerned before raising loans. For other capital expenditure, each authority receives an annual loan authorization within which it determines what sums to borrow and what projects to undertake. Special provisions apply to the GLC, which applies annually for parliamentary authority to raise the money it needs for capital expenditure. In Scotland and Northern Ireland the government department responsible for the service also issues the appropriate loan approvals.

Local authorities may raise long-term loans by means of private mortgages, and by issuing stock on the Stock Exchange and bonds which may or may not be quoted on the Stock Exchange. The bonds may be for any period, though local authorities normally issue them for one year. Local authorities have a right to apply to the Public Works Loan Board, financed by the Exchequer, or, in Northern Ireland, to the Government Loans Fund, for long-term borrowing to finance a proportion of their reckonable capital payments, and may borrow temporarily for a limited proportion of their current outstanding loan debt.

A finance committee, appointed by a local authority, is charged with the function of keeping the financial policy of the council under constant review. However, following reorganization in April 1974, local authorities in England and Wales will not be required to appoint a finance committee (though some will continue to do so) but the authorities will have to make proper arrangements for the administration of their financial affairs. These accounts are open for public inspection and are subject to that special form of control called audit which we consider next.

Audit. The accounts of all local authorities are made up annually, usually to 31 March. These accounts are subject to audit and checking by district auditors, appointed by the Secretary of State for the Environment.

The district auditors are independent officers in the exercise of their powers and performance of duties conferred on them by statute. One auditor is assigned to each of the fifteen districts into which England and Wales are divided for audit purposes. The work of the auditors is co-ordinated by the Chief Inspector of Audit, who is ultimately responsible to the Secretary of State for the Environment.

Grants from Central Government to local authorities in the financial year 1973/4 amounted to over £5000m. Of the total amount of local government expenditure in that year the Central Government underwrote 60 per cent. With government aid comes government control, and one of these in the form of checking receipts and payments by local authorities is audit. District auditors are required to disallow every item of account which is contrary to the law (except for items sanctioned by the Secretary of State for the Environment), and until the *Local Government Act, 1972*, to surcharge the amount of any expenditure disallowed upon the person or persons responsible for incurring or authorizing it. They could also surcharge upon the person responsible any item which had not been duly brought into account, or any item of loss or deficiency caused by negligence or misconduct.

As from 1 April 1974, the *Local Government Act, 1972*, abolishes the district auditor's powers of disallowance and surcharge. He must now refer any question of the legality of payments to the Court for a ruling.

A citizen may still raise objections regarding the accounts before the district auditor, but instead of the auditor himself having the power of disallowance it will be for the Courts to decide whether or not a particular item of expenditure is legal. Thus a citizen can continue to enjoy the power of questioning the accounts, but he himself will not be burdened with the job of taking the matter to court.

Under the 1972 Act the District Auditor will not have the responsibility of surcharging. That power is reserved for the Court, which may make an order of restitution. The effect of this is the same as surcharge, but no order shall be made where the court is satisfied that the person concerned had acted reasonably or in the belief that the expenditure was authorised by law. The Court must also consider all the circumstances before ordering restitution, including a person's ability to pay. So members of councils and officers who have acted in good faith will not be penalised. Surcharging under the old scheme had, it was felt, an inhibiting effect on local authorities. Where there has been a failure to bring money into account or there has been loss of money, the district auditor will certify the amounts due to be repaid by the defaulting member or officer. Any appeal against the certificate of the auditor (or incidentally, any appeal by any citizen regarding the failure to issue such a certificate) will be for the Courts to decide.

Approved Auditors. So far we have been referring to district auditors. The 1972 Act allows local authorities the alternative of themselves appointing an auditor to carry out the necessary audits. The appointment is subject to the approval of the Secretary of State for the Environment and the term used to describe the person so appointed is 'approved auditor'.

Electors may question the approved auditor about local accounts in the same way that they may question the district auditor, but if an elector wishes to make objections to the accounts he must make application to the Secretary of State, asking that the district auditor hold an extraordinary audit. Generally the approved auditor's powers are not so far-reaching as the district auditor's, but for those local authorities wanting to divest themselves of Central Government control it is an alternative.

Inquiry. Where a local authority proposes to take some action which may infringe the private rights of an individual or a section of the public generally, the Minister may hold a local inquiry to ascertain the facts, so that he may be able to make up his mind as to the most convenient course to take. Under the *Town and Country Planning Act, 1971,* an inquiry may be held where a Private Bill is promoted in Parliament. The Minister may wish to ascertain local feeling, for or against the measure, before coming to a decision. Where there is local disquiet over the efficiency of a particular service, such as the police, the Minister may appoint inspectors from his Department to visit the force and hold an inquiry to ascertain the facts, so that he can be assured that there is no corruption or inefficiency or maladministration. Some statutes provide for these inquiries, but where statutory powers do not exist a Minister may set up an inquiry of his own volition.

Inspection. The two services which have a notably strong inspectorate are (i) education, and (ii) the police. Inspectors of Education are 'the eyes and ears' of the Minister and visit all types of schools and colleges gathering ideas, co-ordinating schemes, advising principals, headmasters, and similar officials, and inspecting buildings and equipment to ensure that good standards are maintained. The Inspectors are, as it were, ambassadors sent out from the Ministry to ensure more efficient administration of the educational service. Formerly, these officials were looked upon with some awe and fear. Nowadays, they are regarded as helpful figures in the main, but they do have powers of control and can report adversely.

The police is a uniformed service, with rigid standards of discipline, and has a hierarchy of ranks. The powers of individual police officers have already been examined (see p. 242). The increasing number of crimes, the spread of vandalism, student riots, and similar social disturbances impose a great strain on the forces of law and order. The Inspectors of the Home Office visit each force at least once a year: again advising, co-ordinating, looking at new local experiments, inspecting the whole of the force of the area and sometimes visiting out-stations. The Inspectors make a report to the Minister, who may declare the particular force efficient and make the financial grant (one-half) to the police authority.

Other Ministries have their inspectorates, and the Ministry of Agriculture and Fisheries is an important one. Essentially the same functions are carried out on behalf of the Minister, although the problems, such as animal diseases, increasing food production, advising farmers, etc., are of course, quite different.

Disputes between Authorities. Where a dispute arises between two local authorities (e.g. between a district council and a county council) reference to the Minister will settle the matter. By such means the Minister (a disinterested party) exercises a quasi-judicial control.

Approval of Schemes. Where a local authority embarks on a comprehensive scheme, e.g. slum clearance, or the construction of new roads to ease the growing congestion in a town, a scheme is prepared which is sent forward to the Ministry for approval. Frequently there have been consultations before final submission so that the difficulties are ironed out so far as possible before final decision is made.

Default Powers. Some statutes empower a Minister to act in place of a local authority where that authority is not fulfilling its task or performing its duty. Thus, where a local education authority is not complying with the *Education Act, 1944*, the Minister may declare the authority to be in default.

Early statutes empowered a Minister to make an **Order**, which was enforceable in the courts, compelling the authority to perform its duty. If the authority failed to carry out its task the Minister could appoint some person to do so in place of the defaulting local authority.

Where a duty in relation to public health is imposed on an authority, which fails, in spite of an Order being made by the Minister, the members of the defaulting local authority can be arrested. This is an extreme measure, and rarely occurs.

The modern expedient, when a local authority is in default, is for the Minister to transfer (by law) the functions of, say, a district council to the county council. Where a county council defaults, the Minister may appoint members of his own Government Department to take over the administration and carry out the task on behalf of the community. The cost is charged to the defaulting authority.

Most local authorities are composed of sensible men and women and prefer to negotiate their difficulties and to resolve matters amicably. Hence, default powers are rarely used.

Appointment and Dismissal of Officers. While local authorities are free to employ or dismiss their servants in the normal way (subject to the *Trade Union and Labour Relations Act, 1974*) there are certain important staff members who may only be appointed or dismissed by the local authority, provided the Minister has given approval.

The appointment and dismissal of a Chief Constable must be approved by the Home Secretary (the *Police Act, 1964*). This operates as a check on the police authority. The Minister vets the names of applicants, and ensures that a police authority does not dismiss a chief officer on frivolous or unjust grounds.

The *Education Act, 1944*, empowers the Minister to inspect the list of applicants for the post of Chief Education Officer of a local education authority.

It must not be assumed that Government Ministers operate the foregoing list of controls autocratically. These are reserve powers: there to be used if need be. Generally a spirit of **partnership** prevails, which involves mutual respect and a common desire to make the administrative machinery work smoothly and well, in a spirit of co-operation. This indeed is the spirit of democracy, which in the final analysis is quite as important as the letter of the law, and can be contrasted with the authoritarian control by the dictatorships.

Judicial Control. Local authorities are corporate bodies, created by statute and exercising powers conferred by statute. They are subject to the rule of law and can sue and be sued in the courts.

In the field of private law a local authority is subject particularly to the law of contract and the law of tort (e.g. nuisance, negligence, etc.).

Normally a local authority endeavours to act as a model person and complies with the law, but irregularities occur from time to time. In regard to the services or other function which a local authority is required to perform, a local authority may:

(i) Exceed the lawful powers of a statute. Where it does so it acts *ultra vires* (i.e. beyond its powers).
(ii) Fail to perform the service or functions required.

Where, therefore, any citizen or group of persons are prejudiced by the action, or inaction, or a local authority he or they have recourse to the Courts of Law to seek redress. Action is begun by taking out a writ against the local authority.

The various forms of control which exist are as follows:

(i) **Injunction.** An application may be made to the courts for an injunction restraining the local authority from proceeding on the course it proposes. The grounds for a successful application are usually that the local authority is acting *ultra vires* the statute under which it purports to be acting.

(ii) **Mandamus.** An application may similarly be made to the courts for an order of mandamus where it is averred that the local authority is not doing what it is required to do by law. Mandamus means 'we command' and the order is sufficient to secure compliance.

(iii) **Prohibition.** This order may be sought where a local authority threatens to perform some act which it has no legal power to do, or threatens or proposes to do some lawful act in an **unlawful manner.**

The above three special forms exist in addition to the ordinary right to sue or prosecute a local authority. Again it is necessary to bear in mind that recourse to law indicates that the usual channels of negotiation have broken down. However, circumstances may arise where judicial action is the only way out, for example, where the action complained of has already been taken by the local authority, e.g. where a house has been pulled down or a fence removed.

Judicial control is a final safeguard. Ministers of the Crown, local authority members and officers sometimes take wrong decisions. Where a private person seeks a judicial remedy he knows that his case will be heard by an impartial judge who, from his independence, is above the local feeling, personalities and pressure groups and is able to adjudicate without fear or favour, affection or ill-will.

Party Politics in Local Government

Until 1918 most local authorities were composed of independent councillors and aldermen. 'Party politics' had not manifested itself in local government. Most members were independents, local public-spirited persons, who used their special skills and abilities in the interests of the local community and the common good.

Since 1918, there has been an increasing tendency for local government to be dominated by party politics. This growth has coincided with the rise of the Labour Party and its political activities. The Labour Party regarded the local councils as one of the main instruments through which their policies could be fulfilled. In 1945 the Labour administration under Mr. Attlee stimulated further interest in the local councils, which were the necessary agencies or institutions through which many of their social measures were implemented. Not unnaturally the Labour Government wanted Labour-controlled councils (i.e. those with a majority of Labour councillors and aldermen). The Conservative Party was, therefore, compelled to look to its machinery and party organization to stimulate its own candidates to seek election. Today, therefore, most councils comprise (i) Labour members, (ii) Conservative members, (iii) Liberal members, and (iv) Independents. The main division is between Conservative and Labour and the independent councillor, with limited resources, is being squeezed out of the arena.

Opposition to Local Parties

Many thinking people regard this development as unfortunate. Party politics is regarded as discreditable by some. The main arguments of those who oppose local political parties in local government are:

(i) Local matters should attract the best men and women, who are primarily interested in the localities and in rendering public service for its own sake.

(ii) Councillors who are subjected to the 'party whip', similar to that operating in Parliament, must frequently sacrifice their own judgement for that of the leaders of the local party or national leaders.

(iii) Many local issues tend to become affected by party politics. Such matters should be settled or decided by disinterested citizens independently of party loyalties.

(iv) The majority party in local councils sometimes arranges chairmanships of committees along party lines.

(v) Pre-council party meetings, i.e. meetings of councillors before the main monthly meeting of the council, prevent discussion of matters in the full council meeting where they are reported in the Press.

The Case for Local Parties

The main arguments for local parties in local government are the following:

(i) Parties ensure greater unity and purpose among council members. Individual members know they have a common bond of basic political beliefs.

(ii) Decision making in the full council is quicker. A leader of a party group may speak with authority on a particular matter in the council.

(iii) Party politics rouses interest in local government elections and matters affecting the community.

(iv) Political parties give support to individual candidates, e.g. by advice literature, information and encouragement.

(v) Where a council is composed of exclusively independent members there is a tendency to indecision and delay. Independents tend to have independent policies.

(vi) Parties have declared policies. The electorate know their votes will ensure continuance of a declared and known policy. (A vote for an independent is virtually a vote for a person, not a policy or political doctrine.)

(vii) If parties are essential for Parliament (see p. 39) it is illogical to argue that they are harmful to local government. The same problems in essence exist locally as nationally at Westminster.

(viii) Councillors who intend to become M.P.s get valuable experience in local councils as party members. This assists them in the more difficult work at Westminster.

(ix) Party members (councillors) sometimes meet before the full council meeting, exchange views and formulate policy. They thus save time in the full council meetings. Spokesmen are appointed whose views are authoritative, and business in the council is expedited.

(x) Party politics educate new councillors. Many are amateurs and have scant knowledge of the basic principles of the British Constitution, in which local government acts in partnership with the central Government.

(xi) A Government whose party members are also councillors will be assured that its policies will be implemented and not obstructed or delayed.

Summing Up

The general attitude in most local councils is that party politics plays a less important and crucial role than it does in Parliament. The whip system is less stringent and the local issues are not so controversial. Planning, markets, amenities, and leisure, highways, refuse collection, and such matters are not politically 'charged'. It matters little to what party one adheres in dealing with these routine matters in the various committees. The sensitive areas are education and housing. Common sense and a readiness to grasp the realities of the ordinary situations in life are far more useful than doctrinaire ideas and generalities in the council chamber or the committee meetings.

Managing a Local Authority

In Central Government a Minister has, as we have noted, a Permanent Under-Secretary of State as his chief adviser and chief executive of the department. Formerly a county council had its clerk and an urban district council had its town clerk. These two figures were the chief administrative officers of the respective local authorities.

The chief officers were paid a higher salary than any other employee of the council. Hitherto the chief officer was almost invariably a lawyer, usually a solicitor. The advantage of this was that as local authorities were (as they still are) created by statute and derived all their powers from statutes, it was wise to appoint an official learned and skilled in law to advise the council. Many of the problems in local government—e.g. purchase, sale, letting of land; the making of highways; control of nuisances; compulsory purchase orders and the like—could only be resolved if the chief adviser had a sure grasp of the legal technicalities involved. However, lawyers are not necessarily good managers, and some attention was paid to the question of management, not only of the staff but of the affairs of the local authority as a whole.

The City Manager

There are many ways in which a local authority may be run. The 'City Manager' form of local government was first used at Staunton, Virginia, U.S.A. Since then many American cities have adopted the system. Broadly speaking, the elected council is empowered to make city ordinances and to decide general matters of planning. The council is empowered to hire, as head of the city organization, a professional administrator who is specially qualified by experience and training for that kind of work. The council picks the best man, whether he lives in the city or not. The City Manager appoints the heads of departments and some of the other officers. The Manager is responsible for the enforcement of the ordinances passed by the council. He reports to the council on the needs of the city and suggests plans as to how the city's money shall be spent and how improvements shall be made, and he holds his post for as long as the council is satisfied with his work.

In the United Kingdom, Newcastle-upon-Tyne decided in 1965 to appoint a City Manager and offered a good salary (£10,000). The appointee was formerly a Production Planning Manager with the Ford Motor Company. He became the senior officer of the City Corporation and was made responsible to a special Management Committee of the Council. This practice has certain dangers in that younger ambitious officers in local government would move out to other fields of work if the top jobs were given to persons unfamiliar with the tasks facing local authorities. However, it does re-emphasize that forward-looking authorities are free to appoint those with proved managerial ability.

Reports on Management

Various official reports have been issued on the subject, and we name:

(1) The Mallaby Report on 'The Staffing of Local Government' (Chairman Sir George Mallaby)—(1967);
(2) The Maud Report on 'The Management of Local Government' (Chairman Sir John Maud, now Lord Redcliffe-Maud)—(1967);
(3) The Bains Report on 'The New Local Authorities: Management and Structure' (Chairman M. A. Bains, Clerk of Kent County Council)—(1972).
Each committee was set up at the instance of the Minister.

The Mallaby Report recommended, *inter alia*, that:

(i) The clerk to the authority should be recognized as head of the local service.
(ii) a Central Staffing Organization should be created.
(iii) There should be a reduction in the number of departments in local authorities.
(iv) Local government should attract more graduates in its service.

The Maud Report recommended, *inter alia*, that:

(i) There should be one Chief Executive Officer of local authorities. He should have general managerial ability and should use this to supervise and co-ordinate the activities of all other chief officers.
(ii) There should be a Management Board of Councillors co-ordinating functions, comparable to that exercised by the Cabinet in central Government.
(iii) In large authorities there should be paid councillors.
(iv) There should be substantial delegation of minor decisions from committees to the permanent officials.

The Bains Report recommended, *inter alia*, that:

(i) The **corporate approach** was vital. This is the opposite of departmentalism, under which each department (education, surveyors, planning, housing, amenities, taxation, etc.) operated under a committee and was staffed by a chief officer with subordinates. This made for fragmentation, unco-ordinated effort, confusion and the usual personal frictions operating in most human groups, such as a college or factory. The corporate approach looks at an authority's affairs as a whole rather than as a series of isolated services. An overall plan can be formulated, carried through with resources most effectively deployed. 'Departmentalism' should be discouraged.

(ii) A **Chief Executive Officer** should be appointed (see p. 305).

(iii) **A Policy and Resources Committee** should be appointed (The Maud Committee Report similarly recommended a Management Board, as did the Royal Commission). The functions of the Policy and Resources Committee should be:

(a) To aid the council in setting its **objectives** and **priorities** by providing it with a comprehensive and co-ordinated service.

(b) To co-ordinate and control the implementation of the major policy decisions reached by the Council in the light of the Policy and Resources Committee's advice.

(c) To have ultimate responsibility, under the council, for the major resources of the authority (finance, manpower, land, buildings).

(iv) **Committees based on Programme Areas.** There were too many committees before 1972; consequently (although some are still compulsory) a reduction could be made if the authority divided its work into **spheres of activity**, each having its own objectives and programme for meeting these objectives. Thus in a Metropolitan District 'Recreation and Amenities' could be a programme area, and in this field the following would be dealt with: recreation and tourism; entertainments; commons; allotments; country parks; caravan sites; gipsy sites.

In a district council let us suppose housing is a programme area. The committee would be charged with: letting of houses; assessing future needs; acquiring land and new dwellings; slum clearance; improving private dwellings: caravan sites; accommodation for aged and infirm and disabled people; assistance in providing private dwellings through housing associations and housing societies; advances for purchase; operation of a Rent Rebate Scheme, etc.; enforcement of Rent Acts, etc.; dealing with homelessness; advisory services for those in need of housing.

You will know that each local authority has discretion to frame its own committee structure.

(v) **Community Approach.** The Bains committee used this phrase to imply and urge close co-operation between county councils and district councils within their areas; between new local authorities and the voluntary agencies (Red Cross, housing associations, civic societies etc.) and other public bodies and in particular with the new area health and regional water authorities.

District joint committees should be set up consisting of members of a county council and a district council within its area. The joint committees would be deliberative and advisory. This sort of committee could be used where, for example, a district council is exercising planning functions on behalf of a county council. Joint committees provide a forum for the exchange of valuable information to both authorities.

The community approach would most usefully meet the needs of the area it serves.

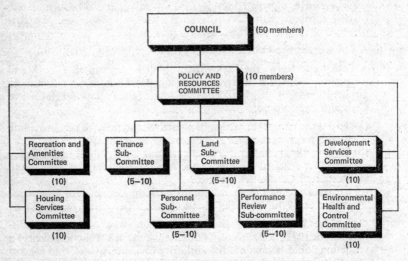

Committee structure of non-metropolitan district. (*Note:* committees and numbers are suggested only. Each authority will determine the committees and constitution itself.)

The Greater London Council have taken steps to implement certain of the recommendations contained in the above reports, and the new local authorities are, from 1 April 1974, following suit. The result, therefore, is rationalization and streamlining of administrative procedures. Certain authorities have invoked the aid of management consultants to examine the work and objectives of the particular authorities and the methods adopted to secure their attainment. Management is a continuous process and must adapt itself to the changes and challenges which are the inevitable accompaniment of modern life.

Co-ordination in Local Government

The committee system is the accepted form in which local administration is carried on. Committees are parts of the whole, and local government works well, therefore, only when the efforts of the various committees are well co-ordinated to produce the desired objectives of effective and convenient local government. Co-ordination is achieved by various means, as follows:

Through Officers. The Chief Executive Officer (and often the treasurer) attends all important committees. Any inconsistencies arising in the various committees will be pointed out by one of these officers. Thus the Planning Committee may adopt one policy which inevitably affects a Highways Committee (or sub-committee) or the Estates' Committee (or sub-committee) or vice versa. The Chief Executive Officer keeps the records and will note the points of difficulty.

Through the Council. All committees report to the Policy and Resources Committee or to the full Council. Councillors note the decisions of those committees of which they are not members and should ensure that the policies or decisions made are consistent with the general or strategic policy of the council as a whole.

Through the Policy and Resources Committee. The object of this committee is co-ordinative. It is made up of a number of councillors who form a sort of 'cabinet' with managerial functions somewhat similar to the Cabinet of the Central Government. These functions have already been discussed (see p. 319).

Through Joint Committee Meetings. Where a matter is of common interest to two or more committees of a local authority they meet together to discuss and resolve the matter. We have mentioned that joint committees exist; the county council and the district council may appoint a joint committee to ensure both councils act in concert.

Through Finance. Formerly a separate Finance Committee was common. Now finance will fall within the province of the Policy and Resources Committee. Where a Finance Committee exists independently (some authorities may feel this matter is so important as to justify separation) the committee must arrange priorities in the spending of money and arrange for its collection through rates, etc.

Through Members. Councillors will find themselves on three or four constituent committees. Each member should know what is done in at least two other committees and he or she can, by knowledge and experience, ensure that each committee's activities are consistent and co-ordinated.

Through Definition of Powers. Where a clear definition of powers and responsibilities is laid down (e.g. in Standing Orders or other documents) each committee will know its function and should not exceed its powers. Where overlapping occurs this leads to confusion and friction unless efforts are sensibly co-ordinated to ensure smooth administration.

Through Chairmen. Meetings of chairmen of committees or sub-committees, official or unofficial meetings, can smooth over difficulties and co-ordinate the work of the respective committees and thus the council as a whole.

Through Party Meetings. Where one political party has a clear majority it follows that power lies in that party's hands. Agreed policies are laid down and members usually act in accordance with the decisions reached.

Complaints of Maladministration

The *Local Government Act, 1974,* establishes machinery for the investigation of complaints of maladministration by local and other authorities. It provides for the appointment of

   (i) a Commission for Local Administration for England,
   (ii) a Commission for Local Administration for Wales, and
   (iii) a Commission for Local Administration for Scotland (*Local Government (Scotland) Act, 1975*).

Local Commissioners are appointed charged with responsibility for particular **areas** and with a **duty** to investigate any claim by a member of the public that he has suffered injustice through maladministration resulting from an administrative action or decision. The Commissioners will work on the lines of the Parliamentary Commissioner for Administration (see p. 266).

How the Commissioners Work

The commissioners will act on a complaint made:

(i) In writing;
(ii) Within 12 months of the time when the aggrieved person first had notice of the matter of complaint;
(iii) Received through a member of the authority concerned, e.g. a councillor.

The object of (iii) is clearly to enable a councillor when approached by the aggrieved person to take the matter up with his own local authority to enable the authority to put matters right.

The Commissioner for the area will not proceed to investigate until the authority has had a reasonable chance to look into the matter and to reply to it. However, a local Commissioner may deal with a matter directly if satisfied that a member of the authority concerned has been requested to refer the complaint to him and this has not been done.

Reports. Where a complaint is investigated, the Commissioner will send a report of his findings to: (a) the complainant; (b) to the member (i.e. councillor) concerned; (c) to any person complained of; and (d) to the authority complained of. Copies of the report are available for public inspection, and public notice of this fact is notified in the press. It is the responsibility of the local authority to tell the Commissioner what action has been taken, and if nothing happens the Commissioner may make a further report and the process of publication is repeated.

An annual general report must be made by the *local* Commissioners to the Commissioners (the central authority) and each year the commissions are required to review the operation of the complaints system of machinery. Local Commissioners are empowered to convey to local authorities, through the local authority associations, or to government departments, any recommendations or conclusions reached in the course of their reviews.

Matters precluded from Investigation. A local Commissioner is precluded from investigating any of the following particular matters:

(a) Any action in respect of which the complainant has a right of appeal to a statutory tribunal.
(b) Any action in respect of which the complainant has or had a right of appeal to a Minister.
(c) Any action in respect of which the person aggrieved has or had a remedy in law.

Nevertheless a local Commissioner may in fact conduct **any** investigation into any of these situations if he is satisfied that in the particular circumstances it was not reasonable to expect the complainant to have taken advantage of the remedies open to him.

Further, a local Commissioner may not look into cases where the complainant claims to have suffered from a decision affecting the public at large, or into legal proceedings, the investigation of crime, certain commercial transactions, and issues relating to appointments, pay, discipline and other personnel matters.

The following authorities are subject to investigation: local authorities; joint boards, consisting of local authorities; police authorities; and water authorities.

Local Authorities and the Public

We have already mentioned the lack of public interest in the work of local government shown by the poor turn-out for local government elections. There are many in the divisions and wards who do not know the names of those holding the keys of power as councillors and many more who understand little of the structure and function of the local authorities in the total scheme of government.

Public Relations. The Bains Working Group observed that the public have a positive right to information about what their elected representatives do and they should have access to committee meetings as well as to the full council meetings. Local authorities for their part had also a positive duty to inform the electorate about the council's activities and to communicate to the public its views on subjects which were of concern to the community.

The Bains Report suggested that public-relations officers be appointed. These officers should be skilled in the presentation of local news and could be most useful in highlighting those matters in which the public ought to be interested and informed. Some authorities have established information centres, and some have habitually issued news-sheets about the council's activities. These were usually drab documents, ill-presented and inefficiently distributed. Many local authorities had taken no positive action at all to improve their relationship to the public.

The Bains report advocates that in the largest authorities a public-relations unit under a suitably qualified public-relations officer be established. In the smaller authorities there might well be one officer specially deputed to do this work, but in all there ought to be some machinery for the proper dissemination of information which the public should know or be interested in. In any event some positive action should be taken by local authorities generally to improve the relationship between themselves and the public, if vital democracy is to be achieved.

Exercises

1. Describe the constitution of county councils, and indicate how the Chairman and councillors achieve their respective offices.
2. What are the arguments for and against the principle of co-option?
3. Describe the Greater London Council. How are the functions distributed between the GLC and the London Borough Councils?
4. Describe the qualifications of (*a*) an elector, and (*b*) a candidate for the office of councillor. What are the disqualifications for election as councillor?
5. The county council is responsible for certain services which are described as 'Protective', 'Environmental', and 'Personal'. Describe what services fall under each head.
6. What is the 'committee system' when applied to local government?
7. How is local government financed?
8. What are rates? What provisions exist for those persons with small incomes? How are rates levied and collected?
9. How is the work of a local authority co-ordinated?
10. What were the terms of reference of the Royal Commission on Local Government Reform (1966–9)?
11. Describe the main recommendations of the Commission.
12. What are the advantages of the new structure of local government?
13. Explain how complaints of maladministration in local government are dealt with.

CHAPTER TWELVE

MODERN DEVELOPMENTS

Devolution

Devolution of power from Parliament at Westminster to assemblies in Scotland and Wales has been in question for some time. The Scottish National Party (10 M.P.s 1974) and Plaid Cymru (3 M.P.s) press for more political power and independence from Westminster.

Successive governments have published reports (1970 Douglas-Home Report; 1973 Crowther/Kilbrandon Report; 1974 White Paper; and 1975 Government White Paper: 'Our Changing Democracy: Devolution to Scotland and Wales'). Mr. H. Wilson stated that a Bill will be introduced in Parliament at the start of the 1976 session, and has asked that there be a 'great national debate' on devolution plans.

The 1975 White Paper proposes a single-chamber Scottish Assembly, initially with 142 members, and a Welsh Assembly with 72 members. Each Assembly will have a Chief Executive who will ordinarily be the leader of the majority party in the Assembly and who will form an Executive which will command the support of the Assembly.

Matters to be devolved include: local government; health; social work; social security; education, science and the arts; housing; physical planning and the environment; roads and transport, and control of local authority airports; development and industry; natural resources; tourism.

The Government's proposals envisage powerful and wide-ranging new systems of democratic control to meet the desire of the Scottish and Welsh peoples for more direct and effective involvement in the running of their own affairs, recognising their distinctive identities within the wider framework of which they will remain a part. The sovereignty of the Westminster Parliament and the duties and obligations of H.M. Government would not be affected. Reserve powers will be retained at Westminster. Disputes arising over the exercise of devolved powers or disputes between Assemblies will be decided by the Government at Westminster or by the Courts. Responsibility for the law courts must remain with the Government at Westminster.

The changed status for Scotland and Wales is not a purely Scottish or Welsh affair. England is implicated, as is Northern Ireland. Dispersal of power will also affect the way England is governed.

Strong advocates within the SNP require 'federalism' in some form, but the exact nature and extent of the devolved powers has yet to be determined. Scottish opinion is, however, divided among three principal parties: Labour, Scottish National and Conservative. Not until the moderates have voiced their opinion can the full extent of the demands and the proposals be known, and not until full debate in Parliament has occurred will change be made. Plaid Cymru similarly advocates large-scale devolved powers; others desire no change or weakening of the U.K.

Because of the division of opinion some M.P.s are recommending that a Referendum be held to make the final decision once the draft proposals have been debated.

Criticism is made that another Assembly would create a four-tier system of government: district councils; county councils, Assemblies and Parliament. This was 'over-government' by more and more officials at enormous cost to the people.

Referendum

The referendum is one method by which the wishes of electors may be expressed with regard to proposed legislation. It is developed in its highest form in Switzerland. Australia and New Zealand have used the referendum, and de Gaulle used it in seeking the consent of the French nation for his policies. In a democracy a referendum should be preceded by a programme of education and public debate.

In early 1975 the issue was Britain's continued membership of the EEC. The *European Communities Act, 1972*, secured our membership of the EEC, which was expressed to be 'of unlimited duration'. On March 10 the Labour Government (which was split over the issue of continued membership) attended an EEC summit meeting in Dublin, and opened renegotiation demands which were met by the other co-members. On April 26, a special Labour Party meeting had approved by 3,724,000 votes to 1,986,000 its NEC recommendation that the U.K. should leave the EEC. To preserve party unity Mr. Wilson decided to order a referendum. The *Referendum Act, 1975*, was passed which fixed Referendum Day as June 5, when all voters in the U.K. on the electoral rolls were entitled to vote. Ballot was by counties (not parliamentary constituencies) and the count was held at Earl's Court, London. Parliament voted £125,000 to each side for campaigning. Other money came from industry and other sources for continued membership, whilst the trade unions subscribed to the anti lobby. The result was:

> For staying in EEC 17,378,581 (67.2 per cent)
> For leaving the EEC 8,470,073 (32.8 per cent)

Some 70 per cent of the total electorate voted in the referendum.
Some points to note are:

1. The referendum is a device which has consequences affecting: (*a*) Parliamentary sovereignty; (*b*) collective responsibility; (*c*) representative Parliament; (*d*) treaty obligations already entered into (e.g. the *European Communities Act, 1972*) and (*e*) subjecting laws to popular vote.
2. The use of the referendum is a major constitutional change which should be used, if at all, only after due deliberation.
3. If the result of a referendum is *binding* on a Government this derogates from Parliamentary sovereignty.
4. The task of Government on major matters is *decision*. If a Minister could not accept the decision of his colleagues in Cabinet he should resign (see below). The referendum may be looked upon as merely 'passing the buck' to the people. That was not 'decision by Government'.
5. If there were a low poll at a referendum it could not be argued that the people had been decisive. Uncertainty would increase.
6. If the referendum were used as a tactical device by one Minister today, it could be used by another Minister tomorrow on a different issue.
7. The people had not asked for a referendum on the EEC issue. (The *European Communities Act, 1972*, had already been passed.) The original

member countries of the EEC had not used the referendum to form the EEC initially.

8. As the U.K. had already passed the *European Communities Act, 1972,* and were bound by the Treaty of Rome (expressed to be of 'unlimited duration'), the holding of a referendum could only damage our standing and cause in the World and in the eyes of EEC co-members. They might query whether we may repeat the exercise of the referendum at a later date.

Cabinet Secrecy

One of the conventions of the constitution is Cabinet secrecy or confidentiality, which is allied to the convention of 'collective responsibility' (see p. 118).

'Achievement of collective responsibility implies that there should be complete frankness between the members, who would not feel free to surrender their departmental and personal preferences for the object of their common policy unless they were confident that the stand they had taken and the points they had conceded would not become public knowledge and be used to their embarrassment.' (*The Cabinet Office to 1945,* by S. S. Wilson, H.M.S.O.)

The above broadly justifies the convention and need for cabinet secrecy. There were three classes:

1. Detailed discussions in Cabinet or Cabinet committee, the record of such discussions, and papers prepared for or arising out of those discussions;
2. Detailed discussions or communications between Ministers and their advisers concerning the development or formulation of policies and their execution;
3. Detailed discussions between ministers and their advisers and between persons responsible for the appointment and transfer of senior members of the public service and their fitness for positions of responsibility.

The law which could have been invoked is the *Official Secrets Act, 1911,* and the *Public Records Act, 1950* (which permits the opening to the public of official documents after 30 years).

The late Richard Crossman, former Cabinet minister, 1964–70, kept a detailed diary during the time he was a Minister. This gave details of Cabinet matters and of conversations and relationships within the Cabinet and with senior civil servants, notably Dame Evelyn Sharp (now Baroness Sharp), formerly Permanent Secretary of the Ministry of Housing and Local Government of which Mr. Crossman was Minister.

Mr. Crossman's literary executors proposed to publish the diaries. The Attorney-General sought an injunction in 1975 to prohibit the publication, and the Courts dismissed his application. Extracts from the diaries were published in the press later in 1975.

Baroness Sharp, who by then had retired from the Civil Service, thereupon published her account of the particular issues described by the late Richard Crossman, and refuted certain of his statements.

Mr. H. Wilson then appointed a Committee of Privy Counsellors to inquire into the operation of the convention of Cabinet secrecy and the writing of memoirs by Ministers even if the memoirs were to be published after death. Lord Radcliffe headed the committee of seven Privy Counsellors, who reported on January 23, 1976.

The principal recommendation is that ministerial authors should be precluded for 15, instead of 30 years, from publishing information falling into three categories:

1. The author must not reveal anything that contravenes the requirements of national security operative at the time of his proposed publication.
2. He must not make disclosures that would be injurious to his country's relations with other nations.
3. He must not publish information destructive of the confidential relationships upon which the system of government is based; that is, relationships between Ministers and colleagues or advisers in the civil service or outside bodies and private persons.

The committee thought the law did not provide satisfactory machinery for enforcement. New legislation creating a series of new offences was not recommended: they rely on a minister's acceptance of an obligation of honour, reinforced by a rule that on taking or leaving office he should have his attention drawn explicitly to his obligations in relation to memoirs. A former Minister will also continue to submit any manuscript about his ministerial experience to the secretary of the Cabinet, with the right of appeal to the Prime Minister.

The Prime Minister has confirmed that Ministers will in future be invited to sign an appropriate declaration so that a transgressor would be known to be breaking an official obligation he had undertaken.

A Written Constitution and a Bill of Rights

The devolution of power to Assemblies in Scotland and Wales; electoral reform; the use of the referendum; the doctrine of the Rule of Law in relation to trade unions and other groups are but some important and topical matters which agitate the minds of responsible figures today. White papers have been published. Lord Justice Scarman in his Hamlyn Law Lectures, 1974, considered, *inter alia*, the need for a Bill of Rights, and Lord Hailsham, ex-Lord Chancellor, put forward his views on and the case for a written constitution for the U.K.

First, a written constitution can exist independently of a Bill of Rights. The U.S. Constitution was drafted in broad terms, but was then followed by amendments, the first ten of which constitute a Bill of Rights which are the bedrock of the individual liberties that have been jealously guarded in the U.S. for two centuries.

The First amendment guarantees freedom of religious worship, of speech, and of the press, and the rights of peaceable assembly, and of petitioning the Government.

Chief Justice Marshall said in 1819 that a constitution written to cover all eventualities 'would partake of a prolixity of a legal code and could scarcely be embraced by the human mind. . . . Its nature, therefore, requires that only its great outlines should be marked.' He added that the American Constitution was one 'intended to endure for ages to come and, consequently, to be adapted to the various crises of human affairs'.

Any Constitution must necessarily be drafted in broad terms; so too, a Bill of Rights.

It is impossible here to deal comprehensively with so vast a subject, but the following notes may highlight some problems involved in the question of a written constitution:

1. *Evolution and need for change.* Our constitution has evolved over 700 years, and changes and adaptations have been made *ad hoc*. But a constitution may wear out or become obsolete, in which case reform on thoroughgoing lines may be inevitable.

2. *The Crown.* Over the years the Crown has increased in prestige and popularity, and the Monarch's position within the constitution should unreservedly be preserved.

3. *The House of Lords.* The reform of the Lords has been discussed on p. 53. The fundamental weakness of this Chamber is that it is not popularly elected.

As a revising chamber the House is ineffectual. The *Parliament Acts, 1911 and 1949* formally restrict its powers (see p. 46). Nowadays a Finance Bill, e.g. capital transfer tax, imposing novel taxation, is never *discussed* by convention in the Lords.

The administration is not prepared to treat the Lords' amendments to legislation (even those which the House can legitimately revise) on their merits. There is an acceptance by all three major parties of the principle that the policies of the Government, when implemented by the House of Commons, should not be obstructed or impeded. A second chamber which is to be effective must be granted greater powers than it has at the moment, in particular to limit attacks on human rights, for example, were a Bill of Rights to be enacted.

4. *The Commons.* Lack of space prevents further comment on this chamber, which is considered on p. 55.

A Bill of Rights

Almost every country with a 'written' constitution attempts in some manner to entrench certain rights designed to protect the individual or minority groups. Where *entrenched* rights are so framed it follows that they cannot be overridden by an ordinary *statute*. Where any subsequent statute conflicts with the entrenched rights disputes will inevitably arise, and the courts would have to adjudge accordingly. We are then faced with the prospect of judges pronouncing on the *validity* of Acts of Parliament. Once judges are given the power so to pronounce we are faced with the prospect of a *political* judiciary. We have so far managed to avoid this. But if a Prime Minister were so minded he could fill judicial appointments with those nominees holding the same political views as himself. In any case, conflict between the judiciary and Parliament may often arise.

The enactment of a Bill of Rights presupposes that the judges will be the guardians of the constitution. If the House of Lords is to be reformed then a Constitutional Court could be created as an ultimate court of appeal on all constitutional matters.

Form of Change

Clearly the above questions relating to fundamental matters of state will require long and patient consideration. If change is to occur then it should be preceded by education and, if need be, a referendum. The whole project should extend over five or perhaps ten years, so that in the end we should retain our traditional institutions of the Queen in Parliament, a bi-cameral legislature, and an independent judiciary, but in a new form with a written constitution.

SPECIMEN LEGISLATIVE DOCUMENTS

(a) Parliamentary Bill

Representation of the People

A

B I L L

TO

Amend the law about the qualification of electors at   A.D. 1968
elections to the Parliament of the United Kingdom
or at local government elections in Great Britain,
and the qualification for election to and membership
of local authorities in England and Wales, about the
conduct of and manner of voting at those elections
and about candidates' election expenses thereat, and
otherwise to make provision about matters incidental
to those elections, and for purposes connected there-
with.

BE IT ENACTED by the Queen's most Excellent Majesty, by and
with the advice and consent of the Lords Spiritual and
Temporal, and Commons, in this present Parliament
assembled, and by the authority of the same, as follows:—

5   *The franchise and its exercise*

1.—(1) For purposes of the Representation of the People Voting age.
Acts a person shall be of voting age if he is of the age of
eighteen years or over; and, if otherwise qualified, a person
who is of voting age on the date of the poll at a parliamentary
10 or local government election shall be entitled to vote as an
elector, whether or not he is of voting age on the qualifying
date.

(2) A person, if otherwise qualified, shall accordingly be
entitled to be registered in a register of parliamentary electors
15 or a register of local government electors if he will attain voting
age before the end of the twelve months following the day by
which the register is required to be published; but, if he will
not be of voting age on the first day of those twelve months—

(a) his entry in the register shall give the date on which he
20   will attain that age; and

[Bill 9]   44/3

ELIZABETH II

1968 CHAPTER 71

An Act to make fresh provision with respect to discrimination on racial grounds, and to make provision with
respect to relations between people of different racial
origins.   [25th October 1968]

BE IT ENACTED by the Queen's most Excellent Majesty, by and
with the advice and consent of the Lords Spiritual and
Temporal, and Commons, in this present Parliament
assembled, and by the authority of the same, as follows:—

PART I

DISCRIMINATION

General

1.—(1) For the purposes of this Act a person discriminates
against another if on the ground of colour, race or ethnic or
national origins he treats that other, in any situation to which
section 2, 3, 4 or 5 below applies, less favourably than he treats
or would treat other persons, and in this Act references to discrimination are references to discrimination on any of those
grounds. *Meaning of "discrimination"*

(2) It is hereby declared that for those purposes segregating
a person from other persons on any of those grounds is treating
him less favourably than they are treated.

Unlawful discrimination

2.—(1) It shall be unlawful for any person concerned with
the provision to the public or a section of the public (whether
on payment or otherwise) of any goods, facilities or services to
discriminate against any person seeking to obtain or use those
goods, facilities or services by refusing or deliberately omitting *Provision of goods, facilities and services.*

A 2

(c) Statutory Instrument

STATUTORY INSTRUMENTS

1969 No. 805 (C.18)

MINES AND QUARRIES

The Mines and Quarries (Tips) Act 1969 (Commencement No. 2) Order 1969

Made - - - 12*th June* 1969

The Minister of Housing and Local Government and the Secretary of State for Wales, in exercise of the powers conferred on them jointly by section 38(3) of the Mines and Quarries (Tips) Act 1969(a), and of all other powers enabling them in that behalf, hereby order as follows :—

1. This order may be cited as the Mines and Quarries (Tips) Act 1969 (Commencement No. 2) Order 1969.

2. Part II of the Mines and Quarries (Tips) Act 1969, in its application to England and Wales, shall come into operation on 30th June 1969.

Given under the official seal of the Minister of Housing and Local Government on 12th June 1969.

(L.S.) *Anthony Greenwood,*
Minister of Housing and Local Government.

Given under my hand on 12th June 1969.

George Thomas,
Secretary of State for Wales.

EXPLANATORY NOTE

(*This Note is not part of the Order.*)

This Order brings into operation on 30th June 1969, in England and Wales, Part II of the Mines and Quarries (Tips) Act 1969, which provides for the prevention of public danger from disused tips.

APPENDIX TWO

STUDY AND EXAMINATION TECHNIQUE

Studying British Constitution

The student of British Constitution is dealing with a 'living' subject in which he does not only study past events but observes the objects of the study in action and in the process of change. This is, at once, the attraction of the subject and a major problem of its study. Its attractiveness lies in the sheer dynamism of the political world in which things are not always what they seem and where institutions do not always carry the functions that they originally held—the student has to be prepared to probe beneath the surface to evaluate the actual working of the political system. The problem of the subject is that it *is* so fast-moving and the student is hard pressed to keep up with the changes that are continually taking place. Thus, for example, recent years have seen major reorganization of the Civil Service, the legal system, Government Departments, and the local government structure.

The student has thus to be prepared to direct his study to achieve two major objectives:

(1) He must be able to analyse, discuss and criticize the system of government. In order to do this he must have a thorough factual knowledge of the working system on which to base his analysis. He must be aware of the practical operation of the system behind the legal or constitutional facade.

(2) His knowledge must be up to date. It is the aim of *British Constitution Made Simple* to assist the student in the achievement of these two objectives but no text book on its own is sufficient for the achievement of a successful outcome to a British constitution course. Each individual will need to consult other texts (see bibliography) and refer to a variety of newspapers and journals in order to widen, consolidate, and up-date his awareness of the workings of the system of government. In this regard the following sources are of considerable value:

Newspapers	Journals and Magazines	
The Times	*The New Statesman*	*Public Administration*
The Guardian	*The Spectator*	*The Political Quarterly*
The Daily Telegraph	*The Listener*	*Local Government Chronicle*
The Sunday Times	*New Society*	*Municipal Journal*
The Observer	*The Parliamentarian*	*Public Law*
	Parliamentary Affairs	

Reference

Keesing's Contemporary Archives
Whitaker's Almanac
Local Government Annotations Service

Regular consultation of these sources will keep the student up to date with current events and a further aid is now regularly provided by R. K. Mosley who annually publishes an admirable little booklet called *British Constitution 1972* (year as appropriate) which is a survey of most recent events in the political system and is directed specifically at students about to take examinations in British Constitution.

EXAMINATION TECHNIQUE

Examination Preparation

Thorough preparation is essential and it is important to realise that the most successful candidate is likely to be the person who plans his work over a fairly lengthy period, studies consistently thoughout this period and leaves himself some weeks before the examination for concentrated revision of what he has learned.

At the end of each chapter in this book you will find questions to enable you to test your knowledge. These questions should be used constantly throughout your course and in the concentrated revision period prior to the examination. Thorough learning and revision is an essential prerequisite to success. However able your teacher may be, in the final analysis the examination will test *your* knowledge and *your* learning. The secret of success is thorough preparation.

British Constitution Questions

The types of question set in British Constitution examinations vary according to the *level* of the examination. Thus examinations at G.C.E. 'O' level and similar standard tend to produce questions designed to test the factual knowledge of the candidate. For example, questions requiring a description of the process of Public and Private Bills or asking the student to show his knowledge of the functions of the Prime Minister are by no means uncommon and illustrate the type of question asked.

At G.C.E. 'A' level and in the intermediate examinations of various professional bodies the questions are designed not merely to test **factual** knowledge but also to test the ability of the candidate to **analyse**. Thus analytical questions ask the student for his opinions as to the effectiveness of certain parts of the political machinery, to discuss critically a particular process or to show what point of constitutional importance is demonstrated by a particular event. The general approach to answering such questions is to initially state the factual framework around which the discussion or analysis is to be built then to carry out the analysis and finally reach a conclusion to provide a neatly rounded ending to the essay.

Examination Strategy

In the previous section the importance of planning your study and revision has been stressed. It is also important that you should plan carefully your approach to examinations ensuring that you complete the technical formalities such as putting in your candidate number, etc., as well as answering the questions. In your approach to the examination bear in mind the value of having an overall strategy in dealing with the paper as a whole in addition to having a set procedure for answering individual questions.

The following simple rules will guide you in planning your overall strategy:

(i) Read the instructions printed on your **answer** sheets and be sure to write in the required details (e.g. name, candidate number, centre number, etc.).

(ii) Read the instructions at the top of the **examination** paper very carefully to ensure that you answer the requisite number of questions and that you are aware of the areas of choice available if the paper is divided into sections.

(iii) Aim to answer **all** the questions required. (If, for example, you only answer four out of five, then the maximum mark you can achieve is eighty per cent and your chances of success are diminished by that much.) This will involve planning your approximate time allocation to each question very carefully.

(iv) Read the question paper through and decide which questions you will answer.

(v) When you have completed your paper read it through for errors and omissions, ensure that the sheets (and any continuation sheets) are in their correct order and make a final check to ensure that you have written in the required information on the answer sheets.

(vi) Hand your paper in.

Individual Questions

It may seem to be statement of the obvious but the aim of the candidate must be to *answer the question*, yet we so frequently see examiners' reports in which the main criticism is the failure of so many students to answer the set question or a tendency to ignore completely certain parts of a question. Thus the objective is to answer the set question as fully as possible and in seeking this objective you will find that a fixed procedure will help you as follows:

(i) Read the question **carefully**.
(ii) Read the question again underlining the key words.
(iii) Make **rough** notes of your answer.
(iv) Arrange your points in logical order with 'a beginning, a middle, and an end'.
(v) Write your answer from your plan.

In writing your answer endeavour to excel in three areas:

1. Style

Examiners want clear and concise answers to the point of the question. Do not introduce irrelevant material and avoid facetious comments. Remember the 'ABC Rule'.

A = Accurate
B = Brief
C = Clear
D = Direct (i.e. no irrelevance)

2. Examples

It is important in British Constitution to use examples to illustrate the points that you are making. This will demonstrate that you can relate your knowledge to the actual operation of the system of government. Also use recent examples wherever possible, preferably those culled from a variety of sources thus indicating to the examiner that you have been prepared to extend your reading beyond a single textbook.

3. Presentation

A paper will commend itself to the examiner if it is grammatically correct, well paragraphed and neatly and legibly written, the latter being particularly important since the examiner cannot mark work which he cannot read. Untidy, blotched, and scribbled efforts will create a bad impression and may not justify good marks.

Example 1

Question: Examine critically the procedure for the consideration of (a) Private Members' Bills, and (b) Private Bills.

Rough Notes: (a) Private Members' Bills—definition: methods of introduction (i) Ballot; (ii) Ten minute rule: Process of bills. Difficulties and criticisms. Examples.

(b) Private Bills and definition, examples. Process in Parliament. Discussion of advantages and criticisms.

Model Answer:

(a) Private Members' Bills are public Bills which are introduced into the House of Commons and piloted through their procedure by an individual M.P. Members of Parliament get the opportunity to introduce such Bills in two ways. Under the first method a ballot is held at the beginning of each session to determine the priority list of Bills to be considered on private members' legislation days. Since 1970 twelve Fridays have been allocated to the passage of such Bills which effectively limits the likelihood of a successful passage to the first eight or so M.P.s and their Bills.

Once the M.P. has been successful in the ballot he must then set about drafting his Bill which can be an expensive process though frequently a pressure group will bear the cost, and since 1971 the Government contribute £200 to the drafting costs of the first ten Bills on the list. After this has been completed the Bill will go through the normal stages of a public Bill. The Bill will have a formal First Reading which serves to introduce its purpose to the House, after which comes the Second Reading in which the main principles of the Bill are debated followed by the Committee Stage in which a Standing Committee will go through the Bill clause by clause accepting, amending, or rejecting each. After this the Bill goes back to the House for its Report Stage and purely formal Third Reading and then the Bill will go to the House of Lords where it will go through the same procedure but piloted now by a supporter of the Bill in that House. Finally the Bill will go for the Royal Assent.

The second method by which a Private Member's Bill may be introduced is under the Ten-Minute Rule whereby an M.P. may put forward in a ten-minute speech a motion requesting leave to introduce a Bill after Question Time on Tuesdays and Wednesdays. If the Bill is unopposed, which is rare, the Bill can proceed through its various stages as unopposed business after 10 p.m.

The main problem with Private Members' Bills is that so few of them get through with consequent wastage of time, money and effort. Ten-minute rule Bills, in particular, stand little chance of success since discussion must take place on opposed Bills and the time for such discussion must come out of the Government's allocation, which it is most unlikely to be prepared to give. However, there are occasions when a Bill is so worthy (*Oil Burners (Standards) Act, 1960, Tattooing of Minors Act, 1969*) that it evokes no opposition. Only about two or three such Bills will be successful in each session.

The chances of success of Bills introduced on Fridays are greater though even here there are obstacles. Much depends on the ability of the M.P. to get sufficient support in the House on Fridays which is not always easy to do since M.P.s are eager to get away to their constituencies. Also the M.P. will rarely be able to rally enough M.P.s to get a closure motion accepted which means that a small group of opponents can 'talk out' a Bill. Thus a Bill to abolish Hare Coursing has been introduced each year since 1966 and has not yet been passed. Much also depends on the attitude of the Government who will ensure the defeat of a Bill if it conflicts with their policy.

Despite these difficulties eight to ten such Bills are passed each year and while they are mainly concerned with fairly minor matters the period between 1964 and 1970 saw the passage of important social reforms, e.g. *Murder (Abolition of the Death Penalty) Act, 1965, Termination of Pregnancy Act, 1967,* The *Divorce Act, 1970.*

(*b*) Private Bills are of more limited scope than public Bills and are promoted by public and private authorities in search of additional powers. Most Private Bills are promoted these days by local authorities (e.g. *Somerset County Council Act, 1967*) and rarely excite national controversy though two Bills in recent years promoted by the Greater London Council and Manchester Corporation to introduce lotteries to assist their finances did evoke national interest and concern—they both failed.

The initial part of the process of Private Bills takes place outside Parliament. After the promoters have petitioned Parliament for permission to introduce the Bill they have to advertise its purposes twice in local newspapers and the *London Gazette* and anybody affected by compulsory purchase under the Bill must be notified. Once these formalities are completed the petitions are examined to see that the promoters have complied with standing orders. Opponents of the Bill are then required to submit petitions indicating the basis of their objections.

The Parliamentary process of a Private Bill is the same as for a public Bill but the emphasis is different in that most of the work is not done on the floor of the two Houses but in committee. If a Bill is unopposed by outside interests it will have an easy passage through Parliament where the main aim of the process is to ensure that standing orders have been complied with and that public rights have not been infringed. If the Bill is opposed the passage will be more difficult in that the opponents may ask an M.P. to object at Second Reading, thus leading to a debate, and at the committee stage in the Opposed Bills Committee the promoters will have to justify their Bill on grounds of public interest in the face of opposition from the various petitioners against the legislation. The proceedings of the committee are semi-judicial in character, the promoters and opponents of the Bill may employ counsel to represent them, evidence is given on oath and cross examination is allowed. If the Bill survives this hurdle it will usually be successful though opposition may be maintained in its process through the Lords (or Commons if the Bill begins in the Lords).

The Private Bill process has the advantage of bringing flexibility into legislation since it enables local peculiarities and needs to be catered for in addition to the general needs dealt with by public legislation. However, the procedure is rather cumbersome and slow. The whole process is very expensive especially if there is opposition to the Bill and it does seem ridiculous that opposition should be allowed to continue in the second House after the promoters have 'proved their case' in the House of introduction. Finally there is no guarantee that the Bill will ultimately be successful after all the expenditure. In view of the expense and uncertainty authorities tend to rely on Special Orders rather than Private Bills wherever possible.

Example 2

Question: Analyse and illustrate the different kinds of interest groups active in British political life. How do they exert their influence and with what success?

Rough Notes: Define interest groups. Classification—

(i) sectional—examples, (ii) promotional—examples.

Methods of influence (*a*) Departments, (*b*) Parliament, (*c*) Public—effectiveness of groups.

Model Answer:

Interest groups are organized groups of people who are linked by some common characteristic of occupation, class, opinion, race, language, or religion. An essential part of the activities of such groups is the bringing of pressure or influence to bear on Governmental authorities to achieve changes in public policy for the benefit of the members of the group. Such 'benefit' may be material (e.g. National Union of Teachers seeking improvements in the conditions of service of teachers) or spiritual (e.g. Activities of members of the R.S.P.C.A.). Interest groups do not seek to govern, like the political party, but to influence those who do govern. Such groups can also be distinguished from political parties in that their aims may not be wholly political (e.g. Automobile Association mainly provides a service to motorists but also exerts influence on the Government in its area of concern).

There are many interest groups and broadly speaking they can be divided into two classes. On the one hand there are the sectional interest groups which represent certain sections of society and which are based on the common economic or vocational interests of their members. The function of such groups is to advance and defend the common interests of their members. Thus the employers associations (Confederation of British Industry, Society of Motor Manufacturers and Traders) employees associations (TUC, National Union of Mineworkers) professional associations (Law Society, British Medical Association) and civic associations (such as the Association of Municipal Corporations) are the main groups in this class.

On the other hand there are promotional groups which are concerned with particular causes or principles arising out of beliefs and attitudes held by members and these groups endeavour to persuade public authorities to accept the cause which they are urging. A number of such groups seek a major change in policy, e.g. Campaign for Nuclear Disarmament, while the majority are concerned with watching over administration of policy in particular spheres and achieving slight modifications, e.g. Howard League for Penal Reform, N.S.P.C.C., League against Cruel Sports, R.S.P.C.A.

Interest groups exert their influence through three main channels. In the first place they operate through consultation with Government Departments and the achievement of consultative status is much sought by the interest groups. The importance that the groups attach to being on the 'to be consulted' list merely reflects the fact that in the British political system the main source of power lies with the Government and the Departments that service the senior Ministers. Once the Government has made a decision it is accepted that the Government's supporters in the Commons will vote for it.

The relationship between Government Departments and the groups is reciprocal. The groups know that they will be consulted on any matters or changes in policy likely to affect them and will, therefore, be in a position to influence the proposals at an early stage. Thus the National Farmers' Union will always be consulted on the annual agricultural price review and the National Union of Teachers on any changes in national education policy. On the other hand the Government Departments regard it as proper and necessary in a complex modern democracy to consult the 'affected interests' in the process of administration and gain expertise and information on the advantages and difficulties of Government proposals as a product of the consultative process. Consultation also has the advantage for the departments of securing agreement and reducing criticism of Government policy.

The second channel of influence is through Parliament. A number of trade union interest groups sponsor Labour candidates at general elections and many M.P.s will agree to be spokesmen for particular groups in Parliament, sometimes being paid a retainer for their services. These M.P.s will back up previous consultations with departments by various activities in the House of Commons, e.g. by putting forward amendments to legislation.

On occasions promotional groups seeking major objectives will launch a campaign designed on a short- or long-term basis to get the support of M.P.s on their proposals. Sometimes they are successful, as with the abolition of capital punishment and the law relating to the termination of pregnancy, but if the Government opposes the group's objectives, then it has little chance of success as was the case with the Campaign for Nuclear Disarmament.

Finally interest groups seek the favour of the public in order to gain support in the promotion of their cause at either Departmental or Parliamentary level. Public favour may be sought either by publicity through radio, Press, and television, as a result of demonstrations and mass lobbying of M.P.s, or in a more subtle way by the use of public relations techniques to build up a favourable public image for the group in the long term, e.g. Aims of Industry seeks to build up a favourable image for 'private enterprise'.

However, group campaigns designed to appeal to the general public are the exception rather than the rule in British politics, particularly in the case of those groups normally in contact with Government Departments. Such groups are more likely to achieve their objectives through consultation. Promotional groups which are not recognized by the Government are the most likely to resort to a public opinion campaign but such a campaign has its dangers in that it may antagonize public opinion rather than gain its support, in which case the group's chances of success are remote.

It is thus generally accepted that the most effective way to achieve their objectives is to seek consultative status so that the group is consulted whenever the Government is contemplating measures which may affect the group. The other channels of influence through pressure on Parliament and public opinion, are resorted to either in order to reinforce or supplement consultations or because the groups concerned are not consulted by the Departments.

APPENDIX THREE

TEST PAPERS

The following questions are taken mainly from examination papers set by the Associated Examining Board (A.E.B.), and the School Examinations Dept., University of London (U.L.) at Ordinary and Advanced Level for the General Certificate of Education. The author acknowledges gratefully the kindness of the examining authorities for permission to reproduce them here. The remaining questions are the author's.

Chapter 1: The Nature of the Constitution

1. How far is it true to say that the British Constitution is unwritten? 'O' (A.E.B.).
2. What part do conventions play in the British Constitution? Illustrate your answer with examples of particular conventions. 'A' (A.E.B.).
3. What is meant by the 'separation of powers'? How far is it a characteristic of the modern British Constitution? 'A' (U.L.).
4. What is meant by the phrase 'The supremacy of Parliament'? 'O' (A.E.B.).
5. Critically examine the view that the Rule of Law has been dangerously eroded in this country. 'A' (A.E.B.).
6. The legal Sovereign is Parliament; the political Sovereign is the people. Explain the meanings of these two statements. How far are they contradictory? 'O' (U.L.).

Chapter 2: Elections and the Party System

1. Describe the main changes in the franchise since 1900. 'O' (A.E.B.).
2. Political parties give cohesion to Parliament. Discuss. 'A' (A.E.B.).
3. Discuss the extent to which party political conferences influence the actions of (a) H.M. Government, and (b) H.M. Opposition. 'A' (A.E.B.).
4. What anomalies and what advantages arise from the British 'simple majority' voting system? Discuss the value of other systems which might be substituted. 'A' (U.L.).
5. 'The party Whips are a help, not a hindrance to good and efficient government.' Discuss.
6. 'The party system subordinates individual opinion to organized pressures.' Critically examine this statement. 'A' (A.E.B.).
7. What qualifications and qualities are likely to enable a would-be Member of Parliament to secure (a) adoption as a candidate of one of the main political parties, and (b) election to the House of Commons? 'A' (U.L.).

Chapter 3: The Legislature

1. Give an account of the composition and functions of the House of Lords. 'O' (A.E.B.).
2. Describe the procedure for dealing with Private Members' Bills. Why are such Bills considered desirable? 'A' (A.E.B.).
3. Describe the main functions of the House of Commons.

4. 'The efficient secret of the English Constitution may be described as the close union, the nearly complete fusion, of the executive and legislative powers' (Bagehot). Criticize this statement, and evaluate its truth.

5. 'The House of Lords is a relic from a bygone age, but it still has its uses.' Consider this statement.

6. Write notes on any *three* of the following:

    (*a*) A Private Bill.
    (*b*) The Queen's Speech.
    (*c*) The Report Stage.
    (*d*) A 'Guillotine' motion. 'O' (A.E.B.).

7. Write short accounts of *three* of the following:

    (*a*) The Speaker;
    (*b*) The Lord Chancellor.
    (*c*) Prorogation of Parliament.
    (*d*) The Queen's Speech.
    (*e*) Standing Committees of the House of Commons.

8. Describe the composition and functions of the various committees of the House of Commons. 'A' (A.E.B.).

9. Describe the role that Select Committees play in the House of Commons. 'A' (A.E.B.).

10. 'Matters affecting national security and Parliamentary privilege should be decided by the courts and not by a committee of Parliament.' 'A' (A.E.B.).

11. Discuss the necessity of the privileges of the House of Commons. Should these privileges be enlarged or reduced? Give reasons for your answers. 'A' (A.E.B.).

12. Describe what happens at Question Time in the House of Commons. What is the purpose of this procedure?

13. Describe a Parliamentary session in the House of Commons.

Chapter 4: The Executive

1. Describe the role of the Queen in the British Constitution today. 'O' (U.L.).

2. Describe the composition and work of the Privy Council. 'O' (U.L.).

3. What is meant by the 'Royal Prerogative'? How is it exercised in modern Britain? 'O' (A.E.B.).

4. What factors does a British Prime Minister have to bear in mind when he chooses his Cabinet?

5. Give an account of the composition and functions of the Cabinet. 'O' (A.E.B.).

6. Examine the reasons for the growth in the power of the Executive during this century. 'A' (A.E.B.).

7. 'A British Prime Minister's powers are varied and enormous, but not without limits.' Discuss. 'A' (U.L.).

8. How is the Prime Minister of Great Britain chosen? What are his main functions? 'O' (A.E.B.).

9. What powers are still possessed by a British Monarch in the Constitution of this country? 'A' (A.E.B.).

10. 'Few Ministers have administrative ability, but they don't need it because they have the Civil Service to administer for them.' Discuss. 'A' (U.L.).

11. Describe and assess the importance of the conventions relating to the Cabinet. 'A' (A.E.B.).

12. 'Cabinet government has been replaced by government by the Prime Minister.' 'Parliamentary sovereignty is supreme.' 'Sovereignty is vested in the electorate.' How far can these statements be reconciled? 'A' (A.E.B.).

13. Describe the work of **either** the Treasury **or** the Foreign Office. 'O' (U.L.).

14. Describe the system of recruitment to the Civil Service.

15. What precisely is meant by the 'expertise' of the civil servants? In what are they expert?

16. 'Despite all the criticism we can still be proud of our Civil Service.' Discuss. 'A' (U.L.).

17. 'There is not enough contact between the Civil Service and the community it is there to serve.' How far do you consider this statement justified? 'A' (A.E.B.).

18. Describe the means whereby the House of Commons controls public expenditure. How effective is House of Commons control? 'A' (A.E.B.).

19. 'The Home Civil Service is still fundamentally the product of the nineteenth-century philosophy of the Northcote–Trevelyan Report.' Discuss. 'A' (A.E.B.).

20. What do you consider to have been the most important changes in the British Constitution in the last ten years? 'A' (A.E.B.).

21. Write notes on three of the following:

(*a*) The Cabinet Secretariat.
(*b*) Ministerial responsibility.
(*c*) Collective responsibility.
(*d*) The Attorney-General.

Chapter 5: The Public Corporations

1. What financial controls do Government Departments impose upon public corporations? To what extent are these controls justified? 'A' (A.E.B.).

2. How does a public corporation differ from a Government Department. 'A' (U.L.).

3. 'Public corporations are not public. We learn more about them from the Press than through Parliament.' Discuss.

4. Why did the major public corporations develop in their present form? How successful have been the arrangements made for their control by Parliament? 'A' (U.L.).

Chapter 6: Public Opinion, Pressure Groups, and the Mass Media

1. What importance may be attached to (*a*) public opinion polls; and (*b*) by-elections in Britain? 'A' (U.L.).

2. What 'interest groups' are active in British political life? By what means and with what success do they operate? 'A' (U.L.).

3. By what means can public opinion express itself on political issues? To what extent can it influence the Government? 'A' (U.L.).

4. How would you distinguish between a political party and a pressure group? How do pressure groups operate in the British system of Government? (L.G.T.B.).

5. What public control is there of (*a*) a county grammar school, (*b*) a university, (*c*) the British Broadcasting Corporation, and (*d*) *The Times*? 'A' (U.L.).

6. 'We take pride in having a "free" Press which is an essential feature of the British Constitution.' Discuss.

Chapters 7 and 8: The Law and the Courts: Judicial Officers and the Legal Profession

1. Give an account of the structure and composition of the High Court of Justice. 'O' (A.E.B.).

2. Compare and contrast the composition and functions of a Crown Court with those of a county court.

3. Describe and comment on the organization of the civil courts in England. 'A' (U.L.).

4. Give an account of the part played by laymen in the administration of justice in England today. How does the English legal system benefit from this use of laymen?

5. Give an account of the courts which administer the criminal law. 'O' (A.E.B.).

6. Write notes on any three of the following:

    (*a*) The Attorney-General.
    (*b*) A puisne judge.
    (*c*) The Chancery Division.
    (*d*) The Lord President of the Council. 'O' (A.E.B.)

7. 'The office of the unpaid, lay magistrate should be replaced by a system of paid, legally qualified magistrates.' Discuss. 'A' (A.E.B.).

8. Give an account of those criminal offences which are described as 'crimes against the State'. 'A' (A.E.B.).

9. Compare and contrast statute law with common law. 'O' (A.E.B.).

10. What functions are performed by the Law Officers of the Crown? 'A' (A.E.B.).

11. 'Justice must be seen to be done.' By what means is this dictum realized in this country? 'A' (A.E.B.).

12. Explain the difference between a crime and a civil wrong. Illustrate your answer with examples. 'A' (A.E.B.).

13. Describe the method of appointment of (*a*) Justices of the Peace, and (*b*) jurors. What are the rules regarding majority verdicts in criminal cases tried in Crown Courts?

14. Discuss the main agencies and committees specially concerned with law reform.

15. Describe the main provisions of the *Legal Aid Act, 1974.*

16. Describe the composition and jurisdiction of Crown Courts established under the *Courts Act, 1971.*

17. Write notes on **three** of the following:

    1. Lord of Appeal in Ordinary.
    2. Stipendiary Magistrate.
    3. Circuit judge.
    4. Recorder.

18. State the main arguments for and against the establishment of a Minister of Justice in Britain.

19. Distinguish between solicitors and barristers as regards their training and their work. Discuss the usefulness of this division of the legal profession.

20. Describe the composition and jurisdiction of the Judicial Committee of the Privy Council, **or** the House of Lords.

Chapter 9: Liberties of the Subject

1. What limitations are placed upon freedom of speech in Britain? 'O' (A.E.B.).

2. Write notes on any **three** of the following:

    (*a*) Writ of *Habeas Corpus*.
    (*b*) Bail.
    (*c*) The doctrine of *ultra vires*.
    (*d*) The law of defamation. 'O' (A.E.B.).

3. In what ways are the rights of the accused safeguarded in British courts? 'O' (A.E.B.).

4. What limitations are placed by law upon the right to hold public meetings? To what extent are such limitations justifiable? 'A' (A.E.B.).

5. What is meant by saying that there is freedom of association in Britain? To what extent, if at all, should this freedom be modified? 'A' (A.E.B.).

6. What limitations are imposed upon freedom of expression in Britain at the present day? To what extent, in your opinion, are such limitations necessary? 'A' (A.E.B.).

7. What safeguards does the British citizen have against tyranny? 'A' (U.L.).

8. 'The liberty of the individual can best be measured by the safeguard he enjoys in relation to the police and the magistrates.' What are these safeguards in Britain?

9. 'The organization of the police is a difficult problem for any democratic society and one which in Britain has not yet been satisfactorily solved.' Discuss. 'A' (U.L.).

10. Discuss the merits and demerits of the present organization of police forces in England and Wales.

11. What are the Judges' Rules? Of what importance are they in relation to the traditional freedoms of British subjects?

12. Discuss the rights which a private citizen has against the misuse of power by a police officer? How are complaints against the police dealt with by the authorities?

Chapter 10: Administrative Law and Justice

1. Define and illustrate what is meant by delegated legislation. What are the advantages of this method of law making? 'A' (U.L.).

2. 'Delegated legislation is essential for speedy and efficient government.' Discuss. 'A' (A.E.B.).

3. For what purposes are Royal Commissions and Committees of Inquiry appointed? To what degree have such Commissions and Inquiries influenced government action? 'A' (A.E.B.).

4. Why was the office of Parliamentary Commissioner for Administration

created in 1966? To what extent, if at all, has he altered the role of the M.P. in relation to his constituents? 'A' (A.E.B.).

5. What is meant by the phrase 'administrative tribunals'? Give varied examples and discuss their contribution to the public welfare. 'A' (U.L.).

6. Distinguish between: (*a*) a bye-law; (*b*) an Order in Council; and (*c*) a Statutory Instrument. Give examples of the use of each type of legislation.

7. John comes to you with a complaint against a Government Department which has bungled an application of his. Advise him of the steps to be taken to bring the case before the Parliamentary Commissioner for Administration.

Chapter 11: Local Government

1. 'Local government in Britain is essentially government by committee, with all the advantages and defects inherent in committees.' Discuss.

2. Examine the part played by permanent officials in local government in England. 'A' (U.L.).

3. Describe and assess the relative importance of the various sources of income of the local authorities in England. 'A' (U.L.).

4. How are local councils financed? 'O' (A.E.B.).

5. In what ways are local councils controlled by the central government? 'O' (A.E.B.).

6. Write notes on any three of the following:

(*a*) the Chief Executive Officer.
(*b*) the Director of Social Services.
(*c*) District Auditor.
(*d*) Chief Education Officer.

7. Why was the *Local Government Act, 1888*, an important landmark in the history of local government in England and Wales? 'O' (A.E.B.).

8. How are Councillors elected? What functions do they perform in local government? 'O' (A.E.B.).

9. 'Judicial control of public authorities is inadequate.' Discuss. 'A' (A.E.B.).

10. 'Party politics educate the public and make local government understandable to the electorate.' Discuss. 'A' (A.E.B.).

11. Explain the significance of the doctrine of *ultra vires* as applied to local government. 'A' (A.E.B.).

12. The Redcliffe-Maud Commission's Report (1966–9) noted four basic faults in the local government structure existing in 1969. What were they?

13. The purposes of local government, according to the Redcliffe-Maud Report (1969) were fourfold. Name the purposes.

14. What advantages did the Redcliffe-Maud Commission (1966–9) claim for its proposed system?

15. List the main functions of county councils and district councils under the *Local Government Act, 1972*.

16. There are six metropolitan counties. Name them, and describe broadly how these authorities are run.

TABLE OF STATUTES

Table of Statutes

INDEX

349